The Iranian Revolution

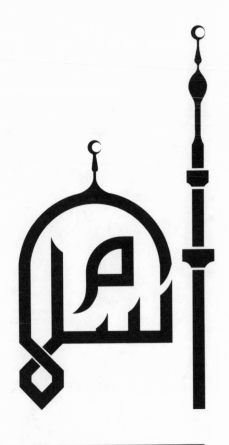

The

Iranian

Revolution

Its Global Impact

EDITED BY JOHN L. ESPOSITO

FLORIDA INTERNATIONAL UNIVERSITY PRESS / MIAMI

This volume was prepared under the aegis of the Middle East Institute, the Johns Hopkins School for Advanced International Studies, and the Royal Institute of International Affairs.

The Florida International University Press is a member of University Presses of Florida, the scholarly publishing agency of the State University System of Florida. Books are selected for publication by faculty editorial committees at each of Florida's nine public universities: Florida A&M University (Tallahassee), Florida Atlantic University (Boca Raton), Florida International University (Miami), Florida State University (Tallahassee), University of Central Florida (Orlando), University of Florida (Gainesville), University of North Florida (Jacksonville), University of South Florida (Tampa), University of West Florida (Pensacola).

Orders for books published by all member presses should be addressed to University Presses of Florida, 15 NW 15th St., Gainesville, FL 32611.

Library of Congress Cataloging-in-Publication Data

The Iranian revolution: its global impact / edited by John L.
    Esposito.
        p.   cm.
    ISBN 0-8130-0998-7 (alk. paper). — ISBN 0-8130-1017-9 (pbk.:
alk. paper)
    1. Islamic countries—Relations—Iran.   2. Iran—Relations—
Islamic countries.   3. Islam—20th century.   4. Islamic countries—
Politics and government.   I. Esposito, John L.
DS35.74.I7173   1990
327.55017671—dc20   90-3083
                    CIP

Contents

Preface

THE YEAR 1989 was a turning point in the history of the Islamic Republic of Iran. In February of that year, Iran celebrated the tenth anniversary of its revolution. On February 14, the Ayatollah Khomeini, precipitating a worldwide furor, called for the execution of Salman Rushdie, author of *The Satanic Verses*, and subsequently condemned Iranian liberals, pragmatists, and the West. On March 28, Khomeini's hand-picked successor, Ayatollah Hussein Ali Montazeri, was removed by Khomeini and the issue of true leadership of the republic dramatically reopened. Scarcely two months later, on June 3, Iran's supreme religiopolitical leader and guide died from complications while recovering from surgery. In the aftermath of Khomeini's passing, issues of leadership, ideological orientation, domestic policy, and international relations endure. This is clearly an important time for Iran and its relationship with the international community.

This volume grew out of an international conference on the global impact of the Iranian revolution held in Washington, D.C., on February 4–5, 1989, ten years after Ayatollah Khomeini returned in triumph to Iran. The conference was sponsored by the Middle East Institute, the Johns Hopkins School of Advanced International Studies and the Royal Institute of International Affairs. Experts from Iran, Europe, Africa, and the United States were asked to assess the worldwide effects of the Iranian revolution, focusing on the following questions: Has the Iranian revolution influenced Islamic revivalism elsewhere, or is the Islamic resurgence in other countries due to indigenous factors? To what extent has the Iranian experience shaped the politics, economics, and cultures of other countries? What factors have so far accounted for the failure of the Iranian revolution to replicate itself in other countries? These questions are the issues taken up on a region-by-region basis in the chapters of this book.

We are indebted to our colleagues who participated in the conference, especially those who provided chapters for this volume and those others whose comments informed the understanding and analysis in the introductory and concluding chapters: Cesar Adib Majul, R.K. Ramazani, Mumtaz Ahmad, Shahrough Akhavi, Philip Robins, Gerard Chaliand, Hermann F. Eilts, David E. Long, Lisa Anderson, Congressman Lee Hamilton, Fred R. von der Mehden, Ibrahim Gambari, John O. Voll, Farhang Rajaee, Nikki R. Keddie, Gary Sick, Kenneth D. Taylor, Martha Brill Olcott, Augustus Richard Norton, and Olivier Roy. In addition, Stephen Grummon, Ambassador William Rugh, John O. Voll, and Jeanette P. Esposito read and made valuable comments on portions of the manuscript. Carleton Coon, Jr., provided valuable editorial assistance for the introductory and concluding sections. Mary Sebold of the Middle East Institute effectively and cheerfully coordinated many aspects of the conference and postconference publications. Mary C. Boiver and Barbara D. Letourneau of the College of the Holy Cross provided valued secretarial support. Finally, we are indebted to the Ford Foundation for its generous funding in support of the conference and its publications, and we are grateful to the Middle East Institute and the Johns Hopkins School of Advanced International Studies and their staffs for their sponsorship, support, and assistance.

John L. Esposito, College of the Holy Cross
James P. Piscatori, The University of Wales
Christopher Van Hollen, Middle East Institute

PART I

Iran

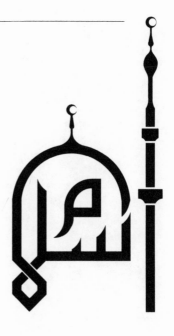

1

Introduction

JOHN L. ESPOSITO

JAMES P. PISCATORI

FEW EVENTS IN THE second half of the twentieth century have provoked as much disquiet as the Iranian revolution of 1979. Iran has since seen many changes: the establishment of a clerically dominated Islamic republic, the elimination of opposition groups, the political and social institutionalization of the revolution, and an eight-year war with Iraq with its devastating human toll and economic consequences. Universally surprised by the form the revolution took, policy makers and academicians have struggled to make sense of an infinitely complex and fluid situation that has affected large parts of the world. Although simplification of this complex reality has all too often been the result, three basic schools of thought have emerged.

In the first wave of writing on the revolution, scholars compensated for the earlier lack of concern with religious officials (mullahs) by according them great influence and power. But this was really overcompensation, and mullah-dominated politics became as unidimensional as the preceding Shah-dominated politics. Unyielding export of the revolution abroad became the complement of intolerant Islamization at home. Some warned that the domino effect of the revolution would topple traditional regimes in the Middle East and beyond.

A second school of thought on the revolution has sought to right this imbalance by stressing the permanence of Iranian state interests and the conventionality of decision making. The revolution has thus been seen as consistent with the longer history of Iranian nationalism. Moreover, the Iran-Iraq war and the export of the revolution are thought to be a continuation of the Shah's hegemonic designs and derived only in a subsidiary way from the particular commitments of the mullahs.

A third school of thought combines elements of the preceding views by emphasizing the extent to which the clergy has definitely recast the mold of Iranian politics, the entrenchment of the revolution, and the commitment of most of the elite to winning the Iran-Iraq war and to exporting the revolution. But this view differs from the others by a greater willingness to explore the infighting of the elite. In this approach, the mullahs are seen as neither monolithically zealous nor monolithically conscious of *raison d'etat*.

There is something to recommend in each of these approaches, especially the third. But a proper assessment of the Iranian revolution requires more than an evaluation of the nature of the regime. It also requires placing this particular revolution in historical perspective and comparing its impact across a variety of societies and regions stretching from the Middle East to Africa and Asia.

This volume assesses the impact of the Iranian revolution within the context of the global resurgence of Islam, focusing one of Iran's major goals, the export of its Islamic revolution. Case studies examine the myths and the realities of Iranian influence and intervention from Africa to Southeast Asia. While describing the impact of direct Iranian influence, the case studies also reveal how the tendency to view Iran as the major source of "Islamic fundamentalism" worldwide has undervalued the indigenous sources of Islamic revivalism in the Muslim world. As a result, the extent to which the Iranian revolution spurred indigenous trends rather than created them has too often been overlooked, even by U.S. policy makers. The final chapter considers the complex nature of relations between Iran and the other nations; including the enduring geostrategic importance of Iran to U.S. interests.

Export of the Revolution: Islam, Ideology, and Foreign Policy

During its first ten years, the Islamic Republic of Iran remained committed to the twin goals of the Khomeini regime: the institutionalization of the revolution at home and its export abroad. As John L. Esposito observes in "The Iranian Revolution: A Ten-Year Perspective," Iranian history and institutions have been intertwined with Shiism since Islam was established as the state religion in the sixteenth century, and, to varying degrees since then, Shii belief, leadership, and institutions have been an integral part of state and society. Politically, the relationship of the clergy to the state has varied from cooperation to opposition and revolt. Thus, at times the ulama have been co-opted servants of their royal patrons, and at other times, such as during the Tobacco Concession protest and the constitutional revolts in the nineteenth and early twentieth centuries, they have raised their voices against the monarchy. During the twentieth century, the Pahlavi dynasty's reforms secularized clergy-dominated sectors of the state, eroding much of the clergy's power and privileges. Nevertheless, for a variety of reasons the fall of the Shah during the 1970s affirmed the continued political and social force of Islam in Iran and the ability of political figures to mobilize opposition and revolt by the use of religious symbols and ideology.

In the aftermath of the revolution, the Iranian clergy moved quickly to entrench its power and institutionalize the revolution. Esposito describes the transformation of Iran from a monarchy to an Islamic republic in terms of its constitution, law, parliament, political party system, and revolutionary committees. Iran's schools and universities, the police, military, government ministries, and opposition parties and groups were purged; dissident clerical and lay voices were silenced.

The second goal of the regime, the export of Iran's revolution, is embedded in the ideological worldview and religious interpretations of Ayatollah Khomeini and his ideologues, who have combined a religiously rooted brand of Iranian nationalism with belief in a transnational mission to spread their version of revolutionary Islam. Farhang Rajaee, a U.S.-educated Iranian professor teaching in Teheran, provides insight into this worldview, identifying its major characteristics and the sources of Iran's rationale and commitment to the export of its revolution during the past decade. In particular, Rajaee outlines the multiple meanings and methods advocated by Khomeini and many of Iran's clerical leaders and ideologues. He underscores the debate over which approach should predominate—that of Iran serving as inspirational model or of Iran actively propagating and disseminating its ideas abroad. While the more radical "volcano" approach predominated

upon the removal of the provisional government, in the period immediately following the Iran-Iraq war (mid-1988 to early 1989) the pendulum seemed to swing toward model building, that is, creating the
"ideal city" that would inspire the emulation of others. However, the
Rushdie affair upset this shift, and it remains to be seen which approach will predominate in the post-Khomeini era.

In "Iran's Export of the Revolution: Politics, Ends, and Means,"
R. K. Ramazani complements Rajaee's ideological approach by analyzing both the theory and the reality of the export of the revolution
within the overall context of Iranian foreign policy and its factionalized
leadership. As the United States and the Soviet Union developed rationales for spreading the ideals of their revolutions and societies, so too,
Ramazani tells us, Iran has sought to "make the world safe for Islam."
He describes Iran's foreign policy as rooted in Khomeini's understanding of Islam, the presupposition that the revolution is divinely guided,
and the Irano-Islamic quest for justice. Like Rajaee, Ramazani emphasizes the multiple ideological meanings and various methods of exporting the revolution, but he also recognizes the diverse actors employed
to realize this goal: soldiers, other liberation movements, student athletes, diplomats, and foreign clergy.

There has also been an almost constant jockeying for power within
Iran's elite, as the Iran-Iraq war and Iran-Contra affair made apparent.
Iran's foreign policy has alternated between international isolation and
cooperation, but the realists more often and pragmatically advocated
an improvement of relations with Western powers in the face of the
persistent resistance of the more hardline idealists. In the end, however, the Rushdie affair won the day for the idealists as Khomeini condemned liberals, pragmatists, and the West alike. Thus, Ramazani concludes that despite a unity of commitment to the revolution itself, in
the first decade after the revolution no broadly based consensus on the
fundamental principles, institutions, and policies of an Islamic policy
emerged. Moreover, he maintains that Iran's realization of its social
and economic goals requires economic relations with the West and a
less militant interpretation of the export of the revolution.

Other chapters in this volume show that the global impact of Iran's
revolution has been both direct and indirect. Indeed, the revolution has
more often served as a broad inspirational example than a precise
model. Muslim activists in many parts of the world were elated by the
success of their Iranian brothers and sisters and took heart in their own

struggles. In this way, Iran's revolution has more commonly reinforced or accelerated preexisting trends in Muslim countries rather than initiated and led revolutionary efforts.

In the immediate aftermath of the revolution, the outlook was more grim. All eyes turned to the Gulf as Shii uprisings erupted in Saudi Arabia, Bahrain, Kuwait, and Pakistan. Could Iraq, with its Shii majority governed by a Sunni minority and sharing a common border with Iran, be far behind? Iran's broadcasts to the Gulf states and its sending of emissaries to other countries and liberation movements enhanced the image of a potentially expansionist Iran, inciting a Muslim world already in the throes of an Islamic resurgence. Yet while many anticipated other Irans, none materialized. Chapters surveying the Middle East, South and Central Asia, Southeast Asia, and Africa reveal the myriad and often subtle but significant ways in which Iran has had an impact upon Muslim politics during the past decade.

The Middle East

The Middle East provides the clearest examples of both direct and indirect Iranian influence on Muslim politics. As David E. Long points out in "The Impact of the Iranian Revolution on the Arabian Peninsula and the Gulf States," many in the region and in Western capitals "perceived all the conservative monarchies in the Gulf as miniature Irans, susceptible to revolution and destined to collapse. . . . one could not give away good news about the Gulf." Initially these fears seemed confirmed by communal riots in Saudi Arabia and civil disturbances, terrorist acts, and hijackings in Kuwait. In addition, Bahrain witnessed several coup attempts that were directly linked to Iran. During the 1970s, the Iranian Hojjat al-Islam Hadi Mudarrisi had created a network in Bahrain to support Khomeini, then still in exile. Soon after Khomeini's return to Iran, several hundred Shii Bahrainis demonstrated in favor of Iran's revolution and clashed with authorities in August 1979. Mudarrisi, who had been expelled from Bahrain in 1980, made regular broadcast appeals from Teheran for an uprising against the ruling dynasty. In December 1981, the government thwarted an attempted coup and arrested seventy members of the Islamic Front for the Liberation of Bahrain, a movement inspired by Mudarrisi and financed by Iran.

Despite these early trouble signs, Long concludes that Iran's influence has proved to be less of a danger than originally anticipated.

Sunni Muslims in the Gulf have shown little receptivity to revolutionary movements as a means to redress grievances. While the Iranian revolution did raise the consciousness of many Shii, making the younger generation in particular more politically aware and assertive of their identity and rights, Iran's intellectual and doctrinal impact has been limited. Moreover, grassroots uprisings among Shii have not materialized at all. Indeed, Long maintains that for a variety of reasons (the excesses of the Khomeini government, Shii concerns that Iranian policies in the Gulf during the Iran-Iraq war threatened their well-being, increased internal security measures, and greater government sensitivity to some Shii grievances), Shii communities have remained perhaps surprisingly quiet.

Few states were as fearful of the impact of the Iranian revolution as was Iraq, a country geographically contiguous with Iran. Saddam Hussein, Iraq's Sunni ruler, governs a Shii majority, many of whom are concentrated in southern Iraq, the home of two of Shii Islam's holy cities, Najaf and Karbala. By the middle of the Iraq-Iran war (1980–89), it looked as if Iraq's worst fears would be realized by its military collapse. Yet as Philip Robins notes in "Iraq: Revolutionary Threats and Regime Responses," by the time of the cease-fire in 1989 many wondered at the marginal impact of the Iranian revolution on Iraqi politics and society. Robins demonstrates how a combination of Iranian misconceptions (about the cohesion of the Shii community in Iraq and about "the supposedly brittle nature of the [Iraqi] regime") and Iraqi policies (which crushed militant Shii leaders while rewarding the quiescent majority with massive development projects) effectively blunted the appeals of Khomeini's regime to Shii coreligionists in Iraq and blocked the export of the revolution to what originally appeared to be Iran's most vulnerable neighbor.

The most direct, forceful, and sustained Iranian influence has taken place in Lebanon. Lebanon's Shii community, essentially apolitical until after the Second World War, became increasingy politicized in the 1960s and 1970s. During the 1970s Musa al-Sadr, the Iranian-born and educated religious leader, reinterpreted Shii symbolism, which paralleled Khomeini's revolutionary interpretation of Islam during his exile from 1964 to 1978, to support an activist movement of social and political reform (the Movement of the Disinherited) out of which grew the militia, the Amal. The movement escalated in 1978 with the Israeli invasion of Lebanon and the disappearance of Musa Sadr, events which fit comfortably into the traditional Shii doctrines of martyrdom and the occultation of the Twelfth Imam, who is in seclusion but will return to restore a just order.

The second Israeli invasion of Lebanon in 1982 and the massacres at Chatila and Sabra further radicalized Shii politics and set the stage for the influx of significant Iranian resources. Augustus Richard Norton's "Lebanon: The Internal Conflict and the Iranian Connection" describes how Iran raised significant sums and created an infrastructure in Lebanon to spread the Islamic revolution. These funds (estimates have ranged from $10 million per month to as high as $30 million per month in late 1987 and early 1988) have been used not only to underwrite Hezbollah but also to run an array of social services. Iran also provided a successful example of an ulama-guided revolution, offering inspiration and guidance for armed struggle against political oppression, imperialism, and tyranny. Posters of Ayatollah Khomeini appeared on houses and in the streets, and Hezbollah publications (in particular the masthead of the newspaper *Al Ahd*) were adorned with his picture. Yet as Norton points out, while Iran influences, it does not always determine the course of Lebanese politics. One needs only to look at Muhammad Husain Fadlallah, the spiritual guide of Hezbollah, who, while recognizing Iran's role as a model of Islamic revolution, has acknowledged that an Islamic republic in Lebanon must remain a goal which for the foreseeable future is "impossible."[1]

Egypt has experienced a more indirect Iranian influence; it is among those states in which the inspiration of the revolution has reinforced existing Islamic opposition without significant intervention by the Iranian government. During the 1970s Anwar Sadat tried to use Islam to bolster his political legitimacy, producing instead an Islamic backlash. The Muslim Brotherhood and Islamic student organizations became increasingly critical of his open-door economic policy (*infitah*), reform of Muslim family law, support for the Shah of Iran (Sadat referred to Khomeini as a "lunatic"), and advocacy of the Camp David Accords and peace treaty with Israel. New, more radical Islamic groups mounted a violent revolutionary challenge to the regime and its accommodation to Israel.

Following the Iranian revolution, both the more moderate Muslim Brotherhood and extremist groups rejected the official Islamic establishment's endorsement of the treaty and called upon Egyptians to "follow the example of Iran and wage holy war against Israel."[2] As Shahrough Akhavi demonstrates in "The Impact of the Iranian Revolution on Egypt," in the first flush of enthusiasm surrounding the early years of the revolution, the Muslim Brotherhood, radical groups, student organizations, and the Islamic left all concluded that Egypt too could radically transform its political order if only there were a cohesive vanguard to propagate the message and mobilize the masses. They were inspired by the spirit and example of the revolution, not by a desire to replicate the Iranian model. This attitude was reflected in the early response of the Muslim Brotherhood: "[The Iranian revolution will] turn political theories and contemporary political forces on their heads . . . [it is] a matchless, powerful, and vital example of the *Islamic* revolution . . . and the important thing is not to put our hands at our sides and wait."[3] As the years have passed, the support of Egyptian activists for many of Iran's actions and policies has waned, though admiration for the revolution itself has not.

Outwardly, Tunisia and Libya could not appear to be more different. Under President Habib Bourguiba, Tunisia was generally regarded as the most secular government in the Arab world. In contrast, Muammar al-Qaddafi had introduced Islamic laws and reforms in Libya in the 1970s. Similarly, Bourguiba opposed Iran while Qaddafi supported it during the Iran-Iraq war. Yet Lisa Anderson, in "Tunisia and Libya: Responses to the Islamic Impulse," argues that Bourguiba and Qaddafi shared some common responses to Iran's revolution. Both leaders regarded the example of the revolution as a threat to their political leadership, and opposition groups in both Libya and Tunisia saw in the Iranian example the general need to make political leaders Islamically accountable. While the Iranian revolution did not lead to direct intervention or new Iranian-supported activist groups, it accelerated oppositional trends already present in both countries. Qaddafi's individualistic, seemingly unorthodox interpretations of Islam alienated both the religious establishment and militant opposition groups. At the same time Qaddafi, who had cultivated his image as the primary revolutionary in the Muslim world, found it necessary to ally Libya with Iran during the Iran-Iraq war. However, as Anderson observes, "This was a relationship based less on common values than on shared antipathies—principally to what both regimes believed to be the terrible influence of Western imperialism—and if it obscured the profound differences between the two regimes for Western observers, it fooled no Islamists."

Esposito and Piscatori

Tunisian Muslim activists were encouraged by Iran's experience and emboldened to assert their own demands. Dissatisfaction with the overwhelming secularization of Tunisian society and education had prompted the emergence of Islamic reform groups like the Koranic Preservation Society. The government's attempt to co-opt and control these organizations was initially successful, but as the economy steadily worsened in the mid-1970s, less accommodating and more political groups such as the Islamic Tendency Movement (MTI) appeared. The Bourguiba government, equating the Islamic revolution with extremism, first attempted to malign these activists with the label "Khomeinist" and then arrested and imprisoned their leaders. The government continued in its efforts to discredit the Islamic opposition by associating it with Iran, yet there was little evidence to suggest such a linkage. Moreover, by 1981 Rashid Ghannushi, leader of MTI, had modified his support of the revolution and rejected the use of violence for political change in Tunisia. Anderson demonstrates that although events in Iran may have confirmed and heightened Islamic-based opposition, Iran's influence in Tunisia and Libya was indirect at best.

South and Central Asia

Like few other issues in the Muslim world, the Soviet invasion and occupation of Afghanistan in 1979 has been one that both the West and the Muslim world have equally opposed. In "The Mujahidin and the Future of Afghanistan," Olivier Roy maintains that despite Afghanistan's proximity to Iran, the overall impact of the revolution on the Mujahidin, the majority of whom are Sunni, has been minimal. Among the Shii, who constitute approximately 15 percent of the population, Iranian influence has been much more pronounced.

As in many parts of the Islamic world, Muslims in Afghanistan were influenced by the writings of the Pakistani Abul Ala Mawdudi, founder of the Jamaat-i-Islami (Islamic Society), the Egyptian Sayyid Qutb of the Muslim Brotherhood, and the Iranian Dr. Ali Shariati. Although the background of most Muslim commanders in Afghanistan is similar to that of activists in other Muslim countries (young, educated urbanites), Roy emphasizes that the success of the Afghan Mujahidin, unlike most other Islamic movements, has been based upon the peasantry and in joining Islamic intellectuals and local traditional mullahs.

Iran's influence in Afghanistan has been limited. The regime took a

strong stand against the Soviet invasion and urged the Afghan Mujahidin to implement an Islamic revolution. Iran also exercised influence
through the Iranization of Shii clerics between 1950 and 1980 when
they studied under Iranian ayatollahs and by encouraging pro-Iranian
political parties to form the Alliance of Eight, established in 1986 and
based in Iran as a counterweight to the (Sunni) Alliance of Seven,
which is based in Pakistan. However, certain circles within Iran regarded the Mujahidin as too pro-Western because of their acceptance
of aid from the United States. Roy maintains that Iran's anti-Americanism was in fact stronger than its Muslim solidarity and so "Iran consistently avoided any direct involvement on the side of the Mujahidin."

Like all religions in the Soviet Union, Islam has long been under
rigorous state control. Restricted access to data prevents an accurate
assessment of the nature of Islamic revivalism and the impact of the
Iranian revolution in the USSR. Nevertheless, we do know that in the
1960s Soviet Muslims increasingly turned to Islamic values and traditions, and informal Islamic schools, institutions, and secret societies
developed. When the Iranian revolution occurred, its impact among
Soviet Muslims was enhanced not simply because of prevailing receptivity to Islamic ideas but because it coincided with the troubled wan-
ing years of the Brezhnev era. Political immobilism, economic failure,
widespread corruption, and deterioration in central control contributed to the entrenchment of local traditional interests and new informal institutions among the 50 million Soviet Muslims. The concomitant development of Islamic revivalism in the Muslim world and the
explosion of Iranian sentiment across the Soviet border affected both
the Muslims and the regime. In "Soviet Central Asia: Does Moscow
Fear Iranian Influence?" Martha Brill Olcott notes: "Certainly the Iranian revolution had some effect; at the very least it provided those Central Asians who had access to short-wave transmissions a contemporary
model of an Islamic society to go along with their more attenuated
knowledge of their own Islamic past."

Both the Iranian revolution and the Gorbachev reforms operated to
intensify Muslim demands against the state. Islamic revivalist sentiment
was already a viable force, but information and education on Islam increased significantly after the Iranian revolution, especially in Turkmenistan and Tadzhikistan. With *glasnost* came additional demands for
the formal reinstitutionalization of Islamic education and ritual prac-

tices. The general upheaval that the reforms created has also intensified ethnic tensions in such provinces as Azerbaijan, Uzbektistan, and Tajikistan and has led to increasing Muslim self-assertiveness. Some activists, located in rural areas and concentrated in Sufi (mystical) brotherhoods, have even turned to violence to advance their goals. But there is no evidence of an Iranian link.

Ironically, an enduring legacy of the Afghan invasion is likely to be the displacement of Shii Iran as exemplar and greater attention to political and religious trends in a Sunni-dominated Afghanistan. Nevertheless, it seems probable that Iran will not disappear entirely from the scene but will continue to play an important, if somewhat secondary, role within Soviet Muslim circles. It is worth noting, for example, that in the November 1988 clashes between Armenians and Azerbaijanis, Azerbaijani demonstrators prominently displayed posters of the Ayatollah Khomeini. In the riots of late 1989 and early 1990 in the same area, Muslim Azerbaijanis called for the dismantling of the formal border with Iran, but the government in Tehran showed as little enthusiasm for this idea as did the government in Moscow.

Southeast Asia

The impact of the Iranian revolution upon the Muslim communities of Southeast Asia has been primarily indirect. In Malaysia and Indonesia, the revolution has both stimulated Islamic political ideas and ideology and enhanced the local government's ability to justify the control and suppression of Islamically oriented opposition movements. In the Philippines, Iran has reinforced preexisting political trends, providing morale and support for the Moro National Liberation Front's struggle against the Manila government.

Like their counterparts, Muslim activists in Southeast Asia applauded the revolution of 1979 and hastened to Teheran to pay their respects to the Ayatollah. However, within a short period of time, activists in Malaysia and Indonesia soon distanced themselves from Khomeini because of concerns about the direction and excesses of Iran's clerical government and because of the Malaysian and Indonesian governments' charges of "Khomeinism" or "radical Islam" to discredit any Islamic opposition. As Fred von der Mehden shows in "Malaysian and Indonesian Islamic Movements and the Iranian Connection," while some predicted "another Iran" in states like Indonesia, in fact the record has proven less subversive. As in other Muslim contexts, the revolution "had a major effect on the religiously conscious elements . . . It fed into a series of other forces that were lending strength to the Islamic revival in the region. While the perceived excesses of the new regime in Teheran and the long Iran-Iraq war weakened the original emotional attraction of many activists to the Iranian experience, the revolution itself is still upheld by a wide spectrum of Southeast Asian Muslims as one of the most important phenomena of the twentieth century. Nowhere else has Islam been so decidedly victorious over the economic, political, and moral forces of the West."

While Khomeini may symbolize the power and force of the Islamic revolution, Iran's impact in Malaysia and Indonesia has been due more to the writings of Ali Shariati than to those of Khomeini. Shariati's writings are widely available and freely discussed in such influential journals as *Prisma, Risalah,* and *Dakwah.* His ideas and orientation have influenced students, intellectuals, and political activists.

If Iran's revolution has been a source of inspiration to some, it has also been used by governments to legitimate their control and suppression of local Islamic opposition movements by explicitly linking them to the image of an extremist Iran, intolerant and in turmoil. The Indonesian government has warned of the dangers of a "deviant Islam" exported by Libya and Iran and has accused its opposition of Iranian backing. Both the Malaysian and Indonesian governments have contrasted "true" Islam with a "deviant" or "extremist" Islam responsible for antigovernment activities, bent upon the fomenting of revolution and establishing an "Iran-type" Islamic state.

The impact of Iran on Muslim politics in the southern Philippines was vividly manifest during the twentieth anniversary celebration of Bangsamoro Freedom Day on March 18, 1988, as placards of Nur Misuari, leader of the Moro National Liberation Front (MNLF), and of Ayatollah Khomeini were paraded side by side. Muslims (the Moros), who comprise about 5 million of the Philippines' 55 million citizens, are concentrated in the south. Their long-established independence movement receives aid from many Muslim countries, including Saudi Arabia and Libya.

Beginning in the early 1970s, however, the Shah and Ferdinand Marcos strengthened diplomatic ties so that by 1978 more than 2,500

Iranian students were enrolled in Philippine universities and some 6,000 Filipinos labored in Iran. The fall of the Shah was greeted with enthusiasm by many Filipino Muslims, who regarded it as a manifestation of God's punishment of an un-Islamic ruler and a possible foreshadowing of the fate of Marcos. This identification was reflected in demonstrations led by Moro students, who carried posters with such slogans as "Long Live Khomeini's Republic," "Unite for Jihad," and "Down with American Imperialism." By the end of 1979, Iranian religious literature entered the country, exposing Muslim faculty and students to the writings of Iranian intellectuals and theologians.

A more substantial linkage was that forged between the MNLF and Iran's leadership. In "The Iranian Revolution and the Muslims in the Philippines," Cesar Adib Majul analyzes the close political ties between the Islamic Republic of Iran and the MNLF, the growth of pro-Iranian sentiment, and the crackdown on the Muslim movement by the Marcos government. He demonstrates that the example of the Iranian revolution, the propaganda that Iran has distributed as well as the official support it has extended to the MNLF, and Iran's encouragement of pro-Khomeini student activists in the Philippines have all made Ayatollah Khomeini, for many Moros, the archrepresentative of political opposition in the name of Islam. Thus, within a short period of time Iran has been able to win the admiration of MNLF leaders and to enjoy support in many Muslim households of the southern Philippines.

Africa

Africa is home to many of the world's Muslims and continues to be the fastest-growing Muslim area today. The African Muslim tradition includes a long heritage of Islamic revivalism and reform, such as the eighteenth-century Fulani movement in Nigeria and the nineteenth-century Mahdist movement in the Sudan. Therefore, it should not be surprising that in recent years Sudan and Nigeria, the former the largest country in Africa and the latter its most populous state, have experienced along with other parts of Africa the rise of the tide of Islam.

In September 1983 President Jafar Numayri formalized his attempt to Islamize Sudan's state and society. Numayri had come to power in 1969 in a coup d'état. Like Muammar Qaddafi, he was an admirer of Egypt's Gamal Abd al-Nasser and placed his revolution under the umbrella of Nasser's Arab nationalism. Also like Qaddafi, Numayri in the 1970s turned to Islam to buttress his regime and its nationalist ideology as well as counter and co-opt his Islamic opposition. In 1978 Dr. Hasan al-Turabi, leader of the Sudanese Muslim Brotherhood, was appointed attorney general, and from 1978 to 1983 Sudan's government became progressively more Islamic. From 1983 to 1986 Numayri implemented his own program of Islamization, which included the introduction of Islamic laws, institutions, and courts.

Numayri's turn to Islam was clearly brought on by indigenous factors, but it was also influenced by the broader realities of the resurgence of Islam in Muslim politics among Sudan's neighbors (Egypt and Libya) and the greater Muslim world. The Iranian revolution reinforced existing trends and developments but did not play a formative role in the reassertion of Islam in Sudanese politics. Although Muslim leaders like Turabi and Sadiq al-Mahdi (Mahdist leader and prime minister of the Sudan in 1966–67 and from 1986 to 1989) visited Khomeini in Iran shortly after the revolution, their purpose was to express solidarity with the aims and ideals of the revolution rather than to align themselves with Khomeini or seek Iran's support. Indeed, the intellectual outlook and orientation of both Turabi and Sadiq al-Mahdi were much closer to that of Ali Shariati than of Khomeini.

As John O. Voll demonstrates in "Islamization in the Sudan and the Iranian Revolution," the Sudan has a rich Islamic tradition. The historic role of Islam in the formation and development of the modern Sudan; the presence of Islamic organizations such as the Mahdiyyah, Khatmiyyah, and Muslim Brotherhood; the tradition of Islamic rule as well as Islamic protest and opposition—all predate the Iranian revolution. As a result, neither the Numayri government nor the opposition found it necessary or useful to rely heavily on the support of Iran or to discredit opponents by attacking the influence of "Khomeinism." Voll concludes that Sudan's Islamization experiment was not tied to Iran, countering those hypotheses that overemphasize notions of international revivalist or Iranian-controlled conspiracy.

Nigerian Muslims, concentrated in the north, constitute 40 percent of the country's 116 million citizens while Christians make up 35 percent of the total population. Some estimates indicate that by the year 2050, Nigeria's population will be the third largest in the world, after China and India. Islamic revivalism in Nigeria, as in other Muslim countries, is primarily homegrown. Nonetheless, Ibrahim A. Gambari in "Islamic Revivalism in Nigeria: Homegrown or Externally Induced?" notes that "Ayatollah Khomeini's leadership and the idea of Islamic revolution touched responsive chords in Nigeria's Islamic community, especially among the downtrodden Muslims in the north . . . [and] was skillfully used by local leaders of Islamic revivalism to galvanize the struggle against the growing corruption and excessive materialism of Nigeria's political establishment."

Nigerian Muslim activists embrace a spectrum of positions, as do activists in other Muslim countries. At one extreme, one finds the millenarian Maitatsine sect founded by Muhammadu Murawa, which staged violent, bloody uprisings from 1980 to 1984 and which continues to exist today. The movement revolted against the acute negative impact on traditional sectors of society that Nigeria's oil boom (1974–83) produced. A less extreme band of the spectrum is represented by student activists and university faculty like the European-educated Dr. Ibrahim Suleiman, whose message is reminiscent of other Islamic reformers such as Iran's Ali Shariati. They challenge the Western orientation of the political and social establishment, regard Islam as an alternative to the excessive materialism and consumerism of Western capitalism, and demand the implementation of Islamic law. Meanwhile, more traditional religious leaders such as Sheikh Abubakar Gumi (former Grand Khadi or chief judge of northern Nigeria) denounce un-Islamic innovations in society and the corruption of Sufi (mystical) brotherhoods while calling for a return to the Koran and Sunna (model example of the Prophet).

Many Nigerian Muslim leaders were encouraged and inspired by the success and example of the Iranian revolution. They welcomed many of its themes, including its condemnation of official corruption, rejection of excessive materialism, denunciation of Westernization, and implementation of Islamic law. However, as Gambari tells us, the majority of Nigeria's Muslims, while favoring some introduction of Islamic law, remain committed to a pluralistic state rather than to the creation of an Islamic republic.

As these case studies demonstrate, the impact of the Iranian revolution has varied from place to place and from time to time. Always significant, Iranian influence has run the gamut from inspiration to intervention and must therefore be appreciated, as this book sets out to do, within the contexts of specific countries and societies. But the reader will also wonder about the revolution's implications for Iran's future international relations, particularly with the United States. In the final chapter, Esposito and Piscatori examine the Iranian revolution from a policy perspective. Highlighting the misunderstandings about Iran that have plagued the recent past, they argue that the long-term interests of both the United States and Iran lie in a normalization of political and economic relations. The post-Khomeini period portends uncertainty but may also be a time of opportunity.

Notes

1. Muhammad Husain Fadlallah, "Islam and Violence in Political Reality," *Middle East Insight* 4, nos. 4 and 5 (1986); 10.

2. *Middle East International* 95 (March 16, 1979): 2.

3. As cited in Shahrough Akhavi, "The Impact of the Iranian Revolution on Egypt" (this volume).

2

The Iranian Revolution:

A Ten-Year

Perspective

JOHN L. ESPOSITO

IN FEBRUARY 1979, the world witnessed the first successful modern, religiously led revolution, in which Iran replaced its Western-oriented, dynastic monarchy with a clerically led Islamic regime. Nothing symbolized that revolution and the contrast of modernity and tradition more clearly than the two opponents of that struggle; the suave, imperial Shah of Iran—self-proclaimed *Shahanshah*, "king of kings," and ruler of a 2,500-year-old dynasty who departed quickly and without fanfare—and the bearded, ascetic, and turbaned Ayatollah—named Ruholla, "the spirit of God," who, after years of exile, returned triumphantly to Iran to a tumultuous welcome.

Appreciating the significance of Iran's revolution and its domestic and global impact requires an awareness of the historical background and context of the politics in Iranian history and society in particular. Such awareness will enable us to understand better the Islamic Republic of Iran—its revolutionary ideology, leadership, institutions, and policies.

Shiism in Iranian History

Shiism has been the state religion of Iran since the sixteenth century. At critical points, Shii belief, leadership, and institutions have played

17

an important role in Iranian politics. However, Shii Islam itself has been embroiled in politics since its inception and Shii history and belief are the underpinnings of modern Iran's revolutionary ideology. Throughout Islamic history, the Shii have been a minority, often disenfranchised and oppressed, within the Sunni-dominated Muslim world.

The origins of the Shii community, which today constitutes approximately 15 percent of the world's Muslims, date back to the early centuries of Islam. The division of the Islamic community (*ummah*) into Sunni and Shii branches resulted over the issue of succession and leadership. While the Sunni believe that the Prophet Muhammad died without designating an heir, leaving his companions to select his successor or *khalifah* (caliph), the Shii contend that Muhammad did indeed indicate that Ali, the senior male of the Prophet's family (Muhammad's cousin and son-in-law), should succeed him. For these *Shia* ("the party" of Ali), the infallible religiopolitical leader (*Imam*) of the Islamic community must always come from the family of the Prophet. However, for most of Islamic history, the Sunni caliphate rather than the Shii imamate has been the prevailing form of government. Living as they did in a Sunni-dominated world, some Shii formed revolutionary groups who resisted Umayyad and Abbasid caliphate rule, but in time most Shii reluctantly acquiesced to their Sunni rulers.

Shii aspirations were thwarted both by having to live under a Sunni caliphate and by the disappearance or occultation (seclusion) of the Imam. Early on, Shiism split into several communities based on differences over Ali's legitimate successors. Twelver Shiism (*Ithna Ashari*, the dominant community in Shii Islam and in Iran) acknowledges a line of twelve Imams. The Twelfth Imam is believed to have gone into seclusion in 874; his followers await his return as a *Mahdi*, or messianic guide, who will bring an end to tyranny and corruption and restore just rule.

While awaiting the appearance of the Mahdi, both temporal rulers (the Shahs) and religious leaders (the *ulama*, or religious scholars) have asserted their role as deputies of the Hidden Imam and their right to guide the community during his absence. Unlike Sunni religious scholars, Shii ulama never acknowledged the religious legitimacy of temporal rule. In practice, however, the reality of imperial rule was accepted. Thus, when Shah Ismail Safavi, founder of the Safavid dynasty (1501–1742), established Shii Islam as the official religion of an Islamic empire and claimed to be the Imam's deputy, the Shii acquiesced

Esposito

to his royal title "Shadow of God on Earth" and accepted government appointments. At the same time, the ulama carved out their own niche as religious leaders of the Shii community. Although not claiming the authority of religious inspiration of the Imam, the ulama affirmed their role as guardians and interpreters (*mujtahids*) of religion and as living sources of emulation (*marja-i-taqlid*) whose example and teaching should be followed until the coming of the Mahdi.

The relationship of the ulama to the state varied depending upon the sociopolitical context. Their authority and leadership were often subordinated to and limited by Iran's rulers; at other times they expressed their guardianship of religion in opposition to the government. Under strong Safavid rule, the ulama were co-opted, exchanging quietism and cooperation for royal patronage as government advisers and administrators. However, under the weaker Qajar dynasty (1794–1925), the ulama reasserted their independence and oppositional role as guardians of religion and a curb on the excesses of government. During the nineteenth and twentieth centuries, the ulama protested the threat to Iranian independence posed by the selling of commercial concessions to European colonial powers (e.g., the tobacco protest of 1891–92); later they joined with *bazaaris* (merchants and artisans) and modern reformers (intellectuals and secular nationalists) in demanding constitutional reforms (the constitutional revolution of 1905–11) to limit royal absolutism.

The issues of foreign domination, preservation of national identity and autonomy, constitutionalism, and the place of Islamic law in the state would resurface during the Pahlavi dynasty (and in postrevolutionary Iran). And the pattern of religious-lay alliance, in particular of mosque and bazaar, under the banner of Islam would be resurrected during the late 1970s in Iran's "Islamic" revolution. However, in contrast to the tobacco protest and the constitutional revolt, in the revolution of 1979 the clergy would not assist but would dominate and rule.

Modern Iran

The history of modern Iran is dominated by the Pahlavi dynasty (1925–79). Under Reza (Khan) Shah Pahlavi (1925–41) and his son Muhammad Reza Shah (1941–79), modern Iran took shape. During the late 1920s and 1930s Reza Shah, influenced by the example of his Turkish contemporary Mustafa Kemal (Atatürk), focused on modernization and the creation of a strong centralized government based on a modern army and bureaucracy. Reza Shah's dynastic monarchy aimed at national integration through such policies as containment of rebellious tribes, centralization of military and judicial power, creation of a national bank, and the building of a modern infrastructure.

Although Reza Shah paid lip service to Islam and in the early years of his reign enjoyed the support of Shii leaders, a number of his policies progressively alienated many of the ulama: the establishment of Zoroastrianism alongside Islam as the state religion, the choice of a pre-Islamic name (Pahlavi) and symbols (the lion and the sun), and, most important, the adoption of Western-based legal and educational reforms. The ulama lost much of their power and wealth as they were replaced by modern secular courts, lawyers, judges, notaries, and teachers. The ulama and traditional classes were especially irritated by dress codes that restricted the wearing of clerical garb, mandated Western attire for men (1928), and outlawed the veil (1935), and by the government's takeover and control of religious endowments (1934). Many of these reforms suited and benefited the upper and new middle classes, widening the social and cultural gap between these Westernized citizens and the majority of Iranians.

Although Muhammad Reza Shah's reign began in 1941, when the British put him on the throne in place of his father, it was not until after his U.S.–orchestrated and British-backed return from exile in 1953 that he began to consolidate his power effectively with assistance from Western governments (in particular the United States and Britain) and multinational corporations. Increasingly dependent on the West, the Shah relied upon the protection of his Western- and Israeli-trained military and police as he pursued an ambitious, Western-oriented socioeconomic modernization program. Implementation of this "White Revolution" (1963–77) was accompanied by co-optation and repression to control dissent. As the Shah became more autocratic during the 1970s, he turned to the U.S. Central Intelligence Agency and his own Mossad (Israeli)-trained secret police (SAVAK) to suppress the opposition of liberal nationalists and Marxists alike.

Like his father, Muhammad Reza Shah had at first enjoyed the support of the ulama. Many remained apolitical during the early years of his rule, regarding the monarchy as a protector against unmitigated secularism and the threat of communism. Although an effective opposition did not take shape until the 1970s, there were early critics of the regime's excesses as religious institutions began to come under gov-

ernment attack in the 1960s. Pahlavi policies had progressively extended state control over many areas previously under ulama domain.
Government reforms of education, law, and religious endowments in
the 1930s were followed by land reforms in the 1960s, which further
limited the property, revenue, and power of the ulama. Moreover, as a
class whose status and power had long been reinforced through intermarriage with the political elite, the ulama suffered from the bifurca-
tion of Iranian education and society as a significant difference in identity and outlook developed between the secular elites and intelligentsia
on the one hand and the religiously minded clergy on the other. As
power became more concentrated in the hands of the Shah and secular,
Westernized elites, ulama-state relations slowly deteriorated. The religious class found a natural alliance with the traditional merchant (*bazaari*) class and identified with populist political, economic, and social
issues.

In the early 1960s, Ayatollah Ruhollah Khomeini emerged as a key
antigovernment spokesman among a growing vocal minority of ulama
who viewed the Shah's modernization program (in particular land reform and women's suffrage) and Iran's close ties to the United States,
Israel, and multinational companies as a threat to Islam, to Iranian
Muslim life, and to national independence. Khomeini began to speak
out from his pulpit in Qum expressing uncompromising opposition to
absolutism and foreign "rule" or influence. He denounced the United
States as "an enemy of Islam in all its policies, this hostility being particularly apparent in its support for Israel and the nature of its influence in Iran."[1] In 1963 clashes in Qum (March 22) and Mashad (June
3) led to Khomeini's arrest on June 4 (the tenth day of Muharram, the
Islamic anniversary of the martyrdom of Imam Husayn). A series of
ulama-led popular demonstrations and disturbances in major cities
were brutally suppressed. Khomeini was released from prison but
within a short time began to speak out again. When Iran's parliament
passed legislation granting capitulatory rights to Americans several
days before Iran received a $200 million loan from the United States,
he bitterly declared:

> The government has sold our independence, reduced us to the
> level of a colony, and made the Muslim nation of Iran seem more
> backward than savages in the eyes of the world! . . . If the reli-
> gious leaders have influence they will not permit this nation to be

The Iranian Revolution

the slaves of Britain one day, and America the next . . . they will not permit Israel to take over the Iranian economy; they will not permit Israeli goods to be sold in Iran—in fact, to be sold duty free! . . . Are we to be trampled underfoot by the boots of America simply because we are a weak nation and have no dollars? America is worse than Britain; Britain is worse than America. The Soviet Union is worse than both of them. . . . But today it is America that we are concerned with.[2]

Khomeini was exiled to Turkey in 1964; he moved to Iraq in 1965 and then to France in 1978. While in exile he continued to teach, write (*Islamic Government*), and speak out against the Shah, condemning his "un-Islamic" policies. Tapes and pamphlets of his speeches were smuggled into Iran and distributed widely through the mosques. The safety of exile enabled Khomeini to remain an outspoken, uncompromising critic and eventually to become the primary symbol of opposition to the Shah. In a sermon he preached in Iraq, Khomeini succinctly articulated his vision of Islam and the role of the clergy: "Islam has a system and a program for all the different affairs of society: the form of government and administration, the regulation of people's dealings with each other, the relations of state and people, relations with foreign states and all other political and economic matters. . . . The mosque has always been a center of leadership and command, of examination and analysis of social problems."[3]

Opposition to the Shah grew throughout the 1970s, encompassing a broad spectrum of Iranian society: writers, poets, journalists; university professors and students; liberal nationalists and Marxists; secularists, traditionalists, and Islamic modernists. They shared concerns about the lack of political participation, the erosion of national autonomy, and the loss of religiocultural identity in an increasingly Westernized society. The clergy was joined by secular and Islamically oriented intelligentsia whose message was particularly influential among political thinkers and students. Jalal-Al-e-Ahmad, a former member of the Tudeh (Communist) party, warned of the dangers of Iran's fixation on the West. His initial acceptance of Iran's modernization program had become tempered by his wariness and finally bitter criticism of what he called "Weststruckness":

I say that [Weststruckness] is like cholera . . . It is at least as bad as sawflies in the wheat fields. Have you ever seen how they infest wheat? From within. There's a healthy skin in place, but it's only a skin, just like the shell of a cicada on a tree. . . . We're like a nation alienated from itself, in our clothing and our homes, our food and our literature, our publications and, most dangerously of all, our education. We affect Western training, we affect Western thinking, and we follow Western procedures to solve every problem.[4]

Another influential voice was that of Dr. Ali Shariati, a Sorbonne-educated intellectual who represented a new breed of religiously minded thinkers whose reformist views combined Third World anti-imperialism, Western social scientific language, and Iranian Shiism to produce a revolutionary Islamic ideology for sociopolitical reform. Shariati also denounced "Weststruckness": "Come friends let us abandon Europe; let us cease this nauseating, apish imitation of Europe. Let us leave behind this Europe that always speaks of humanity, but destroys human beings wherever it finds them."[5]

Shariati's reinterpretation of Islam incorporated the outlook of such Third World socialists as Che Guevara and Frantz Fanon. Like liberation theologians, Shariati differed from those who rejected traditional religions. Instead, he insisted that the defeat of Western imperialism required Iran's reclaiming of its national Islamic religiocultural identity. The dual focus of his revolutionary vision was national unity/identity and social justice. Only a movement dedicated to this program could hope to break the grip of "world imperialism, including multinational corporations and cultural imperialism, racism, class exploitation, class oppression, class inequality, and *garbzadegi* [Weststruckness]."[6]

The ideas and outlook of Jalal-Al-e-Ahmad, Ali Shariati, and Mehdi Bazargan (an engineer, a politician, and an Islamic modernist thinker) influenced a generation of students and intellectuals drawn from both the traditional and modern middle class. Many were graduates of secular universities; they included scientists, engineers, and other professionals. Most were from urban areas, although many had migrated from villages and rural areas to the cities for higher education and employment. These Islamically oriented students and professionals would later join with the clergy, seminarians, and *bazaaris* in opposition to the Shah.

By the mid-1970s, the political situation in Iran had deteriorated dramatically. The Shah's repressive policies affected the intelligentsia,

The Iranian Revolution

liberal nationalists, Marxists, clergy, merchants, and landowners alike, providing common cause for a broad-based opposition movement. Shii Islam proved to be the most viable, indigenously rooted vehicle for mobilizing an effective mass movement. It provided a sense of history and identity, common symbols and values, strong religiopolitical leadership, and organizational centers. Moreover, Shii Islam offered an ideological framework that gave meaning and legitimacy to an opposition movement of the disinherited and oppressed with which a variety of factions could identify and within which they could function. Clergy like the Ayatollahs Khomeini, Mutahhari, Taleqani, and Beheshti along with lay ideologues such as Bazargan and Shariati developed Islamic reformist and revolutionary ideologies. Influenced by the writings of Sunni Islamic activists such as Hasan al-Banna and Sayyid Qutb of the Egyptian Muslim Brotherhood, Mawlana Abul Ala Mawdudi of the Jamaat-i-Islami, and Muhammad Iqbal of Pakistan, the Iranian opposition members reinterpreted Shii history and belief in light of their own circumstances.

As a result, Iran's revolutionary ideology was distinctively Iranian and Shii. The martyrdom of Ali's rightful heir, his son Husayn, by the Sunni "usurper" caliph Yazid at Karbala in 680 was the religiopolitical paradigm for the Iranian revolution. This metahistorical event offered the central sacred story and symbols of oppression and revolt, suffering and martyrdom, and righteous struggle (*jihad*) against the forces of absolutism and social injustice. The army of God, of the good (Husayn, the Shah's opposition), was marshaled against the forces of the satanic opponent, the Shah.

The religious leadership remained untainted, neither cooperating with the government nor being silenced by it. It is true that a number of charismatic ayatollahs—Khomeini, Taleqani, Baha al-Din Mahallati— had suffered under the Shah for their opposition stance: "The royal court's tactics in dealing with the clergy . . . included virtually the entire range from harassment and administrative obstructionism to imprisonment, torture, and even execution."[7] But the government was less successful in suppressing the influence of the clergy, which spread throughout Iran from the pulpits of thousands of mosques, than it was in stifling the leadership of the secular opposition. Islamic lay reformers like Shariati and Bazargan were respected by many, especially by an alienated and increasingly militant younger generation. The ulama-mosque system provided a nationwide network of centers for communication and political action as well as a vast reservoir of grassroots leadership.

The year 1978 was a watershed in contemporary Iranian history. Politicized intelligentsia, ulama, students, and merchants were galvanized by the brutality of the government's response to a series of political protests from late 1977 to September 1978. Although many demonstrations remained peaceful, other protest meetings and strikes turned into riots as police and the military clashed with demonstrators, killing and wounding many. As the backbone of the movement, the ulama, merchants, and students closed down the bazaars and universities; mosque services became a time for prayer, political sermons, and mobilization. In the first half of 1978, demonstrations in Tabriz, Yazd, and Qum turned violent as government forces fired on the crowds of protestors. In turn, protestors attacked symbols of Pahlavi rule and its "Westernized" state: statues of the Shahs, liquor stores, cinemas, and luxury hotels. The crowds became more militant, shouting "Death to the Shah," "Cast out America," and "Husayn is our guide and Khomeini is our leader." Events came to a climax in September 1978 in Teheran. On September 7, more than 500,000 demonstrators protested the imposition of martial law. On September 8 (Black Friday), 75,000 protestors staged a sit-in in Jaleh Square. The crowd was fired upon by soldiers and tanks as well as helicopter gunships supplied, in large part, by the United States.

Black Friday proved to be the turning point in the revolution, uniting the opposition and mobilizing diverse sectors of the population under the banner of Islam. Professionals and white- and blue-collar workers joined with the ulama, seminarians, intellectuals, students, *bazaaris*, and urban poor. Islamic symbols, slogans, and ideology and the clergy-mosque infrastructure formed the core of the revolution. Millions of Iranians poured into the streets, shouting "Allahu Akbar" (God is Most Great), the traditional Islamic battle cry. Believer and unbeliever, secularist and religious activist, traditionalist and modernist attended Friday prayers, marched under the banners of Islam, and carried pictures of Khomeini and Shariati. Women who had worn Western clothes and enjoyed Westernized lifestyles joined their more traditional sisters in donning the *chador* as a symbol of protest. A wave of strikes mobilized support across the country as urban and rural peo-

The Iranian Revolution

ples, modern and traditional classes, and white- and blue-collar workers joined the opposition. By late October strikes had closed down shops, schools, government offices, oil fields, and refineries.

In December, during the Islamic month of Muharram, religious processions commemorating Husayn's martydom turned into protest marches. In Teheran, the *Ashura* (the tenth day of Muharram) procession drew two million people who marched through the streets of the capital calling for the death of the Shah, the return of Khomeini, and the establishment of an Islamic government. The embattled Shah, unable to count on American support and no longer able to control his country, left Iran on January 16, 1979. On February 1, 1979, the Ayatollah Khomeini returned on a chartered Air France jet, accompanied by an entourage of his followers and the Western press, and was greeted by millions of jubilant Iranians at Teheran's airport.

From Monarchy to Islamic Republic

Despite the chaos that accompanies all revolutions, the Islamic Republic of Iran took shape within a relatively brief period and began addressing its twin goals: domestic institutionalization of the revolution and its export internationally. By 1981 the Islamic Republic was institutionalized and the militant clergy emerged in full control of the government. Operating from a revivalist perspective, the new regime took quick measures to purify a corrupted society: Alcohol and gambling were banned; nightclubs and bars were closed down; prostitution, drug trafficking, and other forms of "corruption" were subject to capital punishment. The mosques and the media were employed to propagate the state's Islamic ideology. Most important, substantive institutional changes were undertaken. A referendum in March 1979 transformed Iran's government from a monarchy to an Islamic republic. A clerically dominated Assembly of Experts drafted a new constitution that was ratified by a popular referendum at the end of that year.

The constitution, which is based on Khomeini's concept of Islamic government, establishes direct clerical rule and guidance of the state. While accepting the doctrine of popular sovereignty, the constitution enshrines the principle of government of the jurist (*velayat-e faqih*), stipulating that the *faqih* is to be assisted by a Council of Guardians also composed of Islamic jurists.

Khomeini had developed his doctrine of rule by the jurist many years earlier in his seminary lectures and writings. In the absence of the just ruler, the Hidden Imam, Shii doctrine taught that Muslim society should be guided by Islamic law, the *Sharia*. Accepting the requirement that the true Muslim ruler should be noted for his "comprehensive knowledge, justice and moral character," Khomeini argued that instead of Islamic jurists merely advising the ruler, they should rule directly since, as experts on the *Sharia*, they were best equipped to assure governance according to Islamic law. Khomeini maintained that guardianship or governance by the jurist is similar to that exercised by the Prophet Muhammad. The jurist has the same authority, though not the same status, as the Prophet to govern and administer the affairs of state. Such governance may be exercised by a group of jurists or even a single individual.

The constitution names Khomeini the *faqih* for life. Upon his death, the office is to pass to a qualified successor or to a council of three to five jurists. This occurred when, shortly after Khomeini died on June 3, 1989, President Ali Hussein Khamenei was chosen to succeed Khomeini as the *faqih*. The *faqih* is invested with final authority as the supreme religiopolitical leader of the state: He is the final interpreter of Islamic law; he appoints the Council of Guardians, made up of heads of the judiciary, the military, and the Revolutionary Guards; and he serves as a check on the president, prime minister, and parliament. Against the adoption of the *faqih* system were modernist lay leaders like Mehdi Bazargan and Abul Hasan Bani-Sadr as well as such senior ayatollahs as Shariatmadari and Taleqani, who regarded Khomeini's interpretation of direct clerical rule as an unwarranted innovation of Shii doctrine. But the clerical majority in the Assembly of Experts supported the *faqih* system. Those few who feared that the institution could lead to dictatorship were offset by the many who saw the *faqih* as a barrier to dictatorship. As one delegate put it: "The *faqih*, like the Prophet, brings mercy, kindness and justice to the people, not absolutism."[8] In the end the majority of the Assembly apparently agreed with Khomeini's judgment: "The *velayat-e faqih* is not something created by the Assembly of Experts. It is something that God has ordained."[9]

The supremacy of Islamic law, and thus of jurists (the *faqih*, the Council of Guardians, and the judiciary), provided the basis for the consolidation of clergy dominance of the state. From its inception the government of the new Islamic Republic of Iran bore the seeds of dissension. The revolution had brought together a cross section of religious and secular elites, social classes, parties, and guerrilla movements which represented a variety of political and religious orientations. Although the opposition had a common enemy (Pahlavi depotism and foreign control) and a common purpose (a more just and egalitarian society), there had been no agreement on the form or leadership of the new government. Many were not prepared for what was to transpire in the early days of postrevolutionary Iran, and most were unaware of Khomeini's writings and views on the nature of government and politics. His criticisms of the Shah and his call for a new sociopolitical order had sounded not unlike that of many other critics of Pahlavi rule. Moreover, his advisers in Paris and in Iran immediately following his return had included French-educated Abul Hasan Bani-Sadr and U.S.-educated Sadeq Qotbzadeh, Mansur Farhang, and Ibrahim Yazdi—all modern lay thinkers influenced by the outlook of Ali Shariati. Even as Khomeini emerged as the principal symbol and leader of the revolution, many opposition members had expected that the clergy would return to their mosques and *madrasas* (seminaries) after the revolution.

Since Khomeini's appointment of Mehdi Bazargan as the prime minister of the provisional government in February 1979, tension and competition existed between two contending factions within what almost seemed to be a dual government: the militant clergy who controlled the Revolutionary Council and Bazargan's cabinet. By 1980 Bazargan had resigned, Bani-Sadr was elected Iran's first president, and the clerically controlled Islamic Republican party (IRP) had won a majority of seats in the parliamentary elections. But Bani-Sadr's belief that clerics should have an indirect rather than direct role in government put him at odds with the IRP, led by Ayatollah Muhammad Beheshti. Although a popular protégé of Khomeini, Bani-Sadr failed to build his own political organization and constituency. By June 1981 Khomeini's "devoted son" was impeached by the IRP-dominated parliament and, with the Ayatollah's approval, removed from office.

The clergy consolidated their power during the early 1980s as the broad-based coalition that had brought about the revolution disintegrated. At the apex of power were the *faqih*, the Supreme Judicial Council, and the Council of Guardians of the Revolution. They controlled the executive, legislative, and judicial branches of government, the media, and the Islamic Republican party. The Revolutionary Guards (*Pasdaran*) provided internal security and served as a check on the power of the military. Revolutionary committees (*komiteh*) and organizations (the Foundation for the Disinherited, the Jihad for Reconstruction, the Commission for Reconstruction and Renovation of the War Zones) engaged in a host of activities from security to social services. Officials and members of the old regime's institutions (the military, police, ministries, universities, and schools) were purged; secular, Islamic, and leftist dissidents were silenced. Appointments were based on revolutionary credentials and ideological rectitude as determined by the ruling clergy, while the slogan "Death to Bazargan" and "Death to Bani-Sadr" joined the cries of "Death to America." Bazargan and Ibrahim Yazdi were often harassed; the offices of their Freedom party were raided, ransacked, and finally closed down. Bani-Sadr fled to Paris. Sadeq Qotbzadeh, who had held a number of posts including that of foreign minister, was executed for his participation in a plot to assassinate Khomeini. Other clerics, including ayatollahs Taleqani, Tabatabai, and Shariatmadari, who had not accepted Khomeini's "rule of the jurist" or who were critical of the growing excesses of the Islamic republic were coerced and silenced. Moreover, Shariatmadari, a learned and revered senior ayatollah, was officially "demoted," stripped of the title Grand Ayatollah in the spring of 1982.[10]

Dissident clerical and lay voices were offset by a critical mass of committed clergy and laity and by the government's steps to foster and assure ideological purity. The Society of Militant (Combatant) Clergy was charged with identifying and confirming true, as distinct from dissident, clergy. Secular court judges were replaced by such "true" clerics, and a network of mosque preachers who served as the Ayatollah Khomeini's representatives throughout Iran was created. Each Friday they led Iranians in prayer and preached religiopolitical sermons intended to Islamize and mobilize the people according to the regime's ideology.

Since the early 1980s, the militant clergy has been supported by members of the "lay second stratum of the Islamic Republic,"[11] who accept clerical rule, serve in government, and fill many of the key positions in the state bureaucracy. These lay bureaucrats generally share a common social and educational background: Most are under forty years of age, come from lower middle class and *bazaari* families, and are often the first generation to obtain university education (mostly in science and medicine) at home and abroad.[12] They are represented by men like Prime Minister Hussein Musavi, Foreign Minister Ali Akbar Velayati, and a host of ministry officials, civil servants, and members of parliament. Thus, the Islamic Republic has been based upon a clerical-lay alliance committed to Khomeini and the revolution despite some differences in vision and policy.

Finally, the regime eliminated leftist parties and organizations. In the first years after the revolution, the relationship of the government to the left (the Marxist Tudeh party and Fedayen-e Khalq as well as the Islamic leftist Mujahidin-e Khalq) was one of mutual toleration if not support. But, shortly after Bani-Sadr's impeachment in 1981, the Mujahidin rebelled against the government. They clashed with Revolutionary Guards throughout the country and assassinated prominent clerics. Mujahidin were believed to be responsible for bombings of the IRP headquarters (June 1981), which killed party founder Ayatollah Beheshti and other party leaders. A subsequent bombing (August 1981) claimed the lives of President Muhammad Ali Rajaee and Prime Minister Javad Bohonar. The government countered with mass arrests and executions; more that seven thousand Mujahidin lost their lives. As a result, by 1982 the internal Mujahidin threat had been effectively neutralized; its leader, Masud Rajavi, fled to Paris, where, with Bani-Sadr, he formed the National Resistance Council.[13]

The Tudeh party had worked within the system and had not supported the Mujahidin. However, in the wake of warmer relations between the Soviet Union and Iraq during the Iran-Iraq war, the government cracked down on the Tudeh in the spring of 1983. Many of its leaders and members were arrested and the party was disbanded. Thus, by the mid-1980s it was clear that the militant clergy had consolidated its rule and effectively suppressed or destroyed all opposition, including secular nationalist, liberal, Islamic, and leftist rivals.

Export of the Revolution

The promotion and spread of revolutionary Islam was a primary foreign policy objective since the inception of Iran's new regime. This objective was rooted in the Koran's mandate to Muslims (and thus the Muslim mission) to realize and propagate God's message throughout the world. The goal of exporting the revolution paralleled the historic expansion and conquests of Islam (extension of the Pax Islamica) under Muhammad and his successors and was reflected in a worldview that distinguished between *dar al-Islam* (the territory of Islam) and *dar al-harb* (the territory of warfare). Indeed, Iran's new constitution explicitly proclaimed the Islamic rationale for an activist, aggressive foreign policy whose goal was the unity of the Islamic world and the extension of God's sovereignty throughout the world.

Ayatollah Khomeini espoused a nonsectarian or universalist Islamic revolution aimed at bridging the gap between Sunni and Shia Islam and liberating not just Shii Muslims but all the oppressed. A goal proclaimed by the new constitution was "to perpetuate the revolution both at home and abroad."[14] More than any other revolutionary objectives, this mission captured the attention of the media and struck fear in the hearts of Western and Muslim governments alike. Broadcasts of Iran's "Voice of the Islamic Revolution" appealed to Muslims of the Gulf states and beyond to rise up against their governments. Both the acrimonious rhetoric of Iran and the overreaction of its opponents have made it difficult to distinguish revolutionary hyperbole from reality.

The Iranian revolution occurred at a propitious time in an auspicious historical context. In the late 1960s and increasingly during the 1970s, much of the Muslim world experienced a resurgence of faith expressed in both private and public life. Greater attention to religious observances (prayer, fasting, religious dress, family values) was accompanied by a reassertion of Islam in state and society. Governments in Libya, Egypt, Sudan, Pakistan, and Malaysia appealed to Islam to legitimate their rule and policies, while opposition movements aligned themselves under the umbrella of Islam to rally popular support. Islamic rhetoric, symbols, and historic figures became prominent fixtures in Muslim politics, often used by rulers to buttress nationalism or by their opponents to challenge "Western-oriented" and "secular-inspired" state ideologies.

There was much in Iran's revolutionary experience and ideology that resonated with revivalist themes and concerns in other Muslim societies. First and foremost, the revolution was regarded as an *Islamic* revolution from its Islamically informed ideology to much of its clerical and lay leadership, as symbolized most clearly by the republic's primary ideologues, the Ayatollah Khomeini and Dr. Ali Shariati. As such, it was the first modern example of a successful Islamically inspired revolution. Second, the prototype of Westernizing modernization in the Middle East, the Shah's "White Revolution," produced a broad base of dissatisfaction shared by other Muslims as critics charged that Western models of development benefited a privileged urban elite and compromised Iran's sovereignty and independence by fostering political and cultural dependence on the West. Third, this backlash against "West-

The Iranian Revolution

struckness" was accompanied by a renewed sense of pride in past glories and a quest for identity that emphasized authenticity and a return to, or reappropriation of, indigenous values. Fourth, whatever the vast differences among Muslim societies, a return to the past meant a reclaiming of their Islamic history and heritage.

For a time, the Islamic revivalist experience of failure and disenchantment with Westernization had been offset by the newfound pride, power, and economic success of the Muslim community symbolized by the oil embargo of 1973. But Iran gave the world its first successful "Islamic" political revolution—one fought in the name of Islam under its battle cry "Allahu Akbar," based on Shii ideology and symbolism, and led by Islamically oriented clerical and lay leadership. As a result, Muslims around the world could revel in a heightened sense of Islamic identity and enjoy the restoration of Muslim pride and power in a world long dominated by foreign superpowers. Moreover, Ayatollah Khomeini explicitly offered the Iranian experience as a guide to the political and ideological transformation of the worldwide Muslim community (*ummah*); his agenda was to unite all Muslims in a political and cultural struggle against West and East. Victorious in its struggle, Iran now seemed poised to implement its principles at home and promote them abroad.

Islamic activists around the world could in fact readily identify with many of Iran's Islamic ideological principles. Among these were: (1) the reassertion of Islam as a total way of life; (2) the belief that the adoption of the Western, secular model of separation of church and state was the cause of the political, military, economic, and social ills of Muslim societies; (3) the conviction that the restoration of Muslim power and success required a return to Islam, which is the divinely mandated alternative to Western capitalism and Soviet-inspired Marxism and socialism; (4) the reintroduction of the *Sharia* (Islamic law) as the sacred blueprint for the good society, a moral and socially just community of believers; and (5) the willingness to struggle (*jihad*) against all odds, to suffer and to gain martyrdom (*shahada*) if necessary, in the path of God.

While firing the imaginations of many thoroughout the Muslim world, the success of the Iranian revolution made a number of Muslim governments nervous. Delegations of Muslim leaders from North America to Southeast Asia (including Sadiq al-Mahdi of the Sudan, Anwar Ibrahim of Malaysia, and Nur Misuari of the Philippines) trooped to Teheran to congratulate Khomeini. Shii in other Gulf states and Pakistan, who constitute a significant minority under Sunni rulership, boldly asserted their sectarian identity and ritual practices and expressed their discontent with current regimes. Sunni as well as Shii groups from Egypt (the moderate Muslim Brotherhood and radical al-Jihad) to Malaysia (ABIM, the Muslim Youth Movement of Malaysia, and the militant PAS, the Party of Islam in Malaysia) drew inspiration from Iran's example. Yasir Arafat led one of the first foreign delegations to Teheran, where he opened a PLO office in buildings that had previously housed the Israeli mission.[15] At the same time Muslim rulers increasingly branded their Islamic opposition as Khomeini-like or accused Iran of undue influence on domestic politics.

Gulf state rulers were particularly nervous about the appeal of Iran's revolutionary example and rhetoric. In Iraq, where Shii constitute 60 percent of the population, the Baath socialist government of Saddam Hussein was shaken by eruptions in Karbala, Najaf, and Kufa (June 1979). Khomeini had denounced Saddam Hussein as an atheist and called for the overthrow of his regime. Saddam Hussein countered by denouncing Khomeini and appealing to Iranian Arabs to revolt. At the same time, Ayatollah Muhammad Baqr al-Sadr, one of Iraq's most prominent and influential Shii clerics, had welcomed Iran's revolution and Khomeini's jurist-led government. The Iraqi government suspected Iranian involvement with Iraqi Shii activist groups, in particular the Islamic Call Society (*al-Dawa*) and the Mujahidin, formed in 1979.[16] Shii leaders were arrested; Ayatollah Sadr, who had declared the Baathist regime un-Islamic and forbade any dealings with it, was executed in April 1980; and al-Dawa was outlawed. In an atmosphere in which both governments played upon centuries of Arab-Persian hostility and Sunni-Shii rivalries, the situation rapidly deteriorated. On September 22, 1980, Iraq invaded Iran, initiating a war that would last eight years.

Khomeini was particularly critical of the Saudi and Gulf governments, both because they were "un-Islamic" monarchies and because of their military and economic ties with the United States, an influence he disdainfully referred to as "American Islam." Audiotapes of his speeches, leaflets, and daily Arabic broadcasts from Teheran made explicit Khomeini's critique and agenda: "The ruling regime in Saudi Arabia wears Muslim clothing, but it actually represents a luxurious, frivolous, shameless way of life, robbing funds from the people and squandering them, and engaging in gambling, drinking parties, and orgies. Would it be surprising if people follow the path of revolution, resort to violence and continue their struggle to regain their rights and resources."[17]

In November 1979 Saudi Arabia was rocked by two explosive events. On November 20, as Muslims prepared to usher in the fifteenth century of Islam, the Grand Mosque at Mecca was seized and occupied for two weeks by Saudi-led Sunni militants who denounced the Saudi monarchy. Khomeini's accusation that Americans were behind the mosque seizure led to attacks against U.S. embassies; the embassy in Islamabad, Pakistan, was burned down. While Saudi Arabia reeled from the seizure of the Grand Mosque, riots broke out a week later in the oil-rich Eastern Province (El Hasa) whose 250,000 Shii constitute 35 percent of the population. Pent-up emotions and grievances among Shii, who felt discriminated against by their Sunni rulers and called for a fairer distribution of oil wealth and services, had exploded earlier in the year in response to Iran's revolution and Khomeini's triumphant return.

Events in the early 1980s did nothing to lessen concern among Muslim and Western governments. Statements by Iran's leading ayatollahs, which called for an aggressive expansionist policy, exacerbated the situation. President Ali Khamenei called upon prayer leaders from forty countries to turn their mosques into "prayer, cultural and military bases [to] . . . prepare the ground for creation of Islamic governments in all countries."[18] The Iran-Iraq war inflamed relations between Iran and its neighbors. The Gulf states organized the Gulf Cooperation Council (GCC) and threw their substantial financial support to Iraq. Khomeini called upon the GCC to "return to the lap of Islam, abandon the Saddam Hussein regime in Baghdad, and stop squandering the wealth of their peoples."[19] The Saudis countered such statements: "Ever since the Iranian and Islamic peoples were afflicted by the Khomeini regime, this regime has failed to render any noteworthy service to Islam, and the Muslims. . . . This regime has tried to create schism among Muslims, not only in their politics but also in their mosques. The Khomeini regime sends its agents everywhere to foment discord."[20]

Iran used the annual pilgrimage (*hajj*) to Mecca to propagate its revolutionary message. Ayatollah Khomeini and other senior clerics rejected the Saudis claim to be the keepers of the holy sites and maintained that the *hajj* had a rightful political dimension. Iranian pilgrims, displaying posters of Khomeini and chanting slogans against the United States, the Soviet Union, and Israel, clashed with Saudi security in June 1982. The tensions continued during subsequent years and climaxed in 1987 when more than four hundred people were killed in a confrontation between Iranian pilgrims and Saudi security forces.

Bahrain and Kuwait have also been threatened by Shii unrest. In 1981 the government of Bahrain foiled an Iranian-inspired coup by the Islamic Front for the Liberation of Bahrain. Kuwait, 30 percent of whose population is Shii, was troubled by car bombings of the U.S. and French embassies in 1983 and cracked down on Shii unrest in 1987 and 1989.

Yet despite these sporadic disturbances and government fears of massive unrest, revolutionary Iran proved to be surprisingly unsuccessful in rallying Iraqi Shii and the populations of the Gulf states. By and large, most Iraqi Shii, who constitute the majority of the rank and file in the military, remained loyal to their nation over their coreligionists in Iran. Pockets of Shii militancy in the Gulf states did not translate into significant revolutionary movements as regimes used a carrot-and-stick approach, addressing socioeconomic grievances while increasing security and prosecuting dissidents.

Lebanon's experience in the 1980s is a sharp contrast to that of the Gulf states. Iran's Revolutionary Guards entered Lebanon, and the republic has supplied training, material, and money to Shii militant organizations such as Islamic Amal, Hezbollah, and al-Jihad who have fought Christian and Muslim militias alike and whose goal is the eventual creation of an Islamic state. Iranian inspiration, if not direct complicity, has been suspected in everything from embassy and car bombings to the taking of hostages. In many ways Lebanon provides the clearest and boldest example of the direct impact of Iran's revolution.

Following the 1988 truce that ended the Iran-Iraq war, Iran turned to the arduous task of reconstruction. The human and economic toll of the war was devastating. The defense of Islam and of the Iranian nation had provided a national rallying point, reinforced a sense of unity and morale, and served as a distraction from serious domestic problems. Failure to achieve victory, a war-torn economy, and a general deterioration in the quality of life brought soul-searching and discontent and exacerbated ideological differences within the government over strate-

The Iranian Revolution

gies for national reconstruction and export of the revolution. Divisions had existed within the ruling elite since the beginning of the Islamic Republic and were manifest in the struggles between militants and moderates, parliamentary debates, and the conduct of the Iran-Iraq war. While the leadership in Iran remained committed to the revolution, rival factions differed over domestic and foreign policy issues such as land reform, nationalization, promotion of the revolution aboard, and relations with the West.

Postrevolutionary attempts to articulate and implement an Islamic alternative to the Shah's modernization program have revealed deep divisions between those who favor private-sector freedom and those who advocate radical socioeconomic reforms through state control of the economy. These divisions are complicated by differing interpretations of Islamic law and conflicting class interests. The parliament has managed to pass legislation that would bring about substantive social change through land reform, the expansion of state control over the economy, and the consequent restriction of free enterprise. But merchants, who had been the financial backbone of the ulama and the revolution, along with landowners (who include many clerical leaders) have strongly opposed such measures and effectively lobbied so that the Council of Guardians has fairly consistently vetoed reform legislation as contrary to Islamic law. While these traditionalists have been content to cite centuries-long norms, more radical reformers have argued that new circumstances require fresh legal interpretations.

Differences over economic policies have been matched by deep political divisions and skirmishes between pragmatists and more radical hardliners. The former are represented by Hashemi Rafsanjani, the speaker of the parliament, Ali Akbar Velayati, the foreign minister, and Ali Khamenei, the president. The latter are led by Mir Hussein Musavi, the prime minister, and Ali Akbar Mohtashemi, the minister of the interior. In October 1986, Mehdi Hashemi, head of the bureau in charge of the export of the revolution, was arrested and executed. Hardliners had leaked to the press information about meetings between Robert McFarlane, former U.S. national security adviser, and Rafsanjani regarding the sale of U.S. arms to Iran for the release of American hostages in Lebanon. Rafsanjani seemed to bounce back when he and others persuaded Khomeini to do the unthinkable, call a halt to the war with Iraq and agree to a truce.

Between August 1988 and February 1989, it looked as if the prag-

matists were in the ascendancy as relations with the West warmed, diplomatic and economic missions from the West increased, and Iran
worked in the United Nations and through international delegations to
shore up its image, particularly in the area of human rights. As most
analysts were speaking of a move toward normalization with the West
and even the possibility of improved relations with the United States
seemed possible, the tide abruptly turned in February 1989 with the
publication of Salman Rushdie's *The Satanic Verses*. Khomeini's condemnation of the book, its publishers, and of Britain and the United
States and his call for the execution of the author precipitated an international crisis. Riots and deaths in Pakistan and India occurred in the
midst of Iran's official celebration of the revolution's tenth anniversary.
The Rushdie affair provided the radicals with an issue that would lure
the regime away from the influence of the more flexible pragmatic
camp, offered Khomeini an occasion to reassert his Islamic leadership
internationally and to rekindle militant fervor for the defense of Islam,
and thus shifted attention away from Iran's pressing socioeconomic
problems and growing social discontent. Iran's break in diplomatic relations with Britain, the forced resignation of Khomeini's designated
successor Ayatollah Montazeri, who had become a leading advocate of
moderation (criticizing the regime's slighting of human rights and calling for reconciliation with liberal elements such as Bazargan's Freedom
party as well as the Mujahidin), the dismissal of a number of moderate
and pragmatists in the government, and the resurgence of radical hardline rhetoric all point to yet another phase in the history of the
republic.

Ten years after the revolution, Iran finds itself at yet another cross-
roads. Internationally, it remains relatively isolated within the international community. Moreover, the excesses of the revolution have dis-
illusioned many of its early supporters in the Muslim world.
Domestically, the death of the Ayatollah Khomeini has provided Iran's
new president, Hashemi Rafsanjani, with new opportunities as well as
challenges for power and leadership. The no-win war with Iraq has
taken its human and economic toll. The suppression of opposition voices
and the regime's at times erratic and arbitrary imposition of its ideological programs and policies have silenced much public dissent but
have also undermined the revolutionary commitment of many Iranians.
The militant clergy had been able to retain power and control government institutions but not without great costs. The return to peace pro-

vides a climate not only for new possibilities but also for the reassertion of unrealized expectations—and thus the potential for serious problems. The need for postwar reconstruction, the obligation to deliver the equitable and just society initially promised by the revolution, and the continued struggle for paramount power within the leadership since Khomeini's death—all constitute formidable challenges to the well-being of the Islamic Republic of Iran.

Notes

1. Hamid Algar, "The Oppositional Role of the Ulama in Twentieth-Century Iran," in *Scholars, Saints, and Sufis: Muslim Religious Institutions since 1500,* ed. Nikki R. Keddie (Berkeley and Los Angeles: University of California Press, 1972), 247.

2. Ruhollah Khomeini, *Islam and Revolution: Writings and Declarations of Imam Khomeini,* trans. Hamid Algar (Berkeley: Mizan Press, 1981), 182–185.

3. Ibid., 249–50.

4 Jalal-Al-e-Ahmad, *Garbzadegi* (Weststruckness), trans. John Green and Ahmad Alizadeh (Lexington, Ky.: Mazda Press, 1982), 11, 59.

5. Ali Shariati, *On the Sociology of Islam* (Berkeley: Mizan Press, 1979), 17.

6. Ervard Abrahamian, "Ali Shariati: Ideologue of the Iranian Revolution," *MERIP Reports* 102 (January 1982), 26.

7. Shahrough Akhavi, "Iran: Implementation of an Islamic State," in *Islam in Asia: Religion, Politics, and Society,* ed. John L. Esposito (New York: Oxford University Press, 1987), 31.

8. Shaul Bakhash, *The Reign of the Ayatollahs: Iran and the Islamic Revolution* (New York: Basic Books, 1984), 85.

9. Ibid., 86.

10. Akhavi, 38.

11. Said Amir Arjomand, *The Turban for the Crown: The Islamic Revolution in Iran* (New York: Oxford University Press, 1987), 164.

12. Ibid.

13. Eric Hooglund, "Iran 1980–85: Political and Economic Trends," in *The Iranian Revolution and the Islamic Republic,* 2d ed., Nikki R. Keddie and Eric Hooglund (Syracuse N.Y.: Syracuse University Press, 1986), 20–21.

14. "Constitution of the Islamic Republic of Iran," *Middle East Journal* 34 (Spring 1980): 185.

15. Delip Hiro, *Iran Under the Ayatollahs* (London: Routledge & Kegan Paul, 1985), 348.

16. See Michael C. Hudson, "The Islamic Factor in Syrian and Iraqi Politics," in *Islam in the Political Process,* ed. James P. Piscatori (Cambridge: Cambridge University Press, 1983), 86ff.

17. Jacob Goldberg, "The Shii Minority in Saudi Arabia," in *Shiism and Social*

Protest, ed. Juan R.I. Cole and Nikki R. Keddie (New Haven: Yale University Press, 1986), 243.

18. Bakhash, 234–35.
19. Hiro, 340.
20. Ibid.

3

Iran's Export of

the Revolution:

Politics, Ends, and Means

R.K. RAMAZANI

"Since its creation following several decades of genuine Islamic and popular struggle the Islamic Republic of Iran has considered it one of its main duties to defend dear Islam, its sacred aspirations, and the oppressed Muslims in every region of the world." [Iran's Ministry of Foreign Affairs, March 7, 1989]

AYATOLLAH RUHOLLA KHOMEINI'S imposition of a death sentence on Salman Rushdie ignited a new global crisis. The move demonstrated that Iran's underlying commitment to "the export of the revolution" (*sodour-e enqelab*) was alive and well. It also demonstrated that an assessment of the relative impact of Iran's export activities compared with the indigenous causes of Islamic resurgence in other societies can have profound implications for not only the Muslim world but also the international system as a whole. Such assessment is the principal burden of this volume, which seeks to inquire into the global impact of the Iranian revolution. The main objective of this chapter is to explore the politics, ends, and means of exporting the revolution in the overall context of Iran's foreign policy.

The appellation "The export of the revolution," unlike such terms as "intervention," "aggression," and "self-defense," is not commonly found in the literature of international relations. Yet the basic idea that underpins the act of exporting revolution is part and parcel of ancient as well as modern international relations when defined broadly and not just Eurocentrically in terms of the post-Westphalia international society.[1] As sacred as the Prophet's Islamic revolution may be, and as secular as the American, French, and Russian revolutions have been, the concept of exporting revolution is a corollary of the phenomenon of the revolution throughout world history. This proposition also holds true for the more recent example of the Iranian revolution. By intervention, America wants to make the world safe for democracy; witness the cases of Iran, Guatemala, El Salvador, and Nicaragua. And by invasion, the Soviet Union wants to make the world safe for socialism; witness the cases of Czechoslovakia and Afghanistan. And by the export of its revolution, the Islamic Republic of Iran wants to make the world safe for Islam; witness the cases of the Persian Gulf, Lebanon, and Soviet Azerbaijan and Turkmenistan.

The Politics

Like the Iranian revolution itself, the emergence of the revolution's export as a fundamental foreign policy principle reflected Iran's domestic political dynamics. The revolt in Iran was a populist opposition to both the Shah's foreign policy and domestic politics.[2] The disparate forces of opposition were as united against the Shah's de facto alliance with the United States as they were against his repressive rule. The revolutionary epithet "the American king" reflected a nationwide resentment of the surrogacy of Iran, especially as the Nixon-anointed "policeman" of the Persian Gulf. Whether one traces the roots of the Iranian revolution to the CIA-engineered overthrow of Muhammad Mossadeq's nationalist government in 1953, or to the bloody suppression of the Khomeini-led anti-Shah uprising in 1963, or to earlier developments in Iranian society, politics, and culture, the fact remains that at no time before the 1972–77 period had the alienation from the Shah's regime and the United States reached such explosive levels of populist expression.[3]

In the early days of Khomeini's regime, from Mehdi Bazargan's appointment as prime minister of the provisional government in February 1979 until Iranian students seized the U. S. Embassy in Teheran in November of that year, the principle of "equilibrium" (*tavazon*) dominated the theory and practice of Iranian foreign policy. Historically, the principle of equilibrium had great appeal to modern-educated Iranians. Mirza Taqi Khan, better known as Amir Kabir, first introduced the principle into Iranian foreign policy during his short-lived premiership in 1848–51 as an antidote to the European balance-of-power principle.[4] He believed that Iran might better ensure its independence by maintaining an equilibrium between rival British and Russian influences than by aligning itself with one or the other imperial power. During his equally short-lived premiership in 1951–53, Mossadeq tried to pursue a policy of "negative equilibrium" (*movazene-ye manfi*).[5] Covert CIA intervention, however, destroyed his government, at which point the Shah's regime allied itself with a vengeance to the United States until it too was overthrown.

Although a devout Muslim, Bazargan attempted, as a modern-educated engineer, to pursue the same policy toward the great powers as had his old friend and colleague Mossadeq. His government terminated Iran's membership in the U. S.-sponsored Central Treaty Organization (CENTO) and the Iranian-U. S. defense act of March 5, 1959, while repudiating the nefarious Articles V and VI of the Soviet-Iranian treaty of 1921.[6] The Bazargan government sought amicable relations with Iran's Muslim neighbors, as evidenced by its desire to strengthen the Regional Cooperation Development (RCD) arrangement of 1964 with Pakistan and Turkey. According to the testimony of the Iraqi ministry of foreign affairs, the Bazargan government also sought improved relations with Baghdad.[7] And when Ayatollah Sadeq Ruhani threatened to annex Bahrain unless it adopted an Iranian type of Islamic government, Bazargan denounced the Ayatollah's unauthorized statement and sent envoys to Bahrain and Saudi Arabia to allay their fears.[8]

The seizure of the U. S. Embassy in Teheran did more than precipitate the resignation of the Bazargan government on November 6, 1979. It also split Iranian foreign policy right down the middle. Until January 20, 1981, when the dispute over the American hostages was settled, the self-styled student followers of Khomeini struggled for control of Iranian foreign policy against government ministers such as Abul Hasan Bani-Sadr and Sadeq Qotbzadeh. Both Bani-Sadr and Qotbzadeh were in effect inspired by Mossadeq's foreign policy orientation, although Bani-Sadr rationalized his policy of "equidistance" in Islamic terms. That is, his conception of Islamic foreign policy accorded first priority to the Iranian national interest rather than to the interests of the Muslim world or the whole Third World.[9] For this reason, he considered the seizure of the embassy contrary to the law of nations and sought to settle the dispute with the United States by peaceful means. Qotbzadeh, on the other hand, simply subscribed to Mossadeq's policy of "negative equilibrium" and did not hesitate to describe his foreign policy in those terms.[10]

The students' hostility toward the United States was paralleled by their friendly attitude toward anti-American and anti-Western liberation movements. According to Bazargan, the students were supported by the leftist elements of the Tudeh (Communist) party and the Mujahidin-e Khalq organization, and this may well have been true at the time of the embassy takeover. Subsequently, however, the Islamicists on the extreme right dominated the student faction, representing what can best be described as the radical idealist followers of Khomeini.[11] Many such idealists were also to be found among Khomeini's clerical disciples. Whether lay or clerical, these radical idealists interpreted the Ayatollah's call for the export of the revolution to mean that it should be put into practice at any price. In defiance of Iranian policy makers, particularly Bani-Sadr and Qotbzadeh, the students sponsored an international conference in Teheran of some sixteen liberation movements from around the world. Other radical idealists, such as Muhammad Montazeri, the son of Ayatollah Hussein Ali Montazeri, took it upon themselves to try to export the revolution by any means, including the use of force. Muhammad Montazeri organized the Iranian Revolutionary Organization of the Masses of the Islamic Republic and wished to dispatch Islamic fighters to Lebanon as early as December 1979, long before the Revolutionary Guards were sent there in 1982. He was opposed by Bani-Sadr and Qotbzadeh just as he had been by Bazargan.

Although, as we shall see, Khomeini's call for the export of the revolution had deep roots in his ideology and in the Irano-Islamic political culture, I suggest it emerged from the crucible of the hostage crisis. The seizure of the U. S. Embassy on November 4, 1979, and the fall of the Bazargan government two days later were dubbed by the Khomeinists as the "second revolution," an event Khomeini himself considered even more significant than the overthrow of the Shah's regime. From the perspective of Iranian domestic politics, this second revolution represented the first successful move by the Islamicists against the centralists or nationalists, who are pejoratively labeled "liberals" by their opponents. The anti-liberal Islamicists consisted of lay and clerical, as well as radical idealist and pragmatic realist, factions. They were opposed by other clerical idealists such as Hussein Ali Montazeri, clerical realists such as Hashemi Rafsanjani, lay idealists such as Mir Hussein Musavi, and lay realists such as Ali Akbar Velayati.

This second revolution also marked the transformation of Iran's fundamental foreign policy principle of equilibrium to one of a struggle between good and evil. Under the equilibrium principle, the government took the international system for granted and tried to protect and promote Iran's national interest by maintaining a balance of power and influence in relation to other states. After the second revolution, the foreign policy makers questioned the very legitimacy of the existing international system; they sought to protect and promote Iran's Islamic interest by rejecting the dominance of both superpowers in the international system and by exporting the revolution throughout the world. In other words, the second revolution introduced into Iran's foreign policy the twin principles of "neither East nor West, but the Islamic Republic" (*nah sharq va nah gharb, faqat jomhoori-e Islamy*) and "the export of the revolution" (*sodour-e enqelab*). We shall explore in the following section the foundations of these two principles. Suffice it to say here that they were essentially incorporated into the republic's new constitution which was ratified in early December 1979, about a month after the embassy takeover.[12]

Because of the secrecy surrounding many of Iran's activities, it is difficult to state with certainty when the principle of export of the revolution was first implemented. One can, however, make the case that it was not fully put into practice until after the "third revolution," that is, after the fall of President Bani-Sadr in June 1981. More specifically, it is possible to argue that the principle was formally adopted during the tenure of Mir Hussein Musavi as foreign minister (July–December 1981). This claim can be substantiated as follows: First, none of the foreign ministers before Muhammad Ali Rajaee, that is, neither Karim Sanjabi, Ibrahim Yazdi, Abul Hasan Bani-Sadr, nor Sadeq Qotbzadeh, believed in the export of the revolution, although Bani-Sadr did talk about the "universal mission" of the revolution. Second, although a lay Islamicist and a believer in the export of the revolution, Rajai was preoccupied with settling the hostage dispute with the United States during part of his short tenure. Third, Musavi was the first foreign minister to envisage the need for creating a committee in the ministry of foreign affairs that would "determine the basis of the foreign policy from an ideological perspective, and the principle of rule of theocracy."[13] Moreover, he decided to draw up a "plan for an Islamic front" worldwide, which he said would be "followed up" by the Iranian ministry of foreign affairs "because the fight against imperialism should take place all over the world."[14]

Of even greater consequence, however, was the establishment of the Islamic Revolutionary Council as an umbrella organization. It included such groups as the Supreme Assembly of the Islamic Revolution in Iraq (SAIRI), the Islamic Revolution Movement of the Arabian Peninsula, the Islamic Front for the Liberation of Bahrain, and a liberation group for Syria and Lebanon. These groups were linked to the Islamic Revolutionary Guards Corps (IRGC) through its Islamic liberation movement unit. According to Iran's constitution, the IRGC itself "will be responsible not only for defending the borders, but also for the mission stated in the Book, of holy war in the way of God and fighting to expand the rule of God's law (*Sharia*) in the world."

The suppression of the liberal nationalists and leftists as a consequence of the second and third revolution ensured the political ascendancy of the Islamicists. But just as the disparate political forces had all joined hands in opposition to the Shah's regime and had then quickly divided after its fall, the Islamicists had at first united their forces against the liberal nationalists and leftists and had then broken up into factions after their triumph against their opponents. In regard to Iran's foreign policy in general, the Islamicists divided into what can best be described as "radical idealists" and "pragmatic realists." Khomeini referred to this division in terms of "two schools of thought" while Hashemi Rafsanjani simply speaks of them as "factions." What is meant by "radical idealist" and "pragmatic realist" should become clear in the light of the following discussion of the ends and means of the export of the revolution.[15]

The Ends

To understand the desired outcome of the export of the revolution, one must examine not only Khomeini's political philosophy but also those aspects of the Irano-Islamic political tradition from which even the Ayatollah could not escape. Space does not permit a detailed exploration of these subjects here, but their relevance to the ends and means of the revolution's export requires at least a brief analysis.

One of the fundamental features of Iranian political culture, which dates back to pre-Islamic Persia, is the incessant quest for the establishment of an ideally virtuous society, defined primarily in terms of universal justice. As noted by Adda B. Bozeman, pre-Islamic Persian statesmen posed "for the first time in historically known terms" the problems of moral principles in international relations in the sixth century B.C. when the tyranny of empires plagued the fabric of community everywhere. The Persian Empire attained "universal" peace for some two hundred years in large part as the result of a "policy of tolerance." Bozeman attributes this tolerance to "the statesmanship rather than . . . the religious ethics of the sixth century B.C."[16] In other words, the foreign policy of tolerance in ancient times reflected a kind of prudent realism rather than religious idealism.

It was indeed prudent for these early statesmen to recognize the cultural diversity of the peoples they ruled as a means of maintaining the Persian Empire, an empire vaster than any preceding it west of China. But I suggest that this realism was inseparable from an essentially religiously based idealism which required that Persian statesmen as well as their subjects observe the norm of justice in their own conduct. Only the just individual and society, it was believed, were good. The government and the governed were equally bound by Zoroastrian ethics to think "good thoughts" (*pendar-e nik*), to speak "good words" (*goftar-e nik*), and to do "good deeds" (*kerdar-e nik*). All this was commanded by the cosmic "Force of Good," Ahura Mazda, which was expected to triumph over the rival "Force of Evil," Ahriman. The ruler no less than the ruled had to abide by the commandment of Ahura Mazda. "By Ahura Mazda's will," said King Darius, "I am of such nature that I am a friend to the just; I am no friend to the unjust. What is right is my desire. I am not a friend to the man that followeth falsehood."

Neither modern Iran nor Islam itself could escape these pre-Islamic cultural values, particularly the ideal of a just society. Western observer Malise Ruthven notes the overriding importance of justice in Islam: "Whereas Christianity is primarily the religion of love, Islam is above all the religion of justice."[17] And, I may add, in the Shia cultural tradition in general and in that of Imami Shiism in particular, justice ranks the highest among all values. The violent and bloody martyrdom of Imam Husayn at Karbala symbolizes the historical injustice suffered by the Shias at the hands of such a cruel oppressor (*zalem*) as Shamr. The heroically oppressed (*mazlum*) Imam Husayn will only be avenged when the Mahdi, or the Twelfth Imam, reappears (*zohur*) to establish justice throughout the world.

This essentially chiliastic hope for a just world order among the deprived Shias (*mahroomin*) was defensive in nature and grew out of the conflict between the Shia minority and the Sunni majority. For Persian Shias this messianic hope was at first a shield against the Arab conquest in the seventh century. Later, in the sixteenth century, when the Safavid dynasty made Shiism a state ideology for the first time in Islamic history, Shiism was still defensive in nature; it was primarily a protective mechanism against the aggression of the powerful Ottoman Empire.

During the two centuries preceding the Iranian revolution, the ancient Irano-Islamic quest for justice underpinned Iran's struggle for independence from Russia, both tsarist and Communist, and from the Western powers, first Britain and then the United States. Led partly by the Shia *ulama*, the popular demand for a "house of justice" (*adalet khaneh*) ignited the constitutional revolution of 1905–11, which sought to limit both the tyranny of absolute monarchy and the Anglo-Russian political and economic domination of Iran. Muhammad Mossadeq viewed his nationalist movement of 1951–53 as an essentially "moral" struggle against the age-old British "enslavement" (*enqiad*) of Iran. Interestingly, the same concept of enslavement was used by Khomeini in characterizing the nature of U.S. domination in 1964, when the Pentagon extracted a humiliating status-of-forces agreement from the Shah's regime. Thus, as different as Mossadeq's essentially secular nationalist movement and Khomeini's religious Islamic movement are in nature, they share the goal of an overriding quest for justice, a hallmark of the legacy of the Irano-Islamic political culture.

What kind of justice did Khomeini envision and how does it relate to the export of the revolution? Khomeini wanted a universal justice and believed that only an Islamic world order could bring that about. Furthermore, only a *faqih*-led Islamic republic such as Iran could pave the way for the establishment of an Islamic world order. This concept of the *velayat-e faqih* (leadership of the jurisprudent) is the innovative contribution of Khomeini's political thought. Traditionally, the leadership of the Shia community belongs to God, to the Prophet Muhammad, and to the infallible Imams (*ma'sumin*), but Khomeini extended that leadership to the *faqih*, to whom belongs temporal as well as spiritual authority which he should exercise in the absence of the Hidden Imam who will appear "at the end of time" (*akhar-e zaman*) in order to establish a just world order. Khomeini was quite emphatic that the goal of Islam is to bring justice to the entire world, not simply to Iran or even to the Muslim world: "Islam is not peculiar to a country, several countries, a group [of people or countries] or even the Muslims. Islam has come for humanity. Islam addresses the people and only occasionally addresses the believers. Islam wishes to bring all of humanity under the umbrella of its justice."[18]

This concern of Islam with mankind is clearly reflected in the Iranian constitution. Although Article 11 provides that the Iranian government "should exert continuous efforts in order to realize the political, economic and cultural unity of the Islamic world," Article 154 states that the "Islamic Republic of Iran considers its goal to be the happiness of human beings in all human societies." Thus, the unity of the Muslim world and the happiness of mankind constitute the ultimate goals of the foreign policy of revolutionary Iran, and the unity of the Muslim world is viewed as the first step toward the eventual happiness of humanity at large. But what constitutes the essence of that happiness?

The answer to that question may be explored in the context of Khomeini's view of the nature of the Islamic revolution in Iran. In contrasting modern revolutions, including the French and Russian, with the Iranian, he contended that those revolutions were inspired primarily by "material" considerations, whereas the Iranian Revolution was motivated mainly by the "divine."[19] Because of this distinctive spirituality of the Iranian Revolution, "Islamic justice for all" can bring happiness to mankind as a whole. This essentially Manichaean dichotomy between the material and spiritual is well known in the intellectual history of the Middle East, but Khomeini was the first in modern times to interject it into the discourse on Iran's international relations.

An example of this effort is found in Khomeini's letter of January 1, 1989, to Soviet leader Mikhail Gorbachev in which he stated in no uncertain terms that both the East and the West are ideologically bankrupt bcause they lack spiritual values. Khomeini offered to fill this "ideological vacuum" with Islamic values, which alone "can be a means for the well-being and salvation of all nations." Marxism "does not answer any of the real needs of man. It is a materialistic ideology, and it is not possible to save humanity through materialism from the crisis of lack of conviction in spirituality which is the most fundamental ailment of human society in the West and the East." While many in the West have welcomed Gorbachev's *glasnost* and *perestroika,* Khomeini advised him: "I strongly urge you that in breaking down the walls of Marxist fantasies [*khialat*] you do not fall into the prison of the West and the Great Satan." Reiterating that the unhappiness in both the West and the East reflects the lack of spirituality, he told Gorbachev categorically: "One should turn to truth. The main difficulty of your country is not the issue of ownership, economics, or freedom. Your difficulty is the lack of true faith in God, the same difficulty which has also dragged the West toward decadence and a dead end. Your principal problem is a long and futile combat with God, the origin of existence and creation."

In trying to introduce Gorbachev to the alternative path of Islam as contrasted with the Western way of life, Khomeini suggested that the Soviets could conduct research in Islam by referring, "in addition to the books of Western philosophers, to the books written by Farabi and Bu-Ali Sina." He also referred him to the books of Sohrevardi regarding "the philosophy of illumination" (*hekmat-e Eshraq*) and to the works of mystics, "particularly those of Muhyiddin ibn Arabi." In conclusion he said, "I openly announce the Islamic Republic of Iran, as the greatest and most powerful base of the Islamic world, can easily help fill up the ideological vacuum of your system. . . . "[20]

The twin foreign policy principles of Khomeini's Iran are implicit in the letter to Gorbachev. First, by rejecting both the Eastern and Western ways of life on the ground of lack of religious spirituality, Khomeini was invoking his favorite principle of "neither East nor West." Second, by suggesting that Iran, as the most powerful base of the Islamic world, could easily fill the ideological vacuum everywhere in the world. Khomeini was actually engaging in the export of the revolution, in this instance to the Soviet Union by means of philosophical discussion. With respect to the first principle, he had declared a decade earlier that "a nation that cries in unison that it wants an Islamic Republic, it wants neither East nor West but only an Islamic republic—this being so, we have no right to say that the nation that engaged in an uprising did so in order to have democracy. . . . "[21] In Khomeini's worldview, "Islamic democracy" is superior to both Eastern and Western varieties. With respect to the second principle, about a decade earlier Khomeini had said:

Export of the Revolution

We should try hard to export our revolution to the world. We should set aside the thought that we do not export our revolution, because Islam does not regard various Islamic countries differently and is the supporter of all the oppressed peoples of the world. On the other hand, all the superpowers and all the powers have risen to destroy us. If we remain in an enclosed environment we shall definitely face defeat.[22]

Thus, when viewed in light of the Irano-Islamic political culture and Khomeini's political philosophy, three overriding goals of the export of the revolution became apparent. In the short term, it is a means for defense of the Islamic Republic led by one supreme *faqih* or three to five *fuqaha*. It is also a means for ensuring the security of the republic internationally, particularly in the Persian Gulf. And in the long run, it is a means for the ultimate establishment of a world order under "the umbrella of Islamic justice." A note of caution is in order, however. While the shorter term goals are relatively unambiguous, it is not clear whether the long-term objective can indeed be termed a "goal," despite the fact that the Iranian constitution obligates the government to exert continuous efforts toward realizing the comprehensive unity of the Islamic world and, in fact, uses the very word "goal" in regard to "the happiness of human beings in all human societies" as the ultimate end. One reason for this lack of clarity is the fact that the Irano-Islamic quest for a just world order is, as we have seen, an essentially chiliastic and largely defensive aspiration. The other reason is that in Khomeini's view the attainment of universal Islamic happiness is a matter of hope and gradual occurrence. In his words, "We hope this will gradually come about."[23]

Coercive Means

Greater ambiguity surrounds the means by which the revolution is to be exported. The first and most important question is whether the use of force is allowed. On numerous occasions, Khomeini and his disciples have consistently declared that "swords" should not be used. Note, for example, the Ayatollah's dictum: "It does not take swords to export this ideology. The export of ideas by force is no export."[24] Or this statement: "When we say we want to export our revolution, we do not want to do it with swords."[25] But does this mean that the use of armed force is prohibited? At first glance, Khomeini's view that the use of force is permissible only in self-defense, a guideline compatible with both Shia legal norms and the principles of modern international law, seems to prohibit the use of military force, presumably in whatever form, for the export of the revolution. But the concept of self-defense in Khomeini's ideology presents the same kind of problem of definition that it does under Article 51 of the Charter of the United Nations: What constitutes self-defense? In fact, Khomeini's idea is even more ambiguous; his worldview accorded the territorial nation-state a lower priority than that granted the abode of Islam, which has no recognizable borders anywhere around the world.

The difficult nature of this theoretical ambiguity is best exemplified by Iran's nearly eight years of bloody war with Iraq. At the outset of the war, Khomeini told the Iranians, "You are fighting to protect Islam and he [Saddam Hussein] is fighting to destroy Islam. At the moment, Islam is completely confronted by blasphemy, and you should protect and support Islam. . . . Every person should defend Islam according to his ability. . . ."[26] Since it is generally agreed that Iraq invaded Iran on September 22, 1980, it may be said that Iran was at the time acting in self-defense as the concept is defined territorially, although it did so in the name of Islam. This impression was reinforced by Khomeini himself in March 1982 when the successful Iranian offensive in the Shush-Dezful area foreshadowed the recovery of Khorramshahr in May and the eviction of almost all Iraqi forces from Iranian territory by July: "Today Iran is still bound by what it said at the outset; we have no intention of fighting against any country, Islamic or non-Islamic. To date we have engaged only in self-defence which is a divine duty and human right enjoined upon all. We have never had an intention of committing aggression against other countries."[27]

And yet on July 13, 1982, Iran carried the war into Iraqi territory, and not until July 18, 1988, did Khomeini decide to stop fighting. Why did he not do so six years earlier? Was the war continued in self-defense or in order to export the revolution? Until February 22, 1989, every Iranian leader had denied that Iran's insistence on "final victory" aimed at exporting the revolution, but on that date Khomeini himself said:

Every day of the war we had blessing, which we utilized in all aspects. *We exported our revolution to the world through the war*; we proved our oppression and the aggressor's tyranny through the war. It was through the war that we unveiled the deceitful face of world-devourers; it was through the war that we recognized our enemies and friends. It was during the war that we concluded that we must stand on our own feet. It was through the war that we broke the back of both Eastern and Western superpowers. It was through the war that we consolidated the roots of our fruitful Islamic revolution [emphasis added].[28]

Short of defensive war, what other coercive means are allowed for exporting the revolution? Considerable ambiguity surrounds this question also. Just as war was denounced, military intervention was also condemned by Khomeini and other Iranian leaders. Ayatollah Hussein Ali Montazeri stated categorically on October 30, 1988, that "the question of exporting revolution . . . is not a matter of armed intervention." But "the Constitution provides the basis for trying to perpetuate . . . this revolution *both at home and abroad*" (emphasis added). Moreover, in pursuing the goal of universal happiness "while practicing complete self-restraint from any kind of influence in the internal affairs of other nations, [the Islamic Republic of Iran] will protect the struggle of the weak against the arrogant, in any part of the world."[29] And Khomeini's assurance that Iran had "neither ambition in, [nor] right, to any country, unless it is solely a matter of self-defense"[30] does not help clarify the limits of Iranian intervention because of the thorny ambiguity of the concept of self-defense. Nor does former President Ali Khamenei's unequivocal statement that the constitution prohibits Iran's interference in the internal affairs of other nations either clarify the ambiguity or stop interventionist actions by radical idealist factions such as that of Mehdi Hashemi, which tried using pilgrims to smuggle arms to Saudi Arabia in the summer of 1986.

In order to point out the theoretical ambiguities surrounding the means of exporting the revolution, I have so far distinguished between the concepts of "defensive war" (*jang-e defai*) and "offensive war" (*jihad*) because in Imami Shia legal thought the latter is the prerogative of the infallible Imams rather than of the *faqih*, who can declare only a defensive war. I have also distinguished between "war" (*jang*) in general and "intervention" (*modakheleh*), particularly military intervention. But in the current literature of international relations, all such distinctions may be subsumed under the general concept of intervention, which includes a whole spectrum of activities, from propagandistic broadcasts to armed invasion across international frontiers[31] to, in my view, the export of revolution.

Accordingly, then, this comprehensive view of intervention includes all export activities of revolutionary Iran during the Khomeini era. The Iranian government has been accused of a wide variety of interventionist acts, ranging from inciting propaganda to protracting war. The principal targets of the export of the revolution have consisted of four major geographic areas: the Persian Gulf, the Soviet Caucasus and Central Asia, Afghanistan, and Lebanon. In the Persian Gulf the specific targets were Bahrain, Saudi Arabia, and particularly Kuwait. In the Soviet area, they were Azerbaijan and Turkmenistan. In Afghanistan and Lebanon, Shia Muslims were the primary targets, although the eight pro-Iranian factions of the Afghan Mujahidin are based in Iran while the pro-Iranian Hezbollah movement is located in Lebanon. Only in Lebanon has Iran maintained a contingent of Revolutionary Guards, with initial Syrian blessing, since the invasion of Lebanon by Israel in June 1982. And only in Lebanon have pro-Iranian factions continued to hold Western hostages, while Iran claims that its own hostages are held by the Phalangists and are still alive, despite indications to the contrary.

Besides hostage-taking by pro-Iranian factions in Lebanon, Iran has been accused of other forcible interventionist acts. These include, for example, the attempted coup in Bahrain in December 1981, the suicidal truck bombing against the Americans and French military contingents in Lebanon in October 1983, and the multiple bombings in Kuwait in December of the same year. The Iranian Revolutionary Guards aided and abetted the local Shia militants and engaged in armed conflict with the Israeli force in Lebanon.[32] One could also add the accusations against Iran regarding the hijacking and bombing of planes and even the March 1989 pipe-bombing of a van in the United States. The van was driven by the wife of Captain Will C. Rogers III, who had ordered the missile firing of an Iranian passenger plane over the Persian Gulf on July 3, 1988, resulting in the death of 290 people. Militant Iranian students in the United States were suspected of complicity in the bombing. But the practice of exporting the revolution by terrorist acts is at times as mysterious as its theory is ambiguous.

Peaceful Means

Is it any less mysterious and more clear what peaceful means are preferable, in theory and in practice, for exporting the revolution? Generally the answer is yes. During the Khomeini period, three such noncoercive means emerged: the export of the revolution by example, by supporting liberation movements, and by propaganda.

Regarding the export of the revolution by example, two approaches stand out. One approach aims at a thorough Islamization of Iran itself. This approach was described by Ayatollah Montazeri in October 1988:

> The question of exporting revolution . . . is not a matter of armed intervention. The aim is, rather, that if we build our country on the basis of Islam, if we make the customs of the Prophet and the immaculate Imams our model, and if we implement the aims, ideals, and values which have been stressed by Islam, then by virtue of that fact, our country and our revolution will become a model for other deprived countries and those countries oppressed by and subject to cruelty from superpowers. They will choose our way in order to liberate themselves from the yoke of arrogance.[33]

The second approach is that of postwar reconstruction of the Iranian society and economy. Hashemi Rafsanjani believes that the world thinks mistakenly that "we wanted to export our revolution by invading other countries, through war and military action." But, he adds, "if under the present [postwar conditions] we manage to create an acceptable type of society and set up a suitable model of development, progress, evolution, and correct Islamic morals for the world, then we will achieve what the world has feared; that is, the export of the Islamic revolution."[34] On another occasion, he expressed a similar thought by saying that the White House "used to think that the Islamic Revolution intended to export itself through conquest." He then added: "This frightened our neighbors [but] now they know that if we claim to export our revolution we intend to present to the world the thought, the idea, and the path of the Koran. After eight years of war we stand more steadfast, more determined, and with more experience concerning our ideals and aspiration pertaining to the revolution."[35]

According to the constitution the export of the revolution by supporting liberation movements applies most particularly to "expanding international relations with other Islamic movements." We need not dwell on this subject because it was discussed previously. Suffice it to add here that the support of liberation movements is the most preferred option of radical idealists. For example, Montazeri, who advocates the thorough Islamization of Iran itself, also maintains that the Iranian revolution "has no limits, no frontiers" and adds:

> I would say that we must make arrangements so that the world of Islam and all victimized and deprived peoples can in some way be connected to the center of this great movement—a movement which has disrupted the existing world balance. They should be helped with ideology and Islamic thought. Eventually, the revolution and leadership must be separated from the framework of the limited regulations of state and government [*keshvar va dolat*].[36]

Another radical idealist, Interior Minister Ali Akbar Mohtashemi, also favors this approach: "We are not an isolated revolution, imprisoned within our borders. We support other Islamic movements in other countries. These include the Afghan Mujahidin, Iraqis, Palestinians, and Lebanese. We feel a responsibility to support these movements."[37]

The export of revolution by propaganda includes a great variety of methods, with implementation not necessarily confined to Iranian officials. For example, on one occasion Khomeini encouraged student athletes traveling abroad to export the revolution by the example of their ethical Islamic behavior: "Your deeds, your action, and your behavior should be an example, and through you the Islamic Republic will go to other places, God willing."[38] But export abroad by propaganda is the special responsibility of diplomats, as Khomeini once explained to the Iranian ambassadors and chargés d'affaires: "We shall have exported Islam only when we have helped Islam and Islamic ethics grow in those countries. This is your responsibility and it is a task which you must fulfill. . . . this is a must."[39] In the words of Foreign Minister Ali Akbar Velayati: "We will continue to export our revolution, but in cultural terms. The Western countries are doing the same thing. They export their culture, their way of thinking, and their values with the help of the mass media or universities where foreign students are trained. . . ."[40]

Iran also uses foreign religious leaders (*ulama*) to export its revolution. In addition to receiving streams of individual foreign clerics, Iran

Export of the Revolution

organizes and hosts international congresses for them. When five hundred foreign ulama gathered in Teheran in May 1983, Khomeini told them: "You should discuss the situation in Iran. You should call on people to rebel like Iran."[41] In addition, both foreign and Iranian scholars are also used for the export of the revolution. For example, more than one thousand Islamic scholars attended a conference on Islamic propagation in January 1989 to analyze "various methods of communication, ways of countering Western propaganda and spreading the message of Islam." Scholars attending this meeting came from such places as Nigeria, Pakistan, India, the Philippines, Egypt, Turkey, Hong Kong, Britain, France, Switzerland, Senegal, and Guyana.[42]

Salman Rushdie's novel *The Satanic Verses* was seen by Khomeini as a conspiracy against Islam. In pronouncing a death sentence on Rushdie on February 14, 1989, he said:

> I inform the proud Moslem people of the world that . . . *The Satanic Verses* . . . is against Islam, the Prophet and the Koran. . . . The issue of the book . . . is that it is a calculated move aimed at rooting out religion and religiousness, and above all, Islam and its clergy. . . . The issue for them [the Western powers] is not that of defending an individual—the issue for them is to support an anti-Islamic and anti-value current, which has been masterminded by those institutions belonging to Zionism, Britain and the USA which have placed themselves against the Islamic world, through their ignorance and haste.[43]

From the Iranian perspective, Khomeini's death sentence not only meted out Islamic punishment for blasphemy and apostasy but also aided the export of the revolution. Even though the forty-six-member Islamic Conference Organization (ICO) did not explicitly endorse Khomeini's death sentence in its resolution published on March 16, 1989, the Iranian press tried to reap a propaganda advantage by hailing the conference as a triumph for the Islamic Republic of Iran. "Declaring Salman Rushdie an apostate by the ICO, a big victory for Iran" screamed the headline on the front page of *Ettela'at. Kayhan, Jomhuri-ye Islami, Tehran Times*, and *Kayhan International* also trumpeted the Iranian victory. The editorial of *Abrar* stated: "Contrary to what the West expected, the ICO . . . in support of the leadership and government of the Islamic republic verified Imam Khomeyni's *fatwa* [religious decree, demanding Rushdie's death] . . . by diplomatic language."[44]

Export of Revolution Redefined?

Axiomatically, Iran's policy of exporting revolution, like any other aspect of its foreign policy, reflects the dynamic interaction between Iran's domestic politics and its external environment. In concluding this study, it is appropriate to specify that the aspect of Iran's domestic politics that most often shaped the government's export-of-revolution policies during the first decade of the Iranian Revolution was the style of Khomeini's leadership. In order to serve Iran's overall interest in "Islamic unity," he consistently played the role of the supreme balancer among the various political factions, including the radical idealists and pragmatic realists. On February 22, 1989, he acknowledged such a leadership style in an officially dubbed "very important" address to the instructors and students of religious seminaries and congressional imams: "For the sake of maintaining balance among various factions I have always issued bitter and sweet instructions because I consider all of them as my dear ones and children."[45]

In keeping with this balancing role, Khomeini threw his weight sometimes behind radical idealists and sometimes behind pragmatic realists, depending on the circumstances. In supporting the taking of American hostages by militant students, he in effect went against the moderate government of Mehdi Bazargan. As a consequence, the hostage crisis became the crucible of Iran's confrontational foreign policy in general and its export of the revolution in particular. In effect, Khomeini also supported the radical idealists when, on July 13, 1982, he decided to invade Iraq with the double goal of recovering pockets of Iranian territory and of exporting the revolution.

And yet, by accepting the cease-fire on July 18, 1988, Khomeini in effect threw his weight behind the pragmatic realists, who had never rejected out of hand UN Resolution 598. For months after the acceptance of this resolution, the power of the pragmatic factions seemed to be on the rise. They began developing diplomatic relations with France, Britain, and Canada, strengthening relations with West Germany, and making postwar reconstruction their first priority. It was then that the idea of exporting the revolution by the example of an economically prosperous, politically progressive, and socially popular Iran gained the support of the realistic factions. Hashemi Rafsanjani acknowledged candidly that "if the meaning of exporting revolution is to bring message to people's ears, I must say that our aims are not yet sufficiently clear in the mind of the people of the world."[46] This apparent rush to open up to the West, however, seemed to have alarmed the radical idealists. The Rushdie affair came to their aid.

Between his pronouncement of Rushdie's death sentence on February 14, 1989, and Khomeini's own death on June 3, 1989, the pendulum once again swung in favor of the radical idealists. In his address of February 22, 1989, mentioned above, Khomeini not only blasted as usual at the "liberals" and the "hypocrites" (*Mujahidin-e Khalq*) but also for the first time admonished the pragmatic realists. The imposition of a death sentence on a British subject residing outside Iran's borders was Khomeini's last effort to export the revolution. In criticizing the seeming haste of pragmatic realists to mend fences with Western nations, he said:

> It is not necessary for us to go seeking to establish extensive ties because the enemy may think that we have become so dependent and attach so much importance to their existence that we quietly condone insults to beliefs and religious sanctities. Those who still continue to believe that and warn that we must embark on a revision of our policies, principles and diplomacy and that we have blundered and must not repeat previous mistakes; those who still believe that extremist slogans or war will cause the West and the East to be pessimistic about us, and that ultimately all this has led to the isolation of the country; *those who believe that if we act in a pragmatic way* they will reciprocate humanely and will mutually respect nations, Islam and Muslims—to them this [Rushdie's novel] is an example [emphasis added].[47]

This criticism of the pragmatic realists coupled with Khomeini's reception of Soviet Foreign Minister Eduard A. Shevardnadze during his visit to Teheran in February 1989 appeared to Washington as a tilt toward the East in Iran's foreign policy. The U.S. government saw the Soviet Union poised to exploit the strain between Iran and Western European nations over the Rushdie affair. It also resented Soviet chumminess with Iran while nine American hostages were still held captive by reputedly pro-Iranian factions in Lebanon. The June 1989 visit of the influential speaker of the Iranian parliament, Hashemi Rafsanjani, to the Soviet Union, his reception by Mikhail Gorbachev as a head of state, and the signing of long-term economic and military agreements all aroused Western, particularly American, suspicion of an Iranian tilt toward the Soviet Union.

And yet, paradoxically for revolutionary Iran, the road to Washington may well turn out to be through Moscow. In following the fundamental tenets of its own foreign policy, Iran will have to balance its cooperation with the East by cooperating with the West to avoid dominant influence by or dependence on either bloc.[48] This is the real meaning of Iran's "neither East nor West" principle as interpreted by every major Iranian leader over the past decade. Even Khomeini admitted in his will that Iran's need for foreign aid was an "undisputed fact," despite his vigorous warning against dependency on either the East or the West.

More critically, the unprecedented opening to the Soviet Union may well signify the beginning of Iran's reentry into the international community, including normalization of relations with the United States. If so, Iran's doctrine of the export of revolution may well be redefined to allow for normal relations with other nations. And that, above all else, will require Iran's renunciation, both in words and deeds, of the use of direct or indirect force as a means of exporting revolution. The prospects for Iran's successful export of the revolution through setting an example of its own "Islamic ethical behavior," to borrow the late Ayatollah Khomeini's words, may be brighter in the near future than they were during the entire first decade of the Islamic Republic. It is likely that the political ascendancy of Ayatollah Seyyed Ali Khamenei as Khomeini's successor and of Hashemi Rafsanjani as the strongest president since the establishment of the republic may result in a non-interventionist definition of the principle of the export of the revolution. Both these leaders have demonstrated a sense of political realism and a determination to base Iran's relations with other nations, including the United States, on the concept of equilibrium rather than on the idea of a struggle between good and evil. To the extent that such a fundamental change may occur, future efforts at exporting the Iranian revolution will be relatively tame during the second decade of the life of the Islamic Republic of Iran.

Notes

1. The modern international system dates back to the Peace of Westphalia, signed on October 24, 1648. The treaty marked the end of negotiations between France and Sweden and their opponents, Spain and the Holy Roman Empire,

which took place in two Westphalian cities in Germany. By its terms the sovereignty and independence of the different states of the Holy Roman Empire were fully recognized, rendering the Holy Roman emperor virtually powerless and hence signaling the demise of religion in politics after the Thirty Years' War. No comparable event has occurred in Islamic history.

2. For details, see R.K. Ramazani, *The United States and Iran: The Patterns of Influence* (New York: Praeger, 1982).

3. Three important events in 1972–77, ignited this populist explosion: President Nixon's decision in 1972 to sell the Shah all the conventional military weapons he wanted; the boom of rising oil prices in 1973 followed by the sudden bust, which transformed the Iranians' rising expectations to increasing alienation from both the Shah's regime and the United States; and the Shah's creation of the Rastakhiz party in 1975, which symbolized the height of political repression and compounded the psychological and financial dislocations that the economic boom and bust had already produced. For the earliest characterization of the Iranian Revolution as a "twin revolution," see R.K. Ramazani, "Iran's Revolution in Perspective," in American Foreign Policy Institute, *The Impact of the Events upon Persian Gulf and United States Security* (Washington, D.C., 1979), 19–37; Ramazani, "Iran's Foreign Policy: Perspectives and Projections," in Joint Economic Committee of the United States Congress, *Economic Consequences of the Revolution in Iran* (Washington, D.C.: U.S. Government Printing Office, 1980), 65–97; and Ramazani, "Iran's Revolution: Patterns, Problems and Prospects," *International Affairs* (Summer 1980): 443–57.

4. See R.K. Ramazani, *The Foreign Policy of Iran, 1500–1941: A Developing Nation in World Affairs* (Charlottesville: University Press of Virginia, 1966), 63–65.

5. See R.K. Ramazani, *Iran's Foreign Policy, 1941–1973: A Study of Foreign Policy in Modernizing Nations* (Charlottesville: University Press of Virginia, 1975), 181–250.

6. The Soviet Union claims that these articles give it the unilateral right to intervene militarily in Iran whenever it judges that its security is threatened from Iranian territory. For decades Iran has vehemently opposed this Soviet interpretation. Reza Shah secretly tried to cancel the articles in 1935, and his son made a similar effort in 1958–59. The Bazargan government's cancellation of these articles was affirmed on November 10, 1979, by the Revolutionary Council. For details, see R.K. Ramazani, "Treaty Relations: An Iranian-Soviet Case Study," in *The Search for World Order*, ed. Albert Lepawsky, Edward H. Buehrig, and Harold D. Lasswell (New York: Appleton-Century-Crofts, 1979), 298–311.

7. Iraqi Foreign Minister Saadoun Hammadi stated: "I should say for the record that Mr. Bazargan was also cooperative and tried to strengthen relations between the two countries." See Ministry of Foreign Affairs, the Republic of Iraq, *The Iraqi-Iranian Dispute: Facts v. Allegations* (New York, October 1980), 65.

8. For details, see R.K. Ramazani, *Revolutionary Iran: Challenge and Response in the Middle East* (Baltimore: Johns Hopkins University Press, 1986), 49.

9. Bani-Sadr believed "that despite the historical and ideological differences between the West and Iran, the two sides' interests were not so far apart." See Foreign Broadcast Information Service, *Daily Reports—Middle East and North Africa* (hereafter cited as FBIS—MEA), November 20, 1979.

10. Ibid., December 21, 1979.

11. See Mohandes Mehdi Bazargan, *Enqelab-e Iran Dar Dau Harekat* (The Iranian revolution in two movements) (Teheran: Chap-e Sevom, 1362/1983–84), 94–95.

12. Neither of these principles is explicitly mentioned in the constitution, but their meanings are incorporated in various provisions. For example, Article 152 in effect relates to the "neither East nor West" principle in the original sense that Iran rejects Eastern and Western domination but not *relations* with the United States and Soviet Union, whose rupture the extremists demand. This article states: "The foreign policy of Iran is founded on the basis of ending any type of domination, safeguarding the complete independence and integrity of the territory, defending the rights of all Muslims, practicing nonalignment with respect to the dominating [U.S. and USSR] powers and maintaining mutual peaceful relationships with non-belligerent nations." The principle of the export of the revolution is implied not only in the phrase "defending the rights of all Muslims," but also under other headings in the constitution such as "Style of Government in Islam," "Army of the Book," "Public Relations and Media," and Article 154. For the text of the constitution, with R.K. Ramazani's introductory note, see *Middle East Journal* 34 (Spring 1980): 181–204.

13. See Foreign Broadcast Information Service, *Daily Reports–South Asia* (hereafter cited as FBIS—SA), July 8, 1981.

14. Ibid., October 28, 1981.

15. See R.K. Ramazani, "Iran's Foreign Policy: Contending Orientations," *Middle East Journal* 43, no. 2 (Spring 1989): 202–17.

16. Adda B. Bozeman, *Politics and Culture in International History* (Princeton: Princeton University Press, 1960), 49. The reason for the disagreement with Bozeman in the following paragraph is that while she recognizes the influence of Zoroastrianism on Iran's worldview, she fails to realize that Zoroaster's call to fight against infidels, Turks, and nomads in order to convert the whole world into the domain of good was an injunction subordinated to the higher norm of a just world order commanded by Ahura Mazda.

17. See Malise Ruthven, *Islam in the World* (New York: Oxford University Press, 1984), 227.

18. FBIS—MEA, December 18, 1979.

19. FBIS—SA, February 11, 1987.

20. Foreign Broadcast Information Service, *Daily Reports–Near East and South Asia* (hereafter cited as FBIS—NES), January 9, 1989.

21. FBIS—MEA, December 10, 1979.

22. Ibid., March 24, 1980.

23. FBIS—SA, February 11, 1987.

24. *Soroush*, March 1981.

25. FBIS—SA, August 25, 1983.

26. *New York Times*, October 19, 1980.

27. FBIS—SA, April 1, 1982.

28. FBIS—NES, February 24, 1989.

29. Ibid., October 31, 1988.

30. *Keyhan* (in Persian), July 26, 1982.

Export of the Revolution

31. See Michael Joseph Smith's excellent article, "Ethics and Intervention," *Ethics and International Affairs* 3 (1989): 1–26.

32. See Ramazani, *Revolutionary Iran*; idem, "Iran's Islamic Revolution and the Persian Gulf," *Current History* 84 (January 1985): 5–8, 40–41; idem, "Socio-Political Change in the Gulf: A Climate for Terrorism," in *Crosscurrents in the Gulf: Arab and Global Interests*, ed. H. Richard Sindelar III and J.E. Peterson (New York: Routledge Kegan Paul, for the Middle East Institute, 1988), 127–51; idem, *The Gulf Cooperation Council: Record and Analysis* Charlottesville: University Press of Virginia, 1988), 33–59.

33. FBIS—NES, October 31, 1988.

34. Ibid., October 17, 1988, and October 14, 1988.

35. Ibid., September 26, 1988.

36. Ibid., February 28, 1989.

37. Ibid., February 8, 1989.

38. FBIS—SA, March 9, 1982.

39. *Soroush*, March 1981.

40. FBIS—NES, September 21, 1988.

41. *Keyhan Hava'i*, May 23, 1984.

42. FBIS—NES, February 2, 1989.

43. *BBC Summary of World Broadcasts*, February 24, 1989.

44. FBIS—NES, March 20, 1989.

45. For the text, see *BBC Summary of World Broadcasts*, February 24, 1989.

46. FBIS—NES, February 14, 1989.

47. See *BBC Summary of World Broadcasts*, February 24, 1989.

48. For details, see R.K. Ramazani's analysis in the *Washington Post*, July 2, 1989, p. C2.

4

Iranian Ideology and Worldview: The Cultural Export of Revolution

FARHANG RAJAEE

IRAN HAS NOW EXPERIENCED a decade of Islamic government.[1] Its official motto has been "the Islamic Republic—not one word less, and not one word more."[2] This motto refers to the ideology of Ayatollah Imam Ruholla Musavi Khomeini, put forward in a general way in his important work on jurisprudence[3] and which he made more concrete in a manifesto presented in a series of lectures he delivered in Najaf in 1971.[4]

There have been various and at times contrasting interpretations of what Khomeini's manifesto means in terms of the political, economic, and social structure of Iranian society and the regime's policies and practices. As a result, there is no clear understanding either inside or outside Iran of the complexity of the new order. The confusion is exacerbated by another factor that relates to the nature of the revolution, namely, that the final outcome is not yet clear because the revolution is still unfolding. Iran's revolutionary government has survived a host of challenges: the assassination of many of its top leaders, nearly a decade of constant economic blockade and pressures, one of the longest conventional wars in recent history, the country's partially self-imposed isolation, and, above all, international misunderstanding of the revolution's message and content. At the same time, the country is experimenting with Islamization in many areas such as banking, cultural revolution, and the revision of Islamic juridical principles. Politically, Iran is striving to establish its own democratic processes (during the past ten years the Islamic Republic of Iran has held at least one election each year) and to maintain and "export" its revolution. The formal ideology of the state and of the revolution reflects a particular interpretation of Shii Islam, and the form of the revolutionary government is known as "guardianship of the jurisconsult" (*velayat-e faqih*), Khomeini's interpretation of Shii political theory.[5]

Thus, the new regime has followed policies and practices derived from the revolution and based explicitly on revolutionary principles. At the same time Iran, like most established states, has followed its national interest as dictated by the geographical position of the country, its national sovereignty, its own political and social traditions, as well as other elements that affect the state's interest. To make sense of this paradox, one needs to understand the internal dynamics of Iranian politics, an issue of great scope. I will analyze one component of this paradox, the export of the revolution, by addressing two broad questions: First, what are the characteristics of Iran's new ideology and the worldview? Second, how does this ideology affect the terms of the export of revolution? With regard to the latter, three related questions will be addressed: What does the export of revolution mean according to Iran's constitution and the pronouncements of the revolution's leaders? What has it come to mean in practice, as manifested in Iran's policies and behavior during the past decade? Has the goal been appreciably realized or implemented thus far?

Ideology of the Revolution

Iran's great mystical poet, Jalal al-Din Muhammad Mulawi Balkhi, proclaimed in one of his verses that "the power of the wine will break the bottle," a metaphor that aptly symbolizes the revolution. The wine may be thought of as the whole social fabric, all the interactions and dynamics of a society; the bottle as the structure of that society; and the breaking of the bottle, the result of releasing the power of the wine, as the revolution. When the revolutionary wine in Iran destroyed the existing body politics, Islam emerged as the dominant framework for state and society, providing the foundation for both the structure and the content of the new order.

We will not concern ourselves here with why and how adhering to

Islam became the dominant force in the wake of the revolution; suffice it to say that the revolution took the form that the Iranian adherent of Islam gave it. Does this fact tell us anything about the dominant ideology in Iran and the form of the ruling government, or does it help us understand the problems encountered in the export of the revolution? The answer is yes if one understands what is meant by Islam in Iran today. This question was put to the leader of the Islamic revolution by Eric Rouleau in a 1978 interview with Ayatollah Khomeini:

> Q: You say that in Iran an Islamic Republic should be established. This is not clear to us the French, because a republic can exist without having any religious foundation. What is your view? Is your republic based on socialism, democratic processes, election, constitutionalism or what?
> A. By republic is meant the type of republicanism at work in other countries. The reason we call it Islamic Republic is that all conditions for the candidates as well as rules are based on Islam, but the choice is that of the people. The form of the republic is that which exists everywhere else.[6]

Although this passage does not state clearly what is meant by Islam, Imam Khomeini's voluminous works tell us that the type of Islam he had in mind is that of the Twelver Shiism developed within the Iranian context. What is at work in Iran today concerning the ruling ethos, norms, frame of mind, and collective conscience is a manifestation of a political culture that has actually preserved Iranian national identity. The messages of the revolutionaries and the policies of the republic have been influenced by and matured within the context of Iranian political culture. The interplay of the revolutionary scheme and that context has exhibited features which, I contend, form the dominant ideology and worldview in Iran today.

IDEALISM

All revolutions at least pretend to aspire toward idealism. The final clash that destroys the old regime stems from the clash between the "ideal city" and the existing one. The revolutionaries do not see the ideal city as either a utopia or an imaginary scheme but as a realizable project. Perhaps this explains why revolutionaries mean what they say and usually act upon their meanings. In the Islamic revolution, this aspiration toward utopianism is far stronger because of two factors; the

Ideology and Worldview

influence of Persian gnosticism (*erfan*) and the idealistic features of political and social thought in Iran during the past two centuries.

Persian gnosticism presents a set of precepts postulating that man may become perfect (*ensan kamel*); Khomeini himself has stated that "a good man can save a country whereas a bad man can destroy it."[7] In this view, the main concern of social life is either searching for or training the good man, and politics is defined in terms of education and a harmonious administering of the state. While the essence of politics has to do with the allocation of scarce and limited worldly resources—and hence power—gnosticism ignores worldly life. As Iranian scholar Javad Tabatabai argues, "The great mystics live in 'the world of astonishment' and consider 'life as a passing phase,' while in politics struggle for life is at the base."[8] Gnosticism plays a significant role in the Iranian psyche, all the more so because of the position and stature of Imam Khomeini, who was himself a mystic. This mentality may be the main reason that politics in its common connotation was seen by the Iranian leader as satanic.[9] In Khomeini's ideology political assumptions are based on optimism, rationalism, and the hope that man may be reformed. Indeed, lack of intensive concentration on institution building in post revolutionary Iran stems from such an understanding of politics. In its place much energy is spent on discovering committed and righteous individuals.

The second reason for idealism in the Islamic revolution relates directly to the history of political and social thought in Iran during the past two hundred years. That thinking has basically been a reaction to the expansive and domineering wave of modernism and to Western culture. Iranian intellectuals have shown great admiration for modernism and at the same time have displayed nostalgia for their own glorious past.[10] They have created an illusory and idealized understanding of their history, thereby imprisoning themselves in their past, a past which has crippled them rather than helped them prepare to face the realities of the modern world.[11] Moreover, according to these intellectuals, the only reason their glorious past could not be realized was because of the satanic power of others, particularly of outside nations. This notion of "the Great Satan" can clearly be understood within this context.

UNIVERSALISM

The dominant feature of the Iranian revolution is its propagation of Islam and its basic tenets. Islam is claimed to be the straight path for the glory of humanity regardless of color, race, and culture. One religious leader, a protagonist of the revolution and one of the top officials of the Organization for the Propagation of Islam, argues that Islamic universalism is best related to the revolution: "The export of revolution manifests itself in the expansion of Islamic culture and the advancement of Islamic sovereignty." But he is quick to note that "the advancement of Islamic sovereignty does not mean the domination of the Islamic Republic of Iran; rather it means the domination of Islam, i.e., rule of Islamic laws and precepts." Asked how it was possible to establish the domination of Islam he gave a clue to the way in which revolution is understood by Iran's top religious leaders:

> The domination of Islam will not materialize unless Islamic solidarity rules, and this is not possible unless there is a revolution. [By revolution] we mean evolution towards God. In this sense, what happened in Russia was not a revolution because it was a move from one materialistic status to another, whereas the French could be considered a sort of revolution because it called for the establishment of a social order in which some basic human rights were secured."[12]

In other words, a process aiming simply at social and economic change should not be taken as a revolution. The following verses from the Koran are cited as proof: "Lo! Allah changeth not the condition of a folk until they [first] change that which is in their hearts" (xiii:11); "Allah never changeth the grace He hath bestowed on any people until they first change that which is in their hearts" (viii:53).[13] Any revolution must therefore start from the self, the individual, and by so doing will bring about social change and transformation. Moreover, that such an attitude must be spread throughout the world is part of Islamic teaching. In short, the export of the revolution is not only a revolutionary move but also a doctrinal duty if and when a revolution considers itself "Islamic." This is why the idea of exporting the revolution has been repeated so often by the leaders of the revolution and is also incorporated within Iran's constitution.

Article 154 of the constitution states that "the Islamic Republic of Iran is concerned with the welfare of humanity as a whole and takes independence, liberty and sovereignty of justice and righteousness as the right of people in the world over. Thus, while refraining from any involvement in the internal affairs of other nations, the Islamic Repub-

Ideology and Worldview

lic of Iran supports the struggle of the oppressed anywhere in the world."[14] When this article was being considered by the Assembly of Experts who reviewed the proposed constitution, there was very little debate over it; indeed, it was one of the few articles that received the consensus of the delegates. Such vast support was taken by many as a mandate for propagating a universal exportation of the revolution. The deputy chairman of the assembly commented: "This consensus is a proof that our revolution . . . is a universal one and contrary to what some may say it will not be limited within the boundaries [of Iran], provided we make a model society out of our own country"[15] Thus, the universality of the revolution and its ideology were taken for granted.

Khomeini's views on the export of revolution are directly related to his characterization of the Iranian revolution. For him the revolution is an Islamic one, by which he means that it is not exclusive to Iran: "Islam is revealed for mankind. . . . An Islamic movement, therefore, cannot limit itself to any particular country."[16] This universalist understanding of Islam is repeated throughout his sermons and writings. Indeed, Khomeini equates the idea that "Islam is for mankind" with the need to export the revolution: "When we say we want to export our revolution we mean we would like to export this spirituality and enthusiasm we see in Iran."[17] It is this spirit and enthusiasm that change "the heart" of the people, causing them to rise up and change the situations in their societies.

This understanding of the export of revolution is reiterated by other key leaders in Iran. Ayatollah Montazeri, for example, emphasizes that "one feature of the revolution in Iran is its Islamicness. . . . It is obvious that when a revolution is based on the liberating teachings of Islam, inevitably it will have a universalistic characteristic." Montazeri considers the export of revolution "the only great characteristic of the great movement of our nation." Taking a position similar to Khomeini's, he argues that "the essence of the Islamic Revolution is only in doctrinal (*maktabi*) transformation and change in the condition of nations who will rise and take charge of their own destiny after familiarizing themselves with godly concepts. . . ."[18] Again, the Koranic concept of "change in the heart" is central to the concept of the export of revolution.

The interconnectedness of Iran's revolution with its export is also found in the views of Ali Khamenei, the president of the republic, and Hashemi Rafsanjani, the speaker of the parliament. Khamenei points out that "the foundation and the idea of this revolution is not limited to our country and this nation,"[19] while Rafsanjani emphasizes that "from early on when the revolution succeeded we realized that a revolution is not a phenomenon which would stay limited within one border."[20] For both these leaders the export of revolution amounts to spreading the ideas, spirit, and enthusiasm of the revolution.[21] Thus, based on the Islamic notion that change in the heart of the individual is a prerequisite of any social transformation, it is safe to conclude that for the top leaders in Iran the export of revolution amounts to the export of feeling, solidarity, spirit, and enthusiasm for Islamic precepts and practices. In that sense, Islamic universalism is directly related to the revolution and its export.

POPULISM

The Persian word *mardomi*, "populism," is an important concept in revolutionary Iran. The revolution was both a popular and a populist movement as practically all segments of Iranian society participated in and contributed to it.[22] The ruling regime still considers itself populist, if not in the sense that it has the support of all segments of society, as many would like to believe, but in the sense that it adheres to the dominant or mass culture. This populism stems from the long history of Shiism,[23] which ironically started as a movement that refused, in the late Hamid Enayat's words, "to admit that majority opinion is necessarily true or right" and instead accepted "the moral excellence of an embattled minority."[24] Because of Shiism minority status through the history of Islam, the Shii ulama, in parting from the ruling Sunni majority, had to rely more and more on the support of the masses. A strong and mutually beneficial interdependence grew out of this relationship. But there are limits to the benefits of populism, as Ayatollah Murtaza Mutahhari observed:

> It is true that relying on the people generates power [*godrat*] for the ulama but it takes away their freedom [*harriyat*]. . . . A religious leadership [*rahaniyat*] which relies on the people is able to struggle against injustices and aggresssion of governments but is weak and unable to fight the ignorance of people, whereas religious leaders who rely on governments are powerful in fighting the habits and customs of the ignorant [masses] but weak in fighting the injustices of governments.[25]

Ideology and Worldview

In terms of modern Iranian politics, the ruling regime can easily mobilize the masses by capitalizing on dramatic events in Shii history, such as the tragic death of the third Shii leader, Imam Husayn, at Karbala more than a millennium ago. But by the same token, the ruling elite is confined within the limits of popular culture. This close association of Shiism with popular religion and culture has not only influenced the structure and function of the Iranian republic but has also greatly affected the projection of its values abroad, a point that will be discussed later.

IRANIANISM

Despite the repeated condemnation of nationalism by Khomeini and other Iranian leaders and their efforts to underestimate the role of Iranian nationalism,[26] the ruling regime has been greatly influenced by what may be termed Iranian political culture. This influence is an old legacy. In his monumental work, Henri Corbin shows the close affinity between ancient Persian ideology and worldview and the Shii interpretation of the *imamate* as a political institution.[27] The *imam* in Shii political thought functions very much like the philosopher-king in the Platonic tradition, and the imamate is in turn very similar to the ideal kingship among the ancient Aryans in the Persian plateau.[28] They are all guardians of a sacred order and ordained by transcendent forces above and beyond ordinary human beings. The ruler's main task is to oversee the proper implementation of the truth, which in the Islamic context has revealed itself in the form of Islamic law, the *Sharia*. The following passage from Khomeini's treatise on government could be easily applied to Platonic as well as traditional Persian thought: "The wisdom of the Creator has decreed that man should live in accordance with justice and act within the limits set by the divine laws. . . . Today and always, therefore the existence of a holder of authority . . . is necessary . . . [as] a trustworthy and vigilant guardian of God's creatures, who guides man to the teachings, doctrine, laws, and institutions of Islam."[29]

According to the dominant ideology in Iran today, this ruler should be a theologian-jurisconsult (*faqih*) who knows the correct path.[30] Moreover, the charismatic element of Khomeini's leadership fits all too well the pre-Islamic Persian belief in the divine grace (*farah-e izadi*), one of the characteristics of ideal kingship.[31] According to Dr. Javad Tabatabai, political thought in the eastern part of the Islamic world has been strongly influenced by the Persian notion of ideal kingship, an influence manifested in the tradition of writing a manual of governance, better known as the "mirror of the princes." In contrast, political thought in the western Islamic world has been primarily a promulgation of the principles of the *Sharia* pertaining to politics. Islamic thinkers in the Persian tradition wrote "books of advice" (*andarznameh*) whereas Muslims outside that tradition wrote "books of *Sharia*" (*shariatnameh*).[32] This Persian-influenced Irano-Islamic understanding of politics makes it difficult for non-Iranian Muslims to understand the essential message of the revolution and the attempt to export it.

Thus, the Islamic revolution propelled by the principle "neither East nor West, but the Islamic Republic" has come to mean "Islamic" as understood within the Iranian context. Now let us examine the effect of this understanding on the exportation of the revolution.

Export of the Revolution

In his classic work on revolution, Crane Brinton discusses the universalistic nature of deep-rooted revolutions. He observes that revolutionaries throughout history "all sought to spread the gospel of their revolution." It is therefore possible to make the generalization that exporting the revolution seems to be a natural outgrowth of revolutionary zeal, particularly because revolutionaries are self-righteous and because "our orthodox and successful extremists . . . are crusaders, fanatics, ascetics, men who seek to bring heaven to earth."[33]

Exhibiting as it does the features of a classic revolution complete with its own crusades and crusaders, the Iranian revolution is no exception to Brinton's rule, despite its unique form and context. There is evidence in the earliest days of the new regime that the idea of exporting the revolution was alive in people's minds. The issue was raised in editorials in Teheran's daily papers and, more importantly, in sermons delivered as Friday prayers, the most important public podium instituted in Iran after the revolution. Note, for example, Ayatollah Montazeri's declaration: "We have a long way to go. We hope to export this Islamic revolution of Iran into all other Muslim countries."[34]

Among the four formerly discussed features of the dominant ideology in Iran, Islamic universalism seems to be the most vigorous and impelling factor in the export of the revolution. An official of the Organization for the Propagation of Islam, responsible for dealing with the export of revolution, explains that "the export of revolution is a natural component of Islam. It is one of the clearly accepted issues in jurisprudence because Islam, as discussed earlier, is revealed for the salvation of humanity as a whole."[35] Universalism is likely to play a significant role in the exportation effort for a long time to come.

Other features of the revolution that caused a great deal of enthusiasm, particularly among oppressed people around the world, are its idealism and its populism. The revolution in Iran raised aspirations and hope among people the world over. During the early days of the revolution, many observers of Middle Eastern politics suggested that other countries in the region might revolt, following Iran's example. But so far Iran's revolution has not been duplicated anywhere. It seems the remaining feature—Iranianism—has had a greater impact if not in limiting the revolution, then at least in giving it a more particular cast and outlook. Many political thinkers, even archsupporters of the revolution, complain about the degree to which it has adopted particular Shii and Iranian traits. Nonetheless, events in the first decade of the Islamic Republic of Iran indicate that the revolution has affected the region as well as the world in many ways not the least of which is that Iran's experience serves as an example for people struggling against oppression.

But what are the methods by which Iran's example presents itself, particularly to other countries? Events of the last ten years reveal that there is no one answer to this important question. A number of institutions have been created and a variety of methods adopted to export the revolution. For example, in his sermons Khomeini repeatedly emphasized the method of "communication, dissemination, announcement, and propagation." I have chosen these few terms to convey the meaning of the Arabic word *tabligh*. In common usage the word means "propagation," but its Islamic connotation derives from the word *balagha*, meaning "to reach," "to get," or "to affect." *Tabligh* also means "proselytizing." Thus, according to Komeini, the enthusiasm of revolution can be exported through cultural transformation, communication, and propagation: "The greatest means by which the revolution can succeed here [in Iran] and can be exported is *tablighat* [propagation, communication, and proselytization], in its proper form."[36]

Khomeini also uses the word *dawat*, meaning "calling" in the same way as used by Martin Luther and explained by Weber.[37] Note the following passage from a sermon Khomeini delivered to the members of government, including the Islamic Consultative Assembly: "We want Islam to spread everywhere and want Islam to be exported. But this does not mean that we intend to export it by the bayonet. We want to *call* everyone to Islam, send our *calling* everywhere. We want to show a sample of Islam, even if it is not a complete one" (emphasis added).[38]

These emphases on calling, communication, and dissemination notwithstanding, one can also find passages in which Khomeini does not rule out the possibility of using physical force and nonpeaceful means: "Iran wants to present and spread its Islam in other 'Islamicate' lands. . . . Islamic ulama must come to the scene, bring Muslims to the battleground through *tablighat* [preaching or propagation]. . . . and to give awareness to governments. If they submitted and agreed to behave in accordance with Islamic tenets, support them, if not fight them without fear of anyone."[39] This excerpt does not, however, indicate the precise manner by which to implement the export of the revolution. Moreover, it is contradicted by other passages that rule out any method of interference in the affairs of other states. It should also be noted that the phrase "fight them" does not mean that Iran should take up arms. Rather this is the responsibility of the other Muslim people led and guided by "Islamic ulama" (religious leaders). In other words, just as the religious leaders in Iran actively revitalized religious sentiment among the Iranian people and encouraged them to fight the regime, so should other religious leaders do the same in their own countries. This is an intricate and complex point not understood by many either inside or outside Iran.

While Khomeini espoused *tablighat*, other methods for exporting the revolution were debated and discussed in Iran during the early days of the revolution—and employed accordingly. Many key leaders, including members of the provisional government, argued for the creation of a "model society" (*madineye nemuneh*). Their logic was that a revolution is not a commodity to be exported or imported. Instead, they argued for the establishment of Iranian society as a model for others to follow. For a time, at least, there seemed to be a general consensus on the model-building approach to exporting the revolution. While emphasizing that exporting the revolution was in the interest of the republic, Muhammad Ali Rajaee said, "When we have materialized the ideals of the revolution in Iran, the revolution automatically will become a model."[40] When Ayatollah Beheshti was asked about the export of revolution, he responded, "Our aim is . . . to build a good society which will be noticed by our neighbors. This will bring about the export of revolution."[41]

Ideology and Worldview

With the removal of the provisional government, the broad guidance of the Imam Khomeini with its twofold interpretations—propagation (*tablighat*) and nonpeaceful struggle—became the dominant modus operandi for exporting the revolution. The record of the Islamic Republic of Iran during the past decade indicates the utilization of both methods. The first method has taken the form of communication and religious dissemination—a cultural export of the revolution, while the second method has manifested itself in the realm of politics and foreign policy. In that realm, the export of the revolution is based on realizing the repeatedly stated principle of "neither East nor West." Not all aspects of Iran's foreign policy are manifestations of this motto; indeed, it is difficult to distinguish between the republic's pursuit of national interest and the implementation of revolutionary principles. Moreover, because Iran's revolution is undeniably a cultural one, concentration on the cultural aspects of the revolution provides a more insightful channel for understanding the impact of the dominant ideology on the issue of exportation.[42]

A number of institutions have been set up to implement the cultural export of the revolution, the most notable of which are the Organization for the Propagation of Islam (*Sazemane Tablighat Eslami*), the Hujjatiyeh Seminary in Qum, the Andishe Foundation (*Bonyade Andishe*), and the Farabi Foundation (*Bonyade Farabi*). While these institutions are all related to the government in one way or another, they have relative autonomy because they are more or less privately founded and funded. Thus, when Khomeini was asked whether one could spend "the share of the Imam" (*sahme Imam*)—a special Shii tax usually paid privately to Shii religious leaders—toward the advancement of the revolution, he responded positively and even recommended it.

The Organization for the Propagation of Islam was established in 1981 as the mechanism through which the voice of the new Islamic resurgence would be transmitted and disseminated both within Iran and outside its borders. This organization is basically involved with "the export of the culture of the revolution" and has been relatively successful. Its annual report for 1987 states that "the export of revolution is one of the aims of the leader of the community [Imam Khomeini] and that of the Islamic Republic of Iran. This holy movement will be possible neither by the sword nor by weapons, but with the use of pen, talking, propagation, and art."[43]

To achieve this aim, the organization publishes books in English,

Arabic, French, German, Turkish, Urdu, Kurdish, Hindi, and other languages; it also publishes the quarterly journal *Al Tawhid* (Unity), with the subtitle of "Journal of Islamic Thought and Culture." The journal's title is significant because it means both unity of Islam and the oneness of God; its articles introduce the basic tenets of Islam while emphasizing the preservation of unity among Muslims. The journal is published in English, Arabic, Urdu, and Hindi. The organization also makes movies and videos on various topics and participates in Islamic seminars, conferences, and other gatherings throughout the world. It arranges an annual international conference on Islamic problems and issues of significance for the Muslim world during each anniversary of the revolution (every February); topics addressed during the past seven years include the characteristics of the Islamic community, the Koran, Islamic government, human rights in Islam,[44] and dissemination and propagation. In the 1989 conference, more than one hundred participants came from abroad.

Hujjatiyeh Seminary (*Madreseye Hujjatiyeh*) is a school originally established by Ayatollah Hujjat, a prominent religious leader in Qum. After the revolution, Ayatollah Montazeri turned it into an international religious school. In the early days of the revolution, students came from all over the world, particularly from African countries, and the school continues to attract students from other countries and other schools of jurisprudence. Its objective is to export the revolution through educational training, and it teaches all five schools of Shii and Sunni jurisprudence.

The Andishe Foundation is an institution operating under the auspices of the Ministry of Guidance (*Vezarate Ershad*). Its main objective is to become the focal point for the propagation of Islam through the publication of books and journals. Presently, the foundation publishes ten journals in eight languages (including Japanese), sending them to more than 140 countries around the world.

Finally, the Farabi Foundation is a semiprivate institution engaged in film production. Discussing the aims of the foundation, its director pointed out that "the foundation wants to make good movies and enhance Iran's cinema industry."[45] In practice, however, the foundation works to project Islamic values and revolutionary ideals through its movies, many of which have been well received in international film festivals.

All four organizations seem to be flourishing. The rationale and spirit that guide their activities are "making models" and letting "Islam and the revolution speak for itself," objectives that reinforce the conclusion that a consensus has emerged in Iran to let the model-building approach dominate. Some may point to the Salman Rushdie episode and argue that such a conclusion will not hold. But this issue angered all Muslims, whether revolutionaries or not, and should thus be seen in that context. Moreover, there are those who argue that in fact the timing was set to upset the process Iran had so painstakingly begun.

We noted previously that in the early days of the new regime there was a debate about the methods for exporting the revolution. While it seemed that the majority spoke of model building, or in fact presented the notion of revolution in one country, there were some who talked about permanent revolution. This debate manifested itself in Iran as that of "volcano theory" (*nazariyeye atashfeshan*) versus "building the home country" (*ummo al-qora*). Upon the removal of the provisional government, proponents of the more radical volcano approach gained the upper hand. No doubt many extremist practices were carried out in the name of the revolution. But as the revolutionaries tried to put their ideal city into practice, they realized the permanent gap between the ideal city and the real city. The realities of power politics and the intracacies of the international system forced a great deal of rethinking, and once again the notion of model building gradually became the dominant view.

In fact, Khomeini's letter to Mikhail Gorbachev in January 1989 is considered by many to be the approach that should have been adopted from the outset. Many compared Khomeini's message to the delegations and diplomatic letters of the Prophet sent to other leaders in the early days of his rule. Refuting both Marxism and Western liberalism while presenting Islam as an alternative, Khomeini invited Gorbachev "to do serious research on Islam."[46] No doubt many also see the message as a political tactic, but regardless of its political intent, it definitely marks the emergence of the view that the proper way of exporting the revolution is by example and model building, that is, through the construction of an ideal society.

Only time will tell whether this shift in emphasis will be successful. But in terms of the last decade, what factors account for Iran's limited success in duplicating or exporting the revolution? The particularly Iranian context of the revolution may be most responsible. While in the early days of the revolution the adjective "Islamic" was taken literally, in practice the revolution took the form of an Iranian/Shii populist movement. For example, when Hujjatiyeh Seminary began to train jurisconsults well versed in the *Jafari* (Shii) school of jurisprudence, the school lost a great number of Sunni students. One student from an African country told me, "Had I been trained well in my own Sunni school of jurisprudence in Qum, I would have been the best agent for the export of the revolution for you. But instead, I simply have to leave because I did not come here to train as a Shii." One official acknowledged this obstacle, bitterly observing that "not only has Shiism been considered the official religion of the state, but it also regularly manifests itself as such in the speeches of various leaders."

Besides the inhibiting effects of Iranianism and Shiism, other factors have hampered the export of the revolution. First, in general, revolutions have rarely been exported, except by military invasion or by indigenous reception, which cannot properly be termed export. The case of socialist and communist governments in the Eastern bloc are the most recent examples. The second, more functional reason lies in the way in which Iran's leaders understand the causes of their revolution. They truly believe that the revolution happened because of the dissemination of various messages among the people. For them "the power of the wine" did not break the bottle; rather someone commanded the bottle to break. Consider one of the most accepted books on the revolution, written by Seyyed Hamid Ziyarati (Rouhani), who currently heads a foundation in charge of writing an official history of the revolution.[47] The book concentrates on the leaders of the revolution, particularly Khomeini. The author does not deny the great role Khomeini played in the revolution, but he does not share the leadership's unsophisticated understanding of Iran's revolution, which proposes that if the truth is disseminated among the Muslims of other countries, they will rise up against the ruling regime. This, of course, did not happen. Despite some indications that the revolutionaries have become more sophisticated and at the same time more realistic, they have not compromised on revolutionary principles, particularly Islamic universalism. Some sort of Islamic interpretation of politics is bound to persist in Iranian life for some time to come.

The revolution began as an attempt to restore Iran's lost identity and national dignity. In my judgment, the reason the dominant ideology displays such features as Islamic universalism, Iranianism, and populism stems from the general characteristic of the revolution as a classic

Ideology and Worldview

popular revolution. My general conclusion is that only the revolutionary zeal and extremism, common to all classic revolutions, are bound to be modified or abandoned altogether. The other features are bound to stay and shape the future political culture of Iranian society, even with the departure of Imam Khomeini from the political scene.

Notes

1. I owe a great deal to my colleague James P. Piscatori for originally suggesting this topic and for his constant encouragement and to John L. Esposito, Ali Reza Sheikholesiami, and Mohammad Reza Amid-Nuri, who read the draft and made insightful comments.

Translations of Persian sources throughout this paper are mine unless otherwise noted.

2. Ruholla Khomeini, sermon delivered on March 10, 1979. See *Ettela'at*, March 11, 1979, p. 8.

3. Ruholla Khomeini, *Kitab al-Bay*, 5 vols. (Najaf: n.p., 1390–91/1970–71).

4. This book was first published in Teheran in 1976 under the title *Name' i az Iman, Kashef-ul-Qita'* but went unnoticed by the Iranian intelligentsia. It has since been published under the title *Velayate Faqih* (Islamic government). A very sympathetic and accurate English translation is also available: Ruholla Khomeini, *Islam and Revolution: Writings and Declarations of Imam Khomeini*, trans. Hamid Algar (Berkeley: Mizan Press, 1981). (Hereafter cited as *Islam and Revolution*.)

5. For Khomeini's views on politics and government see Farhang Rajaee, *Islamic Values and World View: Khomeini on Man, the State and International Politics* (Lanham, Md.: University Press of America, 1983).

6. Paris, *Medaye Haq* (Teheran: Qalam, 1457/1978), 95.

7. Sermon delivered on July 1, 1979. For the text see Ruholla Khomeini, *Ruh Khoda dar Velayte Faqih* (Teheran: Vezarate Ershad, 1359/1980), 189.

8. Javad Tabatabai, *Daramadi Falsafi bar Tarikhe Andisheye Siyasi dar Iran* (Teheran: Daftare Motale'ate Siyasi va Binolmelai, 1367/1988), 138.

9. Rajaee, 52–54.

10. One can give a long bibliography of the works published during the past few decades, including the writings of Dr. Ali Shariati, Jalal al-Ahmad, Ehsa, Maraqui, and Daryoush Shayegan.

11. Note, for example, Dr. Ali Shariati's portrayal of the early heroes of Islam.

12. Conversation with the author on December 20, 1988, in Teheran.

13. English translation adapted from Marmaduke Pickthall, *The Glorious Koran* (Albany: State University of New York Press, 1976).

14. For an English translation of the constitution see *Middle East Journal* 34 (Spring 1980): 181–204.

15. See Surate Mozakerat Majlis, *Barrasiye Naha'ei Qanun-e Asasie Jumhuri Eslami*, vol. 3 (Teheran: Majlise-Shuraye Eslami, 1364/1985), 1520–21.

16. Sermon delivered on November 2, 1979. See *Ettela'at*, November 3, 1979, p. 12. This is a theme repeated in many of Khomeini's sermons. See, for example, *Dar Justejuye Rahe Imam* (Teheran: Amir Kobir, 1362/1983–84), part of a multivolume collection of quotations of Imam Khomeini on various topics. This

volume, subtitled "The Islamic Revolution," is devoted to issues such as the export of revolution.

17. Rajaee, 83.

18. Mostafa Izadi, *Masa'ele Jahaniye Enghelabe Islami dar Bayanate Ayat-llah al-'Ozma Montazeri* (Teheran: n.p., 1361/1983), 32, 33.

19. Ali Khamenei, *Chahar Sal ba Mardom* (Teheran: Hezbe Jumhuriye Eslami, 1364/1985), 354.

20. Payame Shahedan, *Bargozidde'i az Sokhamane HoJat-al-Islam Rafsanjani* (Meshed: Jahade Daneshgahi, n.d.), 8.

21. For the latter see ibid., 255; for the former see Khamenei, 354.

22. Hossein Bashiriyeh, *The State and Revolution in Iran*. (London: Croom Helm, 1984), 111–24.

23. For a history of Shiism see Husain M. Jafri, *Origins and Early Development of Shia Islam* (New York: Longman, 1976); and Moojan Momen, *An Introduction to Shii Islam* (New Haven: Yale University Press, 1985).

24. Hamid Enayat, *Modern Islamic Political Thought* (Austin: University of Texas Press, 1982), 19.

25. Murtaza Mutahhari, "Moshkele Asasi dar Sazemane Rohaniyat," in a collection of essays published after the death of Ayatollah Hosein ibn Ali Tabatabai Borujerdi (1875–1962): *Bagsu darbareye Marja'iyat va Rohaniyat* (Teheran: Sherkate Enteshar, 1341/1962).

26. See, for example, Reza Davari, *Nasionalism: Hakemiyate Melli va Esteqial* (Esfahan: Entesharate Poresesh, 1364/1985).

27. Henri Corbin, *En Islam Iranian: Respects Spirituels et Philosophiques* (Paris: Gallimard, 1972).

28. For an excellent account of the relation between ideal kingship in ancient Persia and Plato's political philosophy, see Fathullah Mujtabai, *Shahre Zibaye Aflatun va Shahiye Armani dar Irane Bastan* (Teheran: Adjomane Farhange Irane Bastan, 1352/1973).

29. *Islam and Revolution*, 53.

30. At least one scholar has discussed the influence of ancient Iranian religious tradition on Khomeini and the struggle between the Islamic forces and the Pahlavi dynasty. See Gudmar Aneer, *Imam Ruhullah Khumaini, Sah Muhammad Riza Pahlavi and the Religious Traditions of Iran* (Uppsala: Acta Universitatis Upsaliensis, 1985).

31. Wolfgang Knauth has documented four basic characteristics of a prospective king, namely, race, genre, proper paedia, and wisdom, all complemented by the divine grace. See Wolfgang Knauth, *Armane Shahriyari Irane Bastan*, Persian translation by Seifuldin Najmabadi (Teheran: Vezarate Farhang, 1355/1976).

32. Tabatabai, 39–72.

33. Crane Brinton, *The Anatomy of Revolution*, rev. ed. (New York: Vantage Books, 1965), 192.

34. Ali Montazeri, *Dar Maktabe Jom'e*, vol. 1 (Teheran: Ershad, 1364), 54.

35. The phrase "clearly accepted issue in jurisprudence" is translation of *Badihiyat-e Feghi*, which means it is an obvious issue on which everyone agrees.

36. Sermon delivered on February 7, 1980. See *Dar Justejuye*, 442.

37. Max Weber, *The Protestant Ethic and Spirit of Capitalism* (New York: Charles Scribner's Sons, 1958), 79–92.

38. Sermon delivered in 1983. For the text see Ruholla Khomeini, *Sahifeye Nur*, vol. 18 (Teheran: Vezarate Ershad, 1364/1985), 129. This is a collection of Khomeini's sermons and speeches published by the Ministry of Guidance. So far nineteen volumes have been published.

39. Sermon delivered on January 2, 1983. For the text see ibid., vol. 17, 140–41.

40. See *Farzand Melat dar Reineye Enqe'abe Eslami*. (Teheran: Vezarate Ershad, 1361/1982), 326.

41. See *Beheshti Ostureye Mellat bar Javedaneye Tarikh* (Teheran: Bonyade Shahid, 1361/1982), 326.

42. The Iranian revolution was a cultural revolution not because the dominant ideology of the ruling government is Islam, but because the revolution was a response to a cultural crisis. I hope to develop this theme in research I am conducting on political trends in twentieth-century Iran.

43. *Negahi be Sazemane Tablighate Eslami* (Teheran: Sazeman Tablighat, 1366), 26.

44. See *Mururi bar Ejlas-haye Qabliye Konferance Andisheye Rsalami* (Teheran: Sazemane Tablighat, n.d.)

45. Conversation with the author in December 1988 in Teheran.

46. The text of the letter appeared in the daily papers of Teheran. For an English translation see *Keyhan International*, January 14, 1989, p. 3. The following passage from Khomeini's letter relates directly to the export of revolution:

> By the way, [is] the religion which had made Iran to stand firmly against the superpowers the opium of the masses? Is the religion which seeks to implement justice in the world and wants to free man from material and spiritual ties the opium of the masses?
>
> Surely, a religion which lays the spiritual and material assets of the Islamic and non-Islamic countries at the disposal of the superpowers and [other] powers and shouts at the people that religion and politics are separated is the opium of the society. But then this is not a true religion. It is a religion that our people call "The American religion."
>
> *In conclusion, I would bluntly declare that the Islamic Republic of Iran is the strongest and the greatest base in the Islamic world and can easily fill the ideological vacuum in your system.* And in any case our country—as in the past—believes in good neighborly mutual relations and respect [emphasis added].

47. See Hamid Ziyarati, *Barrasiy va Tahlili az Mehzate Imam Khomeini*, vol. 1 (Qum: Daftare Entesharate Eslami, 1977) and vol. 2 (Teheran: Bonyade Shahid, 1364/1985).

The Middle East

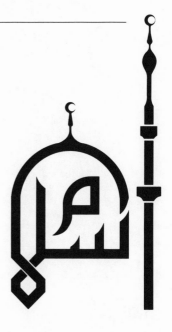

5

Iraq: Revolutionary

Threats and

Regime Responses

PHILIP ROBINS

IF ANY STATE FEARED the impact of the Iranian revolution it was Iraq. This anxiety sprang from two factors. The first is geography. The adjacent location of Iran and the length of the common border between the two states meant that Iraq was likely to be closely affected by changes in the power structure and ideology of its eastern neighbor. The second factor is the overlap in identity between Iranians and Iraqis. Of particular concern to Iraq was the fact that a majority of its people are the coreligionists of Shia Iran, while a large number of its citizens are also of Iranian origin. The Iranian revolution, particularly because of its religious and political appeal to Shii Muslims, appeared poised to cross a porous border and find a readily receptive community within Iraq.

The discomfort felt by the Iraqi government in the wake of the revolution was palpable and manifested itself in the anxious and cautious policies subsequently adopted by Iraq. Initially, the Iraqi government congratulated its Iranian counterpart on the success of the struggle.[1] Moreover, the regime was reluctant to criticize Iran's revolutionary leader, Ayatollah Khomeini, "for fear of the impact of the movement in Iraq."[2] It rapidly became clear from the Iraqi perspective, however, that adopting such a conciliatory policy would not prevent the revolution from having such an impact. By early 1980 the Iraqi view was that "if Ayatollah Khomaini's Shia Islamic republic consolidates itself, it is bound to cover southern Iraq, home of the country's large Shia population and of the Shia holy cities of Najaf and Kerbala."[3]

The initial anxiety on the part of the Iraqi government and indeed many of its citizens over the threat posed by the Iranian revolution was clear enough at the time. However, some ten years later this anxiety may appear curious because of the marginal way in which the revolution has affected Iraqi society. Of course, the war between the two countries dominated the first decade of bilateral relations after the Shah's downfall, and many predicted in the middle of the 1980s that Iraq would collapse militarily, possibly resulting in the dismemberment of the modern state. As we shall see, this prediction involved a major misreading of Iraq's difficulties during that time. But this view was sincerely held, with proponents attributing Iraq's anticipated collapse to the likely success of the Iranian military machine, not to an internal Iraqi uprising spurred by the effects of the example of the Iranian revolution.

This chapter addresses the question of why the Iranian revolution has had a relatively modest effect on the politics of Iraq. The discussion touches upon a number of related themes: the nature of the relationship between the Shia religious hierarchy in Iraq and in Iran; the formative influences on the Iranian revolutionary view of Iraq; and the contemporary policies of the Iraqi regime toward its own Shia community.

The Particularist Appeal of the Iranian Revolution

Initially it was unclear which ideological paradigm would come to dominate the Iranian revolution. In the opposition movement against the Shah's authoritarian regime there was much to attract liberal and intellectual Arabs. Communists and leftist Islamic groups also played a significant role. The religious figures in Iran who came to dominate the revolution emphasized the struggle of all oppressed people. The movement's rallying cry was couched in generalized Islamic terms, not tailored to particular confessional groups. In Iraq, however, the interest in the revolution was more narrowly based from the start as both government and citizenry alike tended to view the movement as specifically Shia in its appeal. This view was at first much more a function of Iraqi political and social dynamics than of the revolution itself. Ultimately the perception was one from which the Islamic rulers in Teheren were unable to escape.

There are two main reasons why the Iranian revolution became so inextricably identified in Iraqi eyes with Shia particularism. The first is the historical experience of the Shia in Iraq, where political discord on the part of the Shia community predates the Iranian revolution. Indeed, self-conscious Shia opposition to the organization of the modern Iraqi state dates back to its very inception. Shia religious and tribal leaders were in the forefront of the 1920 rebellion against the assignation of Iraq as a British mandate. Although the 1920 uprising was characterized by close cooperation between Sunni and Shia notables, this alliance quickly dissipated. By 1922 the moderate Sunni nationalists had by and large been co-opted into the political elite. It was left largely to the Shia leadership, both religious and tribal, to oppose the adoption of an Anglo-Iraqi treaty and elections to the Constituent Assembly that was to ratify it.

This period in Iraq's history is also significant in that it reveals the extent to which certain Shia religious leaders were prepared to appeal to the Persian state for assistance in what was effectively an internal political dispute. The willingness of a number of Shia *mujtahids* to seek support from Persia reveals the topography of their cognitive map: They identified more readily with the larger Shia religious community than with the modern state of Iraq. On this occasion the *mujtahids* involved actually decamped across the border to signal their protest and to attempt to enlist the support of the government in Teheran. Their protest collapsed, however, as Persia refused to become involved.

Direct Shia activity against the Iraqi government dwindled during the next few decades. In the 1950s and 1960s discontented Shias tended to channel their opposition through more generalized political activity. The Baath party and the Iraqi Communist party, both outsider organizations, were vehicles of organized protest by Shias.[4] In these cases particularistic Shia symbols and slogans were sublimated beneath those of Arabism and classism respectively.

Nevertheless, self-conscious protests by Shias qua Shias were on the increase well before to the Iranian revolution. Certainly the identification of Shia religious occasions with antiregime activity had returned by the 1970s. In 1969 the first Shia disturbances "for decades" occurred.[5] In June 1970 the funeral of the preeminent Shia religious authority, Ayatollah Muhsin al-Hakim, became an occasion for antigovernment protest. In 1974 the *ashura* processions also turned into political demonstrations. Several participants in the protests were jailed and five of the leaders were executed. Three years later massive *ashura* demonstrations in Karbala and Najaf resulted in riots that lasted for several days.

The Iraqi identification of the Iranian revolution with Shia particularism also evolved as a natural consequence of the close relationship between Iraq's radical Shia religious leadership, based in Najaf and Karbala, and Iran's Islamic leadership, which came to dominate the revolution. The ties that existed between the Shia ulama in Iraq and Iran remained close regardless of territorial boundaries. Moreover, in the contemporary world of nation-states the precedent had already been set for appealing to external states in internal political disputes. The close historical relationship of Iran to Najaf and Karbala meant that "Persian influence was strong" in these two cities.[6]

In addition, there was a special relationship between the more radical figures in both countries dating back to the early 1960s. Khomeini himself lived in Najaf from 1965 to 1978, as did a number of important Iraqi Shii radicals including Ayatollah Muhsin Hakim, his sons Mahdi and Muhammad, and Ayatollah Muhammad Baqr al-Sadr. Khomeini is reported to have been "very close" to Ayatollah Sadr during his exile.[7] That alliance was broadened by the relationship that developed between the entourages and supporters of both Iranian and Iraqi radical Shia leaders.

The close relationship of Khomeini and his Iranian associates with the radical Shia *mujtahids* in Najaf ultimately proved to be a double-edged sword. Initially the relationship certainly had its advantages for both sides. The Iranian Islamists forged links with senior, established Shia religious leaders inside Iraq, a ready-made support base among a highly respected elite. The Iraqi radicals gained inspiration and ideological development from living and studying alongside Khomeini. The importance of this association increased dramatically with the flight of the Shah and Khomeini's triumphant return to Teheran.

The negative aspects of the relationship, however, were manifested in the inability of the Iranian revolutionaries and their Iraqi Shia supporters to establish leadership authority over the wider political community in Iraq. The closeness of the relationship meant that the radical Iraqi Shia *mujtahids* found it virtually impossible to appeal to the whole of Iraq, a factor that proved crucial in Baqr al-Sadr's downfall. Ayatollah Sadr assiduously attempted to maintain his generalist credentials, both before and during his relationship with Khomeini, and this is nowhere more evident than in his written teachings. One expert has concluded that in Sadr's major works "there are no conspicuous examples of any specifically Shia set of references"; his writings are remarkably universalist.[8] Though it is debatable that Sadr had already lost the battle to be considered a general interconfessional authority within Iraq, his association with Khomeini and revolutionary Iran sealed this perception.

In the end Shia ulama in both Iraq and Iran found it easier to rely exclusively on such an alliance. Iran's Arabic-service broadcasts referred to Sadr as the "Khomeini of Iraq."[9] When the pressure was increasing on Sadr, and there are strong indications that he wished to leave the country, it was Khomeini who insisted that he should remain inside Iraq. Sadr was finally arrested in June 1979 when he attempted to lead a procession to Iran to congratulate Khomeini, an act which symbolized the inextricable links between the two sides.

The execution of Ayatollah Sadr took place the following April after a lengthy period of house arrest. No announcement of his death was initially made, and the news leaked out uncertainly. In describing Sadr's allegiances and the crime for which he had been executed, most newspaper reports made mention of his having been a leader of exclusively Shia protest. The Kuwaiti newspaper *Al Qabas*, which broke the story, reported that the charge against Sadr was leading a pro-Iran secret party, al-Dawa.[10] Western papers, insofar as they reported the death, saw him in the same particularist light; one described him as guilty of "stirring Iraqi Shiite anti-Government fervour."[11]

The succession to Sadr was a contentious issue among Iraq's Shia leaders. The son of Muhsin al-Hakim, Muhammad Baqr al-Hakim, claimed the mantle of Ayatollah Sadr. But his religious credentials were pale in contrast, and the Iraqi Shia community divided its religious allegiance even more than in the past. Fleeing the repression of Iraq's radical clergy, Muhammad Baqr al-Hakim sought refuge in Teheran. This move further associated him with the Iranian revolution and its exclusively Shia nature. It also meant that perceptions of religion and nationality became blurred.

Hakim's position became more difficult once the Iran-Iraq war broke out and the invocation of Iraqi and Arab nationalism increased in Iraq. Any broader credibility Hakim might have had was further undermined when he chose to remain in Iran in July 1982 when the Iranian forces took the conflict over the border and fighting began in earnest on Iraqi soil. Not only did he continue tacitly to support the Iranian war effort, but he intensified his own political efforts in tandem. What was effectively a Shia government in exile, called the Supreme Assembly of the Islamic Revolution of Iraq, was established in 1982 with Hakim at its head. By then it was clear that Hakim had no alternative strategy for furthering his political position in Iraq than the success of the Iranian war effort. Hakim's marginality on the Iraqi political scene is illustrated by the way the Iraqi regime persecuted with impunity other members of his family who remained inside the country.[12]

Iranian Misconceptions of Shia Society in Iraq

By the beginning of April 1980 Iran and Iraq were irreconcilably divided. The Iranian regime brazenly stated its objective as far as Iraq was concerned: "We have decided to overthrow the Baathist regime of Iraq," declared the foreign minister; Muslims of Iran and Iraq would remove the "evil Baathist leaders," stated Khomeini himself.[13] Yet in spite of this uncompromising and unequivocal rhetoric, the Iranian state made virtually no preparations for a conventional war between the two states.[14] This discrepancy can be convincingly explained only by the fact that Iran's revolutionary leadership seriously underestimated the resilience of the Iraqi regime and overestimated the fragmentary nature of Iraqi politics and society. In short, it probably did not occur to Teheran that the Iraqi regime would not collapse under the burden of its own unpopularity.

Many outside observers were mistaken in predicting the likelihood of upheavals in the Iraqi Shia community. Among those to misjudge the political situation were the senior members of the Iranian regime, who held a series of misconceptions about Shia society in Iraq. Their analysis was based primarily on the direct experience that Ayatollah Khomeini and his supporters had gleaned from living in or visiting Iraq. It is probable that the length of time these men spent in the south of Iraq made them confident of having a full and rounded sense of that country's Shia community. After all, these men had resided among Iraq's senior Shia leaders and had shared their teachings and scholarship.

The breadth of this experience was, however, illusory. The Iranian religious figures lived primarily in Najaf. They may have traveled to the Shia shrines, notably in Karbala, on pilgrimage, but they had not traveled widely through other areas of the country. It is safe to say that their experience of the rural Shia areas, the Shia quarters of Baghdad, and the newer Shia cities was scant. Even if they had traveled more widely, the extent to which they would have been able to communicate with ordinary Iraqi Shias is questionable. Khomeini is said to have known only classical Arabic, which helps explain why he appears to have been rather isolated during his stay in Iraq.[15] In turn the Iranian clerics had only a limited awareness of the depth of religiosity and the political consciousness of the bulk of the Iraqi Shias; their knowledge of the patterns of identity which such peoples possessed must have have been negligible.

Consequently, it is likely that the Iranian Islamic leaders took their experiences of Najaf and projected them onto the entire Shia population of Iraq. Yet Najaf proved not to be representative of the larger Shia community. The concentration of radical clergy in Najaf meant that the Shia of that city were more likely to share such an outlook than were their coreligionists elsewhere. In addition, the growing friction between the leading members of this radical movement and the Iraqi regime meant that relations between much of Najaf and the secular authorities had deteriorated considerably further than was the case in other parts of the country.

This greater radicalism, combined with an acute uneasiness with the central authorities, was reflected in outbursts of protest and violence in Najaf that were not comparably replicated elsewhere in the country. This pattern held true through the 1970s, in the aftermath of the Iranian revolution, and even after the arrest and execution of Ayatollah Sadr. Indeed, it is notable that upon Sadr's death "there was no mass protest here [in Iraq], even at the traditional 40th day of mourning."[16]

The radical clergy in Najaf may have encouraged the Iranian revolutionary leaders in their sanguine assessment of the political balance in Iraq. For instance, after his arrest Ayatollah Sadr reportedly claimed: "I am not alone here; there are thousands of real Muslims around me. All of them are one soul in many bodies."[17]

Based on their own vivid but deceptive firsthand experiences and the encouragement they appeared to be receiving from the radical Shia clerics in Iraq, the Iranian revolutionaries no doubt believed that Iraq would soon follow their example. This analysis was repeatedly voiced in their propaganda. An example of such rhetoric amply illustrates the sense of inevitability that the Teheran government seemed to hold in relation to the idea of the downfall of the Iraqi regime: "The holy land of Iraq which is the burial place of the most loved and most noble characters in human history [Ali and Husayn] . . . is now about to raise the call of Islam with its glorious uprising, and by emulating the various stages of the progress and development of the Islamic revolution of Iran, it is about to establish the government of divine justice and the Islamic republic."[18] The Iranians, at least as far as Iraq was concerned, had become seduced by their own rhetoric.

As other outside commentators often do, the Iranian revolutionaries also made the error of generalizing about the nature of Shia society inside Iraq. An enduring misconception is to regard the community as more monolithic than it actually is. At the local level and particularly in rural areas, kinship ties still determine primary loyalties and tend to be more immediate than general ethnic and confessional affiliations. Indeed, contact with the state continues to be mediated largely through tribal leaders.[19] The potency of clan and tribal relations is self-perpetuating since they tend to be important on an almost continuous basis in terms of access to resources and positions of influence.

Another misconception of Iraq held outside the country is that the Baathist regime in Baghdad survives only as a result of government coercion. It is likely that the revolutionaries in Teheran also held this view as a result of their experiences under the Shah; they may also have assumed that under the veneer of Iraqi authoritarianism there was a popular revolt waiting to burst out. Though repression has been used extensively in Iraq, it is reductionistic to conclude that coercion alone accounts for the nation's relative stability.

Such a view ignores the social and political changes taking place in Iraq, especially since the 1970s, as a result of the fairer distribution of far greater resources. The large increase in national revenue and the expanded role of the state in resource allocation has led to rapid changes in society and to the enhanced importance of the state. Massive expenditures on social services, particularly education and health, have improved the standard of living for Iraqis. The broader, more equitable distribution of resources has also ensured increased consumption at all levels of society over a relatively short period of time.

There can be no doubt that the rapid expansion in state spending has benefited the Shia areas of the country at least as much as the other regions, if not more so. As a result the gap between Shias and Sunnis in Iraq has greatly narrowed. For instance, in 1978, just prior to the Iranian revolution, the gap in primary school enrollment had narrowed almost completely between the Shia provinces of the south and the three Arab Sunni provinces. In terms of medical facilities the gap had already been closed. In terms of hospitals the Shia community actually enjoyed the edge; in the Shia provinces there was one institution per 59,000 people, compared to one hospital for every 61,000 people in the Sunni areas.

The strides made in education among the Shia have helped facilitate the further stratification of the community in Iraq. Phebe Marr observes that "a large number of those in the bureaucracy and the professions are *Shii*, and some professions may well be predominantly *Shii*."[20] Such evidence suggests that the regime has been surprisingly successful in integrating the Shias into the Iraqi middle class. Moreover, this process is likely to have changed the values and norms of the Iraqi Shia and to have increasingly differentiated them from their fellow confessionalists.

The Shia areas of Iraq have also benefited from the general policies of economic development and industrialization. Development efforts have focused on improving the quality of village life through the provision of better infrastructure. The state has built roads in agricultural areas, extended rural electrification, and constructed freshwater supply systems. The provision of these resources brought rural Shia peasants into closer contact with the state and may have improved their perception of the central government authority. Such developments certainly increased the dependence of the village on the state and its services and also helped the state to address the rural population directly. The provision of free television sets to southern villagers in the late 1970s to run on the newly installed electric power systems has enhanced the role of the peasant as consumer. It has also increased the ability of the state to talk directly to the Shia peasantry and thereby make the regime less remote.

The industrialization policies of the state and the major infrastructure projects that accompanied them also improved the material well-being of the southern Shia population. In the mid-1970s the Iraqi government attempted to build up the industrial base of the south, concentrating on petrochemicals. Investment was also channeled into improving the vertical lines of communication between the capital and the south, and in expanding the southern port facilities. These projects provided "many Shiite youngsters with relatively high-paying and secure jobs,"[21] which in turn improved these workers' perception of the state, a significant change from the Shia community's generally negative view since the 1920s. The increase in the number of employees dependent on the state for their income in the south indicates the extent to which the state had penetrated the Shia areas. The importance of such salaries in the rural income equation also suggests that the state had increased the dependent position of such areas relative to the center.

When the financial burden of the Iran-Iraq war made it impossible for the Iraqi government to sustain its "guns and butter policy" in 1982, investment in the southern areas, as in rest of the country, naturally lapsed. However, the declaration of a cease-fire was followed by renewed infrastructure development in the southern part of Iraq. One of the first major reconstruction projects has been the rebuilding of the second city of Basra and the town of Faw. The local currency equivalent of some $5 billion was reportedly pumped into the reconstruction of Basra, with priority given to road building and utilities.[22] In fact the process of "reconstruction" has been used as a smoke screen to direct additional resources into making Basra a more modern city than it was before the war.[23] Indeed it is difficult to quarrel with the interpretation that the Shias in Iraq have undergone a process of "integration through economy."[24]

Thus, the notion of the Shia existing almost independently of the Iraqi state both economically and culturally has been rapidly undermined. Significant changes have also taken place in the position of the Shia relative to the political elite. Following the consolidation of the Iraqi state in the 1920s, the Shias were largely isolated from the political affairs of the country. This situation appeared to worsen after the downfall of the monarchy. Between 1948 and 1958, 21 percent of Iraq's top-echelon politicians were Shias. This fell to only 16 percent over the succeeding ten years up to the resurgence in self-conscious Shia protest in Iraq.

More recently the anti-Shia bias appears to have been reversed. One study indicates that between June 1982 and June 1987, 33 percent of the Revolutionary Command Council were Shias. During the same period, some 50 percent of the Regional Command of the Baath Party were Shias, a proportion more representative of the relative number of Shias in the country's population. The author of this study concludes that, "Shiite representation in the political elite under the Baath is indeed unparalleled in the history of the modern Iraqi state."[25] After the cease-fire in the Iran-Iraq war, the trend of greater Shia representation among the political elite appears to have continued. On June 5, 1989, a Shia, Saadoun Hammadi, was promoted to serve as one of Iraq's three deputy prime ministers.

Subsequent analysis of the bureaucracy and military suggests that the position of the Shias in Iraq is improving overall. Of 100 civil servants holding the rank of director general or its equivalent, half were Shias, while only 1–2 percent were drawn from the other group conventionally regarded as being in the political wilderness, the Kurds. Of 60 senior officers in the army occupying the rank of brigadier general or above (perhaps 10–15 percent of the total officer class), 20–25 percent were Shias.[26] Although markedly disproportionate relative to the total number of Shias in Iraq, this is an important statistic given the conventional wisdom that the Sunnis supply the officers in the Iraqi army while the Shias constitute merely the rank and file.

Iraqi Responses to Internal Threats

For all the particularism and miscalculations of the opposition inside Iraq and its backers in Iran, the Baathist regime in Baghdad faced a considerable political challenge. The periodic riots that took place in certain Shia areas in the late 1970s together with the growing assertiveness of the radical Iraqi Shia and the tenor of Iranian rhetoric made the position of the government increasingly uncomfortable. There was also the possibility that the Kurdish dissident opposition might once again begin to stir and cash in on the pressure under which the regime found itself. Of greatest concern were signs of significant divisions opening up within the highest ranks of the Baathist leadership over how to deal with the emerging challenge.[27] The nature and coherence of the leadership's response were likely to be crucial to the stability and continuity of the Iraqi power structure.

The response of the Iraqi leadership to these internal threats involved the employment of two concurrent tactics: an attempt to conciliate the Shias through a variety of means, and an uncompromising policy of confrontation and even destruction of those individuals and organizations that actively opposed or were deemed likely to challenge the regime.

Since 1977 the Baathist government had come to consider the Shia community as an important constituency, one which might eventually present a challenge to the existing status quo. Consequently, the regime had already made some conspicuous attempts to co-opt the Shias by appointing a number of them to membership in the Revolutionary Command Council. This careful attention to the profile of Shias in public life became more scrupulous after the Iranian revolution and during the Gulf war. The National Assembly, which was created in June 1980, was 40 percent Shia; in 1980 and 1984 the speaker of the assembly was also a Shia.

In addition to the general attempt to raise the material well-being of the Shias, through the development policies outlined previously, the regime also moved to target particular problem areas. The Shia cities of Najaf and Karbala were the recipients of considerable injections of extra funds, as were certain Shia areas in Baghdad. Lavish subventions were made available for the renovation of Shia shrines and holy places: In Najaf some $220 million was set aside for spending on the mosque of Ali, while in Karbala $60 million was allocated for the renovation of the shrines of Husayn and Abbas.[28] Such spending, of course, also had a considerable multiplier effect on the local economy, to the particular benefit of local merchants, craftsmen, and construction workers.

Other monies for direct benefit of the population were also allocated. A donation of $52 million was made for the construction of a hospital in Najaf, while in 1981 a host of housing and agricultural projects were financed in Karbala. In Baghdad, the run-down and crime-ridden township of al-Thawra, whose population is 80 percent Shia,[29] also received considerable aid. In 1982 the township's name was changed to Saddam City, and many of its old decrepit buildings were replaced with new concrete structures. A grid system of wide roadways was also constructed, which appears to have improved the policing of the area. Though at night security continues to be uncertain in the township, the level of disturbances seen in the late 1970s has not been replicated.

Central government resources were also used selectively to divide the Shia clergy in the major southern cities. The Shia *mujtahids* were put on the government payroll, while additional funds were made available to benefit those religious leaders who had openly clashed with the radicals. Foremost among these leaders was Ali Kashif al-Ghita, who belongs to an important family of ulama in Najaf.[30] Such investment paid off for the regime: Ghata, together with a second prominent Shia cleric in Iraq, Ali al-Saghir, publicly denounced Ayatollah Khomeini's political philosophy of *velayat-e faqih*.[31]

The Iraqi regime had always been prepared to use force in suppressing disturbances. The army was regularly used to stop violent protest in Najaf and Karbala during the 1970s. In the wake of the Iranian revolution, however, there was a split in the Revolutionary Command Council over the extent to which repression should be used to prevent Shia disturbances. But the swift palace coup in which Saddam Hussein emerged as the formal as well as the informal power in the country, the retirement of President Ahmad Hassan al-Bakr, and the purge of certain senior officials in July 1979 spelled the end of this debate within senior party circles.

The consolidation of the hardliners' position within the ruling party and Saddam Hussein's sudden assumption of power resulted in a greater preparedness to confront the radical Shia movement. Shortly after Bakr's retirement Ayatollah Sadr was placed under house arrest and a large number of his followers were detained. While the exact numbers of those arrested and subsequently executed are unknown, the figures are clearly very large. In mid July 1979 the Islamic Liberation Movement of Iraq estimated that 86 people, many of them Sadr's representatives, awaited execution; 590 had been sentenced to life imprisonment; 11,000 were under arrest; and 36 people had died under torture.[32] Though the numbers quoted are presumably exaggerated, they do indicate the massive scale of the crackdown and show that the regime was prepared to use instruments of repression at will.

When the internal threat intensified once more the following spring, the regime resorted to even more uncompromising methods against those who challenged it. Ayatollah Sadr was executed on April 8, 1980, a momentous and unprecedented decision for the regime. The government sought to legitimize the execution through a Revolutionary Command Council decision making affiliation with the Dawa party punishable by death, a decision that was to be applied retroactively.[33] In tactical terms the execution of Sadr served the regime in Baghdad well. It removed the one opposition Shia cleric of any stature, and in the absence of a well-organized movement with widespread support, the Shia opposition quickly dissipated. One observer noted that "when al-Sadr was killed, the momentum that his charisma had generated was rapidly lost."[34]

The regime also used deportation—real and threatened—to hound its implacable opponents, especially those believed to be most susceptible to Iranian-backed radical Shia activity. The deportations were specifically directed at Iranians residing in Iraq and those Iraqis of Iranian origin. Simply having an Iranian name made one a candidate for expulsion. There are indications that a number of disaffected Iraqi Shias were also deported.[35] Again, the actual number of deportations is unknown; figures range from 30,000 to 350,000,[36] although this latter figure probably includes all the Iraqi exiles in Iran, many of whom would have been expelled in earlier purges.[37]

The deportations of these "Iranians" appeared to be part of a concerted policy of the Iraqi regime to blame the instability of the country on Iran and its agents rather than to accept that there was a domestic constituency that might have genuine grievances. The Iraqi regime stepped up the offensive against the so-called Iranian fifth column with al-Dawa's attempt on the life of Tariq Aziz, a member of the Revolutionary Command Council and a deputy prime minister, on April 1, 1980. The assailant, who was killed on the spot, was described as being an Iraqi of Iranian origin, the release of such information being interpreted as "Iraq blaming neighbouring Iran for the incident."[38] The attack on mourners during the funeral of a student killed in the Aziz incident was grist to the mill. Baghdad radio reported that the second attack occurred while the funeral procession was "going along the street on which the Iranian school and some Iranian houses are located"; at that point "one of the Iranians" hurled a bomb at the procession.[39]

It was clear at least to members of al-Dawa what was happening. In a statement claiming responsibility for the attempt on Tariq Aziz's life, the party accused the Iraqi regime of "trying to disrupt and divert Iraqi public opinion" by holding Iran responsible.[40] But the Iraqi authorities were not to be deflected, and they continued to refer to the perpetrators of subversion as being "of Iranian origin."[41] This recurring reference by government spokesmen suggests that such labels were striking a responsive chord among a significant part of the Iraqi population. Indeed, on the eve of the outbreak of the Iran-Iraq war, Saddam

Hussein reiterated the theme, accusing Ayatollah Khomeini of using Islam as a shield for "Persian expansionist ambition."[42]

Conclusion

From the beginning the perception of the Iranian revolution in Iraq was one of narrow sectarianism. The historical tensions between Shia and Sunni communities in Iraq provided the political and psychological framework within which the revolution tended to be placed. The radical Shia leaders in Iraq were unable to redraw the cognitive map of their fellow countrymen. Though there had been attempts to appeal to Iraqis on a universalist basis, the senior Shia leadership increasingly succumbed to presenting a particularist message. The advent of an Islamic revolution in Shia Iran made generalist appeals by Shia leaders in Iraq subject to suspicion and doubt. Without repudiating the Iranian revolution, the radical Shia opposition could probably never have been successful in mobilizing the non-Shia communities against the Baghdad regime.

There was no retreat from the growing particularism of the radical Shia opposition in the face of the actions and rhetoric of Iran's revolutionary government and religious leadership. The Iranians in turn came to rely exclusively on the Shia opposition in Iraq based on erroneous assumptions about the cohesion of the Iraqi Shia community and the supposedly brittle nature of the ruling regime. These assumptions were based on a superficial analysis underscored by the lengthy but limited experience that some Iranian leaders had of Iraq. The radical Shia leadership in Iraq did not temper such conclusions and indeed seems to have helped feed them.

In spite of the weaknesses in the Shia opposition, the Iraqi regime clearly faced a serious challenge even before but especially after the Iranian revolution. The success of the regime in maintaining power and leading the Iraqi state in a protracted and costly war with Iran owes much to the policies it pursued. With respect to the Shia community in Iraq, the regime has sought to distinguish between those who have organized politically against it and those who are quiescent. The former have been the subject of a campaign of confrontation often resulting in the use of force. But for the vast majority of Iraqi Shia, there have been considerable economic rewards and social advances resulting from an allocative policy that has favored the geographical area in which the majority of Shia are located.

Notes

1. The message sent on March 13, 1979, by the Iraqi government congratulating the Iranian government on the revolution is reproduced in *BBC Summary of World Broadcasts—Middle East* (hereafter cited as BBC/SWB), June 15, 1979.

2. *New York Times*, January 1, 1980.

3. *Observer*, February 2, 1980.

4. While there appears to have been a greater proportion of Shias in the Baath party in its early years and in the Iraqi Communist party than in the ruling political elites, Shias did not numerically dominate these outsider organizations. See Hanna Batatu, *The Old Social Classes and the Revolutionary Movements of Iraq* (Princeton: Princeton University Press, 1978), 650, 699, 748.

5. Chibli Mallat, "Religious Militancy in Contemporary Iraq: Muhammad Baqer as-Sadr and the Sunni-Shia Paradigm," *Third World Quarterly* (April 1988): 719.

6. Phebe Marr, *The Modern History of Iraq* (Boulder, Colo.: Westview Press, 1985), 238.

7. *Guardian*, April 15, 1980.

8. Mallat, 708.

9. Edward Mortimer, *Faith and Power* (London: Faber and Faber, 1982), 364.

10. BBC/SWB, April 16, 1980.

11. *Daily Telegraph*, April 16, 1980.

12. Shahram Chubin and Charles Tripp, *Iran and Iraq at War* (London: I. B. Tauris, 1988), 101.

13. *International Herald Tribune*, April 10, 1980.

14. Chubin and Tripp, 34.

15. Christine Moss Helms, *Iraq, Eastern Flank of the Arab World* (Washington, D.C.: Brookings Institution, 1984), 151–52.

16. *New York Times*, June 26, 1980.

17. BBC/SWB, June 25, 1979.

18. BBC/SWB, April 4, 1980.

19. Chubin and Tripp, 99.

20. Marr, 284.

21. Amazia Baram, "National Integration and Local Orientation in Iraq Under the Baath," *Jerusalem Journal of International Relations* 9, no. 3 (1987): 48.

22. Associated Press report in the *Jordan Times*, June 18, 1989.

23. Interviews with local officials and other analysts.

24. Baram, 47.

25. Ibid., 42.

26. Amazia Baram, seminar given on October 27, 1988, Royal Institute of International Affairs at Chatham House, London.

27. Ofra Bengio, "Shiis and Politics in Baathi Iraq," *Middle Eastern Studies* 21 (January 1985): 7.

28. Helms, 33.

29. Interview with Baghdad-based analyst, November 30, 1987.

30. Chibli Mallat, "Iraq," in *The Politics of Islamic Revivalism*, ed. Shireen Hunter (Bloomington: Indiana University Press, 1988), 79.

31. Pierre Martin, 'Le Clergé Chiite en Irak Hier et Aujourd'hui," *Maghreb Machrek*, no. 115 (January–March 1987): 48.

32. *Daily Telegraph*, July 20, 1979.

33. BBC/SWB, April 11, 1979.

34. Mallat, "Iraq," 82.

35. Bengio, 11.

36. Frederick W. Axelgard, *A New Iraq?* (New York: Praeger, 1988), 23.

37. Helms, 145.

38. *Financial Times*, April 3, 1980.

39. BBC/SWB, April 8, 1980.

40. Ibid.

41. BBC/SWB, April 11, 1980.

42. *New York Times*, September 18, 1980.

6

The Impact of the Iranian

Revolution on the Arabian

Peninsula and the Gulf States

DAVID E. LONG

THE DIFFERENCE BETWEEN MAJOR milestones and déjà vu is often mainly in the eye of the beholder. This is especially true in the Middle East, where time is not linear and can be speeded up, slowed down, stopped, or reversed at the will of the observer.

Ten years after the Iranian revolution, it is still difficult to determine into which of these two categories it falls, much less how it has impacted on the Arabian Peninsula and the Persian Gulf. Not only is there little that is new about the revolution intellectually or ideologically, but Iran's leaders self-consciously extol the old and exhort their followers to turn back the clock to the early years of Islam. At the same time, the Iranian revolution has created a totally new frame of reference for analyzing the political and social developments not only of Iran but of its immediate neighbors in the Arabian Peninsula and the Gulf. Virtually every political study of the Gulf made before the revolution has become obsolete.

Another difficulty in assessing the impact of the Iranian revolution on the Gulf states is perceptual. Prior to the downfall of the Shah's regime, for example, most of the senior policy makers in Washington and elsewhere were convinced that for all the difficulties that confronted him, the Shah had sufficient residual strength to survive. One could not give away bad news about his prospects. In the wake of the Iranian revolution, however, those same policy makers perceived all the conservative monarchies in the Gulf as miniature Irans, susceptible to revolution and destined to collapse. At that point one could not give away good news about the Gulf.

Whatever the past and future impact of the Iranian revolution, there will never be an Iranian-style revolution outside Iran, and never another one in Iran exactly like the past one. Every country in the region is different, and if any one or more of them do have a revolution, it will be in their own mold, not Iran's.

The Iranian revolution is, in fact, two distinct phenomena. On the one hand, it is an Islamic fundamentalist revival movement with roots extending back to the earliest days of Islam. It is at the same time an Iranian nationalist political revolution, the main importance of which is geopolitical rather than religious. In order to assess accurately its impact on the Gulf, the revolution must be viewed in both contexts. The problem, of course, is that this is somewhat like trying to unscramble an egg.

The Iranian Islamic Revival and the Gulf

Before analyzing the impact of the Iranian Islamic revival on the Gulf, several points should be made about Islamic fundamentalism in general. First, it is not a unified, coherent movement. There are many strains of fundamentalism in the Islamic world, all essentially existing independently. Second, militant religious fundamentalism is not limited to Islam. It is part of a worldwide trend to identify with one's roots by attempting to go back to unequivocal "fundamental truths" in the face of a threatening, relativistic world. All major religions, including Christianity, Judaism, Islam, Buddhism, Sikhism, and Hinduism, have fundamentalist strains. Third, revolutionary political movements in the name of Islam (or any other religion) are not so much theologically motivated as politically, psychologically, and sociologically motivated. Although the two overlap, there is a basic difference between theological puritanism and militant political fundamentalism.

There are two principal areas in which the Iranian Islamic revolution has affected the Gulf states: the ideological/intellectual realm and the psychological/political realm.

The Arabian Peninsula

IDEOLOGICAL/INTELLECTUAL IMPACT

The elemental religious difference between Iran and the Gulf states affecting the latter's receptivity to the Iranian Islamic revival is the preponderance of Shia Islam in Iran and of Sunni Islam in the Gulf states. The intellectual and doctrinal impact of the Iranian Islamic revolution on the Sunnis of the Gulf has been virtually nil. Islamic fundamentalism among Sunnis emanates from an entirely different tradition. What ideological/intellectual attraction the revival has had in the Gulf states, therefore, is principally among their Shii communities, which are in most cases minorities and in all cases under Sunni-dominated political systems.[1]

In order to understand better the receptivity (or lack thereof) of Sunnis and Shiis in the Gulf to the Iranian revival, it might be helpful to review quickly the doctrinal differences between Sunni and Shii fundamentalism. Islam is more of a legal system than a theological system, and the differences in Shii and Sunni interpretations of the *Sharia*, or sacred law, are surprisingly small. Therefore, returning to the fundamentals of Islam, whether Sunni or Shia, does not equate to great differences in Islamic jurisprudence.

Although the Sunni-Shia schism was originally political in nature, substantial theological and psychological differences developed over time. In addition to the millenarian promise of the return of the Hidden Imam to restore justice to the world,[2] Shii history has also bequeathed its followers a strong tradition of martyrdom. This martyrdom complex contributes to a lack of moderation among adherents of Shii fundamentalism. The millenarianism of the Hidden Imam has several implications for Shii political theory. First, it assumes an intercessor between God and man (the earthly Imams) not found in Sunni tradition. Second, because the Twelfth Imam is living in a state of occultation, no living temporal ruler can attain that stature. It thus follows that the legitimacy of any temporal leader can be challenged by the religious community, which is the representative of the Mahdi until his return and which retains the right to *ijtihad*, or independent interpretation of sacred law.

Based on this premise, Ayatollah Khomeini developed his concept of *velayat-e faqih*, government by Islamic cleric-jurist, in order to protect society from corruption. This concept is at the core of the Iranian Islamic revival. By extension, the legitimacy of any other political system, whether headed by Muslims or not, can be called into question, includ-

Long

ing the Muslim governments of the Gulf states and particularly the Sunni-dominated, secular Arab nationalist government of Iraq. Moreover, it is the sacred obligation of just Muslims to oppose by force all illegitimate rulers as enemies of Islam; the struggle is known as *jihad* and is the basis for Iran's militant foreign policy of exporting the revolution.

In contrast, Sunnis, who form the majority of Muslims, have come to better terms with temporal authority by legitimizing secular governments in Muslim states so long as they uphold Islamic law. Throughout Sunni Islamic history, however, there have been efforts to purify the religion by returning to the fundamentals of the *Sharia*. One of the greatest influences on contemporary Sunni fundamentalist revivalism is the teachings and writings of Taqi al-Din Ahmad ibn Taymiya (d. 1328 A.D.).[3] Ibn Taymiya was a follower of the Hanbali school of jurisprudence, the most fundamentalist school in Sunni Islam. Not only did he call for reform based on the fundamental teachings of the *Sharia*, but he also claimed, unlike most Sunnis, that *ijtihad* was still valid and that he was a practitioner (*mujtahid*).

Ibn Taymiya contended that the only political legitimacy came from the *Sharia*. He reinterpreted the Islamic concept of *jahiliya* (literally, "ignorance"), which had previously referred to the pre-Islamic age, to include any living Muslim ruler who willfully disregarded God's law. He also claimed that it was an obligation for the Muslim community to rise against them in jihad, an act formerly limited to enemies of God and not previously considered legitimate against Muslim rulers.

This emphasis on the "holy war" aspects of jihad comes very close to Khomeini's use of the term. In both cases, the implication for Muslims seeking to justify violent opposition to secular governments of both Muslim and non-Muslim states is obvious. In their eyes, it raised political violence in the defense of Islam to the religious obligation of jihad.

For centuries Ibn Taymiya's teachings, though known to Islamic scholars, exerted relatively little influence on Islamic political thought. In the twentieth century, however, his ideas of *jahiliya* and jihad have become the doctrinal basis for the rise of militant Sunni Islamic fundamentalism.

In sum, then, despite some theological differences there are great similarities in the intellectual and ideological bases of radical Sunni and Shii fundamentalism: the rejection of legitimacy of both Muslim and non-Muslim regimes that do not rule in accordance with God's law,

The Arabian Peninsula

the use of *ijtihad* to interpret God's law, and the call for jihad in the context of the use of force. Nevertheless, there is more than sufficient intellectual justification for fundamentalism on both sides to obviate either tradition turning to the other for inspiration.

This is particularly the case with Saudi Arabia. Persuaded by Ibn Taymiya's call to reject innovative Islamic practices and return to the original doctrines of Islam, Muhammad ibn Abd al-Wahhab set in motion his revival of Hanbalism in Saudi Arabia. Thus, for the Saudis, not only is the Iranian Islamic revival exclusively Shii, but it comes over two hundred years after their own revival, based on the works of the most revolutionary Sunni fundamentalist of all time, Ibn Taymiya.

The intellectual/ideological impact of the Iranian Islamic revival on the Gulf states is thus limited almost entirely to the Shii communities. It is virtually impossible to judge what if any impact the writings of Khomeini and others have had on Gulf Shii intellectual thought. In Iraq, Ayatollah Muhammad Baqr al-Sadr's fundamentalist writings and preachings were instrumental in the founding of the Dawa (the Call) party in the late 1960s, but this predated the Iranian revolution. Still, the Dawa party did participate in acts of terrorism in Iraq and Kuwait, particularly after the revolution, and was thus obviously influenced by it. Baqr al-Sadr also came in contact with Khomeini when the latter was living in exile in Iraq. (Al-Sadr was executed in 1980).

Whatever influence Khomeini and the Iranian Islamic revival had on Baqr al-Sadr or the Dawa party, it did not incite a significant number of Shiis in the Arabian Peninsula to adopt similar violent political activism. Indeed, based on the rather modest degree of Shii political unrest occurring in the Gulf in the ten years following the Iranian revolution, its intellectual and doctrinal impact on Gulf Shiis has apparently been much less than originally feared by the Gulf regimes.

PSYCHOLOGICAL/POLITICAL IMPACT

Some have compared the psychological impact of the Iranian revolution to the Russo-Japanese War of 1904–5, in which a Third World country humbled a great European power. The facts of the two conflicts are not exactly similar, but facts have never been crucial to perceptions. At any rate, the revolution was seen by many Third World peoples as the victory of an oppressed people against a despotic monarch allied to the United States. That view was not, however, shared by all Third World peoples, and soon after the revolution, the excesses of the Iranian leadership were to breed revulsion among many who had originally been inspired by it.

In order for an event such as the Iranian Islamic revival to have a significant psychological impact, there must be a receptive audience that can identify the revolution, no matter how unrelated, with its own situation—its own frustrations and grievances and its own hopes for redress. Among the Sunnis in the Gulf, there has been little if any receptivity to any kind of revolutionary movement. Whatever their political, social, or economic frustrations, the Sunni societies of the Gulf states are generally stable and do not look upon violence or revolution as a means of remedying their grievances.

In addition, all the Gulf regimes with the exception of Iraq are conservative, and those citizens who were disaffected with established authority have generally chosen Marxism and Arab socialism as their ideological justification for revolution rather than Islamic fundamentalism. The greatest internal security threat in the Gulf in the 1970s came from the left, the Dhufar rebellion in Oman led by Marxist Arab nationalists.

Nevertheless, there was considerable official concern on the Arab side of the Gulf over the potential psychological impact of the Iranian Islamic revival and the potential threat it posed to internal security. From the very start of the revolution, Radio Teheran and Radio Ahwaz broadcast daily invective against the Arab leaders of the Gulf in Arabic-language programs designed primarily for Arab Shii audiences.

In the case of Saudi Arabia, skilled Shii workers had been given some of the most sensitive positions in the oil installations because of their imperviousness to the blandishments of militant Arab nationalists, particularly during the Nasser period. In turn, these workers had always been very loyal to the ARAMCO, which had provided them with jobs and an opportunity to better themselves. But the median age in Saudi Arabia's heavily Shii-populated Eastern Province was only about seventeen years, and it was feared that the younger Shiis, who never knew pre-oil-age poverty, would not share the loyalties of their parents. As a result of the Iranian revolution, the Shii community was seen as a major security threat.

In the years immediately following the revolution, such fears appeared to be well founded. Throughout the Gulf, political discussions increased and intensified at the *husayniyahs*, or Shii meeting places. In November 1979 and again in January 1980, communal riots and disturbances broke out in the Eastern Province. The issue that kindled this activism was the years of benign neglect of the Shii community by the government, but there can be no doubt that the participants were influenced by the Iranian revolution. Also in November 1979, Juhaman bin Sayf al-Utaybi organized the takeover of the Haram, the Grand Mosque in Mecca, proclaiming that a Mahdi had arisen to purify Islam. Although no direct link has ever been established between the mosque incident and Iran, the psychological impact of the revolution was probably an influential factor.

In Bahrain, which like Iran has a Shii majority, at least two coup attempts can be linked to Iranian support. The most serious, in December 1981, led to the arrest of seventy-three people. Kuwait also witnessed a number of civil disturbances and acts of terrorism that can be linked to Iran. These include a series of Shii terrorist attacks in the early 1980s, culminating in the attacks on the French and U.S. embassies and on American and Kuwaiti facilities by members of the Iranian-sponsored Iraqi Dawa party in December 1983, as well as the hijacking of Kuwaiti airliners in 1984 and again in 1988.

Despite these incidents and Iran's avowed policy of exporting its brand of Islamic revolution, substantial growth of Shii political unrest in the Gulf states has not occurred. Although Shii political awareness has increased and the younger population has added a degree of impetuosity and impatience to the political scene, the large-scale, grassroots uprisings by local Shii communities once feared by the Gulf states simply have not materialized. Even the Iraqi army, which is largely Shii, remained loyal throughout the Iran-Iraq war. In many cases, battles did not pit Sunnis against Shiis but Shiis against Shiis.

There is no single obvious answer to why the expected uprisings have not taken place despite the very real political, social, and economic grievances that exist in Shii communities throughout the Gulf. The explanation involves several key factors. First, and most important, the excesses of the Iranian government toward its own citizens were viewed with horror on the Arab side of the Gulf and seen as much less preferable than the policies and practices of the existing local regimes. Life might occasionally seem unpleasant for the Shii communities in the Gulf, but it is not unbearable.

Second, the Iran-Iraq war was generally seen as not merely a threat to the welfare of the Gulf Sunnis but to that of the Shiis as well, for attacks on oil tankers and installations adversely affect the economic well-being of the whole Gulf population. By and large, Shiis through-out the Gulf, not just in the Iraqi army, supported their own countries in the conflict. In other words, the Iran-Iraq war was perceived as more of an Arab-Persian conflict than a Shii-Sunni conflict.

Third, no indigenous charismatic Shii leaders have emerged to arouse the imagination and support of the Gulf Shii communities or to channel vague feelings of discontent into focused, organized dissent. Without organization and leadership, there can be no effective expres-sion of political opposition. There is evidence that the Iranians have tried to encourage organized opposition, but, except in Lebanon where Shii grievances were substantially greater, they have found no significant local leaders with groups of loyal followers.

Fourth, not only have the Gulf states increased internal security measures, particularly in heavily Shii areas and at strategically impor-tant installations, but they have also been more sensitive to legitimate Shii grievances and receptive to Shii demands. For example, following the Shii riots in Saudi Arabia in 1979 and 1980, King Khalid visited the Eastern Province for the opening of the Jubayl naval base and made a special effort to meet with Shii notables and listen to the grievances of the Shii community. The Saudi government has since followed through on increased development spending in predominantly Shii areas.

Fifth, although oil wealth has been distributed somewhat dispropor-tionately to the Sunnis, the Shiis have also shared in the oil boom, and their standard of living is quite high. Moreover, oil company policies have contributed to a strong middle-class mentality in the Gulf, even among the skilled laborers, that is virtually unheard of outside Western industrialized countries.

There may be yet another contributing factor. Shiism is seen all too often in the West as an Iranian-centered religion. The fact is that the original stronghold of the "Followers of Ali" was in present-day Iraq. The two holiest cities in Shii Islam after Mecca and Medina are Najaf and Karbala in Iraq, not Qum or Mashad in Iran. Most of the Gulf Shii clergy receive their training in the Shii seminaries of Iraq, and since the Iran-Iraq war, fewer still venture to Iran. The war, with its Persian-versus-Arab cast, has probably served to reinforce the feeling that it is possible to be a good Arab and a good Shii at the same time.

The absence of broad-based revolutionary Shii movements in the Gulf influenced if not indoctrinated by Iran does not mean that the Iranian Islamic revolution has had no psychological/political impact on the region. One of the most important outcomes of the revolution has been Iran's challenge to Saudi Arabia's tacit claim to spiritual guardianship of the Muslim world and the Islamic way of life.

The Saudi claim is based in part on its guardianship of the two holiest sites in Islam, Mecca and Medina, and in part on the teachings of its own Islamic revival, Wahhabism. Through Wahhabism, the Saudi worldview has essentially conformed to the classically Islamic bipolar division of *dar al-Islam* (those nations living under God's law) and *dar al-harb* (those nations living outside the holy law, i.e., atheists). This bipolar view is paralleled by the Western model of free world nations versus Communist nations; thus, the greatest threat to both the Islamic world and the free world comes from the Communists, who are perceived as atheists.

As a monotheistic country threatening Muslim/Arab nations, Israel is an aberration in the Saudi worldview. The Saudis claim this aberration is the result of secular Zionism, which they avidly oppose, rather than Judaism, which they respect. Their major foreign policy goal has been to persuade the United States to have the backbone to force Israel to grant self-determination to the Palestinians in order to end this divisive conflict and concentrate on stopping the spread of atheistic communism.

Traditionally, then, in the Saudi worldview the greatest threat to the Islamic world in general and to Saudi Arabia and the Gulf in particular comes from the far left of the political spectrum—atheistic communism. The advent of the Iranian Islamic revival, however, which sees the greatest threat to the Islamic world coming from secular Westernism, poses a new threat, not from the far left but from the far right. This is extremely disconcerting to the Saudi regime, which since the Wahhabi revival nearly 250 years ago has considered itself to be the right wing in terms of Islamic puritanism.

The Saudis do not take lightly Iran's claim to guardianship of the Islamic world nor its challenging the legitimacy of the Saudi regime, based as it is on Islamic law. The gravity of the Iranian challenge has been particularly focused on the hajj, or pilgrimage to Mecca, undertaken by thousands of Iranians and nearly two million Muslims annually. The Saudis take their guardianship of the pilgrimage and the holy places very seriously and have traditionally overlooked political differences in welcoming Muslims to perform this obligation of faith.

The Iranians, for their part, have since the revolution attempted to disrupt the hajj to show that the Saudis are unable and unworthy to be guardians of the holy places. Each year, Iranian pilgrims have demonstrated, distributed anti-Saudi literature, and generally tried to incite anti-Saudi sentiment among the pilgrims. The situation came to a head in July 1987 when an estimated two hundred or more Iranian pilgrims were killed in violent demonstrations instigated by Teheran. The incident backfired for Iran as most of the Muslim world sympathized with the Saudis and blamed Iran for the violence. Nevertheless, although the Saudis were exonerated in the incident, they were put somewhat on the defensive. For example, a feature article on Saudi guardianship of the holy places appeared in a 1988 issue of *Ahlan wa Sahlan,* the Saudi Airlines magazine, that was uncharacteristically defensive in tone.

More recently, Ayatollah Khomeini's judgment in February 1989 that Salman Rushdie should die for his book *The Satanic Verses* was at least in part a challenge to Saudi Arabia for spiritual guardianship of the Muslim world. The book is clearly blasphemous in Islamic terms and pits freedom of speech, a Western secular value, against a serious—even capital—offense in Islamic law. The Iranians apparently hoped to trap the Saudis into following Iran's lead or be guilty of condoning blasphemy. Instead, at a conference of Islamic scholars held in Mecca, a consensus was reached that before such a sentence was proclaimed, Rushdie should first be made to appear before an Islamic tribunal. In response to this moderate approach, one of its Saudi supporters—the Muslim imam of Belgium, the Netherlands, and Luxembourg—was murdered with his Tunisian deputy in Brussels on March 29, 1989.

The challenge of the Iranian Islamic revolution combined with what the Saudis perceive as a lack of U.S. responsiveness to their security concerns (through continuing U.S. support of Israel and its refusal to supply basic Saudi defense needs) could in time create a change in Saudi psychology about the West. It is entirely within the scope of Saudi Arabia's own Islamic revival to see the United States and the West not as part of the monotheistic world opposed to atheistic communism but as a secular modernist threat to Islam itself. This is precisely the interpretation given to Ibn Taymiya's teachings by some militant Sunni fundamentalists, including those who assassinated Egyptian President Anwar el-Sadat.

The Iranian Nationalist Revolution and the Gulf

In many ways, the greatest influence of the Iranian Islamic revival on the Gulf has been ethnic and nationalist rather than religious—providing an ideological fervor to reignite the ever-smoldering relationship between Persians and their Arab neighbors.

Prior to the revolution, the primary political confrontation in the Gulf was neither Sunni-Shii nor Arab-Persian but conservative-radical. Iraq was seen as the common threat to both Iran and the conservative Gulf states of the Arabian Peninsula: Kuwait, Saudi Arabia, Bahrain, Qatar, the United Arab Emirates, and Oman. Iraq's single-party Baathist regime espoused an amalgam of socialism, or at least state capitalism, and Arab nationalism, which mixed nostalgia for the golden age of Arab caliphs (for Iraqis, that meant the Abbasid caliphs of Baghdad), enmity toward Israel and Zionism, and xenophobia toward Western imperialism. In 1972, Iraq signed a treaty of friendship with the Soviet Union.

The Arab Socialist Baath (Renaissance) party was actually founded in Syria and had become the single party of that state also. But political differences between Iraq and Syria outweighed ideological ties, and both claimed orthodoxy and that the other was heretical. The split did not become regionally significant, however, until after the Iranian revolution.

As an anti-Western, pro-Soviet Arab state, Iraq was also perceived as a threat to the United States, which attempted to build its Gulf policy around the two largest conservative states in the region, Iran and Saudi Arabia, in the so-called two-pillar policy. Often failing to see the underlying ethnic-national rivalries and confessional division between the Sunni Arab regimes and the Shii Iranian regime, the United States and its allies have often overestimated the degree of cooperation that is possible among them.[4] Nevertheless, the conservative-radical confrontation, both in regional and global perspective, dominated geopolitical thinking about the Gulf prior to the Iranian revolution.

For the other Gulf Arabs, the Iraqi threat was viewed both territorially and in terms of Gulf state subversives harbored by the Baghdad regime. Kuwait in particular was sensitive to Iraq's claim to two strategic Kuwaiti islands on the Kuwaiti border, Warba and Bubiyan.

For Iran, the two primary issues of contention—its support of Kurdish dissidents in Iraq and its challenge of the old Ottoman-British delineation of the Iran-Iraq border along the Shatt-al-Arab river, which gave Iraq sovereignty to the Iranian shore—were both temporarily settled in 1975. In an agreement signed in Algiers, the Shah agreed to cease support of the Kurds and Iraq agreed to Iranian claims to half the Shatt-al-Arab as the common border. Thus, until the eve of the revolution the state of regional stability and the level of Iranian cooperation with its conservative Arab neighbors were about as good as could be expected.

The entire conservative-radical frame of reference was swept away by the Iranian revolution. The Islamic Republic of Iran was seen as a threat to the conservative Gulf states as much as it was to Iraq. In reaction to Iran's militant foreign policy dedicated to spreading its brand of Islamic revolution, the old nationalist and confessional rivalries resurfaced.

Iraqi-Iranian tensions began to mount almost immediately, leading ultimately to the outbreak of the Iran-Iraq war in September 1980. The Iraqis, who invaded Iran, claimed they did so because of the escalating armed clashes instigated by Iran on the border. Nevertheless, Iraq probably calculated that Iran's usually superior military capability could be defeated in the wake of the military purges that took place after the Shah was ousted.

The resilience of the Iranian military and of the new regime was underestimated by nearly every outside observer. Khomeini and his clerics became well entrenched, and Iran's military forces, spearheaded by thousands of shock troops who gave their lives for the cause, drove Iraq out of Iran. The war then turned into a stalemate.

Iraqi strategy was to win a quick victory, for it did not have the resources to fight a protracted war. As the war reached a stalemate, both sides were increasingly hard pressed economically, but Iraq was at a greater disadvantage. The Iranians not only had a larger economic base, but because of their emotional commitment to Khomeini and his regime, they were willing to put up with a great deal more hardship. For them, the war had taken on the aspect of a crusade, a jihad. In addition, the Iranians were initially able to cripple Iraqi oil exports more effectively than the Iraqis were able to cripple Iranian exports. (Later in the war, the expansion of the Iraqi-Turkish pipeline and the tanker war partially evened out this initial Iranian advantage.)

The Arabian Peninsula

It is not the purpose of this paper to discuss in detail the eight long years of the Iran-Iraq war. What is important for our purposes is that the war, as a direct consequence of the revolution, contributed to a totally new alignment of the Gulf states. The prospect of Iraq losing the war set off a chain of major policy shifts in the Arab world and beyond. The conservative oil-producing states of the Arabian Peninsula, which had previously viewed Iraq as a dangerous threat, became major underwriters of the Iraqi war effort. Jordan also opened its borders for shipment of war material, and Egypt's support of Iraq contributed to the gradual reversal of its isolation in the Arab world following the Egyptian-Israeli treaty. Indeed, the war might have taken on completely the character of an Arab-Persian conflict had not Syria, an arch and bitter rival of Iraq, sided with Iran in a virtually unprecedented breaking of Arab ranks against an outside enemy. As it was, the Arab-Persian aspects of the confrontation did become paramount in the Gulf.

In terms of Arab world politics, the war, while tending to isolate Syria, brought Iraq back into the Arab political mainstream after years of isolation and contributed to making Egypt less of a pariah in the eyes of its Arab brethren. In addition, the bitter split between Syria and Iraq divided the Arab radicals most opposed to peace with Israel and placed the moderates in ascendancy. Unfortunately, the split in Arab ranks plus concomitant divisions in Israeli politics allowed for no progress in the Arab-Israeli peace process, but it did make the likelihood of renewed military conflict more remote.

Ironically, the war also temporarily placed the United States on the same side as the Soviet Union as neither nation, for different reasons, desired an Iraqi defeat; as a result, the regional war actually contributed to a lessening of global tensions in the Gulf area. Later, the Kuwaitis asked both superpowers to protect neutral Gulf shipping.

For the Soviets, the war also meant the ticklish job of juggling its close relations with the Syrians and with the Iraqis, antagonists in the conflict. For the United States, it meant reestablishing diplomatic relations with Iraq, the last major Arab state still outside its diplomatic reach following the 1967 Arab-Israeli war.

For the Gulf states, however, probably the greatest impact of the Iranian revolution has been their increased cooperation, exemplified particularly by the Gulf Cooperation Council (GCC). The need for such cooperation was seen as early as 1968 when the British first announced their intention to end by 1971 the treaty arrangements by which Britain was responsible for the defense, finance, and foreign affairs of Bahrain, Qatar, and the seven Trucial States. But the British were unsuccessful in their attempts to unite all nine emirates into a single federation; by the time the British departed in 1971, Bahrain and Qatar had opted for independence while the Trucial States became the United Arab Emirates. Nevertheless, efforts toward collective cooperation continued.

In November 1976, a meeting of the Gulf foreign ministers was held in Muscat, Oman, to discuss a regional cooperation organization. The effort foundered over the representation of both Iraq and Iran at the meeting, as Iraq was seen as a major threat to the security of the others and Iran was not totally trusted by the Arab states. Resentment was still high over real and perceived examples of what the Arab states took to be Persian imperialism. Sections of the median line down the Gulf to delineate Iranian and Arab oil drilling rights were still being negotiated in an occasionally heated atmosphere; Iran's occupation of three small islands in the Gulf claimed by the United Arab Emirates was seen as an affront to Arab sovereignty even though Iran had dropped its claim to Bahrain; even the name of the Gulf (Arabian versus Persian) was contested.

Not only did the outbreak of the Iran-Iraq war create a common security threat to the Arabian Peninsula and Gulf states, but by removing Iran and Iraq from the deliberations, the way was cleared to create a regional cooperation organization. At the Islamic foreign ministers' meeting in Taif, Saudi Arabia, in January 1981, six Arab Gulf states—Kuwait, Saudi Arabia, Bahrain, Qatar, the United Arab Emirates and Oman—agreed to the formation of the Gulf Cooperation Council. The organization officially came into existence when the member nations' heads of state met in Abu Dhabi on May 25–26, 1981.[5]

GCC cooperation extends far beyond mutual security considerations. Indeed, some states such as Kuwait initially wished to downplay the security aspects of cooperation in favor of political, economic, and cultural aspects. Nevertheless, it was the military threat of the Iran-Iraq war and the combined military and subversive threat of Iran's militant foreign policy of spreading its revolution that became the catalyst for the final creation of the GCC. With time, the whole has exceeded the sum of the parts: As its members have become accustomed to the idea of cooperation as an effective means of addressing regional interests and accomplishing regional goals, the GCC has grown in stature. Its

The Arabian Peninsula

importance, therefore, should long outlast the current political, military, and ideological confrontation between Iran and its Gulf neighbors.

Conclusions

Ten years after the Iranian revolution, it is still difficult to assess its true impact on the Gulf. As a justification for seeking revolutionary change in the Gulf, the doctrines of the Iranian Islamic revival have been decidedly lacking in intellectual or ideological appeal. Moreover, there has also been a decided lack of the politically disaffected in the Gulf who might be drawn to such doctrines.

This is not to say that this will always be so, even in the near term. Many of the basic building blocks of disaffection still exist, particularly among the Shii communities. Politically there is a feeling among the Shii of second-class citizenship; socially there is a feeling of being discriminated against by the Sunni majority (minority in Bahrain and Iraq); and economically the distribution of oil wealth generally favors the Sunni business community in fact if not by design. What is lacking are organization and leadership. The rise of a charismatic leader calling for revolution and capturing the imagination of masses of people could rapidly change the situation.

Such an eventuality is still a worst-case scenario, however. Even with the Gulf states' slightly reduced standard of living as a result of the oil glut, the level of popular social, economic, and political discontent appears on the whole to be manageable. Moreover, in most Gulf states, the Shii communities might have the ability to create civil unrest, but they would have a much more difficult time threatening their respective regimes. If there were a challenge to a Gulf regime, and this does not seem likely at the present time, it would most likely come from the Sunnis; and if the challenge were fundamentalist, it would be influenced more by the writings of Ibn Taymiya, Mawdudi, and Qutb than by those of Shariati and Khomeini.

The political impact of the revolution has been more visible, largely because of the Iran-Iraq war. As a result of the war, Gulf politics are now dominated by a pronounced Arab-Persian antipathy. But it is impossible to say whether the predominance of Arab-Persian ethnic differences in Gulf politics will be any more lasting than the previous predominance of conservative-radical ideological differences.

In short, even after ten years, making more than tentative judgments about the impact of the Iranian revolution on the Gulf is very risky. Most probably, when the revolution is viewed from the perspective of one or two hundred years in the future, ten years simply will not be considered a long enough period of time to judge its full implications for the Gulf region and the world.

Notes

1. Both Iraq and Bahrain have Shia majorities. Iraq is ruled by a secular Arab nationalist regime dominated by Sunnis; Bahrain has a hereditary monarchial regime also dominated by Sunnis. The other Gulf states have Shia minorities of generally between 10 and 15 percent of the total population.

2. Muhammad Husayn Tabatabai, *Shiite Islam* (Albany: State University of New York Press, 1975), 211.

3. For a brief discussion of Ibn Taymiya's views, see John Alden Williams, ed., *Islam* (New York: George Braziller, 1961), 205–10.

4. See David E. Long, "Confrontation and Cooperation in the Gulf," Middle East Problem Paper no. 10 (Washington, D.C.: Middle East Institute, 1974).

5. See Erik R. Peterson, *The Gulf Cooperation Council: Search for Unity in a Dynamic Region*, Westview Special Studies on the Middle East (Boulder, Colo.: Westview Press, 1988), 97.

7

Lebanon: The Internal

Conflict and the

Iranian Connection

AUGUSTUS RICHARD NORTON

IRAN HAS DIVERTED an array of resources to Lebanon since 1982 in an effort to export the Islamic revolution and to spread Iranian influence among the more than one million Shii Muslims who account for one-third or more of Lebanon's population. Iran's efforts have been propitiously timed: The last few years have seen Lebanon's economy collapse, political moderation frustrated and discredited, and the general level of misery rising. For numbers of Shii Muslims and many of their Sunni coreligionists, Islam offers a singular and humane alternative to the war system and the long years of killing, as well as a familiar refuge from the trepidations of the daily struggle for existence.

Many, if not all, Shii Muslims revere Ayatollah Ruholla Khomeini as the central contemporary system of Islam, but only a fraction of the Lebanese Shia have affiliated with the groups whose political fortunes have benefited from Iran's support. In fact, Iran's venture into Lebanon has hardly been an unqualified success. The growing militancy and obduracy of the Shia have evoked resistance and resentment in Lebanon's other communities where the consequences of a dominant Shii role in Lebanon are feared, particularly when couched in terms of installing an Islamic system of rule. It is often remarked that there is no confessional majority in Lebanon, but the increased militancy and po-

116

litical assertiveness of the Shia have helped to spawn a working majority of Lebanese opposed to Shii political dominance. Thus, while often at odds with one another, the Maronites, Druze, and Sunnis have been objectively aligned in their commitment to forestall the realization of dreams underwritten by Teheran.

There is no mistaking the fact that the big potential losers in Lebanon are the Sunni Muslims who stand to lose pride of place to the Shia in any likely redistribution of political privileges. Thus, many of the Sunni Muslims believe that Shii demands are direct threats to their status. This belief is reflected not only in the political attitudes of "establishment" Sunni politicians but also, at the popular level, in the appearance of Sunni revivalist movements that are avowedly anti-Shii.[1] Despite Iranian efforts to cast the revolution in broad Islamic terms, it has been perceived as a distinctively Shii endeavor, especially in Lebanon where political privilege is so explicitly bound up in sect.

Some of the strongest resistance to Iran's ambitious efforts has come from within the Shii community itself, where it is understood that the reconstruction of Lebanon, when it occurs, will have to be a cooperative venture. Since 1988 Iran's supporters, loosely gathered in Hezbollah (the Party of God), have found themselves at war with Shia who do not share Iran's political vision. In the tough environs of Beirut the Iranian-supported Hezbollah has won some major victories, but in the Shii heartland in the south, Amal, the more pragmatic and moderate political movement, has won an overwhelming victory. The stakes are not simply abstract religious or political constructs but mundane concerns about how people will live their lives.

Moreover, Iran has faced stiff competition in Lebanon from regional rivals. Syria facilitated Iranian involvement in 1982 in order to undermine Israeli and American designs and to thwart erstwhile Lebanese allies who might be tempted to try to put distance between themselves and Damascus. But Damascus now finds itself often at odds with its strategic ally, and Syria has moved with occasional determination to cap Hezbollah's power. Iraq, no longer encumbered by the Gulf war and an opponent of both Iran and Syria, has become a major supporter of the predominantly Maronite Lebanese forces, and Baghdad has made no secret of its wish to see Iranian influence eliminated in Lebanon. Israel, operating from its euphemistically named "security zone," has learned to distinguish between situational and permanent enemies; thus, it is now better understood in Tel Aviv that Hezbollah and Iran are permanent enemies. For a time, Yasir Arafat's PLO found Hezbollah a convenient ally against Amal, but new opportunities commend new alliances. After nearly a decade of combat, Amal and the mainstream PLO have discovered overlapping concerns in southern Lebanon, where both Shii and Palestinian extremism pose a challenge to their interests. Finally, the often forlorn United Nations Interim Force in Lebanon (UNIFIL), while not usually considered a political actor on the Lebanese stage, plays a key role as a tacit ally of Shii moderation. The upshot is that Iran's foray into Lebanon has been hobbled and circumscribed by indigenous factors as well as regional political competition. These constraints notwithstanding, Iran's influence in Lebanon has grown impressively over the span of only a few years.

Iranian influence has been most visible on the diplomatic stage where its emissaries play an important, if only a supporting, diplomatic role. Foreign Minister Ali Akbar Velayati announced the agreement reached in Damascus in January 1989 that ended brutal clashes between warring Amal and Hezbollah militias. Iranian mediators strove —if only with limited success—to bring the 1985–87 "war of the camps" to a close. In 1985, when the Syrians attempted to quash the Sunni Tawhid (Unity) movement in Tripoli, Iranian mediation (following the intercession of President Ali Khamenei) spawned an agreement between Tawhid leader Shaikh Said Shaaban and Damascus. Shaaban, incidentally, has been an important ally of Iran.

Less visible, but certainly as influential as these diplomatic forays, is the extent to which Iran's revolutionary dogma has reverberated among the Lebanese Shia, providing a rationale for opprobrious misdeeds by local actors enjoying varying levels of autonomy. The kidnapping of foreigners, which has so sullied the reputation of the Shii Muslim in world opinion, owes much to the anti-Western animus spread by Teheran. In southern Lebanon, Iran-fed suspicions of the UN have sometimes jeopardized the stabilizing presence of UNIFIL. The peacekeeping force has often been accused of serving Israel's interests rather than Lebanon's, a charge forged in Teheran, not Lebanon.

Were it not for Iran's intrusive role in Lebanon, there presumably would have been less violence and the Lebanese would be a few steps closer to reconciling their differences. Iran's revolution has cast a long shadow in which moderation has often disappeared from view and factionalism has thrived. Iran's great success has been to affect the tenor of political debate and to circumscribe political options. Shii politicians who resist Iranian influence constantly run the risk of being discredited for being soft on Israel, too conciliatory toward their non-Shii political opponents, insufficiently ardent in protecting the rights of the oppressed, or simply anti-Islamic. Thus, while Iran is nowhere close to seeing an Islamic republic established in Lebanon—a goal which may well have been abandoned[2]—there is no mistaking the potent influence it is playing in the country.

The Shia in Lebanese Politics

Outside observers commonly refer to Lebanon's confessional groups as though they were unified actors, but reality confounds this generalization. Lebanese society is a complex weave of families, clans, and factions for whom political ideology is only of modest importance in defining political behavior. Maronite, Druze, and Sunni politics each subsume a range of adversaries, split loyalties, and competing programs and goals. Any coherent effort to make sense out of who is doing what, to whom, and why must take account of the intraconfessional dimension. This is no less true for the Shii community, which is not united under the banner of a single movement or political party.

Confession (i.e., religious sect) is an inescapable ascriptive fact in Lebanon. The Lebanese is born into a religion, which defines his or her cultural realm and decisively conditions his or her social and political identity. As the state has vanished from view, confessional identity has increased in salience. Political goals are now commonly defined by confessional desideratum. However, to be born a Lebanese Shii or a Lebanese Maronite or a Lebanese Druze does not signify a genetically defined predisposition to paroxysms of religiosity, any more than being born Jewish predicts reliably that a person will keep a kosher kitchen. Religious labels must be disentangled from revivalist sentiments, particularly because too often the confessional label is taken to signify too much. While the confessional label narrows the range of behavioral variation, it is not an unerring predictor of how individuals respond to religious cues, Islamic or otherwise.

Despite strong evidence to the contrary, some scholars have been tempted to give a deterministic slant to the recent history of the Lebanese Shia, to discribe Shii activism and anger as an inevitable byproduct of an antiestablishment religious tradition. Others have simplified this history so as to treat the Shia as an undifferentiated whole, a community of crazed flagellants intent on martyrdom. These perspectives deny individuality to the Shia and ignore the diversity of motives and perspectives that have characterized their political mobilization in the past and in the present.

It is also misleading to argue that the Shii resurgence in Lebanon merely illustrates the rejection of secular authority by Shiism. It is not generally true that the Shia have rejected all temporal authority as illegitimate, though some Shia have interpreted their dogma in this way.[3] In fact, the history of Shiism is replete with examples of political accommodation rather than rejection. Most Lebanese Shia do not deny the legitimacy of the temporal state, though they withhold their approval from regimes that have given short shrift to their demands and needs. As the government of Lebanon has become increasingly irrelevant to the needs and demands of its citizens, attitudes of accommodation have been replaced by attitudes of rejection.

The civil war of 1975–76 was an unmistakable verdict on the Lebanese government, which had failed to meet the demands of many of its citizens. However, from 1976 until 1982 the penchant of many Lebanese was to remake their government, not to destroy it. There was no lack of a consensus that the machinery was broken, even if an agreed-upon blueprint for fixing it remained out of reach. Groups like Amal loudly condemned confessional politics and espoused the jettisoning of the system, but in reality, Amal seemed to be happy to keep the same pie as long as it was cut a larger slice. But since 1982, the government has been increasingly viewed as insusceptible to reform. This is largely the result of the failure of the Lebanese themselves and particularly of the Maronites, who failed to grasp an opportunity early on, when widespread hope and a spirit of give-and-take prevailed.

Indeed, it is difficult to look back on the 1982–83 period without a deep sense of sadness. More than anything else, this period was marked by a great absence of wisdom on the part of many Lebanese leaders as well as the external powers then wielding great influence on Lebanese politics. The politically dominant Maronite Christians were deaf to justified calls for political reform. A few magnanimous gestures would have made a great deal of difference. Instead, President Amin Gemayel and his advisors acted as though they could simply ignore the momentous social and political changes that had already occurred, especially in the Shii community. Rather than embrace the Shii reformers, the government chose a program of intimidation and domination, thereby discrediting the very political figures with whom they might have had a constructive dialogue.

Israel and the United States, caught up in competing strategic opportunities, were too brash in evaluating the Lebanese political scene. In Israel's view, the Shia were but an asterisk in a country whose major threats came from Maronites, Druze, and of course, the PLO. Only as the Israeli army was being defeated by a mixture of Lebanese, including many Shia, did government officials come to understand how badly they had misunderstood Lebanon. For the United States, Lebanon was like found money that one does not want to ask too many questions about lest the real owner claim it. U.S. diplomacy moved at a desultory pace in the autumn of 1982, only really picking up momentum ten months after the Israeli invasion began in June 1982, and then only to negotiate the May 17 agreement. The agreement was so unbalanced in favor of Israel that few serious observers thought it had a chance of being implemented. To its credit, the United States did pressure the government of Lebanon to begin the reform process, but the pressure came too late. The predictable result of all of this was increased anger and frustration among the Shia, not to mention an invitation to Syrian and Iranian adversaries to steal the show.

As time passed and opportune moments slipped away, the government has come to be seen as illegitimate and irreparably flawed. After the abortive presidential election of 1988 and the widening of partition's fissures, the Shii stance became more intractable. Many Shia resigned themselves to living apart in lieu of accepting the authority of a despised government. In earlier years, the political insecurity of the Maronite community was accepted as a given, and calls for deconfessionalism were coupled with a willingness to allow the Maronites to continue their monopoly hold on the presidency provided the system as a whole was reconstructed. That theme of accommodation is now heard less often. Hezbollah has capitalized on this rejectionist mood. It has also promoted it.

The Shia did not appear instantly on the political scene, pulled out of a top hat like so many dumb rabbits by an Iranian magician. They have been groping for their place in Lebanese politics and society for more than thirty years.[4] In fact, like most political events, the saga of the Shii entry into Lebanese politics is a complex one, played out in stages.[5] Only after the Israeli invasion of 1982, as intersectarian alliances evaporated and confessionally heterogeneous political organizations collapsed, have young Shii men and women given their political loyalties to distinctively Shii organizations, and even now there are many exceptions. The important fact is that the political mobilization of the Lebanese Shia as a community of assertive and aware people preceded the emergence of a Shii extremist minority by a margin of decades.

In effect, Iran has been able to tap the frustrations and demands of a collection of people who were politicized well before the fall of the Shah in 1979. The founder of Amal, al-Sayyid Musa al-Sadr, whose disappearance in 1978 was an important turning point in the mobilization of the Shia, espoused an ideology closer to the reformism of Ali Shariati than to the Shii revisionism of Ayatollah Khomeini. Add to this the fact that the years 1978–82, a critical period in the political mobilization of the Shia, were marked by the revival of Amal, a populist movement dominated by nonclerics—including many nouveaux riches—who sought the reformation of the Lebanese political system, not its destruction.

With the revolution in Iran gathering momentum by 1978, many Lebanese Shia took inspiration from the actions of their Iranian coreligionists. Even so, the impact of the overthrow of the Shah should not be exaggerated. Many of the Lebanese Shia adopted a bifurcated view of the revolution. On the one hand, the downfall of the Shah proved that an illegitimate government did not have to be blithely suffered; even the impossible could be accomplished under the banner of Islam. On the other hand, it was widely recognized that Iranian solutions would not necessarily solve Lebanese problems. When discussing the events in Iran it was common for many Lebanese Shia to volunteer precisely this distinction.

If the Islamic revolution was not a working model for Lebanon, it was still an exemplar for action. Amal, as an authentically Shii movement, was the beneficiary of the moment of enthusiasm sparked by the revolution. Amal's growth in the following years owed much to Sadr's revolutionary credentials as a key supporter of Khomeini and a strident adversary of the Shah, although both characterizations deserve to be qualified. It is tantalizing to speculate on the role that a pragmatist and reformer of Sadr's standing might actually have played in postrevolutionary Iran. He may well have been the successor to Khomeini. Several leading Amal officials, notably the Iranians Mustafa Chamran and Sadeq Ghotbzadeh, did take up key positions in the new regime. It is by no means clear, however, that Sadr would have fared any better than Chamran and Ghotbzadeh. Both died violently, the former preportedly in a plane crash on the Iraqi front and the latter by execution following his confessed role in a plot to assassinate Ayatolloh Khomeini.

It is also pertinent to emphasize that the political loyalties of the Shia span a wider organizational and ideological breadth than that represented by the Amal-Hezbollah spectrum. It is not simply a question of whether a Shii adheres to Hezbollah's vision of an Islamic republic established in Lebanon or to Amal's quest for a reformed system in which the political share of the Shia matches their status as the plurality in Lebanon. Not only are there a multitude of trends within Amal and Hezbollah, but by no means are all of the nation's Shia active in either movement. The Lebanese Communist party and the Syrian Social Nationalist party continue to count many Shia as members, while numerous Shia have managed to avoid any organizational affiliation whatsoever.

In a survey of 400 Shii college students (273 men and 127 women) conducted in 1987 at the Lebanese University in Beirut, Professor Hilal Kashan of the American University of Beirut found that only one in five men (as opposed to one in three women) acknowledged involvement in Hezbollah, and a little less than one in three men (versus one in fourteen women) acknowledged involvement in Amal.[6] (As might be expected, Hezbollah members reported a higher level of religiosity as measured by fasting during Ramadan, reading the Koran, or the frequency of praying.) Twelve percent of the male and female respondents acknowledged involvement in the Lebanese Communist party, and 8 percent in the Syrian Social Nationalist party. Over one-quarter of all men and more than 40 percent of the women claimed no political affiliation at all. While Kashan's findings do not purport to represent definitive proportions for the Shia in general, they do illustrate that among a significant segment of Shii youth there is much more political diversity than may often be presumed.

The last half-dozen years have been marked by radicalization and factionalism within Lebanon's Shii community. Amal, which promised in the early 1980s to become the dominant organizational voice for the Shia, has faced a steady erosion in its following. Ineffective and even incompetent leadership, corruption, and more than a modicum of arrogance have undermined Amal's support, especially in the teeming urban quarters around West Beirut.

Hezbollah, the Iranian-funded alternative to Amal, has emerged as a competent, dedicated, and well-led challenger. Although young Shii clerics dominate the party's leadership, Hezbollah has been especially effective in recruiting members and sympathizers among well-educated Shia from secular professions, many of whom have lost confidence in Amal. The May 1988 fighting in the Beirut suburbs (*al-dahiya*), in which Hezbollahis triumphed over Amal militiamen, underscored Hezbollah's steady success in enlisting the Shia, including many disgruntled ex-Amal members. Symptomatic of Amal's declining support in the suburbs were the widely circulating rumors that Hezbollah conquered some of the Amal positions through the simple expediency of paying off the local Amal defenders. Whatever the truth of such rumors, it is reliably reported that many Amal defenders simply deserted their posts rather than fight. Amal's support was further reduced when it reflexively shelled the quarters from which it had been displaced.

Though Amal still claims the larger membership and a firm base of popular support in Jabal Amil, Hezbollah has become firmly established as a political force in Lebanon. The persistent insecurity, the stalling of political reform, and the near-total collapse of the Lebanese economy have elevated Islam as the solution to Lebanon's problem. Musa al-Sadr once remarked that his most important role was as the custodian of religious symbols, and the insight has not been lost on those who struggle for support among the Shia. Taking a cue from Iran, both Amal and Hezbollah exploit the potent symbolism of Shiism to enlist support. For instance, the *Ashura* processions, commemorating the martyrdom of Imam Husayn in 680 A.D., have become not just a plea for intercession or an act of piety, but a revolutionary statement.

Hezbollah has enjoyed much less success in south Lebanon, where about one-third of the Shia live and where anti-PLO animosity runs deep. Amal's staunch stance against the restoration of an armed PLO presence in the area reflects local sentiment and has assured Amal's popularity over Hezbollah. Amal forcefully demonstrated its supremacy in April 1988, when it eliminated Hezbollah as an organized military presence in the region.

Though it may have had a surreptitious existence before the Israeli invasion of 1982, Hezbollah became a visible and attractive movement thereafter. With its cadre of strident young ulama, virtually all in their thirties, Hezbollah was vehemently opposed to the conciliatory stance of Amal and its leader, Nabih Berri. With Beirut under siege, Syrian power in retreat, and the PLO extricated from southern Lebanon, Berri agreed to join the National Salvation Committee, whose members included the Druze leader Walid Jumblatt and Bashir Gemayel, the Maronite militia chief who then appeared to be the main beneficiary of the Israeli invasion. Though the committee proved ineffectual, Berri's participation earned him scorn from three sides: Syria, Iran, and his militant Shii rivals. In its 1985 program, Hezbollah described the committee as "no more than an American-Israeli bridge over which the Phalange crossed to oppress the downtrodden."[7]

With the sufferance of the Syrians, who were anxious to short-circuit Amal's attempt to go its own way, Iran deployed a contingent of about one thousand Pasdaran (Revolutionary Guards) to Baalbek in the Bika Valley in 1982.[8] The Pasdaran has functioned as an important conduit of Iranian arms to Lebanese allies, as well as a training force for Hezbollah militiamen.

But the roots of the Hezbollah movement run not only to Iran but to Iraq as well. Historically, the sacred city of Najaf (the burial site of Imam Ali, thought by the Shia to have been the rightful successor to the Prophet Muhammad) has been the training ground for Lebanese Shii ulama in the Islamic sciences. In Najaf, the young ulama came into contact with the Ayatollahs Muhsin al-Hakim, Muhammad Baqr al-Sadr (the Iraqi cousin of Musa al-Sadr), and Ruholla Khomeini, who spent most of his exile in Najaf (from 1965 to 1978). Musa al-Sadr, Muhammad Mahdi Shams al-Din, the vice president of the Supreme Islamic Shii Council in Lebanon, and Muhammad Husain Fadlallah, whose writings and sermons provided an ideological framework for Hezbollah, all trained in Najaf in the 1960s. If the Shii seminaries in Najaf published yearbooks, they would contain pictures of Ibrahim al-Amin, Abbas Musawi, Hasan Nasrallah, Subhi Tufayli, and Raghib Harb (assassinated in 1984), leading figures in Hezbollah who studied in Najaf during the 1970s.

Amal was riding high by the spring of 1984. In February of that year, the Lebanese army's Sixth Brigade in West Beirut dissolved and then reconstituted in support of the opposition. By April President Amin Gemayel, having failed to subdue the opposition, had no choice but to bring Nabih Berri and his Druze ally of the moment, Walid Jumblatt, into the National Unity government. Berri's new trappings were not an unmixed blessing: His ministerial position brought with it heightened expectations of solutions as well as patronage. Joining a government usually signifies at least a minimal commitment to its survival, and for his opponents in Hezbollah and even within Amal, Berri's support for the government was just another proof of his duplicity. Despite his government post, Berri's power was seriously eroding. By 1986 an accumulation of death threats prompted him to move to Damascus, where he remained until February 1987 when the introduction of Syrian troops into West Beirut enabled him to return to Lebanon.

Amal is totally committed to preventing a reestablishment of the Palestinian armed presence that existed prior to the 1982 invasion. Thus, as Palestinian fighters were reinfiltrated into Lebanon, often with the assistance of government officials, Amal began the "war of the camps" with enthusiastic support from Syria. The Beirut refugee camps, principally Burj al-Barajinah, Sabra, and Chatila, lived under relentless Amal siege from 1985 until December 1987, and in southern Lebanon, Rashadiyya was besieged until 1988. But the siege was very costly in terms of manpower, matériel, and prestige, because Amal ultimately failed to subdue the camps. The anti-Palestinian offensive was a splendid opportunity to dissipate Amal's power, and the opportunity was grabbed, in different ways, by Maronites, Druze, and Sunnis, as well as by Hezbollah.

Iranian Support

Since 1982, Iran has poured a significant amount of money into Lebanon, probably at least half a billion dollars, in order to promote Iranian influence among the Shia and spread the Islamic revolution.[9] These funds have been used to arm and underwrite Hezbollah and to run an array of social services, including hospitals, schools, and sanitation services.[10] The Pasdaran contingent deployed to Baalbek in 1982 has provided military training for Shii militiamen and transferred arms to Hezbollah. The Iranian Embassy in Damascus plays a directive role in guiding Hezbollah's activities and, according to published accounts, has also been the planning center for sensational acts of political violence, such as the 1983 attacks on the U.S. Embassy in Beirut and the U.S. Marine contingent of the multinational peace-keeping force.[11]

Ali Akbar Mohtashemi, the former Iranian ambassador to Damascus who returned to Teheran to take up the post of interior minister, has been described by Nabih Berri as the kingpin in the embassy group that "wrote, composed, and directed" Hezbollah.[12] Mohtashemi lost his ministerial post in August 1989 when President Hashemi Rafsanjani named his cabinet, but he continues to maintain close relations with Hezbollah. In November 1989 he traveled to Lebanon to meet with Hezbollah officials and, in the process, emphasized that he continues to be powerful in his own right in Iran.

Iran's monetary support of Hezbollah has averaged about $10 million per month, though recent reports indicate it has fallen to as little as $1 million per month since the end of the Gulf war.[13] However, upon his return from Iran in November 1988, Shaikh Fadlallah told the Hezbollah newspaper *Al Ahd* that Iran's generous support will continue.

A sampling of recently funded projects illustrates the functional breadth of Iran's support. In November 1988 the Jihad Construction Company announced that it is financing repairs to four hundred dwellings in Yohmor, Zalya, Libia, Sohmor, Ain Tine, and Mashgara. The company is also constructing or restoring schools, *husayniyahs*, and shelters in these villages, as well as clinics in Ain Tine and Mashgara. Ain Tine will also get a water system. The company has opened a store in Mashgara selling agricultural equipment and supplies as well as medicine at heavily subsidized prices.

The Islamic Health Council has organized a civil defense and first-aid course in the Bika Valley. The Iranian-sponsored Committee of the Imam loaned out L£25 million (Lebanese pound) in the fall of 1988. Sixty-four loans totaling L£6,255,000 were for marriages; 18 loans totaling L£4,875,500 were for school expenses; and 72 loans totaling L£ 14,131,500 were for small business ventures. Since the establishment of the fund, the committee has provided 846 loans totaling L£50,-194,525. In 1988 the exchange rate was approximately 500 Lebanese pounds to one U.S. dollar.[14]

Iran has sought to maintain a relationship with a number of Shii personalities and groups, even outside Hezbollah. These efforts may be construed to reflect intraregime rivalries in Iran, but recent developments actually indicate a tilt toward a middle path in Lebanon, to the disadvantage and open dissatisfaction of Hezbollah. The December 1988 visit of Mufti Shams al-Din to Iran enraged Hezbollah spokesmen and prompted Shaikh Fadlallah to remark caustically that the visit was useless since solutions were to be found in Lebanon, not Iran. There have been tense moments in the relationship between Fadlallah and Iran, but in the past they stemmed from Fadlallah's judgment that Iran did not understand the complex social conditions in Lebanon and was pushing much too hard for the establishment of an Islamic republic. Fadlallah has a relatively restrained view of how quickly change may take place in Lebanon, but ironically, as key decision makers in Iran have come to share this assessment, they may actually be willing to accept an accommodation that will disadvantage Fadlallah and Hezbollah.

The Tarbrush of Terrorism

Terrorism has been a public relations disaster for the Lebanese in general, but the Shia have paid the heaviest price for the opprobrious acts of a few terrorists. All Lebanese, but especially the Shia, find that they are often presumed guilty by consular officials, police forces, and customs agents. Indeed, it is quite clear that the majority agree with the proposition that terrorism has been grossly counterproductive. In a 1987 poll of Lebanese Shii college students, 92 percent expressed strong disapproval of hostage-taking, and 93 percent agreed that the hostages should be released immediately with no strings attached.[15]

Although Hezbollah spokesmen have been keen to dissociate the party from the kidnappings of Westerners, it is widely believed that the Islamic Jihad organization, which has claimed responsibility for some of the kidnappings, is merely a label of convenience masking Hezbollah involvement. This is not to say that there are strictly ordered lines of authority all flowing back to a central leadership. Much ink has been spilt on the issue of who leads Hezbollah, but the only conclusive statement that can be made is that the movement is directed by a collegial leadership that subsumes many factions and cliques. In such an environment, even Iran must cajole and persuade rather than direct and order. In other words, despite their links to Iran, it would be erroneous to assert that the cliques within Hezbollah lack considerable freedom of action.

On the other hand, there have been several hostage incidents linked rather clearly to Iran. For instance, when Charles Glass was kidnapped in June 1987, NBC reported that U.S. officials had said that there was conclusive evidence that the action was ordered by Iran. The charges were based on diplomatic communications intercepted between Iranian officials and Hezbollah: "At first, U. S. officials were not sure which American in Lebanon was to be seized. When the intercepts finally pointed to Glass, officials tried to warn the American reporter. It was too late."[16]

A number of alleged terrorists have also been linked to Iran. Among the most notable is Abd al-Hadi Hamadi, the chief of security for Hezbollah.[17] Hamadi travels regularly to Iran, which he visited for two months in early 1987. His brother, Muhammad Ali Hamadi, was convicted by a German court for his role in the 1985 hijacking of TWA flight 847.

Another Shii with close ties to Iran is Imad Mughniah, who is widely believed to play a leading role in Hezbollah-originated terrorism. One news report credits him as the mastermind of the TWA 847 hijacking.[18] Mughniah, who is about thirty years old, is said to have close ties to both Iranian and Syrian intelligence.[19] His cousin and brother-in-law, Mustafa Yusif Badr al-Din, is currently imprisoned in Kuwait for his role in the December 1983 attacks on six foreign and Kuwaiti facilities, including the U.S. Embassy. It is noteworthy that the seventeen prisoners held in Kuwait for the December incident have figured in many of the demands of the hostage holders. (Two of the seventeen prisoners have been released after serving their sentences.)

Iran has attempted to distance itself from the opprobrium earned by Lebanese Shia acting in the name of Islam, and over the past couple of years authoritative Iranian figures have denounced hostage-taking in clear language. President Hashemi Rafsanjani, for instance, notes that "hostage-taking is wrong; we concede this."[20] In some measure, Iran seems to be responding to the anger of Lebanese Shia who resent being painted with the terrorism tarbrush. The Jafari Mufti al-Mumtaz Abd Amir Qabalan, a strong supporter of Amal, has described the kidnapping of hostages "as a wicked action which is not designed to serve Islam." He argues that "the country [i.e., Iran] which instigates kidnappings should carry out such an act in its own country."[21] Nabih Berri, who believes the dignity of the Shii struggle has been trampled by terrorism, has been similarly outspoken: "The name of the Shii has become synonymous with terrorism, whereas it really is a crown of the struggle and resistance. A very fine thread separates terrorism and the struggle, and we must not cut it."[22]

Shii against Shii: The 1988 Explosion

Even before open warfare erupted in 1988, Hezbollah's relationship with Amal was marked by dozens, if not hundreds, of the sort of petty clashes that are seldom reported in Western newspapers but that kindle anger and resentment on the street. The spark that ignited the gruesome fighting was the February 1988 kidnapping of U.S. Marine Lieutenant Colonel William R. Higgins, who had been seconded to the United Nations Truce Supervision Organization as an unarmed military observer. The kidnapping may have been timed to mark the fourth anniversary of the assassination of Shaikh Raghib Harb of Jibshit, an important Hezbollah leader.

Long viewed as an instrument of international legitimacy, the United Nations has come to be castigated by Hezbollah as an instrument of U.S. and Israeli influence. By 1986 there had been a series of attacks on UNIFIL soldiers, much to the dismay of many residents of southern Lebanon who depend on the force to provide a semblance of normalcy in their lives.

The attacks on UNIFIL are part and parcel of the struggle between Hezbollah and Amal. Given Amal's goal of restoring a stable security setting in south Lebanon, an objective that reflects the popular attitudes of those who live there, UNIFIL is a natural ally. Indeed, there is a special symbiosis between UNIFIL and Amal—not because there is an international plot, as Hezbollah has alleged, but because the two parties serve one another's interests. For Amal, UNIFIL is a vestige of legitimacy. It represents an international listening post, more than a modicum of security, and an important source of indirect economic assistance. Faced with a mandate it cannot fulfill, UNIFIL has settled into the task of preserving the security of its soldiers and the zone they occupy. It is hardly surprising that the UNIFIL soldiers should welcome an indigenous force that offers cooperation and support for its task and which, unlike the South Lebanon Army, is regarded as a legitimate player in Lebanese politics.

The Amal position was clearly stated by Nabih Berri in 1987: "We continue to support the UNIFIL, who watch over our rights and the continued existence of our people on their land. Any attack against the UNIFIL means an attack against the resistance and homeland, and consequently, against man himself. Enough trading with religion. With due respect, not everyone who dons a turban has acquired the knowledge of the scholars. Enough attacks on the UNIFIL."[23]

Hezbollah, for its part, has described the UNIFIL presence as just another example of superpower arrogance, a force that does not serve Lebanon's interests but Israel's, since UNIFIL soldiers impede the movement of armed men intent on attacking Israel's security zone. The political rhetoric may be at least a bit disingenuous. The real issue is the fact that Amal is buttressed by its association with UNIFIL. Though the attacks have since stopped, that is due less to changing attitudes within Hezbollah than to the negative popular reaction to the attacks.

The kidnapping of Colonel Higgins was probably the work of Mustafa Dirani, a former sergeant in the Lebanese army's intelligence bureau. Though an Amal official, Dirani is widely known to be sympathetic to Hezbollah. He created an autonomous force known as the Believers' Resistance, which successfully opposed effective control by the local Amal leader, Daoud Sulaiman Daoud. (Following the Higgins kidnapping, Dirani was expelled from Amal.)

Daoud took the kidnapping as a direct affront to Amal and to his efforts to maintain a stable security environment in the south. Conscious of local sentiment, Daoud clearly demarcated the realm of permissible resistance attacks against the Israeli occupation of the south. These lines are not merely a policy decision by Amal but are also a true reflection of the attitudes of the people of the south who do not want to live in a state of warfare. Amal's position has been that no attacks could be mounted on the security zone from the "liberated zone," or the area under Amal's direct influence. Militants like Dirani chafed under Daoud's restrictions and were angered when his followers and allies were intercepted by Amal militiamen.

In the wake of the Higgins kidnapping, tensions quickly escalated until Amal launched a campaign to eliminate the Hezbollah presence in the south. Amal succeeded in its aim, though the success cost Daoud his life. (He was killed in an ambush near Beirut on September 22, 1988.) The Hezbollah response was to launch its own offensive in June, when it scored a series of decisive victories in the Beirut suburbs, prompting a major Syrian intervention.

Clashes continued until November, when fighting again erupted around Beirut. This time Amal recouped many of its territorial losses, but at a terrible cost in civilian casualites. Though some Iranian papers described the fighting as a Syrian attempt to wipe out Hezbollah,[24] the ferocity of the conflict prompted Rafsanjani to lash out at both sides, accusing them of "committing crimes in the name of Islam." He said he was "disgusted and washes his hands of all those who direct their guns at fellow-Shiis instead of the enemy, Israel."[25] The heaviest fighting did not end until late January 1989, when Syrian and Iranian diplomacy managed to patch together an agreement between Amal and Hezbollah.

The eight-part agreement, announced by the foreign ministers of Syria and Iran, includes a number of significant clauses: Amal's authority in the south is recognized, though Hezbollah is to be permitted to conduct political, cultural, and informational programs there. There is to be no return to the pre-1982 situation, referring to the armed PLO presence, and it was agreed that United Nations and humanitarian personnel would not be attacked. To seal the agreement, the killers of Daoud were handed over to Amal.

The agreement notwithstanding, skirmishes between Amal and Hezbollah continue. But Hezbollah no longer enjoys a monopoly on Iranian support, as illustrated by an important statement issued by the Iranian Embassy in Beirut: "The embassy, which is authorized by Islamic sharia, extends its hand to all the hands of devout people who are working hard to extinguish the fire of sedition. It will support every step that is trying to reconcile the two sides and end the war. The Embassy of the Islamic Republic belongs to all and is capable of listening to anyone to end this bloody dispute."[26]

Syria, Iran, and Lebanon

Damascus played a major role in permitting the Iranians to establish themselves in 1982, at a time when Syria was weak and eager to undermine those elements, like Amal, that were playing a moderate hand and striving to improve relations with the United States. Since 1982, Syria's most delicate balancing act has been to maintain its strategic relationship with Iran while simultaneously keeping the pro-Iranian Hezbollah under control. As early as 1984, Damascus turned the screws on Hezbollah, since the movement had outlived it usefulness as a counterbalance to Amal, which from 1982 to 1984 had tried to keep Syria at arm's length. After the withdrawal of the multinational force from Beirut in early 1984, Amal thrust itself into Syria's arms, but by then Hezbollah was well entrenched among the Shia.

There is little sympathy in Damascus for Hezbollah's or Iran's declared goal of establishing an Islamic republic in Lebanon, but Syria has resolutely avoided a decisive head-on clash with Hezbollah. Time after time Syria has walked to the edge of the precipice but has refused to jump. The deployment of the Syrian army into the Beirut suburbs in June 1988 had precisely this tentative character. All militia offices were supposed to be closed, but only the signs were removed; the weapons were not given up. One of the casualites of the December 1988 fighting was the Syria security plan in West Beirut.

Conclusions

Through years of internecine battles, Lebanon's battered governmental institutions survived, if only as mementos of less difficult times. Now, more than ever before, the institutions of the state are in pieces, like the society. Though the symbols of legitimacy have been shattered, the intercommunal and intracommunal competition for the fragments has intensified. Gruesome battles, especially within the Maronite and Shii communities, have become a persistent feature of Lebanese "events." The Maronites have found a hero in General Michel Aun, who, through a combination of military competence, surprisingly resonant bombast, and Bonapartist self-delusion, has stymied the Arab League's reform efforts. Aun stood up to the Syrian army through six months of heavy shelling from March to Sepember 1989. In the process he built a deep base of support among the Maronites, but only at the cost of alienating most of the rest of the population. If Aun has garnered credit among his coreligionists for his stiff-necked resistance to Syrian force, the "Aun phenomenon" is taken as proof by his opponents that the Maronites will not accept any diminishment of their political power.

The rather predictable result is that a state-in-fragments no longer seems such a bad choice in the view of many Lebanese. In fact, the idea of a unified Lebanon no longer evokes the automatic support that it did just two or three years ago. Apprehensions and doubts cloud the political future. In this context the significance of Iranian support for the Shia of Lebanon should not be underestimated. But this is by no means to assert that there is any prospect for an Iranian-style revolution in Lebanon. The special circumstances of prerevolutionary Iran, in which the Iranian people were united in their hatred of the Shah if not in their political prescriptions for the post-Pahlavi state, are hardly replicated in Lebanon where the Shia are divided against themselves. Moreover, even leading Lebanese Shii clerics are equivocal and often skeptical about the applicability of Ayatollah Khomeini's innovative dogma of the *velayat-e faqih* (rule of the jurisconsult) for Lebanon.[27]

Though numbers of poor Shia trapped in the misery of Beirut's suburban slums may see an Islamic republic as the road to salvation, there is little support for the idea among the young men and women who have escaped poverty. In his 1985 dissertation, Ahmad Nizar Hamzah polled 400 Lebanese college students studying in the United States, asking which country they felt had the most favorable political system. Only about 3.4 percent of the Shii respondents (who made up 16.2 percent of the sample) named the Islamic Republic of Iran. (About 63 percent of the Shii students reported that their fathers were illiterate, and almost 68 percent identified themselves as members of the lower social class, so the Shii respondents were reasonably representative of the Lebanese Shia community.) Hamzah produced similar results in a survey of 150 students at the American University of Beirut. In that poll, about one-third of the students, irrespective of confession, favored the U.S. political system, while over 41 percent of the total sample (and almost 52 percent of the Shia) named Switzerland, notable for its system of culturally homogeneous cantons, as the country with the best political system.[28]

Despite the recent successes that Hezbollah has enjoyed in the suburbs of Beirut, Iran has not succeeded in persuading a majority of the Lebanese Shia that Iranian answers are appropriate for Lebanon. In fact, the Hezbollah victory seems to have had much more to do with the failings of Amal and a general sense of exasperation than with the attraction of the Iranian revolution. While desperation and anger have proliferated, it remains true that most of the Lebanese Shia do not aspire to live in an Iranian-style Islamic republic. They do wish to live in a setting in which their culture is respected and in which they enjoy the same access to political privilege and right as their countrymen. Indeed, it is important to remember that the fighting—both within and without the Lebanese Shia community—is about the distribution of power.

Iran misunderstood Lebanon and exaggerated the susceptibility of the country to its message. The Iranian model is not only inappropriate, but Iran has had to eat some of its strident rhetoric, a fact not unnoticed in Lebanon where graffiti speaks volumes about popular attitudes: "Will you now release Higgins so that he can be the chief of observers on the Iran-Iraq border?" and "No to [Resolution] 425, but yes to [Resolution] 598?"

Iran's archenemy Iraq, no longer tied down in the Gulf war, has reappeared on the Lebanese scene in the guise of arms supplier to the Maronites. Iraq's indirect but significant challenge to Iranian (and Syrian) influence in Lebanon has no doubt helped to focus Teheran's attention. In the face of the Iraqi challenge, Syria and Iran—despite their different objectives in Lebanon—have clung to their strategic alliance (though strains remain evident).

Throughout 1989 it was plain that Iran was groping for a new policy in Lebanon and moved to broaden its web of relationships there.[29] In July 1989 Teheran was the site of a conference of fourteen Lebanese and Palestinian groups united less by ideological stance than by a chance to win Iran's support. In October, aging Lebanese parliamentarians met in the Saudi city of Taif—with the Arab League mediation of the Saudi, Moroccan, and Algerian foreign ministers—in order to reach an agreement for political reform. Pointedly, Iran simultaneously hosted a meeting of Lebanese personalities not generally known for their munificent praise of either the Arab League or the Saudis. Attenders at the Teheran meeting included leading figures in Amal and Hezbollah; Shaikh Said Shaaban, an old ally of the Islamic Republic and the leader of the Unity movement; Walid Jumblatt, the Druze leader; and a couple of radical Palestinian leaders.

But Iran's efforts to unify its Lebanese allies failed. Hezbollah predictably rejected the Taif agreements and called instead for more radical changes in Lebanon, following Iran's lead. In contrast, Amal, which has consistently aimed for reform rather than revolution, accepted the accords, though with some reservations. General Michel Aun's total rejection of the agreement, which he viewed as defective because it failed to specify a prompt Syrian withdrawal from Lebanon, made the Hezbollah-Amal differences purely academic. Nonetheless, these differences help to emphasize the fundamental ideological divisions within the Shii community. Within two months Amal and Hezbollah were again at war with one another, this time in the Iqlim al-Tuffah (north of Sidon). These differences will continue to confound and frustrate

Iranian political dreams in Lebanon, where unfortunately, the present continues to be a rough sample of what lies ahead.

Notes

1. For a pithy account see Asad AbuKhalil, "Druze, Sunni and Shiite Political Leadership in Present-Day Lebanon," *Arab Studies Quarterly* 7, no. 4 (Fall 1985): 28–58.

2. Hints of an evolving change in Iranian policy were published in the *Tehran Times*, December 18, 1988:

> Although Iran prefers Hizballah to other groups in Lebanon due to its ideological coordination and harmony, it does not intend in whatsoever way to shoulder all the responsibility on this wing.
>
> Recent steps taken in Lebanon, including the appointment of a new Iranian ambassador to Beirut and inviting different Lebanese Muslim groups to visit Tehran are all indicative of Iran's new move to adopt a new foreign policy in Lebanon. It seems that Tehran has admitted some mistakes in its foreign policy in Lebanon. . . .
>
> According to some political observers, there are still some active anti-Islamic elements in Amal leadership who are the bottlenecks in the way of establishing ties between Tehran and this Shiite group. It is hopeful and optimistic that the upcoming visit of Nabih Berri to Tehran could pour cold water on the hopes of the enemies and also bring it out of its puzzling dilemma.

3. Cf. Abbas Kelidar, "The Shii Imami Community and the Politics of the Arab East," *Middle Eastern Studies* 19 (January 1983): 3–16. Kelidar observes: "The [Shii] community has shown a marked tendency for rebellion stemming from its general attitude and belief that the authority of Muslim rulers, with the exception of Imam Ali's, could not be recognized as legitimate" (p. 3).

4. See Augustus Richard Norton, *Amal and the Shia: Struggle for the Soul of Lebanon* (Austin: University of Texas Press, 1987).

5. For a summary account see Augustus Richard Norton, "Religious Resurgence and Political Mobilization of the Shia of Lebanon," in *Religious Resurgence and Politics in the Contemporary World*, ed. Emile Sahliyeh (Albany: State University of New York Press, 1990), 235–47.

6. Hilal Kashan, "Antiwestern Perceptions among Lebanese Shii College Students," Ph.D. diss., 1987.

7 The program, issued on February 19, 1985, in the form of an open letter, is reprinted in Norton, *Amal and the Shia*, 167–87. The quotation is found on p. 172.

8. In mid-1989 the Pasdaran were estimated to number as many as two thousand; however, there were reports in August and September 1988 that the Pasdaran were being withdrawn. The reports seem to have been premature. See Cairo Middle East News Agency; August 3, 1988, citing *Al Ittihad*, translated in Foreign Broadcast Information Service, August 3, 1988, p. 34; and *Al Majallah*, August 31–September 6, 1988, pp. 8–9.

9. Nabih Berri claims that the Amal budget for one or two years is equal to what Hezbollah has received in a month. See Berri's interview in *Al Sharq al Awsat*, January 22, 1989, p. 3.

10. See Jim Muir, "Buying Hearts and Minds," *Middle East International*, no. 315 (December 19, 1987): 6–7.

11. David C. Martin and John Wolcott, *Best Laid Plans: The Inside Story of America's War Against Terrorism* (New York: Harper & Row, 1988), 105, 133.

12. From an interview in *Al Sharq al Awsat*, January 22, 1989, p. 3.

13. *Al Shira*, September 19, 1988, p. 9.

14. Personal communication, November 1988.

15. Khashan, "Antiwestern Perceptions."

16. Associated Press report in the *Times-Herald Record* (Middletown, N.Y.), June 2, 1987.

17. *U.S. News and World Report*, February 9, 1987, p. 27.

18. Ibid.

19. Jim Muir, "Hostage Fate Tied to Syria's Will to Confront Radicals," *Christian Science Monitor*, June 25, 1987.

20. From a Friday sermon reported by Teheran Domestic Service, December 9, 1989, translated in FBIS, December 12, 1989, p. 64.

21. Beirut Voice of National Resistance, December 21, 1988, translated in FBIS, December 22, 1988, p. 43.

22. Remarks at a rally in Tyre to mark the ninth anniversary of the disappearance of Musa al-Sadr, Beirut Voice of National Resistance, August 31, 1987, translated in FBIS, September 1, 1987. p. N2.

23. Ibid.

24. See, for example, *Abrar*, January 11, 1989, as cited in the *New York Times*, January 12, 1989.

25. Quoted in Jim Muir, "Shiite Clashes Widen Lebanese Rift," *Christian Science Monitor*, January 18, 1989.

26. Beirut Voice of the Oppressed, Lebanon, January 13, 1989, translated in FBIS, January 13, 1989, p. 49.

27. For an insightful analysis of the thought of three important Lebanese Shii clerics, Muhammad Jawad Mughniyya, Muhammad Mahdi Shams al-Din, and Muhammad Husain Fadlallah, see Chibli Mallat, *Shii Thought from the South of Lebanon*, Papers on Lebanon, no. 7 (Oxford: Centre for Lebanese Studies, 1988).

28. Ahmad Nizar Hamzah, "Conflict in Lebanon: A Survey of Opinions and Attitudes" (Ph.D. diss., University of Southern California, 1986).

29. See, for example, Robert Fisk, "Rafsanjani Arms New Beirut Ally to Curb Hizbollah," *Independent*, August 22, 1989.

8

The Impact of

the Iranian Revolution

on Egypt

SHAHROUGH AKHAVI

THE IMPACT OF IRAN or Shiism upon Egypt is a fascinating topic, given the importance of both societies in Middle East history. In fact, however, the two societies have kept their distance from one another, and Egypt has been influenced by Arab and Indian subcontinent themes far more than by Iranian ones.

In the medieval period, a Shiite dynasty ruled Egypt from 969 to 1171 A.D., but this had nothing to do with Iran. The dynasty disappeared—and with it, almost all traces of Shiism—hundreds of years before the Safavids established a centralized Shii state in Iran in the early sixteenth century. Thereafter, Egypt and Iran apparently coexisted without much interaction beyond some mutual trade. In the late nineteenth century, Jamal al-Din "al-Afghani" traveled to both countries and urged Islamic unity among Shiites and Sunnites in the struggle against Western imperialism in the Middle East. But this unity proved elusive, and the various internal movements against the British in both countries went forward without any coordination or mutual support.

In the late 1940s a new and more organized movement emerged to effect a rapprochement between Shiism and Sunnism. This movement had the endorsement of the *marja-i-taqlid* (literally, "source of emulation") of the Shiis, Ayatollah Muhammad Husayn Burujirdi, resident in Qum (Iran). Other Shii supporters included the Najaf (Iraq) *marja*, Muhammad Husayne Ali Kashif al-Ghita and the Lebanese *marja*, Sayyid Abd al-Husayn Sharaf al-Din. In Egypt the movement was endorsed by Shaykh Abd al-Majid Salim of al-Azhar, a number of his students (including the future rector of al-Azhar, Shaykh Mahmud Shaltut), and by the leader of the Muslim Brotherhood, Shaykh Hasan al-Banna. To institutionalize the Shii-Sunni rapprochement, the Dar al-Taqrib bayna al-Madhahib al-Islamiyyah (Center for the Reconciliation of Muslim Sects) was established in Cairo in 1947.[1]

There is some indication that not all al-Azhar leaders favored reconciliation, which may explain why it took at least a decade for a major step to be taken in that direction. In the late 1950s, President Nasser and the Shah of Iran collided over Iranian relations with Israel. In an effort to strengthen his position against the Iranian regime, Nasser turned, inter alia, to al-Azhar, led then by Shaykh Shaltut, in an effort to drive a wedge between the Shah and the Iranian clergy. Disagreements were soon to emerge in Iran between the monarch and the ulama over the Shah's proposed land reform. On 17 Rabi al-Awwal 1378 H.Q./October 1, 1958, Shaltut issued a *fatwa* (authoritative opinion) acknowledging Twelver Shiism as a legitimate school of Islam. In the wake of this *fatwa*, a chair for Shii jurisprudence was established. And between that time and his death in March 1962, Burujirdi apparently continued to maintain an active interest in Shii-Sunni rapprochement.

Despite these efforts, which included the founding of the Dar al-Taqrib's official journal *Risalah al-Islam* (*The Mission of Islam*), to which both Shiite and Sunnite clergy contributed, it is fair to say that the reconciliation did not warm up to the degree desired by the parties involved. In the early 1960s, Egypt and Iran broke diplomatic relations over Iran's relations with Israel and Nasser's efforts to stir up unrest in Iran's oil province of Khuzistan. After the June War of 1967, when Iran condemned Israel for its role in the conflict, the grounds for bitter enmity between Cairo and Teheran were lessened. In the Sadat period, Egyptian-Iranian ties greatly improved, but still the reconciliation between Shiism and Sunnism did not quicken. Throughout the 1960s and 1970s, the Iranian government made it clear it would not tolerate the reconciliation movement in general and the Dar al-Taqrib in particular to be employed as instruments of political influence.[2]

Egyptian Islamic Groups

As noted above, rapprochement between Shiism and Sunnism in the 1940s through the 1960s was the work of what we may term the establishment clergy of both Iran and Egypt, with some input from important lay figures such as Hasan al-Banna, who met the Iranian activist cleric Ayatollah Abu al-Qasim Kashani in the Hijaz in 1948. Egyptian Muslims have given the Iranian revolution a mixed reception. This is understandable in light of the fact that there is no single, monolithic Islamic movement in Egypt, as is clear from the literature on the sociology and social thought of Egyptian Islamic groups over the last decade or so. According to Rudi Mathee's analysis, with respect to the impact of the Iranian revolution the Islamic opposition to the Cairo government takes three main forms: the more conservative Muslim Brotherhood; the view of such radical groups as Takfir wa al-Hijrah, Jihad, and others; and the so-called Islamic left, which has become increasingly interested in Islamic solutions to many of Egypt's social and economic problems.[3]

Leonard Binder, while not specifically interested in the image Egyptian Muslims have of Khomeini and the Iranian revolution, distinguishes among the Egyptian ulama, the "fundamentalists," and the "Islamic liberals." He maintains that the ulama, or the "religious establishment," are hostile to Iran and its revolution:

> The institutional interests of the ulama are clearly tied, not only to the other state structures of which they are a part, but also to the bourgeois parliamentary system, which sustains both institutional pluralism and the system of "positive" law . . . Under present circumstances, in Egypt at any rate, it is the constitutional system itself which sustains the role of the ulama in interpreting the Sharia, even if that function is shared with the parliament and "public opinion." Some ulama are doubtlessly willing to accept the extremist fundamentalist formula . . . Most, however, cannot conceive of themselves in the role of a Khomeini, and they fear the consequences of the emergence of a charismatic leader of a clandestine band of violent revolutionaries who would overthrow the present institutional amalgam and establish a millennial Islamic regime.[4]

It is interesting that the Egyptian establishment ulama, which was willing to attempt a reconciliation with the Iranian clergy prior to the revolution, should be hostile to that same clergy after Khomeini's seizure of power. Part of the explanation for this is that those Iranian clergymen who had worked for rapprochement in the earlier years were not enthusiastic about—eventually even openly antagonistic to— Khomeini. They have been marginalized by the Khomeini partisans, leaving the Egyptian ulama without their erstwhile Iranian interlocutors.

If al-Azhar has consequently rejected the Khomeini model, this still leaves the Muslim Brotherhood, the radical groups, and Mathee's "Islamic left" (Binder's "Islamic liberals"). Mathee correctly notes that the radicals have been legally forbidden to publish their views in the press, and thus it is very difficult for an outsider to reconstruct their impressions of the Iranian revolution. In contrast, more evidence exists of the Muslim Brotherhood's impressions of Khomeini and his revolution, as reflected in the Egyptian religious opposition press until the latter was suppressed in late 1981. The impressions reflected there were strongly positive, although they became somewhat more diffuse after the outbreak of the Iran-Iraq war. Regarding the impressions of the Islamic left, the picture is less clear.

THE RADICAL ISLAMIC GROUPS

In listing the motivating ideas of the various militant groups in Egypt, Nazih Ayubi specifies "support for the Islamic Revolution in Iran and condemnation of Egypt's hospitality toward the ex-Shah."[5] In this connection, one of the earliest responses to the Iranian revolution by emergent Islamic associations in Egypt was that of the Islamic Student Association (al-Jamaah al-Islamiyyah) of Cairo University. The association issued a laudatory declaration in 1979 that was categorical in tone, arguing that the spirit behind the revolution was like the spirit that animated the first converts to Islam. The statement reminded its readers that in Islam no separation exists between religion and politics: Islam is "a comprehensive religion that legislates for this world and the next and organizes all of life." Manmade laws are ipso facto rejected by the people because these laws always invest the government with the power to dominate them. Thus, it is to the Islamic clergy that the people must turn, since the ulama have always been their refuge in the past and their leaders in modern Islamic liberation movements. Caveats are entered that some of the ulama have betrayed the Muslims by collaborating with the enemies of Islam, but generally speaking the ulama are the guardians of the people. Additionally, the declaration notes the bankruptcy of seeking to please the superpowers, warning that the latter will eventually seek new leaders to do their bidding and thus suggesting the impermanence of service in their employ. The final point is made that the enemies of the true believers will seek to exploit differences between Sunnites and Shiites in order to weaken the *ummah* (Islamic community). And the Egyptian government is cautioned not to be so overwrought by the events in Iran as to try to suppress the Egyptian Islamic groups.[6]

The Iranian influence on the militant, violence-prone Islamic groups thus appears to be based on a need to replicate the *spirit* of the Shii revolutionaries, not any particularly Shii organizational forms, doctrinal principles, or eschatological ends. Saad Ibrahim reports that the militants he interviewed claimed they were influenced in the main by the example of the Kharijites (an early Islamic schismatic sect) and by the writings of various Islamic thinkers: the two Muslim Brotherhood leaders, Hasan al-Banna (d. 1949) and Sayyid Qutb (d. 1966); Abul Ala al-Mawdudi (d. 1979, the Pakistani activist, thinker, and founder of the Jamaat-i-Islami); Ali Shariati (d. 1977, the Iranian ideologist); Ibn Taymiya (d. 1328, the harbinger of the Wahhabi movement); Muhammad Abd al-Wahhab (d. 1744, the founder of the Wahhabi movement); and Jamal al-Din "al-Afghani" (d. 1897, the famous anti-imperialist activist).[7]

In short, the Egyptian militants were overwhelmingly influenced by Sunnite not Shiite, writers. It is fair to say that Shariati's inclusion in this group is due more to his anti-imperialism, his call for Islamic solidarity, and the emphasis he placed upon laypersons in the mobilization of the word and deed against imperialism, rather than to the more traditional Shiite themes on such matters as justice, welfare, solidarity, authority, and so on. Notably absent from the list is Khomeini, whose writings must have been circulating in Egypt at that time. (It is true, however, that Ibrahim and his associates conducted their interviews with these militants prior to the Iranian revolution—indeed, the government canceled their interviews precisely because of Khomeini's return and seizure of power.)

Statements made by spokesmen of the more radical groups suggest, then, that Sunnite models are more important. But what about the revolutionary praxis that the Iranian revolution represents? Cannot the Egyptian radicals gain some insight from the Iranian revolutionary example? Emmanuel Sivan notes that Lieutenant Colonel Abbud Zumur, the military leader of the al-Jihad group, testified at his trial that the Iranian revolution showed the futility of Muslim rebels seeking to recruit supporters from the armed forces. Calling instead for a popular uprising, Zumur averred that "Iran taught us that the army and police cannot stand against an insurgency of the masses."[8]

For their part, the Egyptian authorities held that one of the groups that they had discovered in 1979 was the *Ansar Khomeini* (Khomeini's Helpers).[9] Moreover, "during the trials of the Islamic Jihad following the events in Asyut [in March 1980] Iran was pointed to by militants as one of the escape routes open to them, and contacts between the Jihad and Iranian officials were admitted to."[10] Indeed, the prosecutor of the assassins of Sadat claimed that they had intended to establish a Khomeini type regime.[11] A year later, in September 1982, the Cairo authorities announced the arrest of a number of militants who had reconstituted the Jihad organization. The regime charged that these militants had "successfully managed to contact al-Jihad members in prison, and received three smuggled letters from Abbud al-Zumur advising on the group's operations. [They were] also reported to have attempted to contact the Iranian government through Abbud al-Zumur's younger brother, Muhammad Abd al-Salam al-Zumur."[12]

Even more recently, Egyptian authorities announced the arrest of forty-one individuals in August 1989. The Egyptian attorney general declared that these people belonged to a secret Shiite movement that began when four militant Egyptian Sunnites converted to Shiism and then broadened their base through recruitment. In the regime's version, the four were helped by Muhammad Hasan Ramadan al-Awad, an expatriate Saudi Shiite living in Damascus. It is alleged that Awad had created a small revolutionary cell in 1986 to which the four Egyptians adhered for the purpose of overthrowing the regime of President Husni Mubarak. Apart from the forty-one Egyptians arrested, the secret movement purportedly also included another eleven Egyptians (still at large), four Saudis, and one Iranian. Of those arrested, most were university professors, students, or physicians. Their training is said to have occurred in Syria, Iran, Cyprus, and India.[13]

THE MUSLIM BROTHERHOOD

The Iranian revolution occurred at a time in which a "return to Islam" was already under way in Egypt. This "return" had been detected by observers as early as 1967, following the country's disastrous defeat by Israel. Ayubi regards this phenomenon both from the negative perspective that losing this war finally drove home to the Egyptians the failure of secular nationalism and from the oddly positive perspective that the country that had defeated Egypt was one that had drawn its strength from religion, providing an important lesson for the Egyptians themselves.[14]

Thus, for the Egyptians the Iranian revolution has been secondary to the indigenous overall trend of "back to Islam." In fact, the authors of a survey of the Egyptian press on the question of the Iranian revolution have argued that whenever the Egyptian religious opposition mentions that revolution, it places it in the larger context of Islamic movements throughout the world.[15] This suggests that the Egyptian image of the revolution is similar to the image that Khomeini himself wished to project about his movement, namely, that it is a manifestation of the vitality of *Islam* and not that it is a particularly Shiite phenomenon.

In his book *Khomeini: The Islamic Alternative*, Fathi Abd al-Aziz declares that "Khomeini's revolution" is not a revolution of one sect of Islam against another; rather, the core of common values and beliefs that unites all Muslims is what the Iranian revolution is all about. Aziz urges his readers not to equate belief in the imams with infidelity: "It is only a question of persons, and nothing that the Sunnites consider as the foundations of Islam is implicated [by Shiite beliefs in the imams] . . . they do not consider as miscreant or non-believer him who would refuse to agree [with them about the imams]."[16]

At the start of the revolution, Abd al-Munim Jabbara, in an article published in the Muslim Brotherhood journal *Al Dawah*, expressed astonishment that elements in the Arab world were concerned about the challenges to the Shah's rule, "as though [the situation in Iran] were a danger for the Gulf and the whole Arab world."[17] Some seven months later, the same author, witnessing the intensification of the Iranian revolution, approvingly recalled the memories of Navvab Safavi, founder of the Iranian Fidaiyan-i Islam in 1945 and executed by the monarchical regime in the 1950s, and of Ayatollah Kashani (d. 1962), a one-time spiritual guide of that movement. Jabbara claimed that the

Shah tried to use Safavi's execution and Kashani's death as a way to stop the Islamic movement in Iran.[18]

Strong support for the Iranian revolution is reflected in comments by the Muslim Brotherhood about its impact regionally and worldwide. In a hyperbolic commentary, one Muslim Brotherhood member maintains that the revolution will "turn political theories and contemporary political forces on their heads." Moreover, the revolution has demonstrated the futility of trying to establish stability at the expense of freedom or democracy. In fact, the Iranian revolution represents a "matchless, powerful, and vital example of the [larger] *Islamic* revolution," and "the important thing is not to put our hands at our sides and wait."[19]

Upon Khomeini's return to Iran in February 1979, Egyptian opposition religious leaders who supported the Muslim Brotherhood were asked their opinions about Iranian developments. In at least one case, a *fatwa* was requested from Muhammad Najib al-Mutii. In complying, Mutii made the following points: The motives of the Iranian revolutionaries were noble; the causes of the revolution could not but have led to the consequences that Egyptians were witnessing at that time; the Shah was responsible for the oppression of many Muslims; "we can forget neither the martyr, Navvab Safavi, nor the struggler, Imam [*sic*] Kashani, nor Muhammad Musaddiq"; the Koran admonishes that "you are not charged with constraining them" (IV: 45)—i.e., a call for consultation, a standard violated by the Shah; a government that behaves in ways condemned by the prophet deserves to be cast low; and "if Muslims overthrow such a regime and vow obedience to those who merit it, to the ulama, to men of knowledge and to people of great piety and asceticism, the duty of Muslims in all parts of the world is to support them."[20]

Mutii's *fatwa* contains several significant ideas. First, the causes of the revolution include misrule by a secular Shah. Second, something akin to a doctrinal justification is given for the revolution—i.e., if the ruling power fails to consult the Muslims, that can be grounds for revolution. Third, implicitly stated is that a government of the clergy is the appropriate form for an Islamic state. Finally, and unexpectedly, Mutii mentions Musaddiq (a secular Iranian nationalist prime minister overthrown by pro-Shah forces in 1953) approvingly in the context of the anti-Shah struggle. Note, however, that Musaddiq is bracketed with religious leaders, and Mathee is correct to say that the Muslim Brotherhood view is that Musaddiq operating independently of the clergy would have failed.

By the end of 1979, the Muslim Brotherhood was already claiming that Allah had made Iran part of the Eastern defense line of Islam, and that if Islamic Iran were to fall, "it is one of the principal ramparts of the Holy Places [of Islam] that would collapse."[21] Somewhat later, *Al Dawah* viewed Iran's revolution as a logical ally of the Arabs against Israel, and it projected a future alliance of Shiites from Pakistan through the Gulf states to the Eastern Mediterranean. *Al Dawah* stressed that the revolution rescued the people from moral dissolution and loss of identity, but it admitted that class conflicts also had something to do with the Iranian events.[22] Meanwhile, other writers were expressing great concern that the outside world was warring against the Iranian revolution. Their fear was that external interests were attempting to extinguish the expression of hope that the revolution betokened among the Muslims of the world.[23]

The outbreak of the Iran-Iraq war in September 1980 posed a dilemma for the Muslim Brotherhood. Its head, Umar al-Tilmisani, declared that Iraq was no doubt responsible for the war's outbreak, but Iran, in its turn, allowed itself to be dragged into the conflict.[24] Tilmisani excoriated "the governors of Iraq [who] are making war against Islam."[25] This language is identical to the language Khomeini used against the Iraqis when he said that it is not Iran that is Baghdad's target but Islam itself.

Specific references to Iranian history and culture are made only infrequently, as when *Al Dawah* declared that the revolution was merely the most recent in a legacy of collective protests that Iran has known since the nineteenth century,[26] or when the constitutional revolution of 1905–9 is explicitly mentioned as an example of the worldwide Islamic movement of the modern period.[27] Mathee cites a fascinating instance in which specifically Shiite themes are mentioned by a Muslim Brotherhood publication. The incident involved an article that appeared in the official journal of al-Azhar, *Majallah al Azhar:*

> The [*Majallah al Azhar*], in an article on the principle of mahdism in connection with Shiism, argues that mahdism is an undecided issue in Islam. The magazine manages to avoid a final verdict on the issue, noting that most traditions referring to it are

rather weak, and delegates it to a secondary [*fari*] position. It uses the topic, however, to lash out at the Shii interpretation of mahdism as an absurd and heretical expectation of a superhuman iman at the end of time.[28]

But the Muslim Brotherhood publication *Al Mukhtar al-Islami* angrily attacked the author of the Mahdism article for lacking any knowledge of the issue.[29] Indeed, since Mahdism is so indissolubly a part of Shiism, one might infer that the official publication of al-Azhar was repudiating the historical *fatwa* of its own leader Shaltut on the legitimacy of Shiism as a school of Islamic law.

The issue takes on still another dimension in light of Binder's characterization of al-Azhar as highly dependent on the Egyptian state, which, of course, is wholly antagonistic to the Iranian revolution. Nonetheless, the Mahdi principle is itself a very uncomfortable one for the Muslim Brotherhood as well. Its publications usually finesse any analysis of specifically Shiite themes by saying that Sunnism and Shiism have too many points of convergence to zero in on points of divergence—that Mahdism "is a controversial issue which it is not expedient to rake up at this moment."[30]

On balance, Muslim Brotherhood publications could not take too strong a pro-Iranian stand in the Iran-Iraq war, given the Sadat regime's pro-Iraq posture. But the brotherhood anathematizes the secular Baathist regime, with which, *Al Dawah* claims, "America has considerable financial relations"[31] and which, according to *Al Mukhtar al Islami,* is led by a gang of Christians.[32]

What troubled the brotherhood regarding the Iran-Iraq war was not only the fact that Iraq was an Arab country but also that Iran had as one of its staunchest allies the Syrian regime of Hafiz al-Asad. Thus, *Al Dawah* and *Al Itisam* pleaded with Iranians to pressure Teheran to abandon its relationship with the "Shah of Syria," who had savagely tried to exterminate Syrian Muslim Brethren in 1982.[33]

In Mathee's analysis, the Muslim Brotherhood's view of the Iranian revolution, up to late 1981, can be examined in three phases. The first phase was "the period immediately preceding the triumph of the revolution . . . and the roughly one-and-a-half years after the inauguration of the Islamic regime [roughly December 1978 to August 1980]." Mathee calls this a period of "unqualified enthusiasm and unconditional euphoria." This was followed by a period of apologia and defensiveness, but Mathee does not say when it ended, indicating only that it gradually merged into the third phase and that the outbreak of the Iran-Iraq war marked that merger. Since the war broke out in September 1980, Mathee seems to be claiming that the second stage lasted only a month (from August to September 1980). But leaving aside the precise chronology, this third period (September 1980–October 1981) was one of increasing obliviousness caused by the discomfort the brotherhood may have felt about the accumulating excesses committed by the Teheran regime.[34]

THE ISLAMIC LEFT

The Islamic "liberals" believe that the Iranian revolution, which they originally supported, became perverted over the course of several years. The chief spokesman for this position, according to Mathee, is Hassan Hanafi, a former member of the Muslim Brotherhood and currently professor of philosophy at Cairo University. Criticizing the brotherhood for having departed from its earlier concern with social justice, welfare, national dignity, and anti-imperialism, Hanafi has declared: "And what is Khomeini but Musaddiq sent anew?[35] In Hanafi's opinion, the Brotherhood is overly taxed by demands for the literal implementation of Islamic law. The rather remarkable identification of Khomeini with Musaddiq shows that the Islamic left emphasizes the importance of nationalism and sees Islam as contributing to its reinforcement. Khomeini, of course, would vehemently reject such a notion, affirming instead that he stood for a nonsectarian Islamic system. But his efforts did not always convince. Muhammad Abd al-Mumin, a professor of Iranian studies at Ayn Shams University, points out that although Khomeini's "methods follow many Sunnite and Shiite reformers," he remained convinced that "reform can only come through an Islamic government in the Shiite meaning of that term."[36]

Mumin has some other views that would be rejected by the *maktabi* (Khomeinist) clergy in Iran. He warns against blaming Khomeini for all the errors of the revolution, saying that the Ayatollah has been its linchpin, perhaps, but not a daily decision maker. In fact, according to Mumin, "Khomeini was not the real planner of the revolution, but the masses raised him to the peak of rule, and he became a symbol of the unity of the revolutionary forces, not a leader [*zaim*]." In fact, Mumin places a good deal of the blame for revolutionary excesses on the Islamic Republican party, which chose Khomeini as its theoretician, but "he failed to control it." Finally, Mumin claims Khomeini is not the originator of the idea of *velayat-e faqih* but is merely the legatee of the thought of the Safavid *mujtahid* Muhammad Baqir al-Majlisi (d. 1683).[37] This is a somewhat novel interpretation, especially to those who would argue that Baqir al-Majlisi would never have accorded the sobriquet of the imams, *wali al-amr* (lord over matters), to a *mujtahid*.

The Iranian revolution represents for the Islamic left a broadly based social movement that has struck a blow for the anti-imperialist cause. Such a view is expressed, for example, by Abd al-Sattar al-Tawilah in an October 1979 article in the leftist Egyptian weekly *Al Ruz al-Yusuf*: "We support every struggle against colonialism . . . we supported the Iranian revolution because one of its affirmed objectives was to remove Iran from the American ascendency." But hostage-taking is "shameful"; moreover, the Iranian revolution has "shown itself incapable of realizing its slightest objectives," and its leaders have resorted to dictatorship worse than that of the Shah to divert the masses from understanding their plight.[38] (This view differs from the official Egyptian government position, of course, in that the regime had supported the U.S.-Iranian connection).

Hanafi, the chief proponent of the Islamic left, claims that "Islam is capable of serving as an umbrella for all political trends in [Egypt]: liberation, Marxism, and Arab nationalism. The Iranian revolution did it and succeeded. The question is not would an Islamic revolution, Khumayni-type, succeed in Egypt. Revolutions are not copied."[39] But Hanafi is critical of the Muslim Brotherhood for transforming itself from what he regards to have been its founder's (Hasan al-Banna) more tolerant institution to "a more closed and fanatic view of the world" in the 1960s and afterward.[40] Nonetheless, he criticizes the Sadat regime, "frightened of the remote possibility of a Khomeini type Islamic revolution," for trying to ingratiate itself with this "new" brotherhood. Hanafi's objection is not to the regime's pandering efforts per se but to his conviction that the brotherhood uses Islamic law "to obstruct the process of social change."[41]

Hanafi contrasts Egyptian and Iranian societies by saying that Egyptians, unlike Iranians, never experienced an identity crisis as a consequence of the impact of Western culture. He holds that "the rediscovery of Islam . . . among certain committed intellectuals . . . may have been a result of their anger against stereotyped images of Islam and the Muslim in Western culture." Thus, an inferiority complex—not an identity crisis—is more characteristic of Egypt:

Islam, the most attacked religion by Western scholars, would be the best tool to reverse the inferiority complex to a superiority complex. Islam would give the whole culture a sense of dignity.

The rediscovery of endogenous powers of the masses, after the victory of the Iranian revolution, may have given the masses some self-confidence. While the image of the Iranian revolution has been deformed in the [Egyptian] mass media, its impact on a possible Islamic alternative in Egypt is considerable.[42]

Hanafi warns that in the short run the impact might be dogmatism and confessionalism, since Egyptian society has known a "dominant historical conservatism." But he trusts that "enlightened leadership" will overcome such tendencies and encourage the masses to "discover their endogenous powers."[43] It turns out that what Hanafi means by enlightened leadership is in fact what he calls "popular Nasserism," that is, a return to Nasser's prescriptions of Arab socialism, in which Islam served as a general ethos and set guidelines beyond which the state could not go, rather than determined the government's policies. "When [conservatism] as a historical mood paves the way to progressivism, Islam can be carried on as progress."[44]

Official and Semiofficial Egyptian Views

Sadat's views of the Iranian revolution are well known. He seldom withheld his opinions of it as a disaster both for Iranians and for Muslims everywhere. He frequently declared that Khomeini's model was not "true Islam" and that Khomeini himself was *majnun* (deluded). Since Mubarak became president, public statements by the Egyptian government regarding the Iranian revolution have been less frequent. Despite the lower level of rhetoric, few doubt that the current regime views developments in Iran similarly to the previous one. On a practical basis, the Egyptian government has extended its political support to Iraq in its conflict with Iran. Indeed, Teheran has charged that Egyptian labor migrants in Iraq were seconded to the front to fight for Baghdad, the mirror image of Baghdad's accusation that Afghan refugees in Iran were conscripted for the war by the Iranian government.

The nonopposition press—for example, *Al Ahram* and *Al Akhbar*—

has served as a forum for discussions about the role of Islam in the country's politics. Although these papers are not, strictly speaking, government mouthpieces, they frequently provide an outlet for official thinking. It is fair to say that much of the writing in these papers conveys the standard image: Shiites are extremists (*ghulat*); their doctrines mystify rather than clarify Islam; the sect is based on elitism; what drove Iranian foreign policy under Khomeini was Persian neoimperialism; and so on.

Among the more sophisticated views is a recently published work entitled *Iran from Within* by Fahmi al-Huwaydi, who writes for *Al Ahram*.[45] This is a popular book in Egypt, and the publisher has now run at least a second and possibly a third printing. Huwaydi is impatient with the overdrawn depictions of the revolution, which, he notes, have not been absent from the pages of the Egyptian press. His goal was to write a more balanced assessment, basing the project on five different visits to Iran between 1979 and 1986. Like other Egyptians in the popular press (for example, Abd al-Sattar Tawilah), Huwaydi felt a certain attraction to the Iranian revolution in principle. Unlike Tawilah, however, Huwaydi continues to be attracted by the Iranian experience.

Huwaydi draws a number of interesting conclusions: The Shii imams were mainly quietist; Khomeini's theory of *velayat-e faqih* is not acceptable to many Shii, including a goodly number in Qum itself, and the views of Lebanese Hezbollah leader Muhammad Jawad Mughniyya are cited as the doctrinal basis for rejecting it; the Karbala paradigm of martyrdom is partly responsible for motivating the Iranians during the Iran-Iraq war; Sunni and Shii have tried to bridge their differences over the last forty years or so; the clerics have ended up ruling Iranian society because no other qualified group of Iranians could be found, not because they are driven by ambition; and some of the excesses of the Khomeinist clergy are attributable to the fact that the revolutionary experiment is still under way.

This depiction is different from the usual fare one finds in the nonopposition press. Still, Huwaydi does not suggest that Egypt follow the Iranian model, though he seems to imply that some version of cultural identity in which Islam is the centerpiece must be found for Middle East societies. But what kind of Islam does he have in mind? Although he does not specify, his vision appears to be closer to the ideas proposed by Hanafi, Mumin, and others of the Islamic left. Huwaydi argues that the traditional Islamic response to the West was excessively

Egypt

negative, whereas a more positively imbued Islam must be found. He means an Islam must be evolved that provides the anchor of belief for those wholly committed to its literal significations and that represents a general cultural orientation for those less committed to its literal interpretation. What this would mean politically for Egypt is left unclear, but the implication seems to be along the lines of Hanafi's "popular Nasserism."

It is possible, therefore, that a new and more nuanced perspective is gaining currency among the non-Islamic Egyptian media. Huwaydi's ideas may become the basis for a less militantly anti-Iranian image. If so, it will be interesting to compare that image with the depictions of the Iranian revolution portrayed in the outlets of the Muslim Brotherhood.

Conclusions

This chapter has focused on the impact of the Iranian revolution on Egyptian society through an investigation of the nation's press. The consensus seems to be that the Islamic resurgence predated the Iranian revolution by many years. Consider the following evaluation by Hanafi: "Even after the sweeping victory of the Wafd Party in the national election of 1951, the Muslim Brothers continued to be a major force, especially among university students. They were able to win the election of the student's union [at Cairo University?] by more than ninety-five percent of the votes."[46] Ali Dessouki points out that the salience of the Islamic groups on campus continued to be extremely high in 1978, when the Islamic groups dominated—even monopolized—the student syndicates at Alexandria University in the medicine, science, engineering, pharmacy, law, and agriculture faculties.[47]

Various other events in Egypt in 1974 (the assault on the Military Technical Academy) and 1977 (the bread riots, the kidnapping and murder of the minister of endowments, Sadat's trip to Israel) had their own dynamic, apart from what Khomeini was doing in Iraq or Islamic groups were doing inside Iran. Thus, the Iranian revolution has served to quicken, rather than cause, the Islamic resurgence in Egypt. The Muslim Brotherhood and the militant radical Islamic opposition groups have been most influenced by the Iranian revolution. However, it is possible that with the publication of more sophisticated works by authors who are predisposed to the Iranian revolution as a matter of principle (e.g., Huwaydi), the informed lay public may respond more positively than before. Yet there are limits to this potential development, as the doctrinal and other aspects of Shiism will not easily be accepted by Egyptians.

The absence of a Shiite community in Egypt makes more doubtful the possibility of the Khomeini model seizing the imagination of Egyptian constituencies. For most Egyptians, the appealing aspect of the Iranian revolution appear to be its rejection of cultural Westernization and economic dependency on a superpower. Egyptian Islamic activists are more influenced by their own thinkers and by Sunni writers like Mawdudi than by Khomeini. An apparent exception is Shariati, whose attacks on the legacy of Western domination strike a responsive chord. But Shariati's problematics—*intizar* (waiting for the return of the Hidden Imam), *shahadat* (martyrdom), and *imamat* (the Imamate)— are barriers to the further penetration of his ideas among the Egyptian Islamic groups.

Ultimately, the Iranian revolution may have caused an increase in tensions between Muslims and Christians in Egypt. Such tensions date back to the early 1970s and relate to such issues as the construction of churches, strict bans on birth-control practices in the Christian community (thereby promoting fears among Muslims that the Copts were seeking eventual parity in numbers with the Muslims), proselytization, personnel decisions in the bureaucracy, the state's law banning apostasy, and the growing competition between Islamic and Coptic groups in various arenas of Egyptian public life. Although these tensions developed before the revolution, Iran's experience may have added fuel to the flames of conflict between the two communities in Egypt. Consider, for example, the destuction of communal property prior to the Coptic Pope Shenouda's cancellation of Easter ceremonies in March 1980.[48] Some speculate that Coptic insecurity may have increased as a consequence of Khomeini's victory in Iran. On the other hand, given Sadat's antipathy to Iranian developments, it could be argued that the Coptic groups had less to fear than it appeared at first glance.

Sadat wished to solicit the support of Islamic groups when he first came to power because of the narrow base of his popular support, although he apparently felt he had to withhold official recognition of the Muslim Brotherhood. Both he and his successors have sought to project an image of themselves as pious leaders, attending religious ceremonies, invoking Koranic verses, encouraging self-help community groups to build mosques, and so on.

To some extent, however, their strategy has not only been to broaden the regime's popularity but also to split the Islamic groups from one another. But such divide-and-rule policies may not work. For example, Egypt's 1971 constitution refers to Islam as *a* source of law. Some have interpreted this as a gesture to the less militant Islamic groups, such as the Muslim Brotherhood, who chafed under the Nasser period when Islam was relegated to a secondary role. However, the *sharia* movement, which aims to make Islamic law *the* source of law in Egypt, seemingly unites the various Islamic groups. The current regime can only hope that the Brotherhood will continue to refrain from resorting to the wide-ranging violent tactics of the militant Islamic groups. With Khomeini and his idealogues encouraging the Egyptian Muslims not to compromise, to make Islamic law the only basis of law, and to use whatever means possible to achieve this, the Egyptian scene will remain contentious for at least the next several years.

But overall, the Egyptian groups do not need Khomeini to inspire them, for their motivations transcend his message. One cannot help thinking that in the end Khomeini's model will be distilled, and the residue will simply be a constituent element in the edifice that the Islamic groups are seeking to establish in Egypt, not the keystone of the whole structure.

Notes

1. Abd al-Karim Bi Azar Shirazi, *Hambastagi-yi Madhahib-i Islami* (Teheran: Amir Kabir, 1350/1971), xix–xx, 108–12.

2. Ibid., xxi. Shirazi argues that it was decided from the start to keep the reconciliation effort and politics apart from one another (i.e., to keep that effort from being used as a tool in foreign policy).

3. Rudi Mathee, "The Egyptian Opposition on the Iranian Revolution," in *Shiism and Social Protest,* ed. Juan R. I. Cole and Nikki R. Keddie (New Haven: Yale University Press, 1986), 248–49.

4. Leonard Binder, *Islamic Liberalism: A Critique of Development Ideologies* (Chicago: University of Chicago Press, 1988), 258.

5. Nazih N. M. Ayubi, "The Political Revival of Islam: The Case of Egypt," *International Journal of Middle East Studies* 12 (December 1980): 493.

6. Islamic Student Association of Cairo University, "Lessons from Iran," in *Islam in Transition: Muslim Perspectives,* ed. John J. Donohue and John L. Esposito (New York: Oxford University Press, 1982), 246–50.

7. Saad Eddin Ibrahim, "The Anatomy of Egypt's Militant Islamic Groups," ibid., 435.

8. *Al Safir,* May 28, 1982, as quoted in Emmanuel Sivan, *Radical Islam: Medieval Theology and Modern Politics* (New Haven: Yale University Press, 1985), 189.

9. Eric Davis, "Ideology, Social Class and Islamic Radicalism in Modern Egypt," in *From Nationalism to Revolutionary Islam,* ed. Said Arjomand (Albany: State University of New York Press, 1984), 152.

10. Amira El-Azhary Sonbol, "Egypt," in *The Politics of Islamic Revivalism,* ed. Shireen T. Hunter (Bloomington: Indiana University Press, 1988), 32–33.

11. Hamied Ansari, "The Islamic Militants in Egyptian Politics," *International Journal of Middle East Studies* 16 (March, 1984): 125.

12. Tareq Y. Ismael and Jacqueline S. Ismael, *Government and Politics in Islam* (New York: St. Martin's Press, 1985), 120.

13. *The New York Times,* August 22, 1989.

14. Ayubi, 490. But cf. Davis, 153, who says that the Islamic resurgence began almost immediately after the Egyptian government's suppression of the Muslim Brotherhood in 1954 and was certainly evident by the early 1960s.

15. Mohga Machhour and Alain Rousillon, *La révolution iranienne dans la presse égyptienne* (Cairo/Paris: Centre d'Etudes et de Documentation Economiques, Juridiques et Sociales, 1982), 51; also Mathee, 252, 255ff.

16. Fathi Abd al-Aziz, *Khomeini: al-Badil al-Islami* (Cairo: Dar al-Itisam, 1979), 48–49, 59, cited in Machhour and Rousillon, 45, 54.

17. Abd al-Munim Jabbara, *Al Dawah* (April 1978): 7, cited in Machhour and Rousillon, 58.

18. *Al Dawah* (November 1978): 8–9, cited in Machhour and Rousillon, 48.

19. Muhammad Abd al-Rahim Anbar, *Nahwa Thawrah Islamiyyah* (Cairo: Matbaah Abirin, 1979), 101–2, 104, 106.

20. *Al Itisam* (February, 1979), cited in Machhour and Rousillon, 39.

21. *Al Itisam* (December, 1979), cited in Machhour and Rousillon, 49.

22. *Al Dawah* (March 1980), cited in Machhour and Rousillon, 44–45. As Mathee points out, the loss of Muslim spirituality as a consequence of the Shah's Westernization policies is a continuous theme in the Muslim Brotherhood press on the Iranian revolution. See, for example, *Al Mukhtar al-Islami* (August 1980): 26–34, cited in Mathee, 253.

23. Muhammad al-Qaud Hilmi, *Al Itisam* (January 1980): 28–29, cited in Machhour and Rousillon, 60.

24. *Al Dawah* (October, 1980): 4–6, cited in Machhour and Rousillon, 46.

25. *Al Dawah* (October 1980): 4ff., cited in Machhour and Rousillon, 59.

26. *Al Dawah* (March 1980): 44–45, cited in Machhour and Rousillon, 16–17.

27. Mathee, 256.

28. Ibid., 261.

29. Ibid.

30. *Al Mukhtar al-Islami* (January 1981): 8–26, cited in Mathee, 262.

31. Tilmisani, *Al Dawah* (October 1980): 4ff., cited in Machhour and Rousillon, 59.

32. Mathee, 257.

33. *Al Dawah* (September 1980): 16–17, and *Al Itisam,* (February 1980): 6–7, cited in Machhour and Rousillon, 62.

34. Mathee, 263–64.

35. Cited in Mathee, 268.

36. Muhammad al-Said Abd al-Mumin, *Masalah al-Thawrah al-Iraniyyah* (Cairo?: n.p., 1981), 95.

37. Ibid., 103–4.

38. Cited in Machhour and Rousillon, 75.

39. Hassan Hanafi, "The Relevance of the Islamic Alternative in Egypt," *Arab Studies Quarterly* 4, nos. 1 and 2 (1980): 74.

40. Ibid., 61.

41. Ibid., 67, 64.

42. Ibid., 71.

43. Ibid.

44. Ibid., 74.

45. Fahmi al-Huwaydi, *Iran min al-Dakhil* (Cairo: Markaz al-Ahram li al-Tarjumah wa al-Nashr, 1987). This discussion is based on a review of this work by Rudi Mathee, which is forthcoming in the journal *Iranian Studies*.

46. Hanafi, 59.

47. Ali al-Hillal Dessouki, "The Resurgence of Islamic Organizations in Egypt: An Interpretation," in *Islam and Power,* ed. Alexander S. Cudsi and Ali al-Hillal Dessouki (Baltimore: Johns Hopkins University Press, 1981), 108.

48. Hamied Ansari, "Sectarian Conflict in Egypt and the Political Expediency of Religion," *Middle East Journal* 38 (Summer 1984): 397–404.

9

Tunisia and Libya:

Responses to the

Islamic Impulse

LISA ANDERSON

ALTHOUGH THE IRANIAN REVOLUTION did not introduce genuinely new ideas into Tunisia or Libya, nor did new groups spring up at the behest of Iran's revolutionary government, the revolution accelerated trends already present in both countries. In directing the world's attention to Islam and Islamic politics, the revolution raised the hopes of critics and the fears of governments throughout much of the Muslim world. Tunisia and Libya were no exceptions. By so persuasively illustrating the eloquence and power of the Islamic idiom that articulates political rights and responsibilities, the revolution raised the stakes in the disputes over the role of religion and, at least temporarily, lessened the inclination toward tolerance and compromise on all sides.

Although Libya and Tunisia were very different countries on the eve of the revolution, their responses to Iran's experience reveal much about what is a common dilemma in the Muslim world today. At the time of the revolution the governments of Tunisia and Libya, for all their profound differences, shared the conviction that Islam and Islamic traditions must be subordinated to a new, different, and fundamentally secular formula for political authority and legitimacy. In Tunisia, President Habib Bourguiba's government had long enjoyed the reputation of being the most secular regime in the Arab world, following a Western model of separation of church and state that had seemed to many observers, particularly in the West, to be unusually enlightened. The regime's militant laicism relaxed somewhat during the 1970s, a trend seen elsewhere in the Arab and Islamic world, as the government attempted to counter leftist critics of liberal economic policies by encouraging what they erroneously believed to be conservative but innocuous religious politics. By the time of the Iranian revolution the Tunisian government already faced serious criticism from religious quarters; the revolution merely served to widen the gulf and harden the positions of both sides.

In Libya, although the regime inaugurated by the military coup of Colonel Muammar al-Qaddafi on September 1, 1969, had been widely considered the only model of Islamic reform in power, by the time of the Iranian revolution the Qaddafi government had formulated a political ideology that rooted political legitimacy in secular notions of democracy, equality, and revolution. Though grounded in ideas familiar to the West, Qaddafi's ideology nonetheless seemed hostile to Western interests, and it was interpreted there as sharing the same underlying worldview as that of Iran's equally hostile Islamic government. In fact, from the perspective of the role of Islam in politics, Qaddafi shared much more with Bourguiba than with Khomeini. From Qaddafi's point of view, the Iranian revolution constituted an ally—and a competitor—not as an Islamic revolution but as a revolution in the Muslim world. Qaddafi valued his revolutionary image and wanted to be associated with other revolutionaries, but like Bourguiba, he would come to repudiate explicitly the claims of Islam to restrain and guide secular authority.

Thus, as we shall see, the 1980s were marked by increasing conflict between the regime and religiously clad opposition groups in both Tunisia and Libya. In both cases the substance of the disputes—the extent to which religious strictures would constrain and guide policy and policy makers—was homegrown. The Iranian revolution made accommodation more difficult by raising hopes and fears, but it did not create the issues or the parties in dispute. Ultimately, as the revolution becomes routinized, as it settles into the ordinariness and specificity that overtake all such enchanted moments in the modern world, it will likely leave few traces in Tunisia and Libya, for the questions with which they grapple will be formulated and answered in the quite specific historical and social context of each country. To best illustrate this

Anderson

argument, it is well to start with a brief survey of the historical place of religion in politics and society of Tunisia and Libya themselves.

Islam in Precolonial and Colonial North Africa

The populations of both Tunisia and Libya are overwhelmingly Sunni Muslim. There are no indigenous Christian peoples in either nation. Until the middle of the twentieth century important Jewish minorities inhabited coastal cities and inland mountain towns in both countries, but with the establishment of Israel in 1948 even these communities dwindled to insignificance. The few Jews still living in Libya were expelled after the 1969 coup that brought Qaddafi to power; their counterparts in Tunisia still remain, a small and relatively powerless, though symbolically important, community. Small Ibadi Muslim communities exist among the Berber speakers in the mountains of southern Tunisia and western Libya, but there has been no linguistically or religiously based political activity in either country since the 1920s.

Islam is an important part of the history and self-image of both Tunisia and Libya, but the term carries somewhat different connotations in each country. By North African standards, Tunisia's Islamic tradition is a settled, urban one, emphasizing the erudite legal and textual analysis that accompanies the large-scale administrative and commercial life of cities. The ulama, or religious elite, were the scholars, judges, and jurists who elaborated and applied the *Sharia*, the religious law that is to rule all aspects of Muslim life. The city of Kairouan (Qayrawan), founded in the seventh century in northeast Tunisia, is the most important pilgrimage site in North Africa—seven pilgrimages to Kairouan are said to be the equivalent of one to Mecca—and the most important institution of Islamic higher learning between Egypt and Morocco is in Tunis: the famed Zitouna (Zaytunah) mosque.[1]

In contrast, piety in Libya is associated less with urban learning than with the austerity and devotion of brotherhoods based in the mountains and desert. The rigors of nomadic agriculture and pastoralism and the importance of kin over contractual relations among rural tribespeople militated against the Islam of legal scholars. Instead, the emphasis was on simpler, less refined interpretations of religious obligation (often understood as the pure, unadulterated Islam of the Prophet) and the more mystical aspects of relations between the individual and God. With its relatively small urban and large Bedouin population, Libya provided fertile ground for religious brotherhoods, whether mystical or reformist, and it was home to one of the most prominent reformist orders of the nineteenth century: the Sanusiya. In 1843 the founder of the order settled in Cyrenaica (eastern Libya), where he established the brotherhood's first *zawiyah*, or lodge. By the 1880s, the order had adherents all along the trans-Saharan trade routes in Cyrenaica, the Fazzan region in southwestern Libya, Chad, and western Egypt.[2]

This is not to say that there were no legal or religious scholars in Libyan towns and cities or that there were no brotherhoods in Tunisia. On the contrary, the urban religious establishment of Tripoli served the local political administration in Libya throughout the precolonial era, while Islamic religious orders appeared in Tunisian cities and the tribal regions of the mountains and steppes. In general, however, the relative weight of these two forms of traditional Islam was quite different in the two societies, and this had an important impact on the role of religion in the reception of Western influence during the colonial era.[3]

In Tunisia the establishment of the French protectorate in 1881 was met with relatively little protest from either the political leadership or the allied religious establishment. The social elite from which Tunisian rulers and religious notables issued had long entertained close relations with Europeans, and they expected to benefit from European "protection." Ironically, in failing to sound the alarms the old ruling class wrote its own death warrant; the decline of the elite during the protectorate was as irreversible as it had been unforeseen. New social classes, educated *à la française*, eventually provided the ideas and the people that questioned French dominance. The protectorate was challenged and defeated on its own, very secular terms, and the once-dominant political and religious elites were overshadowed by "new men" of petit bourgeois background and French education, of whom Habib Bourguiba, eventually president of independent Tunisia, is a prime example. Largely because of its essentially conservative character—being, as it was, an important part of the old social and political establishment— the urban Islam of Tunisia played a relatively small role in the nationalist opposition to French rule. Although unemployed Zitouna graduates were important in local branches of the nationalist political party during the 1930s and adherence to the party was sworn on the Koran, the rationale of nationalism drew as much from international anti-imperialist ideologies ranging from Marx to Gandhi as from Islam.

Anderson

In Libya Italian pretensions to the territory in 1911 were met by widespread local opposition, much of which was led by men and organizations whose principal claims to loyalty were their credentials as pious Muslims, particularly the Sanusiya. The Italians did not pacify the country until the early 1930s and lost it a mere ten years later to the Allied military governments until UN-sponsored independence in 1951. This continuing upheaval hindered the creation of new classes educated *all'italiana* and reinforced the credibility and prestige of opposition to "Christian" rule. Although there was opposition to Italian rule on almost all grounds, the familiarity of religious rationales together with the unparalleled importance of the Sanusiyyah in rallying support for the resistance dwarfed other ideologies and organizations. In contrast to Tunisia, Libya's exposure to Europe in the twentieth century reinforced rather than undermined the inclination to look to religious legitimation of political power.

Islam and Politics after Independence

By the time the two countries won their independence (Libya in 1951 and Tunisia in 1956) their social and political life, including the role of Islam, diverged dramatically. Although King Idris of Libya and President Bourguiba of Tunisia both set out to subordinate the orthodox religious establishment to the state, they and their compatriots had profoundly different views of the proper role of religion in politics. Idris's sole claim to the throne, apart from his friendship with the British, was his position as head of the Sanusi religious order. Bourguiba, on the other hand, was the leader of one of the few genuinely mass-based nationalist movements in the Arab world, and he had little use for what he viewed as religious obscurantism.

For the eighteen years during which the Sanusi king ruled, appeals for political legitimacy were limited largely to religious justifications (the Sanusi family, like the Jordanian Hashemites and Moroccan Alawis, is said to be descended from the Prophet, and the king himself was well known to be personally pious); only in the late 1960s were a few half-hearted references to Arab nationalism added to the formula. At independence, Libya was among the poorest countries in the world—oil was not discovered until 1959 and exports did not start until several years later—and the domestic administration was little more than a patronage network that served to provide minimal services to the people and maximum political support for the monarch.

Despite its reliance on religious legitimacy, the monarchy began a process of limiting and weakening the role of recognized religious authorities in politics and policy that would reach its logical conclusion under Qaddafi. In consolidating Sanusi control of the state, the regime undermined the position of non-Sanusi ulama.[4] Integration of the *Sharia* courts into the national secular judicial system and incorporation of significant religious positions, like that of Grand Mufti, into the government bureaucracy eroded the independence of the ulama as they became salaried employees of the state. Control of the Sanusi institutions remained in the private hands of the royal household, which permitted religious figures to wield enormous power but discouraged institutionalization of permanent religious authority in government.

Like the king in Libya, though with a very different beneficiary in mind, Habib Bourguiba also supervised the "nationalization" of independent religious institutions. He intended the policy to benefit not a competing religious organization, of course, but rather a secular, "modern" organization—the nationalist political party known as the Neo-Destour—and its leader and his worldview. On the eve of independence an estimated 15 percent of the Tunisian population were card-carrying members of the Neo-Destour, and very diverse interests, including unemployed Zitouna graduates, middle-class farmers, and wealthy merchants, were represented in the party. Indeed, Bourguiba himself had not been above using religious symbolism to appeal to ordinary Tunisians. He defended the veiling of women on the grounds that it was part of Tunisia's cultural heritage; party meetings were often held in a mosque or the *zawiya* of a local brotherhood; Bourguiba himself became known as the *mujahid al-akhbar* (a term that loses its religious connotations in its French rendering as *combattant suprême*) as the nationalist struggle was portrayed as a *jihad*, or holy war. Because the party appealed to such diverse interests, it is perhaps not surprising that as independence approached, its unity fractured. Bourguiba's leadership and judgment were challenged in a virtual civil war that pitted his modernist supporters among the professionals and petit bourgeoisie against the more traditionalist followers of a rival nationalist leader, Salah Ben Youssef, among the religious establishment and old commercial elite.

With French aid, the Bourguiba faction triumphed, but not before Bourguiba and his loyalists became convinced that they could not ignore the threat from Ben Youssef supporters. Thus, by the early 1960s the government was firmly under the control of a Neo-Destour guided by Bourguiba's lieutenants; the precolonial monarchy, which had been retained during the French protectorate, was abolished (its last incumbent was suspected of Youssefist sympathies), and Bourguiba was elected president of the new republic. The *Sharia* courts were disbanded; the Zitouna mosque, where Ben Youssef had announced his break with Bourguiba, and the endowments (*habus* or *waqf*) that supported religious institutions and offices were put under state control; and a Code of Personal Status outlawing polygamy was promulgated. Bourguiba's willingness to tolerate religious influence in politics in the interest of unity during the nationalist struggle had vanished.

In the 1960s little attention was given to religious affairs in both Libya and Tunisia, though for different reasons. In Libya the decade was devoted to what proved to be the monarchy's unsuccessful efforts to absorb the new and, by the Libyan standards of the day, enormous oil income. Clamor against increasing corruption was met with an open letter from the king in which he cited Koranic verses and Prophetic traditions deploring evildoing and theft, an initiative that had little effect on the problem. Criticism of the government's continued dependence on Western patrons and demands for equitable distribution of oil revenues and for greater involvement in pan-Arab causes contributed to virtually universal expectations that the monarchy would not last, and the coup which brought Qaddafi to power in 1969 was met with more relief than surprise.

In Tunisia the 1960s were a period of extension and consolidation of state penetration in the economy and society in the guise of single-party socialism. Like Nasser's socialism in Egypt during the same era, Tunisia's socialism was unorthodox, specifically excluding class struggle in favor of national unity and concentrating on the destruction of what Bourguiba called "archaic modes of production." Secular-style education was strongly promoted as a way of indoctrinating young people with the spirit of liberal rationalism Bourguiba held so dear. By the end of the decade much of the agenda of state consolidation had been met and Bourguiba's own supporters were getting restive. The socialist programs were abandoned as government economic and social policies took a distinct turn to the right in a search for private-sector support for development.[5]

Thus, in the economic realm Tunisia and Libya could hardly have been more different. Libya's laissez-faire monarchy would give way to revolutionary socialism, while Tunisia's developmental socialism was replaced by increased emphasis on free enterprise. In handling religious affairs, however, Tunisia and Libya would look more and more alike as both governments increased their efforts to control and eventually stifle the voice of religion in politics and came to face increasing Islamic protest as a result.

The 1970s were characterized by a growing attention to Islam and its political potential throughout the Muslim world, a revival influenced by many factors. The defeat of the Arab armies by Israel in 1967 and the loss of Jerusalem came as a terrible shock to many Muslims, persuaded as they had been by years of Arab nationalist rhetoric that the liberation of Palestine was imminent. Disenchanted with secular nationalist and socialist ideologies, they turned to beliefs that provided both guidance and solace. For French-speaking North Africa, the 1968 upheavals in France undermined confidence in the rationality and desirability of Western models of civilization. The greater visibility of the religiously conservative Gulf states and of what seemed to be a religiously radical regime in Libya after the oil price inflation of the 1970s further enhanced interest in Islamic politics, both because the ostensibly pious seemed to have been disproportionately blessed with good fortune and because they spent some of their new wealth encouraging propagation of the faith. In some places, including Tunisia and Egypt, the end of an era of socialism and the turn to more liberal economic and social policies were accompanied by government encouragement of religious politics to counter expected leftist criticism.[6] Although the revived interest in Islam shared many common origins, the movements that embodied that interest varied from country to country, reflecting the very different circumstances in which they operated. Nowhere is that better illustrated than in Tunisia and Libya.

Tunisia: "Modernism," Reform, and the Islamic Response

In an important study of the Islamic resurgence in Tunisia, sociologist Elbaki Hermassi connects the revival to the regime's reform efforts:

> To explain the origins of MTI [Tunisia's principal Islamist group], one must refer to a reason so evident that it is rarely taken into account or given its true weight. That is, of all the Arab countries, Tunisia is the only one where the modernist elite deliberately attacked and dismantled the structures of institutional Islam

in the name of a systematic reform of the social and cultural order.[7]

Although, as we shall see, in several critical respects Qaddafi's Libya shares this distinction—with many of the same results—Tunisia's historical efforts at reform contributed in decisive ways to the climate in which the Islamists of the 1980s thrived.

Despite his preoccupation with secular issues such as economic development and social change, during the early 1960s Bourguiba confronted religion directly in one important arena and with a very revealing approach. He declared that fasting during the month of Ramadan, an obligation that constitutes one of the five pillars of Islam, interfered with economic productivity to an extent unacceptable in a country aspiring to industrialization:

> I do not believe that religion should be able to impose such a sacrifice . . . This is an abusive interpretation of the religion . . . All practices of this religion are issues of logical intentions, but when they are incompatible with the necessary struggles of life, this religion must be amended . . . We are obliged to throw out our worst customs. We must be devoted to progress and not lose sight of our goal.[8]

Bourguiba asked the Grand Mufti for a *fatwa*, or legal ruling, that would permit people to postpone the fast until their vacation or retirement. The Grand Mufti refused to issue the dispensation—for which he shortly thereafter lost his job—and Bourguiba declared:

> As Head of a Muslim state, I may also speak in the name of religion . . . Unfortunately our professors belong to a certain category of people who refuse to reason and judge according to past experience and the teachings of the Quran. . . . Insofar as the young prove to be incapable of coping with the effort of work and fasting we must be tolerant. They can then break their fast with a quiet conscience. This is my *fatwa*.[9]

In the face of ample evidence that he was in the minority, Bourguiba continued to press the issue for several years, and the campaign culminated in 1964 with his effort to set an example by drinking a glass of orange juice at a rally during Ramadan. Although many Tunisians were discomforted by Bourguiba's militant secularism, it was not until the

1970s that this sentiment translated into political action. By that time many people were looking to religion for political answers.

The Tunisian Islamists date their activity to 1970 when a cultural association, the Koranic Preservation Society, was founded at the Zitouna mosque.[10] Hoping to counteract leftist agitation, particularly at the university, the government supported the association at the outset, and Tunisia thus experienced a general revival of interest in religion throughout the early 1970s. In 1978, the government's liberal economic policy foundered and labor troubles spilled over into the country's worst rioting since independence; for the first time the army was called out to restore quiet. By then, Islamic sentiment had become politicized and a loose opposition coalesced in a group called the Movement of Islamic Renewal. Within a year one of its constituents, the *Mouvement de tendance islamique* (*Harakat al-Ittijah al-Islami*, known by its initials in French, MTI) led by Rashid al-Ghannushi, emerged as the principal representative of political Islam in Tunisia. For the next eighteen months or so, the MTI organized followers in rural areas, among the poorer classes in towns and cities, and, most importantly, among high school and university students. In June 1981, shortly after the government announced its intention to end twenty years of single-party rule and permit formation of independent political parties, the MTI requested party recognition. The response came within two months: The movement's leaders were arrested.

As early as 1979, the government had given the Tunisian Islamists the ostensibly pejorative label of "Khomeinists." While the Tunisian Islamist movement's claim to be a purely indigenous response to Tunisia's domestic problems is widely credited by nonpartisan observers, the government was correct in suggesting that the Iranian revolution gave hope to the MTI and its leaders, just as it inspired fear and loathing in the militantly secularist political leadership. Dirk Vanderwalle succinctly summarized the Islamist view of the Iranian revolution in Tunisia:

> Ghannouchi initially strongly supported the overthrow of the shah but remained ambivalent about the use of violence, an ambiguity resolved after 1980 when his writings began to stress persuasion and consciousness-raising as a first step toward the establishment of an Islamic state. By 1981 the MTI had distanced itself from the new Iranian regime, arguing that it represented only one

particular way of establishing an Islamic state. In Tunisia, he theorized, the change should come about by working within the system and the use of violence was condemned.[11]

Despite, or more likely thanks to, government repression, the MTI continued to grow during the early 1980s, but perhaps because it was operating underground, the Islamist movement appears to have divided during this period. The growing political activity of the MTI had already led to the secession in the late 1970s of a group of intellectuals more concerned with cultural issues; subsequently some activists apparently grew impatient with the law-abiding and legalistic approach of the MTI. The Islamic Liberation party (*Hizb al-tahrir al-Islami*) appeared on the scene, advocating the violent overthrow of secular governments; it was founded in Jordan in the 1940s and is now thought to be headquartered in West Germany.[12] In 1983 nineteen Tunisian military officers alleged to be members of the Islamic Liberation party were convicted of plotting against the government. A group that called itself Islamic Jihad also appeared in the mid-1980s; it was said to have claimed responsibility for the bombing of several tourist sites during the summer of 1987, but its provenance was unclear.

After serious bread riots in early 1984 many of the MTI leaders were given amnesty and freed, only to be rearrested three years later. In the spring of 1987, hundreds of Tunisian Islamists were rounded up following the arrest in Paris of what press reports described as "seven suspected Iranian-backed terrorists, five of whom were carrying Tunisian passports."[13] Tunisia promptly broke relations with Teheran and trumpeted "evidence" that Iran was backing the growing Islamist movement in Tunisia, a charge that persuaded few of even the government's closest supporters. It did, however, provide the excuse for major show trials that autumn; the failure of the courts to condemn Rashid al-Ghannushi to death (he was given a sentence of hard labor for life) reportedly infuriated the aging President Bourguiba. It was his demand for a retrial that persuaded his prime minister and former security chief, Zine al-Abidine Ben Ali, to engineer Bourguiba's deposition by having him declared senile and incompetent.

Much of the crackdown had been attributed to Ben Ali himself, but as Bourguiba's successor as president, Ben Ali proved to be quite sensitive to Islamic sentiment and, at least at the outset, quite serious about political liberalization. Shortly after coming to power, he went on a well-publicized pilgrimage to Mecca, and Tunisia's state-owned television network began to broadcast religious programming. Within a year virtually all political prisoners had been released, including the most prominent of the Islamists, and although the MTI had not been granted formal recognition as a political party, the president had met privately with Ghannushi.

By then it was apparent to all that the Islamist movement was a response to the Tunisian domestic scene. The militant secularism of the Bourguiba government had left many Tunisians—including many of Bourguiba's admirers—feeling rootless, bereft of a cultural and historical perspective from which to understand and evaluate the world around them, including the government's proposals for the future. That the premature, if not excessive, secularization of political life in Tunisia produced its own "corrective" movement was probably inevitable. That Bourguiba would view that movement with complete incomprehension, portraying both it and the revolution in Iran as evidence of the fanaticism and backwardness he had spent his entire life combating, was equally a foregone conclusion, and it meant that as long as he was president, there was no room for compromise. Bourguiba believed this conflict was a mythic struggle for the very soul of the Tunisian people, and as with so much else in Tunisia over the last fifty years, Bourguiba's conviction very nearly became reality.

Libya: "Revolution" and the Islamic Response

Tunisia was not the only country in which the government had set itself a larger-than-life agenda, where as Hermassi put it, "the modernist elite deliberately attacked and dismantled the structures of institutional Islam in the name of a systematic reform of the social and cultural order." In many important respects, that description also fits Libya under Qaddafi. In Libya, however, two factors intervened to obscure the radically secularist implications of the revolution, particularly at the outset. In its early days in power, Qaddafi's military government appealed to Islam to bolster its legitimacy after having deposed a government that had based its right to rule largely on religion. This gave the pronouncements of the new government a religious coloring unusual among the Arab military regimes of the time. Moreover, unlike the Bourguiba government, which came to power after decades of ideological development in the nationalist movement, the Qaddafi regime developed much of its vision of a new world only while in office; it was not until nearly a decade after he took the reins of government that Qaddafi began to implement his revolutionary vision of the world in earnest.[14]

There are thus two phases in the Qaddafi government's approach to Islam. In the early stages, the regime actively courted "institutional Islam" as a counterweight not to leftist sentiment, as was the case in Egypt and Tunisia during the same era, but to residual loyalty to the Sanusi brotherhood. Even at that point, however, Qaddafi was leaving no doubt about who defined Islam; like many of his secularist counterparts, he distrusted independent religious organizations. He was contemptuous of the Muslim Brotherhood, the reformist group founded in Egypt in the 1930s as one of the earliest exponents of Islamic revival, saying that its members "work against Arab Unity, against Socialism, and against Arab Nationalism, because they consider all these inconsistent with religion. Colonialism allies and associates with them because colonialism is against Arab Unity, against Arab Nationalism, and against Socialism."[15]

Even in its earliest days, there was no question of the Qaddafi regime's order of priorities: Nationalism and socialism came before religion. Once the regime was comfortably entrenched, Qaddafi went further and began to articulate a vision of society in which Islam was explicitly superseded as a guide to action by a broader, more universalistic view of revolution. The Libyan revolution was not an Islamic revolution, as the regime's relations with both the Islamic Republic of Iran and its own Libyan Islamists would demonstrate. In many respects the Libyan revolution was closer to the Bourguibist model of a radical rejection of religious tradition in favor of a new political and social order.

At the outset, however, Qaddafi's regime did concern itself with Islam far more than did any of the other republican regimes in the Muslim world. Very shortly after coming to power, Qaddafi made it clear that despite his embrace of Nasserist Arab nationalism and socialism, he would give a prominent role to Islam in his political formulations. Early decrees of the Revolutionary Command Council abolished the special privileges of the Sanusiya, mandated the use of Arabic and the Muslim calendar in all public forums, prohibited the consumption of alcohol (forbidden by Islam but permitted under the monarchy), imposed Koranic criminal penalties (*hudud*) such as amputation of the hand of a thief, and established the *jam'iyyat al-dawa al-islamiyyah* (Islamic Call Society) to spread the Islamic message.

In taking this activist stance, the new regime served two of its important interests. First, the bid for support among the non-Sanusi religious establishment was an effort to defend the regime's religious probity in having turned out of office a descendant of the Prophet still venerated in some circles in Libya. Second, and more important, the regime defined the boundaries of acceptable religious activity and, as in Tunisia, in doing so gave priority to the state over the religious establishment.

That Qaddafi was a secularist at heart, no more interested than Bourguiba in establishing an Islamic state, would become abundantly clear by the mid-1970s when his Third International Theory was promulgated. This political and economic formulation of a just and democratic society, published in the three slim volumes of the *Green Book*, may have drawn occasionally on Islamic precepts, but its intended audience was much wider.[16] As Qaddafi himself explained:

> The Third International Theory is based on religion and nationalism—any religion and any nationalism . . . We do not present Islam as a religion in the Third Theory. For if we do so, we will be excluding from the Third Theory all the non-Muslims, something which we evidently do not want. In the Third Theory, we present the applications of Islam from which all mankind may benefit.[17]

Implementation of the revolutionary institutions outlined in the *Green Book* did not go smoothly, and the failure of average Libyans to appreciate the complicated revolutionary system of committees and congresses through which they were to rule themsevles was a source of frustration to the leadership. Among the groups that fell out of favor as a result was the religious establishment; like Bourguiba twenty years earlier, Qaddafi attributed popular apathy and opposition to his program of political and economic reform to the retrograde influence of the religious establishment.

As early as 1977 Qaddafi published a newspaper article arguing that representation of the people by religious authorities was incompatible with democracy as he understood it, prompting the resignation of the Grand Mufti he had appointed upon coming to power. The next year a number of ulama voiced objections to the economic socialism of the Third International Theory, arguing that its declaration that "land is not private property" contradicted Islamic tradition and threatened *waqf* (religious endowments), a major source of financial support for the religious establishment. Soon thereafter popular committees were instructed to "seize the mosques" to rid them of "paganist tendencies" and of the religious functionaries who had been "propagating heretical tales elaborated over centuries of decadence and which distort the Islamic religion."[18]

By the end of 1978, while acknowledging that the Koran as the Word of God provides binding precepts for Muslims, Qaddafi declared that the Sunna—the Prophet's practice as recorded in the *hadith* (traditions about his words and deeds)—is not necessarily binding. He did not reject the idea that the Prophet's example is a guide to virtuous behavior but argued that historical inaccuracies and errors had crept into the *hadith*, making them unreliable. In late 1978, he called for a revision of the Islamic calendar, arguing that it should begin not with the *hijra*, or Muhammad's emigration from Mecca to Medina, as it had for nearly 1,400 years but with the Prophet's death ten years later. This, he argued, is a much more significant date for Islam, marking the end of prophecy and ranking in importance with the birth of Jesus for Christianity. Thereafter Libyan Muslim calendars were ten years behind those of the rest of the Islamic world.

The provocation that this represented was reminiscent of Bourguiba's Ramadan glass of orange juice. Qaddafi's rationale for his reformism, particularly his concern to rid himself of conservative religious figures and unveil the "true" character of Islam, was not unlike Bourguiba's earlier criticism of "abusive interpretations of the religion" and call for sacrifice of old customs in light of the demands of progress. Just as Bourguiba could claim the right to issue a *fatwa*, Qaddafi felt free to argue that "as the Muslims have strayed far from Islam, a review is demanded. The [Libyan revolution] is a revolution rectifying Islam, presenting Islam correctly, purifying Islam of the reactionary practices which dressed it in retrograde clothing not its own."[19]

Qaddafi's right to make such pronouncements—like Bourguiba's issuance of *fatwas*—was based on the historical Muslim rejection of a priesthood. John Davis argues that Qaddafi's rejection of the priesthood was inevitable, for "if an Islamic revolutionary leader is not himself a member of the category of religious experts he must assert the direct and unmediated relation of every Muslim to God: he is bound to say that a personally pious man is as capable of understanding as any preacher or lawyer-theologian."[20] Strictly speaking Qaddafi may have been within his rights to proclaim his qualifications as a pious Muslim to interpret Islamic precepts; but in practice he, like Bourguiba, alienated the religious establishment and with his unorthodox conclusions cast doubt on his fidelity to what is conventionally understood as Islam. Ironically, he thus made his regime vulnerable to precisely the same kind of religious opposition that plagued the Tunisian government. George Joffe summarizes the picture at the end of the 1970s:

> Opposition arose not only from traditionalist groups—the al-Azhar school or other urban traditionalists—but also from religious leaders who had also been steeped in the Islamic revival . . . These were people who . . . sought an Islamic solution to the control of a modern state and to the problems faced by Libya itself. They had been antagonized by the regime's incorporation of Islam into its own revolutionary dogma and finally alienated in 1978 by [policies] that seemed designed to destroy their own social and moral relevance. Their power came from the fact that they increasingly articulated the aspirations of many young people in the major urban centres who also rejected the precepts of the [Libyan revolution] and sought, in mosques frequented by such modernizing religious leaders, a viable alternative.[21]

Among the most prominent of the Islamist opponents of the regime was Shaykh al-Bishti of Tripoli, whose critical Friday sermons drew large crowds in the late 1970s. His sudden and unexplained disappearance in 1980 was an indication both of the threat the regime felt he posed and its inability to confront that threat within even its own law. Since then, however, the Friday sermons throughout Libya have been remarkable only for their uniformly uncritical character.

The Libyan Islamists did not benefit from the relatively free intellectual environment that characterized Tunisia in the 1970s and 1980s, and it is thus impossible to assess the importance, to say nothing of the belief, of Libyan counterparts of Tunisia's MTI. There is evidence that such groups exist, however, both among the exile opposition and, if the televised confessions of men on their way to the gallows are to be believed, within the country as well. In 1983 there were reports of arrests of *Hizb al-tahrir al-Islami* members among the armed forces in

Anderson

Libya as well as Tunisia, but it is not clear whether these are branches of the same transnational group or simply separate groups sharing no more than a name.

This ambiguity was not clarified by the hanging in 1984 of two students said to be members of *Hizb al-tahrir al-Islami* and the arrest in October 1986 and eventual (televised) execution in February 1987 of nine members of groups said to be called *Jihad* and *Hizb Allah*.[22] The fact that the latter group shares the name of a prominent Lebanese Shii group may indicate external influence, but as Joffe points out:

Ironically, the only Islamic movement which has been able to attack the regime effectively has been the Lebanese Shia movement *Amal*. The reasons for this is that the Qaddafi regime is held responsible by Lebanon's Shia community for the disappearance of its charismatic leader, Imam Musa Sadr, during a visit to Libya in August 1978. Amal and its specifically anti-Libyan offshoot, the Imam Sadr brigades, have only threatened Libyan interest in Lebanon itself, however.[23]

Qaddafi viewed the Iranian revolution as a challenge not because he was interested in its religious origins and preoccupations but because he was loath to give up his claim to be the principal revolutionary in the Muslim world. Although his initial hopes that Iran would be a second outpost of the political and social order mandated in the *Green Book* were disappointed, his attraction to revolution still dictated his alliance with Iran during the Iraq-Iran war. This was a relationship based less on common values than on shared antipathies—principally to what both regimes believed to be the terrible influence of Western imperialism—and if it obscured the profound differences between the two regimes for Western observers, it fooled no Islamists.

Conclusions

In both Tunisia and Libya the Iranian revolution intervened at a time when each country was embroiled in a struggle over what role, if any, Islam should play in restraining and making accountable political leaders. It came at a time when the ascendance of the secular rulers was being challenged by groups in society who refused to accept the respective governments' formulation of the debate, the pitting of backward and obscurantist Islam against the virtues of modernist or revolutionary government. By so framing the issue, the governments freed themselves of the age-old obligations imposed by Islam on rulers in favor of what proved to be in practice very ambiguous commitments to democracy or socialism. Had the governments allowed themselves to be bound by institutions that expressed the popular will, the impetus to a return to the traditional Islamic precepts that bind rulers might have been deflected, but that was not the case in either Tunisia or Libya nor, for that matter, in most of the Islamic world.

If the reactions to the Iranian revolution on the part of both government and opposition in Tunisia and Libya were more similar than is commonly recognized, it is also true that Qaddafi enthusiastically associated himself with the revolution politically while Bourguiba emphatically did not. For although Bourguiba and Qaddafi shared the conviction that Islam is to be subordinatd to other causes, they parted ways on precisely what those causes should be. Bourguiba's commitment to nationalism and development implied an acceptance of the international system that was a far cry from Qaddafi's enthusiasm for revolutionary revision of the international order. In its refusal to accept the international status quo, the Iranian revolution found an admirer and kindred spirit in Qaddafi, and it was this shared hostility to the Western-inspired international system that led most Westerners to associate Qaddafi with the Iranian leader Ayatollah Khomeini and to distinguish them from Bourguiba. From the point of view of Islam and politics, however, Qaddafi and Bourguiba shared more with each other than with the Islamic regime in Iran.

As neither an example nor a patron, therefore, did the Iranian revolution have a profound influence in Tunisia and Libya. It was the regimes in Tunisia and Libya themselves that generated the opposition they faced. The revolution probably did heighten fears in the Bourguiba government and provided a ready diversion in the search for causes of dissatisfaction: It was easier to blame the Islamic opposition on Iranian provocateurs than to look to the ambitions and failings of the government itself. In Libya the Iranian revolution failed either to retard the division between the regime and the Islamists or, as far as one can tell, to accelerate the development of Islamic opposition.

The Iranian revolution is a reflection of the great and painful dilemmas that test the developing Muslim world today. The resolution of the relationship between leadership and accountability, the identification of the sources of political sovereignty, and the definition of political responsibility are all still to be accomplished—by the Iranian revolutionaries or anyone else—and we can expect the search for satisfactory answers to continue throughout the Islamic world.

Notes

1. For a history of Islam in Tunisia, see L. Carl Brown, "The Role of Islam in Modern North Africa," in *State and Society in Independent North Africa,* ed. L. Carl Brown (Washington, D.C.: 1966); L. Carl Brown, "The Religious Establishment in Husainid Tunisia," in *Scholars, Saints and Sufis: Muslim Religious Institutions since 1500,* ed. Nikki R. Keddie (Berkeley and Los Angeles: University of California Press, 1972).

2. For a history of Islam in Libya, see E.E. Evans-Pritchard, *The Sanusi of Cyrenaica* (Oxford: Oxford University Press, 1949); Salaheddin Hassan Salem, "The Genesis of Political Leadership in Libya, 1952–1969" (Ph.D. diss., George Washington University, 1973); Ettore Rossi, *Storia di Tripoli e della Tripolitania dalla conquista araba al 1911* (Rome: Instituto per L'Oriente, 1968).

3. The history of this period is recounted in Lisa Anderson, *The State and Social Transformation in Tunisia and Libya, 1830–1980* (Princeton: Princeton University Press, 1986).

4. For a discussion of the relations between the Sanusi and the non-Sanusi ulama, see Lisa Anderson, "Religion and Politics in Libya," *Journal of Arab Affairs* 1, no.1 (Autumn 1981).

5. For more on this period, see Clement Henry Moore, *Tunisia since Independence: The Dynamics of One-Party Government* (Berkeley and Los Angeles: University of California Press, 1965).

6. The literature on the sources of the Islamic revival is vast. Among the particularly useful surveys are Edward Mortimer, *Faith and Power* (New York: Random House, 1982); Malise Ruthven, *Islam in the Modern World* (New York: Oxford University Press, 1984). On the impact of the events in France in 1968 on the Tunisian Islamists, see the comments of MTI spokesman Jebali Hamadi quoted by Louise Lief, "Tunisian Leader Grapples with Pro-Islamic Trend," *Christian Science Monitor,* 1987.

7. Elbaki Hermassi, "La société tunisienne au miroir islamiste," *Maghreb-Machrek,* no. 103 (January–March): 40.

8. Cited in Moore, 57.

9. Ibid.

10. On the development of the Islamist movement in Tunisia, see Hermassi, "La société tunisienne au miroir islamiste"; Susan Waltz, "Islamist Appeal in Tunisia," *Middle East Journal* 40 (Autumn 1986); Marion Boulbi, "The Islamic Challenge: Tunisia since Independence," *Third World Quarterly* 10, no.2 (April 1988); Souhayr Belhassen, "L'Islam contestaraire en Tunisie," *Jeune Afrique,* nos. 949–51, (March 14–28, 1979): the articles collected in Rashid al-Ghannushi, *Maqalat* (Paris, 1984).

11. Dirk Vanderwalle, "From the New State to the New Era: Toward a Second Republic in Tunisia," *Middle East Journal* 42 (Autumn 1988): 612.

12. Vanderwalle, 608; Francis Ghiles, "Tunisian Trial Fails to Halt Radical Groups," *Financial Times,* August 28, 1987.

13. Patrick E. Tyler, "Tunisia Targeting Islamic Radicals in an Uncustomary Clampdown," *Washington Post*, April 10, 1987.

14. On religion and politics in Qaddafi's Libya, see Lisa Anderson, "Qaddafi's Islam," in *Voices of Resurgent Islam*, ed. John Esposito (New York: Oxford University Press, 1983); Ann Elizabeth Mayer, "Islamic Law and Islamic Revival in Libya," in *Islam in the Contemporary World*, ed. C.K. Pullapilly (Notre Dame, 1980); George Joffe, "Islamic Opposition in Libya," *Third World Quarterly* 10, no.2 (April 1988); and John Davis, *Libyan Politics: Tribe and Revolution* (Berkeley and Los Angeles: University of California Press, 1987).

15. Muammar al-Qaddafi, *Thus Spoke Colonel Moammar Kazzafi* (Beirut: 1974), 61.

16. Exegesis of the *Green Book* is a required subject in the Libyan university curriculum, which accounts for the substantial body of more or less useful literature. Among the more interesting scholarly discussions are John Davis, *Libyan Politics;* Marius K. Deeb and Mary Jane Deeb, *Libya since the Revolution* (New York: Praeger, 1982); S.G. Hajjar, "The Jamahiriya Experiment n Libya: Qadhafi and Rousseau," *Journal of Modern African Studies* 18 (1980).

17. Qaddafi, 12.

18. See Anderson, "Qaddafi's Islam": Herve Bleuchot and Taoufik Monastiri, "L'Islam de M. El Qaddafi," in *Islam et politique au Maghreb*, ed. Ernest Gellner and Jean-Claude Vatin (Paris: Editions du CNRS, 1981); H. Mammeri, "Libye: Islam et ideologie," *Maghreb-Machrek* 82 (January–March 1979).

19. Cited in S.A. al-Assiouty, "Le Coran contre le fiqh: A propos du mariage d'apres le Livre Vert du M. Al Qaddhafi," in *Le Maghreb musulmane en 1979*, ed. Christiane Souriau (Paris, 1981), 14.

20. Davis, 51.

21. Joffe, 625.

22. Ibid., 629–30; Francois Burgat, "Coran contre Livre Vert?" *Le Monde,* December 30, 1986.

23. Joffe, 631.

PART III

Southwest Asia and Central Asia

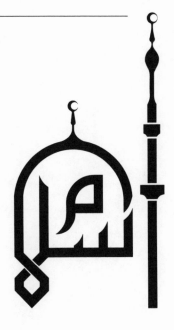

10

The Mujahidin

and the Future

of Afghanistan

OLIVIER ROY

THERE IS A STRANGE coincidence in the chronology of events in Iran and Afghanistan: in 1978, upheavals against the Shah in Iran and against the Communist regime in Afghanistan; in 1979, the triumph of the Iranian revolution and the Soviet invasion of Afghanistan; in 1988, the cease-fire in the Gulf and the beginning of the Soviet withdrawal from Afghanistan. Nonetheless, the impact of the Iranian revolution on the Afghan Mujahidin has been minimal, except as far as the Shii minority is concerned. Even in this case, the assessment of the Iranian Shii influence has to be balanced. The Afghan Mujahidin movement is a part of the "fundamentalist" wave that swept the Muslim world in the early 1980s. This "fundamentalism" is for the most part rooted in and stresses Sunni rather than Shii identity.

Fundamentalism in Afghanistan

Discussions of "fundamentalism" have been clouded by the failure to distinguish between fundamentalism as a political ideology (which I call Islamism) and fundamentalism as the sole desire to return to the *Sharia* (Islamic law) and an authentic Muslim way of life. This distinction separates Islamic revivalism from Islamic revolution. The future of Afghanistan, which now lies in the hands of the Mujahidin, will be determined not by a confrontation between a secular, nationalist, and moderate program on one side versus a fundamentalist movement, whether radical or conservative, on the other. All Mujahidin movements advocate an Islamic state and the implementation of the *Sharia*. Whoever may be in charge in Afghanistan next year, the country will be known as the Islamic Republic of Afghanistan. The question before us is, What is the political meaning of this "Islamization"? And of course, the answer varies a great deal according to the different political actors involved in the issue.

THE TRADITIONAL FUNDAMENTALISM OF THE SUNNI MULLAHS

For traditional Sunni mullahs, an Islamic state means that *Sharia* is implemented, whoever is in charge (a king, a president, a general, or an assembly). They do not care about the political form of the state, nor do they advocate revolution or social change; theirs is a purely legal conception of Islamization. Almost all mullahs in Afghanistan were trained through the private *madrasa* (religious school or seminary) system and share its conservative and legalistic views. The bulk of them joined the *Harakat-i Enqelab-i Islami* party (Movement of Islamic Revolution), which, despite its name, does not advocate an Islamic revolution. It is typical of the confused Western view that this party, led by Mawlaui Nabi Mohammadi, is seen as a moderate and nationalist one, opposed to the so-called fundamentalist parties. But, if the mullahs are not fundamentalist, who is?

THE DICHOTOMY OF THE TRIBAL WORLD

It is also common for outside observers of Afghanistan to stress the secular outlook of Pashtun tribal common law and customs.[1] In fact, the enforcement of daily religious prescriptions often seems stronger in the country's tribal areas than in nontribal areas: The nonrespect of the pillars of the faith, like fasting, can cost one's life, and women are more secluded in tribal areas than in northern Afghanistan. It is true that there is a tension between tribal traditions and worldview (*Pashtunwali*) and strict compliance with *Sharia*; but like the Sunni mullahs, tribesmen advocate the application of *Sharia* as far as everyday life is concerned, even if patterns of both internecine and external warfare as well as political loyalties and affiliations tend to be shaped according to tribal customs. The present jihad enhances this support of the imple-

Roy

mentation of *Sharia*: It is a sui generis move, frequent in Afghan history, where tribesmen engaged in jihad choose mullahs as leaders in place of the traditional tribal aristocracy.[2] In tribal areas, the movement toward an indigenous Islamization has had nothing to do with the Iranian revolution. Indeed, this Islamization has typically given ground to Wahhabism, which, of course, is quite opposed to Iranian influence. (The fact that the Wahhabis came with huge amounts of money made it easier to reconcile booty, or *ghanimat*, and faith.)

The tension between tribal institutions and Islamization rarely leads to open confrontation but usually gives way to a kind of compromise, perhaps because this tension is not so much between opposed vested interests as it is rooted in the mind of every tribesman. In the south of Afghanistan, where most of the Mujahidin groups are headed by mullahs, the coordination among various fronts and factions is typically ensured by *jirga* and *shura*, both meaning "councils," but the former is a Pashtu word and a tribal institution, the latter a Koranic concept. The innovation as far as tribal tradition is concerned is that these coordinating bodies are headed by mullahs, even if they operate as traditional tribal councils. Consensus is the rule, rather than compliance with religious legal regulations as interpreted by mullahs.

The opposition between Islamic and tribal systems is stressed by former khans (traditional local notables) in exile who are dreaming of the past, but that view is no longer valid. Whether the opposition ever really existed or is a kind of reinterpretation for political purposes is open to question. It is accurate to say that the political views of the tribesmen are secular and that they do not advocate an Islamic revolution, but it would be a mistake to say that their *Weltanschauung* is also secular. Islam is a way of life, and tribesmen are very sensitive to the propaganda waged by the mullahs throughout the war against "non-Islamic" behavior (hence the success of Wahhabism in highly tribal areas such as Pech and Kunar valleys).

If tribesmen also support implementation of *Sharia*, do they have the same political views as the mullahs, that is, an indifference toward who applies this program in Kabul? In fact, contrary to the mullahs, Pashtun tribesmen do care about who is in charge in Kabul: It has to be a Pashtun supported by the tribes. At the political level, historical legitimacy plays a bigger role than compliance with *Sharia*. Dichotomy between political interests and everyday fundamentalism is characteristic of the Afghan Pashtun tribes. This explains why a clerical party like

Harakat, which is particularly strong in tribal areas, could favor both the return of the king and the implementation of *Sharia*, even if the constant endeavor of all kings since 1901 has been to edge out the mullahs from the political scene and to build a modern and secular constitutional and judicial system. At the beginning of the war, tribesmen joined with leaders such as Nabi, Gaylani (of the National Islamic Front) and Mojaddidi (National Liberation Front), but Khales (head of *Hezb-i Islami*, or the Islamic party, not to be confused with Hekmatyar's party of the same name) made a breakthrough in tribal areas, as did other Islamist parties (Jamiat and Sayyaf's *Ittihad*). This breakthrough is typical of the reinforcement of the fundamentalist trend in tribal ideology. In 1988 the majority of the tribal commanders around Kandahar belonged to an Islamist party, while the former tribal establishment, royalist and secular, kept control of the Kandahar refugee camps in Pakistan.

THE POLITICAL ISLAM OF THE YOUNG ISLAMISTS

Afghan Islamists are young, middle-class intellectuals educated in the governmental modern school network before the Communist coup d'état. They live in a secular, generally nontribal (or detribalized) environment, and most have studied in scientific faculties, not in the arts or religious faculties. They became politicized in the 1960s and have been influenced by modern political ideologies. Their aim is a political revolution, and they view Islam more as a political ideology than as merely a religion. In this regard, most of them view the Shii versus Sunni opposition as irrelevant. Their three main sources of influence were the Egyptian Sayyid Qutb, the Pakistani Abul Ala Mawdudi, and the Iranian Ali Shariati.

As far as state power is concerned, the Islamists advocate a revolution, a social change, and for them Islamization is more a political process than a legal one. They see the fundamentalism of traditional mullahs as narrow-minded and purely legalistic. They reject the tribal system because it contradicts the nature of the *umma* (Islamic community) and is an obstacle to taking power. The Islamists tend to join one of three political parties, with the main opposition being between the moderate *Jamiat-i-Islami* (Islamic Society) led by Rabbani and Gulbuddin Hekmatyar's radical *Hezb-i Islami* (Islamic party). (The third party is an Hezb-i Islami splinter group that is also called *Hezb-i Islami* and is headed by Yunus Khales.) If we consider the Islamists' ideology,

Roy

the congruence with Khomeinism is obvious; as Imam Khomeini wrote to President Khamenei in January 1988, the achievement of the revolution is more important than the strict implementation of *Sharia*. The relative priority of these goals is the watershed between Islamists and fundamentalists.

But if revolution supersedes *Sharia* it does not mean that reference to *Sharia* is irrelevant for the Islamists. The Afghan Islamists used *Sharia* to legitimize their new power against tribal institutions, but for that they, like their Iranian counterparts, needed to ally with the clergy against the traditional establishment. In Afghanistan this alliance was achieved only through the jihad against a foreign and infidel invasion. Thus, Afghanistan and Iran are the only Muslim countries where Islamists and clerics merged, but the respective historical backgrounds of this alliance gave quite different outlooks to Afghanistan's Mujahidin and Iran's Hezbollahis, which prevents any real affinity between them.

PRESENT FUNDAMENTALISM AND ETHNIC SEGMENTATION

The most notable characteristic of the Afghan Islamist movement is that it achieved its success among the peasantry. This is probably the only such case in the contemporary Muslim world, but it is not due to the peculiar nature of the Islamist movement. In fact, the background of most of the Islamist Mujahidin "commanders" (young, educated urbanites) is not very different from that of their Iranian or Egyptian counterparts.[3] It was the Communist coup and the Soviet invasion that drove the Islamist workers into the countryside, where they had no previous political influence. The exile of most of the former establishment deprived the peasantry of its traditional elite, and the spirit of jihad merged intellectual Islamists and traditional mullahs within the framework of Mujahidin Islamist political parties.[4]

The rooting of Islamism into Afghanistan's peasant society is a consequence of the war, but it produced a backlash in the ideological purity of the movement, which is especially obvious in the Jamiat-i-Islami party, now the biggest political group in Afghanistan. The Islamist workers became more conservative and toned down the revolutionary aspects of their political and social doctrines. This trend was necessary to gain the confidence of a conservative peasant society and was facilitated by a social change that had already been achieved through the war: There were fewer powerful landowners, the aristocracy went into exile, and a better share for tenants resulted from depopulation. In a

Afghanistan

way, the social demands that make the Islamists advocate a "revolution" (perceived injustices, a secular regime, and their own interest in social advancement) have been partly fulfilled. A new generation of leaders has emerged, including intellectuals, mullahs, and tribal fighters, who all refer more to the *Sharia* than to Islamic revolution and who have to adapt the political parties' structures to a traditional and sometimes tribal society. Both tribalism and Islamism lost some ground: The three categories of leaders (intellectuals, mullahs, and tribesmen) tend to adopt a "fundamentalist" conception of the society, the lowest common denominator of the jihad.

Hekmatyar's radical Hezb-i Islami is the only party to retain an Islamist revolutionary ideology, a characteristic consistent with the fact that the party lost influence among Mujahidin fighters inside Afghanistan but won support among the refugees, who, in a way, are the new urbanites of Afghanistan (as it did in Iran and Egypt, Islamism tends to find a social basis among recently urbanized and uprooted peasants, of whom there were relatively few in prewar Kabul). But this homogenization of the political differences among Mujahidin (with the exception of Hekmatyar's followers) does not account for the political game now being played in Afghanistan.

The main issue is not social nor ideological but ethnic. This is not to say that parties now correspond to ethnic groups and that there will be an ethnic civil war in Afghanistan. In fact, to understand the ethnic factor in Afghanistan, we need to distinguish between "macroethnic" and "microethnic" groups. "Macroethnic" groups are those groups that appear on the so-called ethnic maps of Afghanistan and whose existence justified the Soviet endeavor to create "nationalities" in Afghanistan on the basis of a common language, culture, history, and territory. They are mainly Pashtuns, Tadzhiks, Uzbeks, Hazaras, Baluchis, and Turkmen, but even to label all these as "ethnic groups" is questionable.[5] In fact, even if belonging to a particular ethnic group does play a role in political affiliation (Jamiat is 60 percent "Tadzhik," Khales's and Hekmatyar's parties are mainly Pashtun), no political party among the Seven Parties Alliance in Peshawar expresses the interests of one ethnic group.

Ethnic identity is only one of several factors determining political affiliation in Afghanistan.[6] There is another dimension that plays a major role in political attitudes and feuds at the local level: Every Afghan (at least in the countryside) belongs to a "microethnic" group called a *qawm*. *Qawm* is the term used to designate any segment of society bound by solidarity ties; it may refer to an extended family, a clan, an occupational group, or a village, and so on. *Qawm* is based on both kinship and client/patron relationship. Before being an ethnic group, a *qawm* is a solidarity group, which protects its members from encroachments by the state and other groups (*qawm*) but which is also the scene of internal competition between contenders for local supremacy.[7] At the local level *qawm* affiliations are more pertinent than other factors. No political system, including the Islamist one, was able to supersede, not to say destroy, these rules of the game. It explains why a vocal revolutionary approach, stressing the necessary implementation of a new Islamic state apparatus that supersedes traditional affiliations, is doomed to fail in the Afghanistan countryside. It is why the Afghan Sunni Islamists had to water down their ideology; it is why the Iranian revolution did not appeal to the rural Afghans.

Only one ethnic group, the Shii Hazaras, did in fact strengthen its common identity and supersede "microethnic" affiliations throughout the war. But is that phenomenon a consequence of the spread of the Iranian revolution among them? To answer that question, it must be recognized that in contrast to the non-Hazara Shii, the Hazaras perceive themselves and are perceived by others as first an ethnic group, then a religious one. The Hazaras use the word *mellat* to define themselves; the others say *qawm*, while the Pashtuns in particular stress the racial features of the Hazaras (which, in fact, are less evident than, for example, those of the Turkmen). When Shii belong to the same ethnic groups as their Sunni neighbours, they tend to have better relations with them. This is true of the Hezbollahis in Herat, the Kizilbash in Kabul, and the Pashtuns in Kandahar.

The Afghan Shii Community

To assess the impact of the Iranian revolution in Afghanistan, we must draw a clear distinction between the Shii and the Sunni. As we have seen, the Shii/Sunni distinction is perceived by the Afghan peasants as mainly a matter of ethnic identity and by the ulama as a theological split (the Shii being considered almost heretics since Afghan ulama were mostly educated in the Indian subcontinent in a strongly Sunni Hanafi atmosphere). But for the Islamist intellectuals, who used to stress the unity of the *ummah* and to read Ali Shariati, the success of the Iranian revolution was perceived as a good opportunity both to by-pass the segmentation of the Afghan resistance and to get new and effective foreign support in the fight against the Communist regime and the Soviets. The fact that official Iranian propaganda of that time avoided classical Shii references and stressed the unity of the Muslim world facilitated this early enthusiasm for the Iranian revolution. It has been Iranian policy toward the Afghan resistance that has antagonized most of the Sunni Islamist Mujahidin. My own experience traveling from Paktya to Herat in 1982 confirmed that the split between supporters of the Iranian revolution and the Afghan Sunni resistance already existed (1981 was probably the critical year). Before analyzing the reason for this split, let us look more closely at the Afghan Shii community.

Shii Muslims constitute perhaps 15 percent of the Afghan population (the Shii Alliance in Iran recently claimed the figure is 30 percent).[8] The Afghan Shii are mainly Hazaras, a Persian-speaking ethnic group living in the central part of Afghanistan and subdued by the Kabul government in 1892. Most Hazaras are poor peasants, dominated by *arbab* or *mir* (landowners) and *sayyid* (descendants of the Prophet Muhammad), who are far more venerated in Hazarajat than elsewhere in Afghanistan. In Kabul many Hazaras work as porters, cooks, and cleaners, but a majority of them have succeeded in becoming rich traders. Hazaras are generally despised by Sunni Afghans and resent what appeared as a Pashtun colonialism in their lands through central administration and nomads, who bought or seized Hazara lands for pasture. During the 1970s, tens of thousands of Hazaras went to Iran as workers.

In the cities other Shii groups are to be found. The Kizilbash in Kabul, like the Shii in Kandahar, are probably descendants of Iranian soldiers and civil officers established in the mid seventeenth century. Both groups assimilated with the surrounding population in terms of language but have maintained a strong Shii identity. In Herat, the Shii population seems to be indigenous, Herat having once been a part of the Safavid empire. Urban Shii are well educated and assimilated.

In the past, Afghan Shii identified themselves with Iran in order to counterbalance the hostility of their Sunni-dominated environment. During the 1960s pictures of the Shah were to be found where Khomeini's picture is now. But as early as the 1950s a revivalist movement took hold of the community. A new Shii clergy, well educated and activist, regained some influence due to the edging out of the traditional establishment after the nineteenth-century wars, despite King Zaher's efforts to beef up traditional Hazara leadership through the National Assembly elections of the 1960s. This new clergy acquired legitimacy through its direct link with the Iranian ayatollahs established in Najaf: Traditional identification with Iran and religious legitimacy were thereby merged. It is not clear exactly when young Afghan clerics first found their way to Najaf and Karbala. But the migration persisted from the 1950s until the Gulf war, while some lay Hazara emigrated to Iran and Iraq in search of work, sometimes finding the opportunity to study there as well. A milieu of émigrés, both secular and clerical, was thus created, and the group became highly politicized and influenced by contemporary political debates. Most of the present cadres of the Shii movement in Afghanistan are offspring of this generation, politicized between 1950 and 1980.

These travels of Afghan Shii in Iran and Iraq led to an "Iranization" of the Shii community in Afghanistan. Edwards and Kopecki note that typical Iranian Shii rituals (e.g., celebration of *Muharram* and use of tape-recorded sermons on Husayn's battle with oppressors) were introduced in Afghanistan as early as the 1950s.[9] A recent "Iranization" of the Afghan Shii community is obvious in other respects, such as in names and patronyms (use of *agha*, or "Mister," and of patronyms ending in *i*).

The spread of revivalist ideas dates back to 1950 when Sayyid Ismail Balkhi, a cleric recently back from Iraq, engaged in religiopolitical itinerant preaching that eventually led to his arrest. Other Shii clerics became active in the 1960s, including Waez in Kabul and Sheykh Mohseni in Kandahar. All these figures share two important characteristics. First, their religiopolitical activities preceded the Iranian revolution, which means the radicalization of the Afghan Shii community is not a consequence of the Iranian revolution but part of a broader Shii movement more centered in Najaf and Karbala than in Qum.[10] Second, they were mainly disciples of Ayatollah Hakim, until his death in 1970, and then of ayatollahs Khoi or Shariatmadari, not of Ayatollah Khomeini. Today's two most prominent Afghan Shii clerics, Sheykh Assef Mohseni (head of the *Harakat-i Islami*, or "Islamic Movement") and Qorban Ali Mohaqeq (from Turkmen Valley and now living in Iran and not involved in politics), are disciples of Khoi. Only the third and lesser-known cleric in the present hierarchy, Taghadossi, is a disciple of

Khomeini; also from Turkmen, he now heads the Afghan *Pasdaran*, or "Guardians."

The Shii youth were also agitated by leftist (Maoist) and nationalist movements. Strangely enough, for the Hazaras there were no clear-cut distinctions among leftist, nationalist, and clerical movements as there were for the Sunni. The reason is that supporters of all these movements, except for a few clerics like Mohseni, expressed first an Hazara identity. This explains why, at the outset of the upheaval against the Communist regime, the Hazaras were the only ethnic group to establish a political organization on an "ethnic" base, even if this organization (the *Shura-yi Ittefaq-i Islami-yi Afghanistan*, or "Islamic Council of the Unity of Afghanistan") never acknowledged its purely Hazara or Shii identity. The *Shura* was created by clerics like Sayyid Ali Beheshti, *mir* (landowners), and intellectuals in the summer of 1979 when the Hazarajat was almost entirely free of any government presence (except Bamyan, which was evacuated by the Communists in the summer of 1988). On a trip to the area in 1982, I witnessed that the *Shura* was effectively in charge of two-thirds of the Hazarajat. On a return visit in 1984, it appeared that the *Shura* was reduced to a small district (Nawur), which was taken by the radical Shii elements in summer 1988. The change, as we shall see was a consequence of the Iranian policy. But first let us review the Shii political parties.

The Shii parties are divided between independent and pro-Khomeini parties; all of the pro-Khomeini parties except *Harakat-i Islami* are headed by former disciples of Ayatollah Khomeini. When the *Shura* split in 1982, members who were disciples of Khomeini went out to join or create pro-Khomeini parties, while most of the Khoi followers stood with Beheshti, a traditional cleric, disciple of Khoi, and head of the *Shura*. In general, Khomeini's followers among Afghan Shii are younger and of course more radical than Khoi's followers.

THE INDEPENDENT SHII PARTIES

The *Shura-yi Ittifaq-i Islami* (Islamic Council of the Union), headed by "Ayatollah" Beheshti (from Waras and educated in Najaf under Khoi) and by Sayyid Jaglan (a former military officer of a traditional family from Khawat), was not a political party but an administrative council that claimed to bring together the different strata of the Hazara society; in fact the *sayyid* were dominant in the group. The council was founded in September 1979 in Waras, where an Hazara congress gathered after the complete eradication of Kabul administration in the area. This council was not recognized by either Iran or Pakistan. At the beginning Sayyid Beheshti paid lip service to Imam Khomeini, but soon the conservative nature of the group (even if some Maoists were pushing, under cover, for a more radical social approach) antagonized the pro-Iranian elements.

In addition, a small, independent, and effective organization exists in Bamyan, the *Mustazafin* headed by Hashemi, which was influenced by the leftist lecture of Ali Shariati made by the Iranian *Mujahidin-e Khalq*. Another Shii group exists in Nimruz Province on the Iranian border; made up of former Maoists, headed by Parwiz, and known as the "Front of Nimruz," it is said to have adopted a more pro-Iranian attitude, but little has been heard from it since 1982.

THE PRO-IRANIAN SHII PARTIES

Most of the pro-Iranian Shii parties were formed by young clerics and workers returned from Iran. It is worth noting that a young worker returning from Iran to Hazarajat, after having learned to read and write and having participated in the revolution, is perceived by the Hazara peasant as one of the "educated," an "intellectual" rather than a toiler, and so the worker thinks as well. That perception explains the alliance between young clerics and intellectuals; they were both "new people," excluded from the traditional elites (*sayyid* and *mir*) and having a recent urban background.

Iranian influence grew in Hazarajat because of two main factors: first, the traditional link between Afghan Shii and Iran, and second, the social tensions inside Hazarajat, which were worse than in other parts of Afghanistan. In Hazarajat, the *sayyid* are a genuinely endogamic caste to whom people used to pay taxes known as *khums*, and the landowners were stronger than elsewhere in Afghanistan. It was not unusual to have a *mir* owning more than one village, a quite uncommon pattern in Sunni Afghanistan. The rooting of pro-Iranian parties among the Hazara peasantry was made possible by the alliance of the new educated generation back from Iran or Iraq with some of the poor tenants against the old establishment of *sayyid* and *mir*, who were unable to unite against the threat.

The pro-Iran political parties are all members of the Eight Parties Alliance established in 1986 and based in Qum. The alliance includes the following parties:

The *Harakat-i Islami* (not to be confused with the Sunni Harakat-i Enqelab-i Islami) headed by Sheykh Assef Mohseni, a cleric from Kandahar, is the party least dependent on Teheran. Founded in 1979 among urban Shii, it has never been linked with the *Shura*. In 1979, following Khomeini regime's seizure of American documents advocating support for Mohseni, then established in Iran, he was put under house arrest. Once released, his headquarters were reestablished in Qum. But in January 1988, without breaking his ties with the Eight Parties Alliance, Mohseni moved to Islamabad. The Harakat recruited mainly among educated urban Shii of all ethnic backgrounds (Mohseni himself is said to be Pashtun). The party is strong on the eastern fringes of Hazarajat, around and inside Kabul (under commander Sayyid Anwari). Harakat is the only Shii party to maintain constant military involvement against the Soviets. The party kept a moderate line as far as internecine feuds between Hazaras were concerned; like Jamiat, it shifted from a strong Islamist ideology to a middle-of-the-road position. Relations between Harakat-i Islami and Jamiat are good.

Nasr is a purely Hazara party with a radical ideology. It is said to have been founded in Kabul before the war (in 1972 or 1978) and to have included many former young leftists and Hazara nationalists; its cadres are very young. Nasr waged a bloody war against the *Shura*, to which it has never belonged (this war is still going on around Nawar in Ghazni Province). Nasr is also opposed to the big landowning families; it is said to have executed some landowners and former notables such as Haji Nader in Turkmen Valley. The party is headed by a council. Nasr is strong in central and northern Hazarajat.

Sepah-i Pasdaran was founded around 1982 under direct Iranian supervision, apparently as an endeavor by the Iranian Pasdaran to bypass the political divisions among Afghan Shii by bringing together all pro-Iranian elements in the framework of the same movement. As is usual in Afghanistan, the structure created to unite other parties became a party among the others. Sepah came into existence as a splinter group from the *Shura*, headed by two clerics, Akbari from Behsud and Saddiqi from Nili. Sepah has the same ideology as Nasr but claims more clerical cadres. Geographically Sepah is intermixed with Nasr, and some clashes based on local rivalries have erupted between them.

Nehzat is a purely Hazara organization, which has some support in southeast Hazarajat and in the Hazara community in Herat.

Niru is a very small organization, which lost ground after the elimination of Hashemi in Qum in 1986.

Hezbollah is the expression of the Herat Shii. Hezbollah is headed by Qari Ahmad (or Qari Yekdast), a bright young layman from Herat. Hezbollah has hundreds of fighters in the vicinity of Herat and is said to be supported by Iranian President Khamenei.

Two other small organizations are part of the Eight Parties alliance in Qum; the *Jebhe-yi Mottahed-i Islami* (Islamic United Front) and *Dawat*. I have been unable to trace these two groups inside Afghanistan.

Iranian Policy toward Afghanistan

When the Soviets invaded Afghanistan, both Imam Khomeini and President Bani-Sadr took a hard line against Moscow, as did Ghotbzadeh as long as he was minister of foreign affairs. But when Bani-Sadr went into exile in the summer of 1981, the Iranian "radicals" who then took charge suspected the Afghan resistance of being pro-Western and conservative. Anti-Americanism was stronger than Muslim solidarity.

There was no drastic change in Iranian policy toward Afghanistan until the end of 1988.[11] Strongly opposed to the Soviet invasion, Iran pressed the Afghan Mujahidin not to make any concession to the Soviets but discouraged them from obtaining help from the United States, stressing the priority of implementing the Islamic revolution in the fight against the invaders. In fact, Iran consistently avoided any direct involvement on the side of the Mujahidin. But when the Geneva agreements were signed on April 15, 1988, Iran vehemently rejected them. The contradiction between a vocal hard line and a lack of commitment antagonized most of the Afghan Mujahidin, particularly the Sunni but eventually even some of the Shii as well.

The second key aspect of Iranian policy, although it was not publicly advocated, was its exclusive support for the Shii. Iranian policy toward Afghanistan was implemented from Qum until the fall of Mehdi Hashemi, a close adviser of Ayatollah Montazeri and in charge of exporting the revolution, in September 1986. In the wake of ensuing "normalization" effort the ministry of foreign affairs tried to regain control: It officially invited Rabbani, Sunni leader of Jamiat-i-Islami, to Teheran in December 1986 and March 1987, and it organized the first International Conference on Afghanistan in January 1989. But the ministry of the interior, under Mohtashemi, made it clear after the July 1988 cease-fire in the Persian Gulf that relations with Afghan Mujahidin, like relations with Lebanese Hezbollahis and Iraqi Shii, are under its jurisdiction as a part of the Iranian "back yard."

Until 1986, pro-Iranian Shii parties such as Nasr, Sepah, and Hezbollah received some military supplies from Iran under the direct supervision of Iranian *Pasdaran*. But this help could never match the amount and quality of weapons supplied by Pakistan to the Sunni.

The policy implemented first by Qum and then by Mohtashemi was consistent with the logic of Iran's exportation of the revolution. The Shii in Afghanistan, as in Lebanon and Iraq, were not supported for theological reasons but because they were seen as the vanguard of the Islamic revolution from an ideological point of view. The policy of exporting the revolution meant first ensuring the victory of the "radicals" inside the Shii community, then using this community as the revolutionary vanguard that would topple the illegitimate and satanic ruler. The first part of the program was successfully implemented from 1982 to 1984; the revolutionary parties, namely Nasr and Sepah, were able, after a bloody civil war among the Shii, to reduce the *Shura* to a small regional force. The second part never succeeded: The Iranian revolution had no impact among the Sunni. Let us examine why this is so.

REVOLUTIONARY IRAN AND THE SUNNI MUJAHIDIN

There has been some Iranian influence among the Afghan Sunni but in cultural, not political, terms. Revolutionary rhetoric pervaded all Mujahidin discourse; even conservative mullahs call the upheaval against the Communists a "revolution." Symbols were borrowed from Iran (tulips for *shahid*, or "martyrs"). Iranian customs and language became more common, due to long sojourns of Afghans in Iran (and also to the popular BBC Persian service). But as a general rule the identification of Iran solely with the Shii prevented the Iranian political model from spreading among the Sunni.

Iranian policy toward Sunni Mujahidin was ambiguous. Until 1988, without formally denouncing the Sunni parties of the Peshawar Alliance of the Seven, Iran made a distinction between the "Islamic" parties (that is, the "Islamists") and the "reactionary" parties (the so-called moderates), condemning any attempt to reach an agreement with the Soviets or to bring back former King Zaher. The Iranian media referred to the Mujahidin as "Afghan revolutionary Muslims," thus avoiding precise references to the different groups. Iran asked the

Sunni to adapt a "neither East nor West" policy and condemned the reliance on Western arms shipments, stressing the priority of Islamic revolution against military short-term gains. But in fact Iran never provided direct support even to the Sunni "Islamic" Mujahidin (Jamiat or the two Hezb parties). The official distinction between "Islamic" and "reactionary" parties meant only that the former were allowed to have offices in Teheran. Only recently has Iran tried to engage indirect discussions at the highest level with the Sunni parties of the Alliance of the Seven. The Iranians officially met with Rabbani in Teheran in December 1986, March 1988, and December 1988.

Instead of giving direct support to the "Islamic" parties, Iran tried to attract Sunni splinter groups. Some local Sunni fighting groups along the Iran-Afghanistan border were organized as *Hezbollah* groups (it is not clear whether they were part of the *Hezbollah* that we listed as a Shii party); these Sunni *Hezbollah* groups (but not the Shii) were disbanded by Ismail Khan of the Jamiat party in the summer of 1986. Iran also welcomed Sunni splinter group leaders such as Nasrullah Mansur from Harakat-i Enqelab, who was given a warm welcome in December 1987; Mawlawi Moazen, from Mojaddidi's National Liberation Front; and Qazi Amin, a dissident of Hekmatyar's Hezb-i Islami. A local figure from western Afghanistan, the *pir* of Obey, who created an organization called *Jamiat-i-Ulema* in 1980 (which was infiltrated by Maoists) and who left for Iran after clashes with Jamiat-i-Islami, used to play the token Sunni for interviews on Teheran Radio, supporting Iran's position against Saudi Arabia at the end of August 1987. A Jamiat splinter group in Herat, headed by Safiullah Afzali (assassinated in July 1987), received more Iranian support than did the dominant Jamiat leader, Ismail Khan, although in fact the Afzali group was sponsored by Wahhabi organizations.

It does not seem that Iran actually tried to implement a radical Islamic revolution among Afghan Sunni. The Iranians may have thought that the Sunni were too backward politically or that the Shii would be able to "revolutionize" their Sunni brothers without direct Iranian interference. The most reasonable interpretation is strategic: Iran wanted to keep a foothold and a leverage in Afghanistan through the Shii but was not eager to confront the Soviets or to see a premature victory of the Mujahidin, which could bring the United States back to the area.

Iran has always been unwilling to face a strong Sunni resistance and has kept some distance even from the more radical Sunni parties; the

Hezb-i Islami left Iran in 1984 due to disappointment in the lack of privileged support. Today, Jamiat is the only Sunni party to have an overall representation in Iran. The more favorable attitude of Iran toward Jamiat is due to the fact that it is a mainly Persian-speaking party and thus the natural ally of the Shii in case of an ethnic civil war in Afghanistan; but it has been also criticized by the Iranian press for being too conservative and pro-Western. In fact Jamiat is one of the few Sunni parties (along with Gaylani and Mojaddidi) to have friendly relations with Shii and to acknowledge the right of the Shii to have their own jurisdiction. On the field, there is a good cooperation between Jamiat commanders and the Shii Harakat-i Islami. For historical and cultural reasons, Afghan Pashtuns are generally more opposed to the Shii than are the Tadzhiks. Hekmatyar and Khales deny the right to implement a specific Shii system of law.[12]

THE IRANIAN INFLUENCE: WHY DID IT FAIL?

Iran's exclusive support of the Shii limited the country's influence in Afghanistan. In contrast to the Shii of Lebanon and Iraq, the Afghan Shii are a small minority, and they have generally been despised by other ethnic groups. Sunni ulama used to be rather anti-Shii for theological reasons, viewing them almost as heretics. Influence from the Muslim Brotherhood and Wahhabi movement, which increased among Afghan Mujahidin in the course of the war, did nothing to ease the relations between Shii and Sunni schools of thought. The fact that the Shii did little fighting against the Soviets and began plundering Sunni arms convoys in 1986 exacerbated these tensions. Only Mohseni's Harakat-i Islami has maintained good relations with most of the Sunni parties, perhaps because it is not a purely Hazara party.

The second major constraint of Iranian policy was the Gulf war. Iran needed leverage over the Soviets to minimize their intervention on the Iraq side, but the Khomeini regime was careful to avoid any direct or even indirect confrontation; the solution was to maintain the Shii Mujahidin's capacity to resist any Soviet offensive without allowing them to attack the Soviets. This policy succeeded in restraining the Soviets but had very negative side effects in Afghanistan: The Shii seemed to be excluded from the jihad. The result was a frustration among the Sunni who had the impression that they alone bore the war effort. Deprived of weapons, the Nasr and Sepah cadres began to plunder the Sunni convoys.

Roy

Moreover, the Iranians had a restrictive policy toward the Sunni groups fighting on their borders, especially the Jamiat; in particular, authorization to bring weapons from Pakistan through Iran was very rarely given. In 1986, it was forbidden to export any goods from Iran to Afghanistan, thus depriving the Mujahidin of food and medicines. Some Mujahidin commanders went so far as to say that Iran was in fact playing the Soviet card.

Despite these disputes, there have been some cases where the radical Shii united with Hekmatyar's party against more conservative groups, mainly in the northern provinces of Jozjan, Balkh, and Ghazni, but they are the exception. In the south, the strained relations between Hazaras and Pashtuns are now mainly based on traditional ethnic feuds. The Qarabagh and Ghazni incidents of August 1988, when heavy fighting took place between Hazara and Pashtun, were entirely ethnically driven.

The coherence of Iranian policy was also hampered by the factionalism in Iran's government. After the fall of Hashemi in Qum (1986), Afghan affairs were simultaneously handled by the ministry of the interior, which followed the same policy as Qum, and the ministry of foreign affairs, which advocated a more balanced and open policy.

Another obstacle was the opposition evolution of Sunni and Shii Islamism. As we saw, the condition for the rooting of "Islamism" (that is, political Islam) in Afghanistan is to adjust an urban revolutionary ideology to a traditional segmented society. Among Sunni, the Jamiat generally succeeded in adapting to traditional society. The task was in fact more complicated for the Shii parties than for their Sunni counterparts, as opposition in Hazarajat between backward peasants and young clerics returning from Najaf is stronger than between Sunni peasants from the Panjshir Valley and students from Kabul. The Hazara peasants used to be more conservative than those elsewhere, the Hazara students more radical.

Iranian influence was also limited by the recent spread in Afghanistan of an Arab conservative fundamentalism, which strongly opposed both the Iranian revolution and the Shii *mazhab* (school of thought and legislation). This move is, in fact, not so new: Since the 1950s the *madrasas* in Pakistan, where Afghan mullahs used to be trained, were subsidized by Saudi Wahhabi, a particularly strict, literalist, and orthodox sect. But the move toward fundamentalism intensified after the Soviet invasion of Afghanistan. Beginning in 1985, hundreds of

Arab "Muslim Brothers" and "Wahhabis" entered Afghanistan through the Islamist parties to wage a personal jihad. They were recruited mainly from among Saudi migrant workers and were dispatched to Peshawar in Pakistan in order to enter Afghanistan. Sometimes they also participated in religious propaganda, fighting Sufism, Shii influence, and any "deviant" attitude (smoking, laughing, etc.). Wahhabism is now well entrenched in the Kunar Province, particularly in Nuristan (Mullah Afzal) and Pech valleys, though it has been defeated in Badakhshan by local Jamiat leaders. But the influence of the Muslim Brothers has spread among the Sunni resistance, even if there is a strong Sunni Hanafi reassertion against this "foreign" propaganda.

THE CHANGE IN IRANIAN POLICY

Despite its vocal condemnation of the pro-Western policy of Pakistan, Iran never tried to challenge Pakistani control over the Sunni but instead asked for reciprocity. In fact, a de facto repartition occurred, with the Sunni remaining in Peshawar and the Shii in Qum. The Pakistanis avoided excessive interference in Shii affairs: Officially, until 1986 there were no Shii offices in Peshawar (they were established in Quetta), and Pakistan avoided openly supporting one Shii faction against another (although Islamabad indirectly supported some Hazara nationalist secular groups, such as *Ittihadia* and *Tanzim*). This de facto repartition created many logistical problems both for Jamiat, which was established at the Iranian border and generally not allowed to bring weapons from Pakistan through Iran, and Nasr, for whom the reverse was true. The consequence was the existence of two different alliances in Peshawar and Qum.

Until mid-1988, Teheran kept the same vocal hardline policy toward Afghanistan. In April it strongly condemned the Geneva accords signed by Islamabad, Kabul, Washington, and Moscow, which embodied for Teheran the complicity of the two superpowers. Teheran then proposed that the radical Sunni Mujahidin shift their headquarters to Iran so they could continue the fight to establish a true "Islamic state" in Afghanistan. But in the aftermath of the Gulf cease-fire, Teheran undertook an overall reassessment of its foreign policy; the exportation of the revolution was viewed a failure and the various pro-Iran Shii groups were in a difficult position. Differences occurred between Iranian "radicals" and "moderates," but a new trend emerged: Teheran

Roy

wanted to participate in the negotiation process and to reintegrate the Shii in local politics.

As far as Afghanistan was concerned, Teheran decided to join the post-Geneva negotiations and encourage the Shii to merge with the Sunni Alliance to form a provisional government. The direct negotiations between Moscow and the Mujahidin and the coming to power of Benazir Bhutto (more acceptable than Zia ul-Haq to Teheran because she has some familial Shii background and is supposed to be less influenced by Wahhabis and Americans) helped facilitate this change.

At the same time, the new Pakistani government adopted a more balanced policy toward the Sunni groups and Hekmatyar ceased to be the main beneficiary of military and political aid. In fact, the interests of both Pakistan and Iran were converging in creating a "Muslim" belt (Pakistan, Afghanistan, Iran, and perhaps Turkey), which in the eyes of Islamabad could thwart the threats of both India and the USSR, and in the eyes of Iran could prevent the United States from filling the political vacuum left by the Soviet withdrawal. After the renunciation of the "Islamic revolution" for Iran, the new "Muslim neutralism" could benefit both Iran and Pakistan. Both countries feel that to have a stable Mujahidin government in Afghanistan, with Shii and Sunni participation, is preferable to Lebanonization.

The changes of policy were embodied in the first International Conference on Afghanistan, held in Teheran in January 1989. The main "centrist" leaders of the Sunni Alliance (Rabbani, Mojaddidi, and Nabi) attended the meeting, while the radicals (Hekmatyar) and the royalists (Gaylani) were absent. In his inaugural speech, Velayati referred only to the "nonaligned character" and "Muslim identity" of Afghanistan, without any mention of revolution. The Shii were presented as a minority eager to preserve its rights, not as the vanguard of the revolution. Velayati also stressed the necessity of a political solution and of a joint venture between Pakistan and Iran to avoid an American comeback. The negotiations between both alliances pertained to the share of the Shii in the forthcoming Provisional Assembly: The Sunni proposed one-eighth, the Shii asked for 30 percent.

This strategy, consistent with the new Iranian policy, was also welcomed by the Afghan Shii. They were disappointed by Iran's lack of material support in the course of the war, which bore no comparison to the channeling of funds to the Lebanese Hezbollah, and were worried about a potential Pashtun post-war revenge. Heavy ethnic fighting occurred in August 1988 between Hazaras and Pashtuns near Ghazni, and the discrepancy between Western and Iranian aid widened the military gap between Shii and Sunni.

But this move toward a merging of the two alliances met strong opposition from the Pakistani military, the Wahhabi and Muslim Brothers lobby in Pakistan, and more radical Sunni parties (of Hekmatyar, Sayyaf, and Khales). This opposition, which led to the walkout of the Shii from the Provisional Assembly that gathered in Rawalpindi, Pakistan, in February 1989, can be readily explained. First, despite their alleged "radical" ideology, the Shii tended to go along with the Afghan "moderates," mainly Mojaddidi, who negotiated the Shii participation in the assembly, and the Jamiat. That would have weakened the "radicals" who were supported by the Pakistani military and the Wahhabis/Muslim Brothers lobby. More than that, the massive presence of the Shii in the assembly would have reduced the Pashtun share of the seats. The opposition of the more radical Sunni parties toward the Shii expresses as much a variant of Sunni fundamentalism as it does a Pashtun ethnic bias. Conversely, the rapprochement between Afghan pro-Iranian Shii and Sunni moderates indicates the superficiality of systematically identifying Iran with any kind of Muslim extremism.

Appendix: The Shii Policy of the Kabul Regime

The Khalqis used to hate the Shii. Thousands of Shii were indiscriminately killed in 1978 and 1979, mainly after the upheaval of Herat in February 1979, which was wrongly attributed to Iranian influence: hundreds of inhabitants of Chendawol, the Shii quarter in Kabul, were executed in June 1979.

However, Babrak Karmal tried to enlist Shii in his regime. The policy was threefold:

—to give a high visibility to Parcham Shii such as Sultan Ali Keshtmand, the prime minister from 1980 to 1988 and a Hazara from Kabul.
—to recognize the Hazaras as a "nationality" (*melliat*) in the Soviet sense of the word. A "High Council of Hazarajat" was created in Kabul (the chairman was Khadem Husseyn Beg).
—to treat Sunni and Shii equally in the religious institutions. The

Shii were always granted the second place: Sayyid Reza Afshari for the Council of Ulama in 1985; Sayyid Mohammad Ali Shah Tawakoli, deputy chairman of the Department of Islamic Affairs until 1985; Sheykh Mohammad Ewaz Saddiqi, deputy minister for Islamic affairs in early 1989.

But this policy was a failure for several reasons:

—it always lacked a territorial basis; the Hazarajat was almost entirely freed in 1979.
—the Shii enlisted in the regime were unknown among peasants and could not, for lack of roots, be used as a relay.
—the Khalq is mainly seen as strongly Pashtun nationalist; that is enough to prevent the Hazara from joining him. On the other hand, the Parcham regime never dared to proclaim autonomy for Hazarajat, which would have antagonized the Pashtuns and the Khalqis.
—the so-called representatives of the Shii were sometimes Ismailis (like Sayyid Mansur "Kayan"), who were not considered "orthodox" by the Shii clergy.
—the Shii Marxists were Maoists and hated the pro-Soviet communists.
—Generally speaking, the regime has never been able to achieve any credibility.

Prospects

The Afghan war brought both a reassertion of Shii identity through Iranization and of Sunni Hanafi identity, with the exception of Wahhabi pockets of influence. (Ismail Khan in Herat used to put pictures of General Zia on the walls and called the school closest to the Iranian border "Abu Bakr-i Saddid," after a caliph who is seen as illegitimate by most Shii.) A symmetric reassertion of Shii identity is obvious in Hazarajat: The disappearance of Pashtun nomads and Pashtun administration gave all the administrative powers to Shii, who are now armed and in power.

In the course of the war, the Afghan Shii were able to assert their identity and to establish an almost independent state in Hazarajat, although they do not advocate independence. In fact, more than ever the Shii think of themselves as Afghans, but they want a fair share of power and the recognition of Shii law by the state. The Shii already achieved a de facto parity with the Sunni through identification with the Iranian Islamic revolution, but not to the point where they are simply Iranian agents in Afghanistan. But at the same time, Sunni Mujahidin gave up all references to the Iranian revolution and took their most extreme ideological references from the Arab Muslim Brothers and Wahhabi. The Afghan war embodies the "Shii ghetto" in which the Iranian revolution has locked itself. In the future, Afghanistan might be an interesting test case to see how Iran will go along with the conservative brand of Sunni fundamentalism that is now spreading throughout the Muslim world, superseding the more progressive political Islam of the Islamist intellectuals. The Rushdie affair in February 1989 was an unprecedented endeavor from Imam Khomeini to appeal directly to the entire *ummah* on nonpolitical and purely religious grounds, without any reference to political Islam and revolution. Is this just a flash in the pan or the beginning of a long-term accommodation between the Shii brand of political Islam and Sunni fundamentalism?

There will be no Iranian-style revolution in Afghanistan. The more likely outcome is the probable emergence of a conservative, Sunni "Islamic republic," where the problem of relations with the Shii will be based on ethnicity rather than ideological or religious grounds. If there is a strong central state, the Shii will probably be able to retain a large degree of autonomy, even if Pashtun tribes try to regain some of their former privileges on Hazara grasslands and local armed clashes result. If there is no strong central state, Hazarajat will administrate itself with Iran acting as referee in domestic rivalries, and there will be numerous clashes on the Hazarajat borders. But the post–Gulf war Iranian policy will probably allow better relations between the Shii and Sunni in Aghanistan.

Shii Parties

The Eight Parties Alliance based on Qum contains:

Harakat-i Islami: led by Sheykh Assef Mohseni (Kandahar).
Nasr: founded by disciples of Khomeini; leaders are Azizullah Shafaq (Behsud), Abdel Ali Mazari (Mazar), Ghorban Ali Irfani (Yakaolang), Saddiqi (Turkmen).
Sepah-i Pasdaran (a split of *Shura*, in 1981): Akbari (former deputy of Beheshti), Zahedi (Ghazni), Taghadossi (Turkmen, the

most high-ranking after Mohaqeq and Mohseni), Saddiqi of Nili.

Hezbollah: based in Herat; Qari Ahmad, Mahmud Kateb.

Nehzat (close to Montazeri): Ifthekhari (a relative of Montazeri, from Jaghori), Zaki (Jaghori), Musavi (representative in Teheran).

Dawat: Sheykhzade (Ghazni).

Jebhe-yi Mottahed-i Enqelab-i Islami (a regrouping of small groups: Lulenji (Parwan), Alemi (Mazar), Qassemi (Behsud), Naqavi (Kandahar).

Niru (was close to Hashemi): Sayyid Zaher Mohaqeq (Behsud; not to be confused with the religious leader Qorban Ali Mohaqeq).

Other parties are:

Shura-yi Ittefaqh: Sayyid Beheshti, Sayyid Jaglan.

Mustazafin: Hashemi (was close to Iranian Mujahidin-e Khalq).

Notes

1. See Louis Dupree, *Afghanistan* (Princeton: Princeton University Press, 1980), 104.

2. See Akbar S. Ahmad, *Millennium and Charisma among Swat Pathans* (London: Routledge & Kegan Paul, 1976), 14, 54.

3. See Olivier Roy, "The New Political Elite in Afghanistan," paper presented at the Massachusetts Institute of Technology workshop on Political Elites and the Restructuring of the Political Order, Cambridge, November 1988.

4. For the logic of political affiliations, see Olivier Roy, *Islam and Resistance in Afghanistan* (Cambridge: Cambridge University Press, 1986).

5. For example "Tadzhik" is not used by most people who are so labeled on the ethnic maps. For the debate on what constitutes an ethnic group in Afghanistan, see Digard et al., *Le fait ethnique en Iran et en Afghanistan*, (Paris: Editions du CNRS, 1988).

6. For a further explanation, see Roy, *Islam and Resistance*, chapter 8.

7. For the definition of a *qawm*, see Roy, *Islam and Resistance*, chapter 1; Pierre Centlivres, *Un bazar d'Asie Centrale* (Weisbaden: Riechert, 1972), 158–59; Whitney Azoy, *Buzkashi, Game and Power in Afghanistan* (Philadelphia: University of Pennsylvania Press, 1982), 31–32.

8. The best survey of the Afghan Shii political movements is found in Rolf Bindemann, *Religion und Politik bei den schi'itischen Hazara in Afghanistan, Iran und Pakistan*, Occasional Papers *Ethnizität und Gesellschaft*, no. 7 (Berlin: Freie Universität Berlin, 1987). On the Afghan Shii and their politicalization, see David B.

Edwards, "Shii Political Dissent in Afghanistan," in *Shiism and Social Protest*, ed. Juan R.I. Cole and Nikki R. Keddie (New Haven: Yale University Press, 1986).

9. Lucas-Michael Kopecky, "The Imami Sayyad of the Hazarajat," in *Folk*, vol. 24 (Copenhagen, 1982) 91, 95; see also Edwards, 214.

10. See Olivier Roy, "Les Frontières de l'Iran," *Revue du Monde Musulman et de la Méditerranée* (Aix-en Provence), no. 48, 49 (1988): 266–80.

11. For an excellent presentation of the Iranian policy toward Afghanistan, see Zalmay Khalilzad, "Iranian Revolution and Afghan Resistance," in Martin Kramer, ed., *Shiism Resistance and Revolution* (Boulder, Colo.: Westview Press, 1987), chap. 14.

12. Interview with Hekmatyar, March 1987.

11

Soviet Central Asia:

Does Moscow Fear

Iranian Influence?

MARTHA BRILL OLCOTT

Central Asia: A Unique Muslim Region

Soviet Central Asia is probably the most remote of all the Muslim regions described in this book.[1] Since the decline of the great silk routes,
the physical isolation of this region has led to a relatively syncretic relationship between religion and culture.[2] Historically the main currents
of debate in the Muslim world were introduced slowly into this region,
and often through intermediaries who distorted the message in its
transmission. When the Russians annexed Central Asia in the nineteenth century, they furthered this isolation by restricting travel into
and out of the region, by introducing an elaborate system of censorship, and by placing religious schools and courts under state supervision.

The isolation of Central Asia was made more complete after the
Bolshevik takeover. For the past seventy years the Soviet regime has
pursued an avowedly antireligious policy in Central Asia. The severity
of this policy has varied over time. In the first decade of Communist
rule the regime vacillated between policies of religious persecution and
the grudging acceptance of a limited role for the religious establishment. But in the late 1920s Stalin ended this equivocation and em-
barked on a process designed to eliminate the independent religious es-

tablishments and to wipe out the practice of organized religion. All ecclesiastically owned property was nationalized, mosques and *madrasas* (Islamic schools) were closed, and thousands of Islamic clerics were shot or sent to prison camps.

During World War II a state-controlled Muslim religion board known as SADUM was organized in Central Asia.[3] SADUM was charged with reopening a couple dozen mosques and two madrasas to serve the Muslims of the region.[4] These religious establishments, staffed by SADUM-trained clerics, were, until 1989, the only sanctioned Muslim organizations in Central Asia. The SADUM-sponsored madrasa in Tashkent, Uzbekistan, known as the Imam al-Bukhari Institute, graduates less than a dozen young clerics yearly.[5] However, the activities of officially trained clerics are supplemented by those of thousands of "illegal" or self-designated clergy, who lead unsanctioned services in unregistered mosques or other public places. Officials in Uzbekistan have recently admitted that fifteen times more clerics are trained illegally than legally.[6] Others claim that the number of individuals receiving informal religious training is much greater.[7]

Given the extraordinary restrictions on religious life in the USSR, the social and political role of Islam has been different in Central Asia than in much of the Muslim world. This area is still physically isolated. Most of the borders of Central Asia are closed, although the technological revolution has created new ways for ideas to filter into this society.[8] Radio transmissions from abroad, smuggled cassettes, and even photocopy machines have all helped introduce "alien" ideas into Central Asia.

Nonetheless, despite all the official restrictions on the practice of religion, Islam appears to be a dynamic force in the lives of Soviet Central Asians. However, it is very difficult for Western analysts to assess the social and political role of Islam in Central Asia. We have access to many of the largest cities in the region, but long-term residence has been very difficult to arrange. Almost all the smaller cities where Muslim political activities appear to be most intense have been off limits to us, and the countryside is wholly inaccessible.

Thus, we are generally forced to fall back on the written record. But frank discussions of the social and political role of Islam in Central Asia have not been characteristic of Soviet writings, given the state's official claim to be an atheistic society. Even now, in the more open atmosphere of *glasnost* (openness), there are numerous complaints of the continuing restrictions on open discussion of the pervasiveness of religion in society. Nonetheless, some Soviet sources are more useful than others.[9] Scholarly publications and republic-level newspapers provide valuable information, especially if they are supplemented by a judicious use of *samizdat* (illegally printed material) or other forms of clandestine materials.[10] Despite the imprecision of our data base, such sources clearly indicate that there has been a religious revival in Central Asia.

But given the problems with our data base, it is very difficult to describe the precise nature of this revival, and it is really impossible to assess the relative importance of the various internal and worldwide trends that have encouraged it. Thus, it is unlikely that we will ever truly understand the role of the Iranian revolution in encouraging already-existing trends in Central Asia to seek solutions to the failures and inequities of the Soviet socialist system through advocacy of an Islamic order. But certainly the Iranian revolution had some effect; at the very least it provided those Central Asians who had access to short-wave transmissions a contemporary model of an Islamic society to go along with their more attenuated knowledge of their own Islamic past.

The Soviet Union and Iran share two common borders, one in Azerbaidzhan (in the Caucasus) and the other in southwestern Turkmenistan (in Central Asia). Azerbaidzhan, not Central Asia, is the area of the Soviet Union where the greatest direct influence of the Iranian revolution could be expected. There are Azerbaidzhanis on both sides of the Soviet-Iranian border, and historically they have thought of themselves as a single people.[11] Over 70 percent of the Azerbaidzhanis are Shiite Muslims,[12] but they are a Turkic people and are well aware of the harsh or indifferent treatment that their conationals have received from the government in Teheran both before and after the Islamic revolution. The Turkmens, the other Soviet-Iranian border population, are a Sunni population of Turkic extraction. Although there are reported to be about 500,000 Turkmens in Iran, these Tekke, Goklen, and Yomut tribesmen are all Sunni Muslims and have been only peripherally involved in the Iranian revolution.[13] The only major Persian-speaking population in Central Asia is the Tadzhiks, and they too are Sunni Muslims.[14]

Despite the fact that Iran shares a common border with two Soviet Muslim republics, events in Teheran are relatively remote for most Central Asians. Far more immediate are events in neighboring Afghanistan. Afghanistan borders on three Central Asian republics (Turkmen

SSR, Tadzhik SSR, and Uzbek SSR), and all of the principal Soviet Central Asian peoples have conationals in Afghanistan.[15] Afghanistan has had its own Islamic revival, influenced in part by events in Iran. This revival created its own internal political crisis that degenerated into a civil war, which in turn led to a Soviet invasion. Soviet Central Asians have not remained unaffected by these events, but the pressures created by the war are varied and often conflicting.

The Islamic revival in Central Asia has undoubtedly been most strongly influenced by internal changes in the Sovet Union. During the past decade the local population has had to respond to the stagnation of the Brezhnev years, the party purges in Central Asia during the Andropov and Gorbachev succession crises, and the current *perestroika* (reconstruction) campaign. These various official policies have provided climates that have alternatively supported and restricted the forces of religious revival.

The last years of Brezhnev's rule (1979–82) were a period of official benign neglect. Moscow's disinterest in local republic affairs enabled Central Asian party officials to turn a blind eye to the revival of traditional Islamic practices that was going on in the countryside and to ignore the revival of interest among the Central Asian urban elite in the intellectual roots of Islam and Islamic doctrine.

The reformers who came to power upon Brezhnev's death were less tolerant of this religious revival. During Yuri Andropov's brief rule (December 1982–February 1984) there was some evidence of a hardening of official attitudes toward the prevalence of Islamic practice in Central Asia. Moscow's criticism of the local party elite's acquiesence and even participation in the religious life of the Central Asian communities became far more frequent and strident after Gorbachev came to power in March 1985. But over time it became apparent that this attack on religion seemed to be motivated more by power politics than by a desire to stem the tide of Islamic revival within Central Asia. Once Gorbachev managed to dilute the power of the "old guard" of the Central Asian republic party organizations, he began to limit his attack on Islam to a discussion of the dysfunctions that traditional economic practices introduced into the Soviet economy.[16]

However, Gorbachev and the leadership that he put in place soon faced new challenges from nationalist sentiment triggered by the reform programs themselves. The most serious challenges to the nationality policy of the Soviet Communist party have come from the devel-

Olcott

opment of national fronts in the Baltic republics (Latvia, Lithuania, and Estonia) and from the continuing violent interethnic conflict in the Caucasus (Armenia, Azerbaidzhan, and Georgia). But although the political situation in the Central Asian republics is relatively quiet, the local population is aware of what is going on in other parts of the country and has responded by beginning to develop some fledgling reform movements of its own. At the time of writing in 1989, these groups are small, largely informal, and very inchoate in their demands. But there are growing signs of political activism in Central Asia, and while public protest has so far been linked most directly to party politics and public calls for increased national language education, there is a good chance that the already present religious subtext will become more explicit over time.

Islam in Central Asia

Soviet antireligious policy destroyed the dominant traditional Islamic establishment that had been centered in the mosques and seminaries of the medieval cities of Khiva, Bukhara, and Samarkand. However, the Soviets were far less successful in eliminating the more unstructured and informal religion that was practiced in the countryside, the Islam of the *Sufis*, self-claimed *Sufis*, self-trained mullahs, and unofficially trained mullahs. Thus, while the doctrinal basis of Islam has been lost to most Central Asians, much of the traditional Islamic culture of prerevolutionary Central Asia has been preserved. The economic, social, and political life in the region is still heavily influenced by a modified version of the traditional culture, and especially in the countryside this culture more closely approximates the Central Asia of the past than it does the society planned by the Communist social engineers in Moscow.

In recent years official Soviet sources have admitted that virtually all Soviet citizens of Muslim extraction still maintain at least a passive identification with Islam, and it is an identification strong enough to impede many of the Communist party's social goals. The party has admitted that while it can legislate that antireligious lectures be given, it cannot ensure that they are held or that their content is taken seriously. First Secretary K. M. Makhkamov of the Tadzhikistan Communist party recently admitted that in many areas of his republic, even in institutions of higher education, antireligious lectures appear in the official plan but are in fact never held.[17]

The various Muslim nationalities accept Islam as part of their cultural legacy and a source of their moral values.[18] Islam is the faith of their forefathers, and each of these nationalities places a strong emphasis on honoring their ancestors. For all the Muslim nationalities there is a fusion of religion and ethnic identity that is recognized by all who live in the region, regardless of what official position they may hold. Only in Moscow do social scientists or party propagandists seriously argue that the influence of Islam has been substantially curtailed

In Soviet Central Asia, an individual's entry into and departure from the world are commemorated by religious rituals. One's choice of profession is still influenced by a sense of preordained social role, and status is still often conferred by birthright. In the rural areas the party elite is often drawn from the same ethnic subcommunity that dominated in the prerevolutionary period. Religious leaders are drawn from families that claim descent from the Prophet or who have traditionally served Islam. Moreover, a religious establishment has managed to recreate itself. It is unofficial, local in nature, and self-perpetuating. But the population recognizes the religious authority of these leaders. The people fund their activities and allow them to train their successors.

The type of Muslim religious practice that has been preserved in the Soviet Union is generally based more on ritual than on doctrinal content. Because of the small number of clerics, mosques, and religious schools, the uniformity of doctrine and practice that results from supervision by a centralized religious hierarchy is almost completely absent. Consequently religious rituals have become more syncretic, often infused with local pre-Islamic rituals. The Soviet Central Asians consider themselves to be Muslims, even if there are those both inside and outside the Muslim world who reject that contention.

There is an almost definitional link between national and religious identity in Central Asia. Those who claim to be Muslims may be expressing pride in their ancestry rather than asserting their knowledge or acceptance of Islamic doctrine. It is useful to think of three distinct types of Muslim believers: "passive Muslims," "cultural Muslims," and "doctrinal Muslims," although people do not always fit neatly into these categories.[19]

"Passive Muslims" identify with Islam as an expression of their ethnic or national identity; they are Muslims because they are members of an historically Muslim community. These people may practice certain rituals, particularly those that are seen as signs of communal membership, but they do so to show respect for a culture or a national way of life. Virtually all Central Asians have at least this minimal identification with Islam.

Islamic customs centered on the commemoration of life have proved virtually impossible to eliminate in Central Asia. Male circumcision appears to be universally practiced across all sectors of society in the Muslim areas, including the children of party members.[20] The ceremony, generally held when a male child is between five and seven years of age, is a social necessity, for an uncircumcised male child is considered unborn and a family refusing to perform this act may be placed under communal interdiction.[21] In addition, most Central Asians receive ritual burials,[22] and even civil ceremonies for prominent local party leaders include some features of an Islamic burial. There have even been complaints that there are no manuals for how to perform a secular funeral.[23] Memorial rites marking the end of the forty-day mourning period and the first anniversary of a death are also universally observed and can be elaborate in scale.[24]

Most Central Asians seem to have a more active identification with religion than that described above. "Cultural Muslims" want to perpetuate Islamic customs precisely because they are religious rituals, but these believers have little or no awareness of the religious doctrine behind these practices. It is difficult to be precise about the size of this group, although it is clear that a large number of people in both urban and rural areas fall into this category.[25] One problem with Soviet survey research is the imprecision of the questionnaire categories. What one analyst describes as a "believer" another terms a "waiverer."

A 1971 study of rural Karakalpakia, by a scholar named Bazarbaev, reported that 78.5 percent of those surveyed said that they practiced Islamic customs and rituals.[26] Similar findings were reported in Bazarbaev's more recent survey of 1974–77, this time of school-age youth from three rural regions and four cities.[27] (These surveys define religious believers as people who practice religious rituals and celebrate religious holidays.) One should be cautious in generalizing from these results, however, because Karakalpakia is a remote rural region (in the northwest corner of Uzbekistan). There is no study as comprehensive as Bazarbaev's for any other Muslim region of the USSR. Most recent surveys have been far more limited both in scope and aims. But many of these studies still provide a sense of the pervasiveness of Islam. One excellent survey shows that believers are found in all social strata in rural Uzbekistan.[28] Corroboration of this data is found in Baialieva's survey of Kirghiz blue- and white-collar workers and peasants in 1977. Nearly one-third of those interviewed responded that they were believers.

Given the problems of data reliability, Soviet surveys can provide only a partial picture that should be supplemented by field reports of Soviet ethnographers. Many Soviet analysts tacitly acknowledge the contradiction between the data obtained in surveys and in field research. Baialieva claims that religion is dying out, but she admits that almost all the youth of her sample observe the principal Muslim religious holidays of *Uraz bairam* (*id al-fitr*, the culmination of Ramadan) and *Kurban bairam* (*id al-kabir*, the feast of Abraham's sacrifice) because they are now perceived as a national tradition.[30]

Family life, especially in the rural areas, is still strongly influenced by the pervasiveness of traditional values. There have been a number of studies that report continued popular observance of the *nikah*, an Islamic wedding ceremony performed by a mullah. Various surveys have provided contradictory evidence as to how widely practiced these religious rites are. Published reports indicate that about 50 percent of all couples who have their marriage registered at the ZAKS (civil registry) also have a religious ceremony.[31] In urban areas officials simply ignore these religious ceremonies. In rural areas local officials are themselves participants when their friends and relatives throw *nikah tois* (parties to follow the *nikah*) for their children, and until 1985 *Sharia* marriages of Komsomol (Young Communist Youth League) members went without reprimand. A number of other traditional prenuptial customs continue to be practiced, especially in the countryside. The most widespread of these is payment of the *kalym* (bride price), which continues with the knowledge and even the connivance of local rural authorities.[32] There are also reports of the continued existence of polygamy.

Recent Moscow-sponsored campaigns designed to limit such customary practices attack the notion that Islam can be used as a defense against the complete integration of women into the economy. Islamic customary wedding practices are said to reinforce the vision of women as wives and mothers, not the state-desired image of workers and citizens. Moreover, recently published Soviet data support the notion that the gender gap is greater in Central Asia than in other parts of the country. Central Asian women continue to want to have large families,[33] and those with large families usually do not enter the work force.[34]

Nationalism and religion are closely intertwined for the "cultural Muslims." But there is a spiritual dimension to their actions as well. The Soviet Muslims acknowledge that they are practicing Islamic rituals, even if they do not know the doctrinal basis of the customs that they are observing.

The third group of believers, the "doctrinal Muslims," is by far the smallest. It includes people who would be classified as believers by the criteria applied in most other Muslim countries. These are people who have at least some knowledge of Islamic doctrine and who try to work religion into their daily life. Most try to attend weekly prayers, and many pray daily. Some try to proselytize among nonbelievers in the community.

It is difficult to get precise information about the number of these people or to learn much about them in most published Soviet sources. Until recently most authors maintained that interest in religion was declining, but scattered in the literature are surveys that offer the opposite conclusions. Most of this research was experimental, such as the small survey done by a Kazakh ethnographer in the early 1970s, which asked both young and elderly recent converts to articulate why they became believers. Just over 60 percent of the young people surveyed said that they became believers because they had received formal religious instruction or because of the influence of their relatives. The remainder of the young people interviewed, as well as nearly 70 percent of the elderly converts, said that they became practicing Muslims because religion helped them cope with the problems of life and death.[35]

Other authors also point to the multiplicity of reasons that lead people to embrace religion. T. Saidbaev, a well-respected Kazakh scholar, maintains that there are three distinct groups of Muslim believers. The first group, the smallest in number, consists of people whose whole existence revolves around religion. They live close to a mosque and participate fully in its operation. The second group, much larger in size, consists of people who live close enough to a mosque to attend weekly services, but they do not involve themselves directly in the management of religious affairs. The largest group of believers are people who may live some distance from a mosque and who attend services only on an irregular basis. These people have some religious education but also participate fully in the life of the secular community.[36] Saidbaev offers virtually no data on the size of these communities, nor does he deal with their relationship to the official religious hierarchy. However, his argument leaves no doubt that the number of devout Muslims is far greater than those served by the officially trained religious hierarchy.

There is no simple relationship between Islam and society in Central Asia. Virtually all Central Asians maintain some sort of elemental tie with their Islamic heritage. For many, Islam provides the basis of the cultural and social fabric of their lives. For a small group of others, Islamic doctrine serves as a source of spiritual strength. But a political environment hostile to the transmission of formal religious teachings has inevitably warped the type of religion that has been preserved, and the deemphasis on the teaching of formal Muslim doctrine has meant that Soviet Central Asia has undergone its own form of Islamic revival.

Islamic Revival in Central Asia*

Soviet Central Asia began to experience an Islamic revival sometime in the middle or late 1960s. In fact, it may more properly be said to have experienced two religious revivals, one among the intellectuals in the cities and the other among the rural population. These two revivals seem to have been parallel phenomena, at times complementary and at times contradictory, but they have yet to fuse completely. The initial impetus was identical for both revivals. The relaxation of social and political tensions known as the "Khrushchev thaw" did not really catch up with life in Central Asia until the 1960s, after Khrushchev himself was out of office. Once the use of coercion as the primary means of political control was deemphasized in the countryside, customary Islamic practices were openly observed and increased in popularity. Similarly, as absolute central control of intellectual life began to break down, the Central Asian intellectuals began, timorously at first, to assert their right to define their own cultural identities within the general Marxist-Leninist guidelines set down by Moscow. This act of rediscovery included an explicit assertion of their Muslim identity.[37]

*This chapter was sent to the publisher before the Uzbek youths rioted in Ferghana in June 1989, when more than one hundred people were killed, and before the Tadzhik "pogrom" of Armenians in February 1990, in which about forty people died.

The works of Central Asian writers and historians of the late 1960s and 1970s display a political consciousness that integrates their seemingly contradictory heritages, their ethnic identity, their religious past, and a Marxist worldview. Some did this in works of historical fiction about the medieval Muslim civilization.[38] Others wrote about the Soviet period and cautiously signaled the identification of characters with Islam in unobtrusive ways; they exchanged traditional greetings, or casually invoked the name of Allah, and didn't work on Fridays. Prior to the advent of *glasnost* only Chingis Aitmatov, the celebrated Kirghiz novelist, attacked the issue of religion head-on. The plot of his Lenin Prize–winning novel, *A Day Lasts Longer than a Hundred Years*, revolves around efforts of the hero to arrange "proper" burial for his friend. The message of the book was clear: Man should not look to his roots in his quest to live by a well-defined moral code.[39]

Religious revival in the countryside also predates the Islamic revolution in Iran. S. P. Poliakov, head of the Moscow State University Central Asian expedition since the early 1970s, reports a persistent increase in public observance of Islamic rituals and claims that religion is completely reintegrated with the traditional economy. According to Poliakov, observance of customary practices is obligatory for anyone who wants to preserve the respect of the community, and the scale of this observance has grown so grand as to fuel the continuation of a second underground economy. He reproduces archival data from one region in Kirghizia, which show that the amount of money spent in one year on religious funerals, weddings, circumcisions, and birth celebrations represented 70 percent of the legal earnings of the population.[40]

Poliakov's as yet unpublished data go far beyond other sources. However, inklings of the scale of the religious revival were found in the Soviet press well before the current relaxation of censorship. In the mid-1980s the local Central Asian newspapers carried accounts of the increased popularity of religious weddings.[41] There has been even more discussion of the growing incidence and scale of Islamic funerals, including reports that granite and marble headstones adorned with Islamic calligraphy, and sometimes Koranic passages, were being produced "on the side" by those in the construction industry and sold for between 5,000 and 15,000 rubles each.[42]

While some Soviet scholars argue that the popularity of traditional headstones and the great expansion of memorial feasts are no more than signs of a new affluence, others claim they are evidence of the tenacity of Islam. As Saidbeav notes:

> In Islam script carries a holy character. From the very beginnings of Islam the Arabic script became an inalienable component of the Muslim faith, as a symbol of it. The alphabet, according to Islam, was created in order to call to mind the words of God, the prophet Muhammad and the other prophets and angels. The holy character of the script not only demands the careful and accurate writing of religious documents, but also induces Muslims to see in the script an outlet for religious feelings considering the script as a fulfillment of the beauty of God and his creation.[43]

By the early 1980s Soviet scholars were admitting that the principal Islamic holidays of *Kurban bairam* and *Uraz bairam* were major social occasions in the Central Asian countryside and, to a lesser extent, in the urban areas as well. While some authors condemned this as misplaced nationalism, others saw it as evidence of a religious revival.[44] At both *Uraz bairam* and *Kurban bairam* the mosques are filled beyond capacity, with hundreds and sometimes thousands of people gathering near the mosques. The atypically large attendance in the mosques at the end of Ramadan and for *Uraz bairam* has made this period the traditional time for collecting religious taxes (*zakat al-fitr*), which must, according to Soviet law, be a form of self-tithing.[45]

Mavliud, the Prophet's birthday, is also observed in the Muslim regions of the Soviet Union. An Uzbek scholar recently noted that observance of this holiday had all but died out in the period immediately preceding World War II but is now quite commonplace. One survey conducted in northern Kazakhstan reported that 50.5 percent of the believers polled still observe this holiday.[46]

The Soviets had always prided themselves on the virtual disappearance of the practice of fasting during Ramadan. It is now admitted that Ramadan is a period of public religious observance throughout Central Asia. In many areas the traditional evening prayer meetings are preserved. Widespread observance of at least part of the fast is still occurring, especially in the countryside. During the past couple of Ramadans, articles in the Central Asian press complained of declining economic productivity caused by religious fasting. More surprising was the complaint of Tadzhikistan First Secretary Makhkamov that the near total observation of the fast by school children in one rural district came to light only when cafeteria workers lodged a complaint about the wasteful disposal of uneaten food.[47]

There has also been increased interest in learning about Islamic doctrine that predates Khomeini's revolution. Sarsenov, a Kazakh ethnographer, conducted intensive interviews of a small group of believers in the countryside in 1979. He concluded that although the percentage of avowed believers was small, Islam was not a moribund faith. The doctrine being preached accepted modernization as inevitable; the clergy did not denounce the present system but tried to instill in people a conviction that the belief in Allah will enrich their earthly life and prepare them for a future existence from which non-Muslims will be barred.[48]

Although not explicitly stated, it is clear from the context that the believers Sarsenov interviewed were praying in unsanctioned mosques and teaching in unsanctioned schools. The easing of censorship has encouraged a freer discussion of the role of the unofficial clergy in spreading the Islamic revival in Central Asia. While Soviet sources have always admitted the existence of such people in the countryside, press accounts of their activities have stressed that unsanctioned clergy lack a proper knowledge of religion and claim to be pious in order to defraud the population. Such accounts continue to be popular in the Soviet press, especially in newspapers written in the local language.[49]

But *glasnost* has also encouraged a freer discussion of the scale and influence of unsanctioned religious activities. In a 1987 article in the Soviet literary weekly *Literaturnaia gazeta*, a leading journalist specializing in Soviet Islamic affairs claimed that there were some 1,800 unregistered mosques in the USSR.[50] In a recent article, S. P. Poliakov implies a much greater scale; he states that there are 456 "prayer houses" (or simple mosques) in Kurgan Tuibe oblast of Tadzhikistan alone.[51]

In his larger work, Poliakov claims that there are mosques and religious schools in all of the settlements of rural Uzbekistan, Tadzhikistan, and Kirghizia that he has investigated. In some areas, traditional mosques exist; in others someone's house serves as a regular meeting place. In some areas, believers meet for daily prayers; in others only weekly prayers are conducted. Some of the mullahs seem well trained, while others have only the most rudimentary knowledge of Islam. He states that in recent years "schools" have sprouted up to provide for the religious education of children aged seven and older.[52] These facilities vary considerably depending upon the preparation of the mullahs in charge.[53] While Poliakov argues that local religious hierarchies have managed to become more firmly entrenched in the local economic infrastructure,[54] he makes no claim that a formalized religious hierarchy with ties throughout the Central Asian republics has been established. If the scale of the revival reported by Poliakov is accurate across central Asia, then the level of religious learning of the young will be much greater than that of their parents, and religious practice in Central Asia may more closely replicate what was seen in other parts of the Muslim world when the current revival began.

While there is yet no published work on the scale of Poliakov's, numerous articles confirm parts of his thesis. There are accounts of how the number of unsanctioned clerics is growing rapidly,[55] of the illegal construction of new shrines and mosques,[56] of increased religious education[57]—including the "subversion" of the state curriculum by teachers who proselytize religion,[58] and of a revival of Islamic practices designed to suppress women, such as abduction, the payment of *kalyms,* and polygamy.[59] The issue of the relationship of Islam to women's rights has been well publicized in the past two years, with the usual claims that each year over two hundred women in rural Uzbekistan and Tadzhikistan burn themselves to death after being disowned for trying to leave home.[60]

The spread of Islam among young people, a phenomenon of both the city and the countryside, has been a topic of increasing concern throughout Central Asia. Especially troubling is the fact many young believers come from secular homes, which, party officials complain, will mean that the next generation of intellectuals will be even more closely tied to their religious roots than were their predecessors.[61] In the first few years of Gorbachev's rule the Central Asian press was full of warnings that the local religious revival meant that youth were becoming more and more alienated from the ideological goals of the Soviet regime.[62]

For example, there have been complaints that in parts of Uzbekistan up to one-fifth of all ninth- and tenth-graders have *admitted* to being religious believers and that young people in general are no longer embarrassed to identify publicly with religion.[63] Similar charges were made in Turkmenistan. There, as throughout Central Asia, Komsomol officials and educators are said to be helping spur the religious revival.[64] Some of the most serious complaints have come from Tadzhikistan, where Tadzhik State University faculty have been accused of prose-lytizing Islam instead of fulfilling their assigned task of teaching the Arabic language.[65] Religious observance by young people in Tadzhiki-stan has been described as widespread. In a recent survey only 7 percent of the students surveyed at the Tadzhik State Pedagogical Institute claimed to be atheists.[66]

Military officials have also complained about the Islamic revival and the problems it has posed for them in conscripting young Central Asians and getting them to serve in Afghanistan.[67] There have been re-ports of doctors providing fraudulent letters of medical disability and of influential parents buying their children's way out of military ser-vice.[68] In 1987 officials in Uzbekistan reported that hundreds of Kom-somol members had been prosecuted for draft evasion;[69] draft evasion in Tadzhikistan was also widespread.[70] Party officials have also com-plained of "Muslim zealots" who have successfully urged youth not to serve in solidarity with the *dushmen* (the derogatory term used for mu-jahaddin),[71] and of the growing number of young people seeking and receiving exemptions from military service on religious grounds.[72] But it is important to keep a proper perspective on the problem of draft evasion in Central Asia, as the Afghanistan war in its last years was a very unpopular one and reports of draft evasion on religious or moral grounds were common nationwide.[73]

In the mid-1980s most Soviet analysts of Islam believed that the Is-lamic revival in Central Asia was containable and of no direct political threat to the state.[74] But the political realities of the USSR have been changing rapidly since the late 1980s. There is a revival of nationalist sentiment throughout the country, and in Central Asia this has predict-ably taken on a religious tone. Moreover, the religious revivals of the countryside and the city are beginning to come together. In the univer-sities of Central Asia, student protest is helping to place nationalist demands on the Central Asian parties' current political agendas.

The new realities of Central Asian nationalist politics were shown in the Alma-Ata protests of December 1986. Three days of riots in the capital city of Kazakhstan followed the announcement that D. A. Ku-naev, head of Kazakhstan's Communist party and a long-time Polit-buro member, had "retired" and was replaced by an ethnic Russian from outside the republic. Most of those who took to the streets were students, but it is not clear just what they hoped to gain from this pro-test. Most seem to have wanted the old guard of Kazakhstan's Communist party restored, but a small number appear to have used the occasion to call for the creation of an Islamic state in Kazakhstan.[75]

Other smaller skirmishes seem to have been more directly tied to a perceived religious suppression. Throughout 1986 and 1987 republic party officials, quite probably under pressure from Moscow, pushed local officials to enforce laws designed to limit the authority of unofficial clerics.[76] Most of these laws dealt with religion only indirectly; mullahs who sold religious tracts were charged with extortion, and those who sold amulets were charged with faith healing, an illegal practice that is considered an interference with medical science. Some of my contacts talked about how some locally powerful sheiks armed themselves and their followers in this period and remain prepared to defend themselves when necessary. These sheiks are depicted as isolated, with only the most primitive knowledge of the situation in other Muslim countries. But without corroborative evidence from the press it is hard to know the scale of their protests or the threat they represent. Demonstrations in Kurgan Tiube oblast following the arrest of two mullahs were so large that they did receive some press coverage.[77] But through May 1989, religiously inspired mass protests were still quite rare.

However, in the past year more secular, nationalist-inspired protest has become a periodic occurrence in Central Asia, especially in Uzbekistan and Tadzhikistan. In both republics there have been joint efforts by local Russian and Tadzhik intellectuals to form national front organizations modeled after those in the Baltic republics. These efforts have been only partially successful. But they have led to a radicalization of public opinion on cultural issues, which in turn has led to a series of mass demonstrations for making the local language the official state language.[78] Coupled with this have been calls to return to writing these languages in the Arabic script, and others have called for more Arabic-language education, raising the specter that some protestors have a religiously inspired agenda.[79] The Soviet press has also written of the presence of known Islamic activists at the rallies.[80]

Some of my local contacts have claimed that there are at least two types of national fronts being organized in these republics, one secular and one religiously inspired. They dub the religiously inspired organizations "Wahhabi-like," claiming that the young people active in them are trying to create fundamentalist-inspired social and political organizations within the legal framework of the USSR. These young people

Olcott

are said to have come from the Ferghana Valley to Tashkent (Uzbekistan's capital) for their higher education. My contacts have argued that these are not true Islamic fundamentalist organizations because their members have only an elementary knowledge of Islamic doctrine and maintain only indirect contact with fundamentalist organizations in neighboring countries.

Their claims that the Central Asian fundamentalists' political agendas are largely internally inspired became more convincing after students rioted in Tashkent in March 1989 to force the dismissal of the head of SADUM, who, they claimed, was guilty of immoral behavior and not knowledgeable about Islam.[81] Many of the rioters, who, as a new feature of *glasnost,* have been allowed contact with Radio Liberty staff members, claimed to be part of an organization called Islam and Democracy.[82] However, official Soviet sources continue to deny that there is an organized Islamic movement in Tashkent or elsewhere in Central Asia,[83] and they were quick to blame the Ferghana riots of June 1989 and the Dushanbe riots of February 1990 on religious extremists who manipulated Islamic themes. Although these Soviet claims seem manifestly untrue, it is certainly true that the Central Asian population now perceives that it is legitimate to organize to promote nationalist aims, and their protests have both implicit and explicit religious overtones.

The Fate of the Islamic Revival

One's evaluation of the political impact of the Islamic revival in Central Asia is partially dependent upon the assessment of its causes, and there has been considerable debate in the Western literature as to what these are. Scholars like Bennigsen and Wimbush see foreign actors as playing a significant role in encouraging internal Islamic forces to oppose the regime, and they see Islam and communism as set on an ultimately antithetical path.[84] Others, like myself and Muriel Atkin, have maintained that the revival of Islam has largely been an internally generated process, stimulated by external forces but potentially containable should the regime pursue a tolerant policy toward religion.[85]

Certainly Islamic broadcasts from Iran have helped influence the tone and direction of the religious revival in Central Asia, something that the Soviets themselves have long recognized. The Soviet Union's diplomatic response to the Iranian revolution has been cautious but quietly optimistic in the hope that the anti-Western character of the

Khomeini regime would help tip the strategic balance in the Persian Gulf in favor of the USSR. However, Soviets charged with interpreting the implication of the events in the Persian Gulf were sensitive to the potential political implications for Central Asia.

This sensitivity emerges quite clearly in the literature prepared by party ideologists and antireligious propagandists. For example *Argumenty* (*Arguments*), an annual publication aimed at responding to "propaganda" from abroad, has usually contained one article per volume designed to counter the "falsifications" of Islamic activists who try to spread the idea that the Soviet state is persecuting those who practice Islam.[86] Typically Islamic broadcasts from Iran are described as a form of anti-Soviet propaganda, and Islamic fundamentalists are said to be in league with those anti-Soviet forces in the United States who are sponsoring religious broadcasts on Voice of America and Radio Liberty.

Most serious Soviet scholars of Islam, particularly those from Central Asia, have been uncomfortable with the thesis that the rise of Islamic fundamentalism is largely a product of external machinations. They see Islam as part of the national traditions of the Central Asians and therefore worthy of preservation.[87] Moreover, they argue that the moral void of the late Brezhnev years made Islam even more attractive; the state had abdicated its responsibility to provide a coherent ethical code, so the people found their own ways to bring order to their lives.[88] Thus, while acknowledging that broadcasts from Iran have increased the level of religious knowledge of the population in general and of the border population of Turkmenistan in particular, they conclude that local interest in Islam is derived less from foreign "propaganda" than from the Central Asians' deeply held conviction that Islam is a part of their national heritage.[89]

Most Soviet policy makers also seem to have accepted this conclusion. Until Gorbachev came to power, Soviet leaders were not particularly concerned with a potential "Islamic threat" in Central Asia. They tried to minimize the "propaganda" success of foreign radio broadcasts, but there is little evidence that they believed these broadcasts to be seriously undermining Communist party rule in Central Asia. Similarly, Soviet officials concerned with the war in Afghanistan were sensitive to the special problems of fighting against an insurgent Muslim population in a Muslim border region using troops that included representatives of these nationalities. But while they seem to have gone to some length to produce socialization material designed especially for Central Asian conscripts, there is no evidence that they viewed draft resistance by the Central Asians or the threat of their subsequent defection as a more serious problem than the potential disloyalty of non-Muslim Soviet youth.[90]

But when Gorbachev came to power, the Communist party began to reassess its attitude toward the Islamic revival in Central Asia. The party leadership decided that while the revival did not pose a strategic threat to the USSR, it did threaten to undermine the economic and political goals of the regime. Egor Ligachev, speaking for what was then a united leadership, underscored this point in a December 1985 address: "While respecting believer's feelings, it is necessary to assess from a principled Marxist-Leninist standpoint the role of Islam, the role of any religion and any church, in the history and cultures of its people, and to consistently oppose any attempts to identify national, spiritual, and ethical values with religious injunctions and to portray religious rituals as popular traditions."[91]

In the republic and all-union Communist party congresses that followed, party officials from each of the Central Asian republics rose to denounce the "fallacious" linkage of religion with nationalism. But some intellectuals warned that while there had been an increase in "harmful" activity by Muslim clergy who were spurred on by events in the Muslim East more generally, the rise in religion among Central Asian youth was part of an inevitable growth of national self-awareness that accompanied economic and cultural development.[92]

Moscow chose to ignore the tacit warning of such messages and intensified the crackdown on the practice of religion by party officials in Central Asia.[93] A well-publicized drive began; several officials were dismissed,[94] and others were warned that the continued toleration of unsanctioned religious activities within their jurisdictions would make them criminally liable.[95] While some in Central Asia complained that Moscow was going too far, there were others in the capital that complained that Gorbachev was not doing enough to meet the strategic threat posed by the worldwide rise in Islamic fundamentalism.[96] As if to demonstrate the veracity of this position, in March and April 1987 Afghan guerrillas made two armed raids near the border of Tadzhikistan. Though easily disarmed, the guerrilla raids heightened the sense of Soviet vulnerability.

However, by late 1987 it became quite clear to the Soviet leadership that the greatest threats Moscow faced were from "enemies" within the USSR. The rising tide of nationalist protest began to spread throughout the country, and Gorbachev became convinced that he had to rethink his policies toward the national minorities.[97] While a complete elaboration did not appear until September 1989, some changes in policy became apparent.[98] Legislation was drafted to give the national republics greater control of their economies and to make national languages the state languages of the various republics; draft legislation giving greater rights to religious organizations and believers was also prepared.

Changing official attitudes toward religion is particularly important to Central Asians. But while the planned legislation will apply to Central Asia, this is not the population that it was initially designed to appease. Gorbachev's interest in reforming the laws governing religious practice dates from pressure by the Russian population for an official observance of the first millennium of Christianity in Russia, celebrated in 1987. Those lobbying for an expanded role for the Russian Orthodox church and a freeing of restrictions on cultural life more generally have been an important support group for Gorbachev in pursuing his strategy for reform. Adding to this pressure are the actions of those in the Baltics, who have already restored their national churches without waiting for Moscow's approval. The greatest progress along these lines has been made in Lithuania, where since 1988 Christmas has been observed as a national holiday and where religious history has been restored to the curriculum. But in all three Baltic republics and in Armenia and Georgia, the national churches are being given a greater role in public life in the hope that they will help mediate between the party and the nationalists.

Moscow is still less sure of how to treat Islam. The official religious establishment has been periodically called upon (and unsuccessfully) to help quell violent demonstrations in the various Muslim regions. They have been rewarded by plans for a dozen or more new mosques in a number of cities and two new madrasas, but talk of recognizing all unsanctioned religious establishments or permitting unofficial clergy to hold sanctioned services has been discouraged. Nor has there been official endorsement of calls for increased Arabic-language education or for discarding Cyrillic and reintroducing Arabic script as the basis of writing the Central Asian languages.[99]

Islam poses a number of special problems for the Soviets. Gorbachev views Islam as not simply a faith but a way of life, and one that impedes the economic and social goals of the regime. He will not allow the Central Asians the same religious freedoms granted to Christians if that means they will use these freedoms to resist fulfilling what Moscow has defined as their economic responsibilities. Thus, in redefining the interpretation of a "Leninist" and therefore just policy toward Islam, Moscow has made it clear that arguments of religious custom may not be used to inhibit programs designed to produce economic justice for all.[100] Thus, the practice of Islam will only be tolerated when the message preached is consistent with Moscow's reform program.

Moscow also tacitly recognizes that Islam is a supranational faith in a way that Christianity is not and admits more frankly that Soviet Muslims are affected by currents in Islamic thought worldwide. Recent discussions of the role of the Iranian revolution have admitted that events in Iran have had an impact on the religious identification of some Soviet citizens. While Iranian "propaganda" is still attacked, other authors have tried to "educate" Soviet believers to what the Khomeini revolution has meant to those living in Iran.[101]

However, such arguments are likely to be of limited persuasiveness. The national revival that is currently going on in the USSR is sure to lead to a heightened identification of religion with nationalism and eventually to a heightened identification with the worldwide Islamic community. As this occurs events in neighboring countries will become more important. The decision to withdraw from Afghanistan made in 1988 and completed in 1989 has removed some of the immediacy of the threat from that country. But should an Islamic fundamentalist regime come to power in Afghanistan, there will inevitably be reverberations in the USSR as well. The Islamic revolution in Iran, despite its infinitely greater resources, will always play a more remote role in influencing the behavior of Soviet Muslims. As we have seen in the past decade, Iranians can heighten the level of learning about Islam and even make previously suppressed texts available. But they cannot introduce a wholly alien Islamic agenda in Soviet Central Asia.

For now the demands of the Soviet Central Asians are distinct from those of most of their coreligionists abroad. Most do not have an explicitly religious agenda but want to be able to "recapture" their past from the misinterpretation of the Soviet years, which means gaining respect for religion and the role of Islam in framing the development of Central Asian civilization. Others have more explicitly religious goals.

Soviet Central Asia

They want to learn Arabic, to be able to obtain Korans freely, and to have some access to religious education.

For the first time in five decades such demands can be made public. The new multiple-candidate electoral system provides a forum for this debate, and eventually newly elected republic legislatures might be willing to pass legislation that goes far beyond what Moscow has promised. But the Central Asian initiatives from locally generated political reform are far less specific and far less inclusive than those originating in the Baltic republics. And, for now, even the violent demonstrations in Central Asia are smaller in scale than those in the Caucasian republics. For now, the intellectuals of Central Asia are far more concerned with obtaining increased economic investment in the area and with finding solutions to the severe water shortage that could leave the area without potable water within the next five years. At least for the moment, events in the larger Muslim world are more remote than developments in the other republics. But the lessons of activism and organization that the Central Asians are learning from their fellow Soviet citizens are sure to heighten identification with their coreligionists abroad, and as political protests increase in Central Asia, so too will public identification with Islamic causes.

Notes

1. Soviet Central Asia is composed of five republics: – Kazakh SSR, Kirghiz SSR, Tadzhik SSR, Turkmen SSR, and Uzbek SSR. The titular nationalities of these republics are Sunni Muslim. According to the 1979 census there were 6,556,000 Kazakhs, 1,906,000 Kirghiz, 2,898,000 Tadzhiks, 2,028,000 Turkmens, and 12,456,000 Uzbeks in the Soviet Union. Between the 1970 and 1979 census these populations increased 23.7 percent, 31.3 percent, 35.7 percent, 33.0 percent, and 35.5 percent, respectively. As no appreciable decrease in birthrates has been reported, the 1989 census should report considerable increases in each of these populations.

2. For a detailed history of the relationship between religion and the state in Central Asia, see Alexandre Bennigsen and Chantal Lemercier Quelquejay, *Islam in the Soviet Union* (London: Pall Mall Press, 1967).

3. SADUM stands for the *Sredno-Aziatskoe Dukhovnoe Upravlenie Musul'manstvo;* this is the Muslim Religious Board of Central Asia and Kazakhstan.

4. There were 365 registered mosques in the Soviet Union when Gorbachev took power. In the past two years he has promised to increase their number, but no goal for building new mosques has been set.

5. SADUM also runs the Mir-Arab madrasa in the city of Bukhara, which sends graduates on to Tashkent.

Olcott

6. *Pravda vostoka,* October 2, 1986, p. 2.

7. S.P. Poliakov, "Bytovoi Islam," manuscript, 1989. See an English version of his manuscript under the title *Religion and Tradition in Rural Central Asia*, ed. Martha Brill Olcott (Armonk, N.Y.: M.E. Sharpe, 1990).

8. The border with Afghanistan has always been a porous one, although official supervision of that border has been greatly enhanced over the past decade. The Soviet-Iranian border in Turkmenistan is said to be closely patrolled, and the Soviet-Chinese border in Kirghizia and Kazakhstan was closed until early 1989.

9. Source material for this chapter includes Russian-language publications gathered by Martha Brill Olcott on several trips to the Soviet Union, translations of local-language publications, and Olcott's interviews of Soviet contacts.

10. There has been very little *samizdat* coming out of Central Asia, and most of the recent "clandestine" materials are supplied by Central Asian deserters from the Afghanistan war.

11. According to the 1979 census there were 5,477,330 Azerbaidzhanis in the Soviet Union. *Narodnoe khoziaistvo SSSR za 70 let,* "Finansy i statistiki" (Moscow, 1987), 401. The 1989 census results have yet to be released.

12. Shirin Akiner, *The Islamic Peoples of the Soviet Union* (London: Kegan Paul International, 1983), 121.

13. Akiner, 327.

14. About 5 percent of the Tadzhik population are Ismaili Muslims. They live in the Pamir Mountains of the Gorno-Badakhshan Autonomous Oblast in Tadzhikistan and are considered an ethnically distinct population. Ibid., 313.

15. Akiner reports that there are 2,000,000 Tadzhiks, 1,200,000 Uzbeks, 400,000 Turkmens, 25,000 Kirghiz, and 3,000 Kazakhs living in Afghanistan.

16. For a detailed account of politics in Central Asia during the first two years of Gorbachev's rule, see Martha Brill Olcott, "Gorbachev, the National Problem and Party Politics in Central Asia," in *Assessing Soviet Power,* ed. Dan Nelson and Raj Menon (Lexington, Ky.: Lexington Press, 1989).

17. *Kommunist Tadzhikistana,* September 3, 1986, p. 3.

18. Joint Publications Research Service (hereafter *JPRS*), *USSR Political and Social Affairs,* no. 82661 (January 17, 1983): 42.

19. For a more detailed elaboration of these categories, see Martha Brill Olcott, "Moscow's Troublesome Muslim Minority," *Washington Quarterly* 9 (Spring 1986): 73–84.

20. Dzh. Baialieva, *Religioznye perezhitki u Kirgizov i ikh preodelenie* (Frunze, 1981) 75.

21. Kh. Esbergenov and T. Atamuratov, *Traditsii i ikh preobrazovanie v gorodskom byte karakalpakov* (Nukus, 1975), 159.

22. T. Saidbaev, *Islam i obshchestvo,* 2d ed. (Moscow: Nauka, 1984), 210.

23. *Tojikistoni soveti,* July 29, 1987, p. 4. Translation provided by Muriel Atkin.

24. *Tojikistoni soveti,* August 21, 1987, p. 4. The author of the article reported that a modest memorial observance could cost 2,000 rubles, or nearly ten months' salary at official wage levels. Translation provided by Muriel Atkin.

25. For the summaries of a number of different accounts, see Saidbaev, *Islam i obshchestvo*.

26. Zh. B. Bazarbaev, *Sekularizatsiia sel'skogo naseleniia Karakalpakii* (Nukus, 1974).

27. Zh. B. Bazarbaev and S. Sadykov, *Formirovanie nauchno-ateisticheskoi mirovozzrenia molodezhi* (Nukus, 1980).

28. I.R. Khuzhumuradov, *Problemy sekularizatsii v regionakh rasprostraniia islama* (Tashkent: Tashkent State University, 1981), 11–13. In this survey, 36.4 percent of all homemakers and 46.9 percent of all pensioners said that they were believers, while an additional 26.3 percent of all homemakers and 15.3 percent of all pensioners said that they were "waiverers"; 8.2 percent of the intellectuals and 7.4 percent of the party, government, and trade union personnel said that they were believers, while an additional 10.9 percent of the intellectuals and 31.5 percent of the party, government, and trade union personnel said that they were "waiverers"; 16.4 percent of the intellectuals claimed to be atheists, as did 9.3 percent of the party, government, and trade union officials, as opposed to 1.3 percent of the pensioners. No homemakers admitted to being atheists.

29. Baialieva, 73. In this survey, only 2 percent of the intellectuals surveyed who were thirty years of age or older admitted to being believers. Of the twenty- to twenty-nine-year-old intellectuals surveyed, 5.0 percent admitted to observing religious holidays, a figure not significantly different from the 5.2 percent response of workers and 5.9 percent response of farmers.

30. Ibid.

31. *Voprosy teorii i praktiki ateisticheskogo vospitaniie* (Tashkent, 1979), 175.

32. *Turkmenskaia iskra*, May 5, 1987, p. 2.

33. A recently published survey reported that while only 28 of every 1,000 Russian women (aged eighteen to forty-four) planned on having four or more children, 559 Kazakhs, 815 Kirghiz, 855 Uzbeks, 864 Tadzhiks, and 894 Turkmen women planned to have four or more children. *Vestnik statistiki*, no. 9 (1986): 27.

34. For example, the first secretary of the Turkmenistan Communist party reported that there were 332,700 unemployed adults (of working age), of whom 80 percent were women. He further claimed that unemployment of women in urban areas was more severe than in rural areas, where farm labor was often required of them: 97–98 percent of women with four or more children living in small towns or larger urban centers did not work. E.G. Filimonov, *Sotsial'naia politika KPSS i ateisticheskoe vospitanie* (Moscow: Znanie, 1988), 18.

35. Sh. B. Amanturlin, *Perezhitki animizm, shamstva, islame i ateisticheskaia rabota* (Alma-Ata, 1977), 175.

36. Saidbaev, 236.

37. For a good example of this, see Olzhas Suleimenov, "Slovo o literaturnoi kritike," *Prostor* (May 1970): 92–98.

38. For some examples, see D. Doshzhanov, *Trudnyi shag* (Moscow, 1974); idem, *Polyr i tsvety* (Alma-Ata, 1981); idem. *Shelkovyi put'* (Moscow, 1980).

39. Chingis Aitmatov, *A Day Lasts Longer than a Hundred Years* (Bloomington: Indiana University Press, 1983). One of the most powerful images in the book is of "mankurts," legendary people of Aitmatov's own creation who have had their historical consciousness crushed out of their brains.

40. Poliakov, 84–85. The data are drawn from a reym in Osh oblast, the same region about which Baialieva wrote that religious observance was declining. The year is unspecified but appears to be 1985 or 1986.

Olcott

41. In a recent survey, just under half (44.6 percent) of the young workers interviewed in Dushanbe (Tadzhikistan) said that they wanted a religious wedding, and of these respondents, 43.4 percent said that they thought that their wedding should be registered at the ZAKS as well.

42. *JPRS USSR Political and Social Affairs,* no. 77252 (January 27, 1981): 56; ibid., no. 82274 (November 19, 1983): 2.

43. Saidbaev, 178. (This material did not appear in the first edition.)

44. Osipov, *Islam v SSSR* (Moscow: Nauka, 1983), 68; Amanturlin, 175.

45. Saidbaev, 213.

46. Osipov, 68.

47. *Kommunist Tadzhikistana,* September 3, 1986, p. 3.

48. K. Sarsenov, *Kritika modernistskikh tendentsii v ritual'no obriadovoi sisteme islama v sovremennykh usloviakh (na materialakh Kazakhskoi SSR)* (Tashkent: Aftoreferat, 1979).

49. For some examples, see *JPRS Soviet Report: Political Affairs*, UPA-001-87 (June 4, 1987): 61; ibid., UPA 87-30 (April 22, 1987): 64.

50. I. Beliaev, "Islam i politika," *Literaturnaia gazeta*, May 13, 1987, pp. 13, 20; ibid., May 20, 1987, p. 12. I have edited a translation of this article which appears as Igor Beliaev, "Islam and Politics," *Soviet Anthropology and Archeology* (Spring 1988): 82–101.

51. Boris Kalachev and Sergei Poliakov, "Bytovoi islam," *Molodoi kommunist,* no. 2 (1989): 31–38.

52. Poliakov claims that there are separate educational facilities for boys and girls; moreover, he writes that the female-led schools for training women are very recent phenomena.

53. Poliakov, "Bytovoi Islam," 57–65.

54. Poliakov contends that the Islamic religious establishment survives in part because of its ties with the opium growers and traders. Kalachev and Poliakov, 36.

55. *Tojikistoni soveti,* July 27, 1987, p. 2. Translation provided by Muriel Atkin.

56. It was recently announced that an oblast secretary in Uzbekistan had been dismissed for using state funds to build a mosque.

57. *Tojikistoni soveti,* August 21, 198. Translation provided by Muriel Atkin.

58. *Kommunist Tadzhikistana,* June 25, 1987, p. 2.

59. *Turkmenskaia iskra,* May 5, 1987, p. 2.

60. Kalachev and Poliakov, 31.

61. See Saidbaev, 257–58; he reports that young converts from secular homes make up 15 percent of all new believers.

62. Much of the material on youth used in this paper is drawn from Martha Brill Olcott and William Fierman, "Soviet Youth and the Military," U.S. Department of State contract no. 1724-620124, 1988.

63. The data cited are from Khorezm and were published in *Komsomolets Uzbekistana,* February 21, 1987. One implication is that religious weddings and christenings seem to be on the rise republicwide. At a recent republic party congress it was reported that 18,000 religious weddings and 7,000 christenings took place annually.

64. *Komsomolets Turkmenistana,* February 14, 1987.

65. *Kommunist Tadzhikistana,* September 3, 1986, p. 3.

66. This survey was based on a questionnaire distributed at five VUZs (institu-

tions of higher education), the medical institute, and four PTUs (technical high schools). Of those surveyed, 49.6 percent of the VUZ students, 65.4 percent of the medical institute students, and 68.0 percent of the PTU students reported that they observed Ramadan.

67. *Komsomolets Kirgizii,* March 5, 1987.

68. *Pravda,* May 18, 1987; *Pravda Vostoka,* June 4, 1987; and *Komsomolets Kirgizii,* March 5, 1987.

69. *Komsomolets Uzbekistana,* February 21, 1987. Earlier there had been reports of a meeting held by the procurator on how to deal with youths who fail to report for military service; *Pravda Vostoka,* October 4, 1987.

70. *Kommunist Tadzhikistana,* December 30, 1987.

71. *Pravda Vostoka,* June 4, 1987.

72. The reference was unclear as to whether these were Muslim or Christian youths; *Komsomolets Kirgizii,* February 21, 1987.

73. For details, see Olcott and Fierman, "Soviet Youth and the Military."

74. According to Saidbaev, "The absolute majority of contemporary believers do not permit encroachment by the clergy or the religious community on their civil rights and they oppose attempts of isolated dangerous fanatics to lead life within the confines and dictates established by Islam" (*Islam i obshchestvo,* 216); he then goes on in a footnote (p. 283) to describe the antiregime activities of two anti-Soviet groups.

75. *Kazakhstanskaia pravda,* December 18–21, 1986; and interviews with eyewitnesses to the riots.

76. One local contact has argued that Moscow did not direct the Central Asian party organizations to crack down on religion, but that the party organizations did this themselves in order to demonstrate their fitness to rule to a leadership in Moscow that was generally critical of their performance.

77. *Kommunist Tadzhikistana,* January 31, 1987, and February 12, 1987. For an account in English, see Andrew Ilves, "Protest against the Arrest of Mullah in Tadjikistan," *Radio Liberty Research,* RL 101/87, March 11, 1987.

78. *Kommunist Tadzhikistana,* February 27, 1989. In April 1989 both the Turkmen SSR and the Tadzhik SSR announced draft legislation to make Turkmen and Tadzhik the respective state languages of these two republics.

79. Timur Kocaoglu, "Demonstrations by Uzbek Popular Front," *Radio Liberty Report on the USSR* 1, no. 17 (April 28, 1979): 13–14.

80. *Kommunist Tadzhikistana,* March 4, 1989.

81. These riots led to the dismissal of Mufti Shamsuddiankhan Babikhanov, who had been appointed head of SADUM following the death of his father. He was replaced by Muhammadsadyk Muhammadyusuf, rector of Imam al-Bukhari Institute.

82. Annette Bohr, "Background to Demonstrations of Soviet Muslims in Tashkent", *Radio Liberty Report on the USSR* 1, no. 11 (March 17, 1989): 18–19.

83. Foreign Broadcast Information Service, *Daily Report: Soviet Union,* SOV-89-059, March 29, 1989, p. 59.

84. See Alexandre Bennigsen and Marie Broxup, *The Islamic Threat to the Soviet Union* (London: Croom Helm, 1984); Alexandre Bennigsen and S. Enders Wim-

bush, *Mystics and Commissars: Sufism in the Soviet Union* (Berkeley and Los Angeles: University of California Press, 1986).

85. Muriel Atkin, *The Subtlest Battle: Islam in Soviet Tajikistan* (Philadelphia: Foreign Policy Research Institute, 1989); see also Martha Brill Olcott, "Soviet Islam and World Revolution," *World Politics* 36, no. 4: idem, 487–504; "Moscow's Troublesome Muslim Minority," *Washington Quarterly* 9 (Spring 1986): 73–84.

86. See A. Akhmedov, "Pod flagom islama," *Argumenty 1981* (Moscow: Politizdat, 1981), 5–36; idem, "Islamskii faktor' v planakh imperializma i reaktsii," in *Argumenty 1982* (Moscow: Politizdat, 1982) 63–85; idem, "Fal'shivye tesizy," in *Argumenty 1984* (Moscow: Politizdat, 1984), 40–60; idem, *Islam v sovremennoi ideino-politicheskoi bor'be* (Moscow: Politizdat, 1985).

87. According to Saidbaev, "Islam does not only compensate for man's weakness but can also satisfy his requirements which are not connected with religion; it can help a man express himself, to 'find' himself among people, to feel a sense of belonging to a nation, to its history, to satisfy needs in social intercourse." Saidbaev, *Islam i obshchestvo*, 1st ed. (Moscow: Nauka, 1978), 191.

88. This is Osipov's thesis in *Islam v SSSR.*

89. This idea was restated in numerous interviews with Soviet scholars of Islam freed from the restraints of censorship.

90. See Olcott and Fierman, "Soviet Youth and the Military"; idem, "The Political Socialization of the Muslim Conscript," *Soviet Union* 14, no. 1, (January 1987): 65–101. For the opposite viewpoint, see Alexander R. Alexiev and S. Enders Wimbush, "Soviet Muslim Soldiers in Afghanistan," in their *Ethnic Minorities in the Red Army* (Boulder, Colo.: Westview Press, 1988), 237–54.

91. *Bakinskii rabochii,* December 22, 1985, as quoted in *FBIS USSR Daily Report,* January 2, 1986, p. 16.

92. *Kommunist Tadzhikistana,* January 28, 1986, p. 4.

93. See *JPRS Soviet Report: Political Affairs,* UPA-88-017, (May 16, 1988): 41–43, for a reprint of a relevant article from *Sotsialisticheskaia industria,* February 11, 1988.

94. Including the dismissal of the first secretary of Samarkand, to the accompanying protest of some of his subordinates. *Soviet Ouzbekistani,* August 6, 1986, p. 3. Translation provided by William Fierman.

95. *Kommunist Tadzhikistana,* September 3, 1986, p. 3.

96. This is the thesis of Beliaev's "Islam i politika" article.

97. For a discussion of the evolution of Gorbachev's thought on nationality relations, see Martha Brill Olcott, "Gorbachev's National Dilemma," *Journal of International Affairs,* no. 1 (1989).

98. A plenum of the Central Committee of the Communist party of the Soviet Union to discuss nationality relations, first promised in summer 1987, has yet to be scheduled.

99. Plans for eventually allowing Moldavian to be written in the Latin script and the official recognition that Moldavian is simply a form of Rumanian create dangerous precedents in Central Asia, where Tadzhik can be declared to be Persian and the four Turkic languages to be forms of one or two common languages.

100. For a statement of Moscow's recent position, see Filimonov, *Sotsial'naia*

politika KPSS. Filimonov is the deputy director of the Institute of Scientific Atheism of the Academy of Social Sciences of the Central Committee of the Soviet Union. It is interesting to contrast his views presented in this book with those expressed in an interview published in *Komsomol'skaia pravda*, January 25, 1984, p. 2, in which he expressed great hostility to Islamic clergy as definitionally antagonistic to Soviet economic and social programs.

101. For an example, see S. Agaev, "Iranskaia revoliutsiia," *Nauka i religiia,* no. 11 (1988): 26–29.

PART IV

Southeast Asia

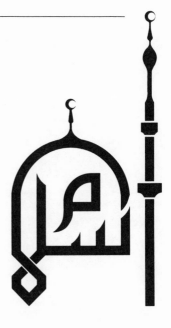

12

Malaysian and Indonesian

Islamic Movements and

the Iranian Connection

FRED R. VON DER MEHDEN

AT THE TIME OF THE Iranian revolution in 1979, some observers of the
Southeast Asian Islamic scene predicted that states such as Indonesia
could well be "another Iran."[1] In reality, the revolution and subsequent
events in Iran have not had the impact initially anticipated. This chapter examines the effect of the revolution on the two major Muslim-
populated countries of Southeast Asia, Indonesia and Malaysia. The
focus of this investigation is on state-to-state relations, government efforts to contain the local impact of the revolution, and popular attitudes toward the revolution. But prior to focusing on the past decade,
it is necessary to understand the environment within which these events
took place, as defined by the type of Islam found in Southeast Asia, the
character of the Islamic revival in the region, and previous patterns of
interaction between Southeast Asia and Middle Eastern Muslims.

The Islamic World of Southeast Asia

Both Malaysia and Indonesia are religiously pluralistic societies. A slim
majority of Malaysia's population is Malay, with the remainder composed of some 37 percent Chinese, 11 percent Indians, and the rest
various other ethnic groupings. There is a close identification of religion and ethnicity, with almost all Muslims being Malay and vice versa.

A relatively small percentage of other ethnic elements have accepted Islam. With this Muslim population there is little difference in faith and practice: Virtually all Malaysian Muslims are Sunni; Shii Muslims are practically nonexistent. Historically, Malaysian Muslims have generally adopted traditionally Islamic religious attitudes and ritualistic practices.

Indonesia's religious pluralism is largely within the Muslim community itself. Approximately 90 percent of all Indonesians are Sunni Muslim; the remainder are primarily Christian, Hindu, animist, or Buddhist. However, within the Sunni community (again, Shiites are almost nonexistent), there are significant differences in belief and practice. The major variation is between those Muslims who follow a more syncretic belief system in which Islam is deeply penetrated by traditional animist and other pre-Islamic elements, often termed *agama Jawa* or *abangan*, and those who attempt to follow a more universal or "orthodox" pattern, who have been termed *santri*. In Indonesia today, the former tend to dominate the upper echelons of civil and military power, while the latter have strongholds in religious schools and Islamic organizations.

The current Islamic revival in Southeast Asia has evolved over the past two decades, although there were antecedents evident even before World War II, particularly in the Dutch East Indies (now Indonesia).[2] This increased influence of Islam has been facilitated by a variety of indigenous factors, including dissatisfaction with Western secular solutions to social and political problems, a rejection of what are seen to be undesirable aspects of modern Western value systems, a greater sense of pride and identity among Muslims fostered by the Islamic world's greater prominence in global economic and political affairs, and the expansion of efforts by foreign Muslim governments and groups to spread the faith. Ironically, the differing policies followed by authorities in Jakarta and Kuala Lumpur to deal with the revival have also given it strength. The more confrontational approach employed by Indonesia has fostered solidarity in the Muslim community, while the effort to co-opt the movement in Malaysia has given it a degree of legitimacy and governmental authority.

The revival has manifested itself in a variety of ways in both Malaysia and Indonesia, although it has been more prominent in the former. Among the obvious signs are the wearing of modest clothing by more and more women; the greater attention given to prayer, fasting, and other Islamic rituals by the public and the political elites; more reli-

von der Mehden

gious programming on television, particularly in Malaysia; the references to Islam in the rhetoric of politicians; and greater involvement in international Islamic organizations. It should be emphasized that while these phenomena are apparent within the Islamic community in Indonesia, the national political leadership has tended to play down the centrality of Islam in both domestic politics and foreign affairs. On the other hand, the Malaysian government has engaged in numerous activities in the name of Islam: establishing an Islamic bank, hosting international conferences dealing with Islamic issues, encouraging Islamic education, and so on. There are compelling domestic political reasons for these differing approaches, which will be discussed later.

In both countries there has been a growth of *dakwah* organizations, including a burgeoning of religious groups on the campuses of local universities.[3] The youth have been particularly attracted to the revivalists' messages and are conspicuously involved in a number of missionary activities. Also highly publicized, though relatively rare, have been the sensational and violent manifestations of the revival. These have included airplane hijackings, bombings of department stores and other public buildings, attacks on government installations, the depredation of religious edifices of other faiths, reported plans to kill cabinet ministers, and alleged plots to overthrow existing governments in order to establish an Islamic state. Despite their notoriety there is a general consensus that these acts have been the work of small minorities with little public support.

There are other significant but less public manifestations of the revival. One of the most important is the growing intellectual interest in religious questions, including revivalist ideas arising from the Middle East. Islamic journals such as *Dakwah* (both the Indonesian and Malaysian editions), *Risalah, Al Nahdah, Panji Masyarakat*, and *Kiblat* present a wide range of religious thought of both local and foreign writers.

The penetration of religious thought from the Middle East is part of a centuries-long legacy of relations between the Middle East and Southeast Asia. Even before the arrival of Islam in Southeast Asia, the region served as a transit point between the Middle and Far East. The expansion of Islam into the region began a new period of contact.[4] Historically, we can identify three epochs of differing relationships between Muslims in the two regions. In the first centuries after the arrival of Islam into Southeast Asia, there was relatively little continuous trade, diplomatic, and intellectual contact with the Middle East. Some Arab traders and religious teachers made their way east, a small number of Malays and Indonesians made the hajj or traveled abroad to study in Muslim centers of learning, in rare cases Turks or Arabs became advisers to local Southeast Asian monarchs, and for a brief time the Turks aided the Achinese of northern Sumatra against their common enemy, the Portuguese based in Malacca.[5] During this period Islamic works from the Middle East became available, initially in Arabic and later in translation.

By the nineteenth century relations had intensified, although the expansion of European colonialism severely limited state-to-state contacts. Still, more Southeast Asian Muslims were making their way to Islamic centers, and Arabs were increasingly found in Indonesia and Malaya. Biographies of noted ulama show that many went abroad, particularly to Egypt, for their religious training, while Arab scholars became more prominent in Southeast Asia.[6] By the early twentieth century so many Indonesians were making the hajj that they became known as the "rice of the Hejaz," and on their return many of these hajjis and ulama became leading spokesmen for Islam at home.[7] Malays making the pilgrimage were relatively fewer but still of significant numbers, reaching a pre–World War II high of 14,000 in 1920.[8] In this period the Egyptian Modernist movement became influential in Indonesia and less so in Malaya, while greater sophistication in Islamic religious schools brought increased demands for instructors competent in both Arabic and religion.[9] There was also an increased interest in Middle Eastern affairs, particularly among Indonesian Muslims. Sympathy for the Turkish cause in World War I was publicly expressed in the islands, and Indonesians participated in international discussions of the future of the Caliphate after the war.[10]

The Great Depression and the Second World War brought this second era to an end. The former led to a sharp decline in travel between the Middle East and Southeast Asia, and the latter isolated one region from the other. (There were still Indonesians and Malays studying in Cairo, however, and as late as 1937–38 there were 10,884 pilgrims traveling to Mecca from the Dutch East Indies.)[11] Thus, until the end of World War II Southeast Asian Muslims were at the periphery of the Islamic world, participating only intermittently in important events in the wider *ummah* (Islamic community). They were essentially outsiders reflecting a dependent position in religious and political affairs. They were largely ignored or unknown by Muslims in the Middle East and, when considered, were viewed as unlearned or even impure religiously.

The postwar years have brought significant economic, political, and intellectual changes, leading to a major intensification of relations between Muslims in Southeast Asia and the Middle East. First, the end of colonialism broke the barriers between official contacts, allowing Muslim states to establish diplomatic relations, trade and investment opportunities, and international Islamic organizations. Second, the combination of more sophisticated international communications systems and better education opened new channels of interaction. Today ideas and events are readily transmitted across the Islamic world. Aiding this exchange has been the newfound wealth of many Muslim countries, which can now afford to increase their contact with other Muslim peoples. Finally, and intimately connected to the other points, leaders in both the Middle East and Southeast Asia have realized political and economic gains from promoting themselves to other Muslims in the name of Islam. Thus, the Saudis have competed with the Iranians and Libyans for the minds of Southeast Asians, and Malaysian and Indonesian spokesmen have played upon religious ties in attempts to increase trade and investment opportunities with the Middle East.

This change in relations has manifested itself in economic, political, and intellectual interactions. Prior to World War II there was relatively little trade between the two regions (most notably, Indonesia was the largest exporter of tea to Saudi Arabia), but in recent years levels of trade and investment have expanded dramatically. From 1975 to 1985 Malaysian trade with the Middle East almost tripled, and from 1979 to 1982 Indonesia's trade with West Asia almost quadrupled.[12] Southeast Asia has also become a major supplier of labor to the Middle Eastern oil fields, with Indonesia supplying 22,000 workers to Saudi Arabia alone. In spite of major efforts by Indonesia and Malaysia to increase exports, trade has been heavily weighted in favor of the Middle East, although the imbalance is somewhat offset by labor and investment income. In the past decade Arab funds have been poured into fertilizer plants, highways, dams, timber, oil refineries, and so on in Malaysia and Indonesia. At the same time, the expected investment boom driven by religious affinity has yet to be realized. As the managing director of the Arab-Malayan Development Bank noted, the Arabs have been "hard-headed businessmen," primarily interested in the profitability of their investments.[13]

Malaysia and Indonesia

Major changes have also taken place at the political level. Almost every Middle Eastern state now has diplomatic relations with Indonesia and Malaysia. Both Southeast Asian states have participated in international Islamic organizations, although Malaysia has been far more interested in developing opportunities to interact with other states in the name of Islam. Tengku Abduul Rahman, former Malaysian prime minister, was the first secretary general of the Organization of the Islamic Conference (OIC). Malaysia was an early host of the World Muslim Congress and the first Asian country to recognize the Palestine Liberation Organization; the state has also been active in the meetings of the Islamic foreign ministers.

There has also been greater public involvement of Southeast Asian states in Middle Eastern affairs. Both Indonesia and Malaysia have opposed Israeli actions in the Middle East and Soviet policies in Afghanistan, and have called for peace in the Iran-Iraq war. Here again, Malaysia has been more prepared to express its views in Islamic terms, while Indonesia has articulated a more secular policy. Jakarta has been less antagonistic to the Israelis and criticized the Soviets in Afghanistan for actions against another Third World state, not another Muslim country.[14] Malaysia has been particularly critical of Israeli actions, and Prime Minister Mohamad Mahathir and his minister have attacked international Zionism for seeking to weaken both Malaysia and Islam.[15]

For their part, various Middle Eastern states have become more interested in events in Southeast Asia. The OIC was a major critic of the Philippine government for its actions against Muslim citizens in the south; later the OIC sent emissaries to the Philippines and Colonel Qaddafi and Imelda Marcos negotiated the Tripoli Agreement as a solution to the problem.[16] A second example of Middle Eastern involvement in the region can be seen in Libyan and Saudi efforts to influence Southeast Asian Muslims through financial aid to Muslim religious organizations and educational institutions. One could argue, however, that these funds were donated partly to counter the potential influence of one benefactor over the other.

Perhaps the most far-reaching changes in relations between the Middle East and Southeast Asia can be seen in the increased intellectual interaction between the Islamic world of Southeast Asia and that of the Middle East. A perusal of books dealing with Islamic subjects by Middle Eastern authors and translated into Malay-Indonesian is revealing. Of the contemporary seminal writers and activists of the revival in the Middle East, the most prominent would probably include the Egyptian Sayyid Qutb, the Iranian Ali Shariati, and the Pakistani Abul Ala Mawdudi.[17] Indonesian translations of these three authors published during the 1980s number over fifty books and tracts, not counting multiple translations and publications. Not only are these authors widely published, but their ideas are frequently noted in religious periodicals, and their works have become required reading in Islamic institutions of higher learning.[18]

Moreover, an increasing number of Southeast Asian students are studying in the Middle East, many of whom return to teach in the religious schools of their home country. At Malaya University, for example, of fourteen lecturers in the Islamic Academy, faculty of Sharia, eleven were trained at al-Azhar in Egypt and three in Baghdad, while at Kebangsaan University almost every professor of Islamic studies received part of his education in the Middle East.[19] Such training is part of a growing sophistication in Islamic education and has helped broaden the religious thinking of Indonesia and Malaysia. For example, in the March 1985 issue of the Indonesian journal *Prisma*, local scholars cited the following Western and Middle Eastern writers: Robert Bellah, Paul Tillich, Gustave von Grunebaum, Nikki Keddie, Edward Shils, Harry Benda, Kenneth Landon, Anniemarie Schimmel, Bernard Lewis, Thomas Hodgkin, Sayyid Qutb, Ali Shariati, Hasan al-Banna, Ismail Faruqi, Yusuf Qardhawi, and a host of others.

State-to-State Relations

It is within this changing pattern of relations between the Middle East and Southeast Asia that the impact of the Iranian revolution must be analyzed. The first part of this investigation is to examine the effects of the revolution on government-to-government relations between Iran and Malaysia and between Iran and Indonesia. If one simply read the formal statements of the governments concerned and noted the comings and goings of officials, it would appear that very little was changed by the revolution. However, this external normalcy masks the serious concerns of Southeast Asian authorities about the effect of events in Iran on their own people. Nevertheless, neither Jakarta nor Kuala Lumpur wished to be seen publicly criticizing a seeming victory of Islam over Western imperialism and secular behavior.

Initially, the official reaction to the overthrow of the Shah in 1979 was silence; no favorable, unfavorable, or neutral statement issued from either the Indonesian or Malaysian regime. It was not until later in the year that the Malaysian foreign minister, in answer to a question in the Dewan Rakyat, stated that relations between Iran and Malaysia were "normal" and that the formation of the revolutionary government in Iran was part of "the internal affairs of Iran." He also noted that diplomatic personnel were carrying out duties as usual.[20] The Indonesian government was even more reticent, carefully avoiding comment on the ousting of the Shah and the release of the American hostages.[21] Even during the Iran-Iraq war, when the Malaysians were prepared to help mediate the conflict and participated in the OIC Peace Committee, the Indonesian government remained silent. Prior to these peace efforts, both Jakarta and Kuala Lumpur maintained a neutral stand toward the two combatants.

It can be argued that there were other equally or more important issues that confronted both governments and held the attention of the press: the flight of great numbers of Vietnamese "boat people," President Carter's Middle East peace talks, the major row over the Malaysian airline strikes, and the Chinese attacks on the northern border of Vietnam. Yet these events do not fully explain the official silence and the absence of local media coverage. As we shall see, the explanation appears to lie in the domestic problems raised by the Iranian revolution.

During the past decade, however, both Indonesia and Malaysia continued to engage in diplomatic missions and official visits with the Iranians. In 1981 Hashemi Rafsanjani, then speaker of the parliament, visited Kuala Lumpur and met with Prime Minister Mahathir; in 1982 an official Iranian diplomatic mission was established in Malaysia; in 1984 an official Indonesian delegation visited Iran and the Iranian foreign minister went to Malaysia; in 1985 Khomeini received the Malaysian envoy; in 1987 the Indonesian foreign minister went to Iran; and in 1988 the Malaysian foreign minister went to Teheran, Rajsanjani again came to Malaysia, and Khomeini received the outgoing Indonesian envoy.

But if diplomatic relations continued in a "normal" pattern, the revolution and the subsequent Iran-Iraq war severely limited trade and investment relations between Iran and Southeast Asia. While other Middle Eastern states were increasing their economic ties to Indonesia and Malaysia, Iranian trade remained the lowest of the major Middle Eastern states, the small Indonesian work force in Iran during 1978–79 disappeared by 1980, and Iranian investment in Southeast Asia was virtually nonexistent.[22] In sum, state-to-state relations were generally quiet politically and stagnant economically.

Government Attitudes toward the Revolution

While diplomatic relations continued at a seemingly tranquil pace, the actions of Jakarta and Kuala Lumpur to control any unfavorable local impact of the revolution demonstrated the concern that authorities had about events in Iran. To understand that concern, one should be familiar with some aspects of the domestic policies of these two Southeast Asian states, particularly those developed to deal with the religious opposition present in both countries.[23]

In Indonesia religious antagonism toward the Suharto regime comes primarily from the so-called *santri* community and includes both more traditionalist and modernist elements. The tension that exists is based on the perception among many of these "orthodox" Muslims that those in power have been polluted by Western influences, and do not reflect proper Muslim values, do not display sufficient interest in the economic and social problems of rural Muslims, and are attempting to foster un-Islamic ideologies. The major complaint has been the government's establishment of the *Panchasila*, the five principles originally formulated under the Sukarno regime and now promoted by Suharto. The crux of the issue is the demand that all groups accept the *Panchasila* as their sole ideology; moreover, its fifth principle calls for belief in a Supreme Being but is formulated so as to include all of Indonesia's religions. This is perceived by many Muslim leaders as a form of agnosticism.

Since the deposition of former President Sukarno in the late 1960s, the only strongly organized opposition to the Suharto regime has come from dissatisfied Muslims. While the leadership of public Muslim organizations has generally favored peaceful opposition and even the withdrawal from politics, there have been elements that have promoted violence or used Islamic foundations for highly critical verbal attacks on what they perceive to be a corrupt and un-Islamic government. To meet this challenge the authorities have sought to weaken Islamic political influence by diluting Muslim party power, meting out severe sentences to those preaching what are termed seditious attacks on the government, and underscoring the dangers of "deviant" interpretations of Islam.

Malaysia is a limited parliamentary democracy in which religion and ethnicity define much of political life. The centerpiece of the party system is the National Front, a coalition that dominates national and most state politics. The National Front is headed by a Malay Muslim party, the United Malay National Organization (UMNO), from which have come all the country's prime ministers and most senior ministers since independence. The primary Muslim opposition to UMNO comes from the *Parti Islam sa-Malaysia* (PAS), whose leadership has continuously emphasized Malay traditions and religious values. It has been incumbent on UMNO to maintain a pluralistic racial policy to meet the expectations of the multiracial coalition while attempting to satisfy its own Muslim party membership and to forestall possible inroads from PAS. UMNO's need to appeal to its Muslim constituency has been one of the reasons for the government's efforts to support Islamic causes at home and abroad. At the same time, the Malaysian regime sees a danger in extremist interpretations of Islam. These fears arise from the more radical stance on Islamic issues held by the PAS and the infrequent cases of even more radical Islamic groups employing violence against the government. Thus, like those in power in Jakarta, National Front leaders in Kuala Lumpur constantly emphasize the danger of "deviant" Islam.

Any analysis of the Indonesian and Malaysian governments' efforts to deal with the impact of the Iranian revolution events is plagued by severe limitations. First, neither regime has publicly delineated its policies, as both are caught in the dilemma of wishing to control undesirable behavior while not openly attacking a movement with strong religious and emotional ties. Second, while there have been numerous charges of possible Middle Eastern interference in Southeast Asian Islamic affairs, there is little concrete evidence. Finally, not all "deviant" interpretations of Islam originate in Iran or are considered by the respective governments to be Iranian inspired. Thus, when accusations are made it is not always easy to identify the target.

Various press reports indicate that the Iranian government has been warned by the Malaysian regime against interfering in domestic matters. In 1979 the press published veiled statements from both the deputy prime minister and the inspector general of police that certain religious groups were seeking to overthrow the government.[24] In 1982 the Penang *Star* reported that the Iranian Embassy had been told to curtail certain links with groups working to set up an Islamic state.[25]

von der Mehden

These groups allegedly included Malaysians arrested in Saudi Arabia during the hajj season for passing out anti-Saudi, pro-Iranian material that had been sponsored by "an Islamic country"; seditious groups and individuals, including several government figures and top officials of "a certain bank," who desired an Islamic state; and visitors seeking to teach and promote the advantages of an Islamic government. A later article in the *New Straits Times*, often an outlet for official policy, stated that the Malaysian home minister had sought to regulate traffic of allegedly revolutionary individuals between Iran and Malaysia.[26] There were also frequent accusations that the main nongovernmental *dakwah* youth group, known as ABIM (Angkatan Belia Islam Malaysia, an organization perceived as a political threat by the government), had links with Iran.[27]

In Indonesia there have been allegations but no firm evidence of the existence of seditious groups seeking support from Iran or Libya. For example, an organization called the Indonesian Islamic Revolution Board was accused of seeking Iranian support to overthrow the Suharto regime. There have also been charges that Muslim radicals have sought to implement an Islamic state in the pattern of Iran. In one well-publicized case, Irfan Suryahadi, editor of the Muslim youth magazine *Al Risalah,* was sentenced to thirteen years' imprisonment for subversion. Among the articles in the magazine that were used against him was one titled "The Advice of Ayatollah Khomeini" ("Wejangan Ayatullah Khoumeini"). It was alleged that this piece incited a "stirring-up of Islamic revolution to destroy governments not based upon Islam, and to invite Muslims throughout the world to bring Islamic revolution to fruition." Suryahadi was also reported to have admitted frequent contacts with the Iranian Embassy in Jakarta. While raiding his office authorities claimed they confiscated the Iranian embassy newsletter *Yaum al Quds*; they asserted that *Al Risalah* was funded by the Middle East and called upon the Iranian Embassy to send copies of the newsletter to the Indonesian government prior to local distribution (somewhat similar controls have been established in Malaysia).[28] But it would be incorrect to state that the Indonesian authorities underscored the Iranian connection in the series of antisedition trials that charged Islamic "radicals" with attempts to overthrow the regime or speak against its policies (particularly the *Panchasila*). A review of the charges and defense of religious defendants during 1985 and 1986 uncover little reference to the Iranian revolution or Iranian influence.

Both governments have also discouraged private visits to Iran and students going to Iran for religious studies. This was an unofficial policy in the first years after the revolution, and those citizens returning from Iran have reportedly been held in suspicion by authorities. However, the Indonesian government has recently barred its citizens from studying in thirty-one countries. Of these countries, twenty-one are Communist, four are states with which Indonesia has no diplomatic relations (Israel, South Africa, Taiwan, and Portugal), and six are defined as "extreme" (Libya, Iran, Iraq, Syria, Lebanon, and Algeria).[29]

There have also been veiled and not so veiled warnings from the governments against "deviant" behavior and ideas, which would appear to include the ideology of the Iranian revolution. These statements have ranged from relatively neutral wording (such as Prime Minister Mahathir's comments that one Islamic country could not be compared with another and that the glory of Islam could not be achieved with slogans)[30] to more direct analyses (characterized by the view of Religious Affairs Minister Haji Munawir Sjadzali that "although the extremist movement became stronger since the Islamic Revolution in 1979, the Muslims generally do not favor the militant approach"[31] and blatant charges that "deviant" religious ideas sought to destroy "true Islam." Such comments seem to have two purposes. One has been to discourage Muslims from becoming interested in ideas that could destabilize the regimes of the two states. While not expecting either state to be "another Iran," both governments see a danger in ideas that might lend support to their radical opposition or that might reinforce the beliefs of mainstream Muslims to the point where inter- or intrareligious friction might be exacerbated. Second, cynics argue that by playing up the extremists and publicizing their statements and rare acts of violence, the authorities will frighten other Muslims away from possibly "subversive" religious ideas; then, by branding less radical opponents as tied to these "deviants," the governments can weaken popular support of the opposition.

Thus, one of the most important effects of the Islamic revolution on the governments of Indonesia and Malaysia was to increase their efforts to control the political role of those Islamic forces seen as detrimental to state policies. Due partly to events in Iran, both Jakarta and Kuala Lumpur became increasingly aware of the dangers posed by religious ideology and sought to contain the negative effects through a combination of co-optation, threats, increased religious observance and rhetoric, and greater surveillance of religious activists.[32]

Popular Attitudes toward the Revolution

This brings us to the core questions regarding the impact of the Islamic revolution in Indonesia and Malaysia: What has been the actual penetration of the Iranian experience within the populace? Are the fears of the authorities justified? How accurate were some of the early pundits when they predicted that Indonesia or Malaysia would become "another Iran"? To answer these questions it is important to consider several key issues, including the viability of a Shiite community in Indonesia and Malaysia that would likely be more vulnerable than the Sunni population to the principles of the revolution, the impact of prerevolutionary and revolutionary religious thinking on the majority Muslim population of those countries, and the degree to which attitudes may have changed over time. Again, there are certain methodological barriers to a complete understanding of these issues. Given the antagonistic views of the governments involved regarding aspects of the revolution and its philosophy as well as the absence of politically sensitive polling, it is difficult to gauge public attitudes accurately. This does not prevent the observer from noting major trends. Nor can it be argued that the absence of sizable pro-Iranian organizations and lack of popular support for a similar undertaking in Malaysia or Indonesia are simply a result of government repression.

As stated earlier, there is no large Shii community in either Malaysia or Indonesia. Most Muslims that have immigrated to the region are natives of the Indian subcontinent or Sunni Arabs, with many of the early Arab arrivals being from the Hadhramaut. There is evidence of Shia influence among the early Muslims coming to the region, and scholars have noted its local expression in art, culture, and, in a very limited way, religion. In an article on Shiism in Indonesia (aptly titled "What Here, Sir, Is Potpourri Syiah") the writer stated: "The amount of Syiah [Shii] teaching which mixed with cultural characteristics of Indonesian society has created 'a unique pattern' here. Perhaps a type of gado-gado [Indonesian mixed vegetable salad] Syiah."[33]

At present, then, there is no sizable self-conscious Shia religious group in either Indonesia or Malaysia, though Shia thought is more prominent in Indonesia than in Malaysia. That is, there are religious schools and teachers in Indonesia who include in their doctrines some elements that might be defined as Shii (although these institutions and individuals strongly emphasize their Sunni foundations) and there are youth, primarily in Jakarta, who are attracted by both religious and political aspects of Shia ideas. However, as we have noted Muslims in Southeast Asia are displaying a much greater breadth of religious thinking, and part of this change has been a consideration of new ideas generated from the Shia tradition. This appears to be particularly evident in Indonesia, where the syncretic nature of the country's Islamic foundations allows greater incorporation of new views.[34]

In order to judge the impact of the Islamic revolution on the Sunni-dominated Muslim communities of Indonesia and Malaysia, we can look at three major indicators: the literature on or by Khomeini and other Iranian religious thinkers available in the two countries; references to the revolution in the press and Islamic journals, and reactions by Islamic organizations and activists. This type of analysis is tainted by government efforts to limit the effect of the revolution, which may lead to understating the actual influence of the Iranian experience.

While there have been many translations of other contemporary Muslim activists in Southeast Asia as well as interpretive articles analyzing their theological and political views, there have been relatively few such works on the premier figure of the Islamic revolution, Ayatollah Khomeini. The shortage of these writings may be partly due to fear of government reprisals. However, it may also be that Khomeini's writings and statements have been seen as primarily Iranian in character and thus of limited attraction to scholars and activists in Indonesia and Malaysia.

If Khomeini's views are being carefully watched and, if possible, contained by authorities, there has been a ready market in Malaysia and Indonesia for the writings of men who were influential in developing the ideology of the Islamic revolution. Perhaps the best example is the works of Ali Shariati, a key intellectual forerunner of the changes that rocked Iran after 1979. Shariati has been credited with going beyond the narrow confines of Arab-based, more secular interpretations of Islam (such as Arab socialism) to provide a more universal religious ideology founded on Islam itself.[35] It may be argued that his views were broader and more universally attractive than those expressed by contemporary leaders of the revolution. Certainly Shariati, along with Qutb, Mawdudi, al-Banna, and others, has been widely published and quoted in both Indonesia and Malaysia. During the 1980s translations of many of Shariati's books and tracts have appeared in Indonesia, including *Islamic Criticism of Marxism and Other Western Fallacies* (1983), *Ideological Intellectuals* (1984), *Nobility* (1987), *The Role of the Intellectual Muslim* (1985), *Islam in the Perspective of Religious Sociology* (1983), *Haji* (1983), *Once More* (1987), and *Holy Book* (1982). There have also been articles by or about Shariati in journals such as *Al Nahdah*, *Prisma*, and *Dakwah*. In some instances his Iranian roots and relationship to the revolution are clearly noted, while in others he is defined as either a contemporary revivalist or radical religious commentator.

Analyses of the religious aspects of the revolution itself have appeared only intermittently in the press and Muslim journals. During the first year after the fall of the Shah, there was a deluge of articles in local-language publications discussing the events in Iran and the religious context of the rise of Khomeini.[36] The English-language press displayed less interest; many articles simply detailed events with little commentary. When they did analyze, Malaysian English-language papers were more likely to underscore the instability surrounding the post-Shah era. In general, the press was cautious about praising the policies of the revolution itself or recommending replication of those policies in southeast Asia. There were, however, published interviews with individuals returning from Iran who explained what was taking place. They often applauded the victory of Islam in Iran but with the qualifier that as a model the Iranian revolution was not applicable to Indonesia or Malaysia.[37]

During the next decade the patterns of reporting and religious analysis changed somewhat. A review of journal and newspaper articles shows a high percentage covering the Iran-Iraq war; their general perspective was that the conflict was disruptive of Islamic unity and could only aid its enemies.[38] The war, along with the character of the regime in Iran, incidents such as the rioting in Mecca, and the obvious governmental discouragement of prorevolutionary rhetoric and support, can largely explain the diminishment in positive articles about what was taking place in Iran. Nonetheless, journal articles noting the importance of the revolution and some of its significant contributions to the people of Iran continue to appear. Yet the overall thrust of these articles has been more objective, critical analyses of the character of the revolution as it has played itself out in Iran.

Malaysia and Indonesia

We can also assess the impact of the revolution through the reactions of Muslim organizations and activists in Malaysia and Indonesia. From the beginning there were demands from some *dakwah* and Islamic political organizations that the local government show greater support for the revolution. For example, the ABIM Federal Territory branch secretary asked the Malaysian government to support the struggles of Iranians to realize an Islamic republic.[39] When ABIM President Anwar Ibrahim returned form a meeting with Khomeini in Iran, he joined with religious leaders from other countries in calling for an "Iranian Liberation/Solidarity Day" to be held on March 16, 1979.[40] In 1982 the ABIM journal *Risalah* praised certain accomplishments of the new regime such as its ability to control drugs, alcohol, gambling, and prostitution.[41] Although more cautious in its support, the Malay-Muslim opposition party PAS was also initially prepared to praise the events in Iran. But like ABIM, PAS was careful not to call for a similar revolution in Malaysia. Both ABIM and PAS have been accused by their political opponents of close links to Iran.

As previously noted, in Indonesia there have been numerous government charges of radical Muslim groups supporting an "Iran-type" Islamic state or advocating the overthrow of the regime to further the Islamic cause. However, there is little evidence of mainstream Islamic organizations going any further than their Malaysian counterparts; that is, they may find satisfaction in the Islamic victory in Iran, but they do not encourage such a model for Indonesia. In fact, a review of numerous recent Islamic religious talks and sermons, many of which have been classified as subversive by the Indonesian government, reveals very little mention of the Iranian revolution or Khomeini. When there are references to contemporary individuals they are more likely to be local scholars or Middle Eastern writers of an earlier era.[42] This lack of comment in sermons deemed subversive runs counter to the assumption that the paucity of pro-Iranian rhetoric has simply been due to government censorship. Nor can it be argued that the Indonesian people know little about events in Iran. Both religious journals and news magazines have featured Khomeini on their covers. One observer even stated that he thought Khomeini was the third most popular figure in Indonesia behind the present and former presidents of the republic. However, I would argue that this interest in Khomeini flourished because he symbolizes the victory of Islam, not because Southeast Asians support the manner in which the Iranian revolution developed.

von der Mehden

Greater credence has to be given to the fact that the more specific characteristics of the revolution as it unfolded have not been easily translated into the Southeast Asian experience.

Yet, based on the comments of a wide range of observers of contemporary Islam in Malaysia and Indonesia, the general consensus is that the Iranian revolution had an important influence on the religiously conscious elements of these countries. It came at a time when the Islamic revival was gaining momentum in the region and Muslims were becoming more aware of their own identities. It was a period when the revivalist interpretations of Islam by men such as Mawdudi, Qutb, and Shariati were beginning to make an impression on many activists. Locally, Muslims were increasing their contact with Western materialism and morality and finding the meeting unsettling and often undesirable. It was also a time when the Western ideological solutions often put forward by the region's secular leaders were found wanting.[43] In this environment the Islamic revolution appeared at first to be an example of the victory of Islam over just those forces of Western materialism, morality, and ideology. That context explains why the initial public reaction to Iran's revolution was so generally positive and why religious leaders were attracted to it. This was not necessarily a vote in favor of the specific institutional structures established in Iran or to the religious laws that were promulgated. To many Southeast Asians, it was the revolution as symbol rather than reality that was so compelling.

The efforts of the Iranian Islamic community to overthrow the Shah also found resonance in the view of many Southeast Asian Muslims of the need to struggle (*perjuangan ummat Islam*) to achieve an Islamic society. While this concept can mean many things—from the formation of an Islamic state to the greater implementation of Islamic principles—the very real, historical requirement of Southeastern Asian Muslims to obtain their goals and make manifest the destiny of Islam gave added impetus to the support of the Islamic revolution in Iran.[44]

However, as we have noted, some of the specific policies adopted by revolutionary Iran after 1979 were difficult for Southeast Asian Muslims to accept. Among those factors that had a generally negative impact were the increased role of the clergy in the Iranian government, the reports of harsh treatment of secular and religious opponents of the regime, the actions of Iranians abroad (such as the demonstrations in Mecca), the bloody Iran-Iraq conflict with the seeming intransigence of both sides, and the alleged state-supported attacks on other Muslims outside Iran. When these perceptions were combined with local government efforts to contain the influence of "radical" and "deviant" forces, the luster of Iran as a model diminished noticeably. But the initial phenomenon is still viewed by many as a major milestone on the road to the inevitable victory of Islam. In terms of its symbolic power, the success of the Iranian revolution is analogous to the Japanese victory in the Russo-Japanese War, which was perceived by many Southeast Asian nationalists as the first real triumph of Asians over Europeans.

Conclusions

Any analysis of the influence of the Iranian experience on Southeast Asia in terms of readily verifiable concrete evidence may miss the depth of the revolution's impact. State-to-state relations have generally been proper, and the intragovernmental tensions that do exist have not broken out of polite diplomatic exchanges and veiled criticisms. At the same time, the Malaysian and Indonesian governments have fully recognized the threats to political and religious stability inherent in Iranian events. This has led both Kuala Lumpur and Jakarta to work to control Islamic ideas perceived to be subversive or detrimental to "peace and order." Thus, while continuing "normalcy" at the official level, there have been active efforts to assure that the ideas of the revolution do not penetrate too deeply into local Islamic communities. Most threatening was that Iran would become a model for the establishment of new Islamic states in Southeast Asia. It can be argued that the indigenous cultures and nature of Islam in the region are fundamentally antithetical to such a movement. Yet both governments have been faced with opponents deeply commited to fundamental religious changes. Admittedly, neither government has experienced mainstream religious opposition that has publicly advocated the establishment of "another Iran," although the formation of a state administered according to more structured Islamic legal and social principles has been espoused by organizations such as PAS. However, to the degree that the revolution touched emotional nerves of religious elements within the population, it gave warnings to the establishment that "radical" Islam needed to be carefully controlled.

While some of the evidence is admittedly impressionistic, it would appear that the revolution itself had a major effect on the religiously conscious elements in both countries. It fed into a series of other forces that were lending strength to the Islamic revival in the region. While the perceived excesses of the new regime in Teheran and the long Iran-Iraq war weakened the original emotional attraction of many activists to the Iranian experience, the revolution itself is still upheld by a wide spectrum of Southeast Asian Muslims as one of the most important phenomena of the twentieth century. Nowhere else has Islam been so decidedly victorious over the economic, political, and moral forces of the West.

There were those who initially thought that Indonesia and Malaysia were possible candidates for "another Iran." Today it would be very difficult to make that prognosis, at least for the foreseeable future. Not only have events in Iran made that less likely, but more importantly those in authority in Malaysia and Indonesia have, at least for the time being, weakened those elements in their countries seeking radical religious solutions. In Malaysia this has been accomplished through co-optation of many of the ideas and even leaders of the religious opposition, combined with the threat and use of state power to limit the influence of those Muslim activists who propound what the government defines as radical or "un-Islamic" views. The Indonesian government has been even more prepared to use its power and authority to assure that dissident religious groups and ideas do not gain paramountcy, and at least for now the larger religious organizations have seen their political power seriously eroded. Beyond state policies, the religious cultures of both countries make questionable the successful transfer of the Iranian model to Southeast Asia. The syncretic nature of Indonesian Islam and the traditional loyalties of the Malay are not fertile ground for "another Iran."

Notes

1. It should be noted that no local or foreign scholar dealing with the region made bald assertions of this nature.

2. For more information on the revivalist phenomenon, see J. Nagata, *The Reflowering of Malaysian Islam* (Vancouver: University of British Columbia Press, 1984); Fred R. von de Mehden, "Malaysia and Indonesia," in *The Politics of Islamic Revivalism*, ed. S. Hunter (Bloomington: University of Indiana Press, 1988); and idem, "Islamic Resurgence in Malaysia," in *Islam and Development*, ed. John L. Esposito (Syracuse: Syracuse University Press, 1980). For details on the prewar antecedents, see D. Noer, *The Modernist Muslim Movement in Indonesia, 1900–1942*

(Kuala Lumpur: Oxford University Press, 1973); and J. Peacock, *Muslim Puritans* (Berkeley and Los Angeles: University of California Press, 1978).

3. See M. Lyon, "The Dakwah Movement in Malaysia," *Review of Indonesian and Malayan Affairs* 13 (December 1979): 34–45.

4. There is considerable literature on dating the first entrance of Islam into Malaysia and Indonesia, but basically the faith was brought to the region by traders beginning at the end of the twelfth century and continued to spread through primarily peaceful means during succeeding generations. See A.H. Johns, "Islam in Southeast Asia," *Indonesia* 19 (1975): 33–55; M.B. Hooker, *Islam in South-East Asia* (Leiden: Brill, 1983); S. Fatimi, *Islam Comes to Malaysia* (Singapore: Singapore University Press, 1963); and H. de Graaf and T. Pigeaud, "De eerste Moslimse Vorstendommen op Java, Studien over de Staatkundige Geschiedenis van de 15e en 16e Eeuw," *Verhandelingen van het Koninklijk Instituut voor Taal-, Land- en Volkenkunde* 69 (1974).

5. For fascinating accounts of Turkish influence, see A. Reid, "Sixteenth-Century Turkish Influence in Western Indonesia," *Journal of Southeast Asian History* 50, no. 3 (December 1969): 395–414; and G.W. van der Meiden, "A Turkish Mediator between Mangkubumi and the Dutch East Indies Company," *Review of Indonesian and Malayan Affairs* 15 (1981): 92–107.

6. See, for example, W. Roff, "Indonesian and Malay Students in Cairo in the 1920s," *Indonesia* 9 (April 1970): 73–87; K. Steenbrook, *Beberapa Aspek Tentang Islam Di Indonesia Abad K-19* (Jakarta: Butan Bintang, 1984), 128–38. An excellent example of an Indonesian religious leader's intellectual contacts is found in M. Nakamura, "Haji Kahar Muzakhir and the Maturing of Indonesian Islam," *Mizan* 1, no. 3 (1984): 87–97.

7. See J. Vredenregt, "The Haddj," *Bijdragen tot de Taal-, Land- en Volkenkunde* 118 (1962): 91–154.

8. K. Kamarun, "Sejarah Haji di Malaysia," *Dakwah* (August 1986): 8–12.

9. See Abdullah Alwi Haji Hasen, "The Development of Islamic Education in Kelantan," in Khoo Kay Lim et al., *Tamadun Di Malaysia* (Kuala Lumpur: Persatuan Sejarah Malaysia, 1980); Muhammad A. Zaki, "Modern Muslim Thought in Egypt and its Impact on Islam in Malaya" (Ph.D. diss., University of London, 1965); and J. Peacock, *Muslim Puritans*.

10. See Fred R. von der Mehden, *Religion and Nationalism in Southeast Asia* (Madison: University of Wisconsin Press, 1963), 159; M. Kramer, *Islam Assembled* (New York: Columbia University Press, 1986), 95–118 passim; and A. Milner, "The Impact of the Turkish Revolution on Malaya," *Archipel* 31 (1986): 119–29. There was even worry among the Dutch that the war would spread to the Indies.

11. In fact, in 1945 Indonesians living in the Middle East were among the first outside the region to support independence from the Dutch. See M. Natsir, "Masa depan Hubungan Indonesia," *Budaya Jaya* 9 (March 1976): 166–181.

12. Malaysia, *Economic Report 1986–87* (Kuala Lumpur: Ministry of Finance, 1986); Indonesia, *Ekspor Indonesia 1982* (Jakarta: Departmen Perdgangan, 1983).

13. *Middle East Economic Digest*, September 14, 1979.

14. For Indonesian views, see F. Weinstein, *Indonesian Foreign Policy and the Dilemma of Independence* (Ithaca: Cornell University Press, 1976), 125–30; and M. Leifer, "The Islamic Factor in Indonesia's Foreign Policy: A Case of Functional

Ambiguity," in *Islam in Foreign Policy*, ed. A. Dawishi (Cambridge: Cambridge University Press, 1983), 144–59.

15. See the *New Straits Times* (Kuala Lumpur), May 5, 1985, and August 17, 1986.

16. See James P. Piscatori, "Asian Islam: International Linkages and Their Impact on International Relations," in *Islam in Asia*, ed. John L. Esposito (New York: Oxford University Press, 1987), 230–61; and L. Pangandaman, "Philippine Diplomatic Relations with the Islamic Countries," *Kasayagan* 5 (1980): 32–36.

17. One analysis of the intellectual antecedents to the Islamic revival noted these three men plus the Kharijites, Ibn Taymiya, and two modern thinkers, Jamal al-Afghani and Abdul Wahhab; see Helena Cobban, "The Angry Children of Islam," *Middle East* 87 (January 1982): 17–19. In another work on the Islamic revival, Qutb, Shariati, Khomeini, and Mawdudi are the featured spokesmen; see John L. Esposito, *Voices of Resurgent Islam* (New York: Oxford University Press, 1983).

18. For example, courses in Islamic education at the Universiti Teknologi in Kuala Lumpur feature the less radical works of authors such as Mawdudi and Qutb.

19. *Universiti Malaya Kalendar 1986–1987* and *Universiti Kebangsaan, Laporan Tahunan KE-12, 1981–82.*

20. Malaysia, *Foreign Affairs* 12 no. 4 (1979): 463.

21. See S. Siddique, "Contemporary Islamic Developments in ASEAN," in *Southeast Asian Affairs 1980* (Singapore: Institute of Southeast Asian Studies), 90.

22. See *Ekspor Indonesia 1982* (Jakarta: Departmen Perdagangan, 1983); and "Five Years of Indonesian Efforts in the Middle East," *Iktisadi* 4, no. 8 (March 1983): 5. In September and October 1980, Malaysian newspapers reported difficulties of Malaysian workers in the war zone and their subsequent return home. (*New Straits Times*, September 29 and 30, 1980, and October 1 and 16, 1980).

23. For details, see Fred R. von der Mehden, "The Political and Social Challenge of the Islamic Revival in Malaysia and Indonesia," *The Muslim World* 76 (July–October 1986): 219–33; and S. Barraclough, "Managing the Challenges of Islamic Revival in Malaysia," *Asian Survey* 23 (August 1983): 958–75.

24. *Straits Times* (Kuala Lumpur), July 7, 1979; *Star* (Penang) July 19, 1979.

25. *Star*, October 7, 1982.

26. *New Straits Times*, December 12, 1984.

27. Barraclough, 961.

28. A detailed account of this case is given in *Indonesia Reports—Human Rights Supplement* 18 (October 1986): 5–7; *Indonesia Reports* 13 (November 1985): 36; and *Indonesia Reports* 16 (June 1986): 45. Amnesty International has come to the defense of the accused, stating that there was no violence intended.

29. *Al Nahdah* 5, no. 3 (1985): 50.

30. *Star*, October 23, 1985.

31. *Berita Harian* (Kuala Lumpur), October 1, 1987.

32. See Barraclough, "Managing the Challenges," and von der Mehden, "The Political and Social Challenge."

33. This article, by D. Siriajuddin and Iqbal Abdurrauf Saimina, appeared in *Panji Masyarakat* and was translated by Mary Fulcher in *Indonesia Reports—Books &*

Biblio Supplement, 19 (December 1986): 4. See also Baroroh Baried, "L'Islam dans l'archipel," *Archipel* 15 (1978): 65–84.

34. For an interesting discussion of the intellectual influences of Shia thought in Indonesia, see the interview with Nurcholish Majid in *Panji Masyarakat* 513 (August 21, 1986). The interview was translated in *Indonesia Reports—Culture & Society Supplement* 25 (1988).

35. See M. Amein Rais, "International Islamic Movements and Their Influence upon the Islamic Movement in Indonesia," *Prisma* 35 (March 1985): 37–38.

36. For example, from March 1979 through early 1980, each monthly issue of the Malaysian Muslim journal *Dakwah* included a story on events in Iran, usually with a picture of Khomeini and once with his picture on the cover.

37. For example, when the former head of ABIM Anwar Ibrahim (now education minister) returned from Iran, he was careful to qualify his praise for the revolution with the recognition that it was not a model for Malaysia.

38. See, for example, "Israel Senang Hati," *Dakwah* 48 (November 1980): 8–9.

39. *Watan* (Kuala Lumpur), May 16, 1979.

40. *Watan*, March 1, 1979.

41. Noted in Muzaffar Chandra, *Islamic Resurgence in Malaysia* (Petaling Jaya: Penerbit Fajar Bakti, 1987), 36. Chandra makes the point that the revolution was a secondary factor in giving impetus to the Malaysian Islamic revival.

42. *Indonesia Reports* has translated a number of these comments in recent years.

43. See Chandra, *Islamic Resurgence*.

44. For a discussion of contemporary Indonesian perspectives on this struggle, see A. Samson, "Conceptions of Politics, Power, and Ideology in Contemporary Indonesian Islam," in *Political Power and Communications in Indonesia*, ed. K. Jackson and L. Pye (Berkeley and Los Angeles: University of California Press, 1978), 196–226.

13

The Iranian Revolution

and the Muslims

in the Philippines

CESAR ADIB MAJUL

AS A MOVEMENT THAT overthrew the Shah of Iran (who was judged as tyrannical by Islamic standards) and aimed to make Islamic law more operative in society, the Iranian Islamic revolution led by Ayatollah Khomeini has had unavoidable political implications in the Philippines. There are several reasons for this. First, in parallel with the anti-Shah movement in Iran, the authoritarian regime of President Ferdinand Marcos, who had imposed martial law since 1972, was increasingly resented if not actually challenged by different segments of the Filipino population. Second, although fragmented in leadership and organization, there is a respected ulama in the Philippines, many of whom were educated in Arab countries. They would inevitably develop a stand on the Iranian revolution (or any Islamic revolution, for that matter), and their influence on Muslim communities can be fraught with religious and political consequences. Third, since the very inception of martial law, there has been a Muslim armed struggle against the regime—a movement directed toward self-determination and independence defined as a prerequiste for the unhindered implementation and enhancement of Islamic institutions among the Muslims in the Philippines. Fourth, after the 1971 celebration of the 2,500th anniversary of the founding of the Achaemenid Empire, the Philippines and Iran commenced closer diplomatic relations (a move both countries were forced to reevaluate after the Revolution). By the end of 1978, there were at least 2,500 Iranian students in various Philippine institutions of learning, principally in Manila, while some 6,000 Filipinos were working in Iran. Finally, the Iranian revolution's anti-imperialist character (more specifically aimed at the United States) gained the approval of anti-American leftist segments in the Philippines.

The Political Opposition to Marcos

When President Ferdinand Marcos imposed martial law in September 1972, he abolished Congress, banned demonstrations, established censorship, imprisoned his severest critics, and so on. Political opponents who were not incarcerated were intimidated, left leaderless and in disarray. Former Senator Benigno Aquino, Jr., well-known leader of the opposition and main rival for the presidency, was among the first to be arrested and imprisoned. Aquino firmly believed that the majority of Filipinos hated martial law and that if free elections were held, he would easily defeat Marcos. But for the moment he was immobilized. Still in prison when the Iranian revolution took place in 1979, Aquino came to entertain the possibility that, analogously to Khomeini, Jaime Cardinal Sin, one of the highest prelates of the country and archbishop of Manila, could weld the Catholic clergy and faithful into a united opposition that would force Marcos to step down or at least lift martial law and permit free elections under a restored democracy.

In October 1979 Aquino wrote a letter to the cardinal suggesting that the cardinal "provide the necessary leadership" for the country in lieu of the old politicians. The cardinal's response in a subsequent press interview was that he would "not play the role of an Ayatullah Khomeini in the Philippines."[1] In his view, the religious and social situation in the Philippines was quite different from that in Iran. At the start of martial law he had even reflected that at least some form of law and order had been reestablished in the land. Moreover, the church had not been persecuted and continued to operate its places of worship, seminaries, schools, and other properties undisturbed. At bottom, the Catholic church represented one of the most conservative institutions in Filipino society and did not wish to be blamed for any social upheaval or disorder. This was the situation in 1979. It would not be long, however, before the cardinal and other leading prelates would number among the foremost critics of Marcos on the issue of human rights, but such criticism did not necessarily imply revolution by force.

The fate of the Shah was certainly foremost in the minds of others fighting the Marcos regime on the issues of human rights and political freedom. For example, on December 8, 1979, the Philippine Civil Liberties Union (CLU) boldly branded Marcos as "the American Shah of the Philippines" and predicted that the United States would "withdraw support from him sooner or later" due to the widespread corruption in the country.[2] Nonetheless, there did not appear to be any charismatic leader to do to Marcos what Ayatollah Khomeini had succeeded in doing to the Shah.

The Ulama and the Muslim Students

Muslims in the Philippines, also called Moros, are concentrated in the southern part of the country.[3] These Muslims are Sunnis who generally adhere to the Shafii school of law (*madhhab*). Most Moros are unaware of or indifferent to the differences between Sunni and Shii; to them, all Muslims are one. It is true that Muslim students who have been exposed to the growing literature on Islam entering the country are aware of these differences, but such awareness does not generally signify much in their daily lives since there has been no history of conflict between Sunni and Shii in the Philippines. In Manila mosques, Sunni and Shii pray together and minor variations in some ritual prayer movements are consciously ignored.

Before the Iranian Revolution, educated Muslims in the Philippines read or had been told about the alleged anti-Islamic actions of the Shah: restrictions on *madrasas* (religious schools), the disregard if not outright persecution of some Iranian ulama, and the rapid introduction of Western institutions in a manner that spelled danger to traditional Islamic values. Consequently, the Shah's overthrow inspired much local popular sympathy for the Iranian revolution. Moreover, the ulama must have felt some collegial sympathy for the ayatollahs of Iran—a form of peer or class identification. When reminded of possible differences between Sunni and Shii, they often responded by saying that any revolution for Islam merited the support of all true Muslims, and that they had heard enough about Muslims being pushed around in many parts of the world. Some ulama viewed the Shah's downfall as not only a manifestation of Allah's punishment but a preview of Marcos's fate as well.

Around the end of 1979, a fair amount of religious literature in the form of booklets, journals, and pamphlets began to enter the Philippines directly from Iran or through the Iranian Embassy and Iranian students. This literature was initially distributed to Muslim institutes, organizations, and students. Many of the English-language publications of the Ministry of National Guidance of the Islamic Republic of Iran, the Islamic Propagation Organization, the Shariati Foundation, the Cultural Revolution Council, and other agencies, official or otherwise, were of a high academic quality. For the first time, Muslim faculty members and students in the Philippines became exposed to the thought and writings of Iranian Muslim intellectuals and theologians. In particular, they came to know more about the historical role of Ali ibn Abi Talib, the significance of the martyrdom of Hussain (the Prophet's grandson) and the meaning of the Mahdi, as well as to gain additional insights into the meaning of Revelation and the Qur'an. At the same time, a great deal of anti-American propaganda began to enter the country, not without overtones of Iranian nationalism. The reception to this was mixed. In general, there was no overt anti-Americanism among the Moros, and the negative relations that ensued between Iran and the United States lacked relevance to them.

Most of the younger ulama are graduates of religious institutes in the Arab world, notably al-Azhar in Egypt. Although these ulama are conscious of some theological differences between Sunni and Shii, they often dismiss them as unimportant. Instead, they emphasize basic similarities among Muslims and the oneness of the *ummah* (Islamic community). Nevertheless, some religious leaders believed that certain Islamic issues hitherto unknown (such as the advent of the Mahdi or qualifications for succession in the Caliphate) would serve to confuse the minds of young Muslims. Consequently, some ulama did not encourage theological arguments between their students and Iranian religious partisans. But all of this did not affect the vast majority of Muslims in the southern Philippines. They were too busy attending to their daily needs while doing their best to perform their religious duties under war conditions brought about by the Muslim armed struggle against the government.

A major source of confusion to concerned Moros was the Iran-Iraq war. Historically, Muslims in the Philippines have tended to side with the Arabs. While sympathetic to the Iranian revolution, the Moros were not too happy about the prospects of an Iraqi defeat, especially when the bulk of the Arab world sided with Iraq. The war between Muslims was indeed a form of religious trauma for the pious. Thus, the explanation that the Western world, and particularly the United States and the Soviet Union, was the ultimate instigator of the war was readily accepted by them.

On November 30, 1979, about 300 Moro students, representing five local Muslim associations, gathered in a park near the U.S. Embassy in Manila. They carried placards bearing such slogans as "Long Live Khomeini's Islamic Republic," "Unite for Jihad," "Down with American Imperialism," and "Carter: Return the Shah." A detachment of 250 riot police came to disperse them, since political demonstrations were prohibited under martial law. Some of the young Muslim leaders explained that they had gathered for the Friday prayer meeting and that the whole affair was to be a peaceful one. The students were then allowed to pray. Meanwhile, armed soldiers had arrived to stand guard before the U.S. Embassy. After prayers, the students were ordered to disperse or go to buses waiting to return them to a Manila mosque. But a few demonstrators refused to leave, wishing to march before the embassy. They persuaded those already in the buses to rejoin them. Chanting "Allahu Akbar" (God is Most Great), waving their placards, and defying the police, the students began to regroup. The police then moved in with nightsticks and fire hoses. About 150 students were arrested and hauled to Fort Bonifacio for interrogation. Eventually most of them were released, but twenty-five demonstrators were detained in the Fort for several months under very unsanitary conditions, much to the shock of visiting students from the University of the Philippines who did not fail to notice that alleged Communists imprisoned nearby had better quarters.

Following this incident, talk in some university quarters that the whole idea of holding a prayer meeting and marching before the U.S. Embassy originated from Iranian students who had also provided funds to a few of the Muslim youth. Some claimed that the original plan called for a group of Iranian students to join the demonstration. The fact is that no such Iranian group appeared, nor was there any subsequent incrimination of Iranians for this alleged failure by other Muslims. Still, the anti-Carter and anti-American slogans may well be evidence of Iranian influence and persuasion. But given the spirited character of the Manila Muslim youth and the enthusiasm of their leaders, the demonstration revealed a genuine sympathy for Imam

The Philippines

Khomeini and the Islamic character of the Iranian revolution. It was also a bid for leadership on the part of a few Muslims. The return of students from the buses to regroup simply reflected the invariant pride of the Muslim youth in belying any charge of cowardice at an event believed to be Islamic.

In any event, government authorities were alarmed at the "bad example" generated by the incident. The press had carried daily reports on the attack by Iranian students on the U.S. Embassy in Teheran and the taking of American hostages. To many Filipino journalists close to the administration, the prayer meeting and intended demonstration were tangible signs of support for what had happened in Teheran. Within twenty-four hours of the prayer meeting, Marcos declared that illegal demonstrations were to be dispersed and students who had broken the law would be prosecuted. Among other things, this policy was one way of informing U.S. authorities that Marcos was their friend.

The Moro National Liberation Front and the Iranian Revolution

To understand Iranian relations with the Moro National Liberation Front (MNLF), a brief historical digression is necessary. For centuries, the Muslims in the southern Philippines constituted independent sultanates. Successfully avoiding Spanish conquest, they gradually fell under U.S. sovereignty. The United States made them become part of an independent Philippines in 1946, a move the Muslims viewed as a betrayal of a trust. Prior to independence, the vast majority did not consider themselves Filipinos and retained their identity as a separate people.

This identity was essentially religious and cultural in nature. Muslim leaders had wished to separate from the rest of the Philippines to form an independent state. For decades, the Muslims had vainly resisted the encroachment of Christian settlers (under government assistance) on their traditional lands. Years of economic neglect and political discrimination had reduced them to the lowest national literacy and economic levels. Unemployment was endemic; law and order had deteriorated in some areas. That Filipino national leaders in Manila viewed Muslims and their lands in much the same way as Spanish and American colonial authorities had done before them was met with deep suspicion and fierce resentment. Significantly, government programs to integrate

Muslims into the body politic were paralleled by the growth of Islamic revivalism.

Events in the late 1960s and early 1970s further alienated the Muslims and forced them to arm themselves: the massacre of some Muslim trainees by the Philippine military in March 1968; communal clashes between Muslims and Christians (in which the constabulary and police often sided with the Christians), the gradual loss of Muslim communal lands to settlers; the effects of the November 1971 elections, which led Christian politicians, with the help of Marcos and the ruling party, to capture many provincial and municipal offices in traditional Muslim areas; and the rise of well-armed Christian paramilitary forces. Beginning in 1969 scores of Muslim youth were trained abroad in the Malaysian state of Sabah in guerrilla and jungle warfare. Their return has helped secure the defense of their communities.

When martial law was declared in September 1972, government attempts to disarm Muslims, who feared Christian armed groups as well as military retaliation, provoked open rebellion. Foremost in this struggle was the MNLF, whose founders were among those Muslim youth trained abroad. The MNLF was guided by a central committee whose original members crossed regional and linguistic lines; its chairman, Nur Misuari, was a faculty member at the University of the Philippines. Even before his training abroad, Misuari had argued that only through a free and independent state could the Muslims free themselves from corrupt leaders and fully implement Islamic institutions. To him, the Moros constituted a separate people—the Bangsamoro people. Misuari's concept had a nationalistic connotation such that non-Muslims who cast their lot with the Muslims were also to be called "Moros" and therefore considered as members of the future Bangsamore Republik.

The war in the southern Philippines resulted in the death of thousands of soldiers and civilians and the flight of several hundred thousand refugees. Charges of genocide gained for the Moros the sympathy and concern of the international Muslim community. Libya provided sanctuary for some of the top MNLF leaders and did not deny that it had provided various forms of aid. The Organization of the Islamic Conference (OIC) and other Muslim international organizations continually exerted pressure on the Philippine government to negotiate for a peaceful settlement with the leaders of the Muslim armed struggle, particularly the MNLF.[4]

In December 1976, due to Libyan intervention and under the auspices of the OIC, Philippine government officials and MNLF leaders were able to negotiate a settlement in Tripoli, Libya. Called the Tripoli Agreement, the settlement called for a cease-fire and the granting of autonomy to thirteen provinces where the majority of Muslims lived. Marcos then set out in early 1977 to provide a form of autonomy in accordance with his own definition of it. Meanwhile, the Bangsa Moro Liberation Organization (BMLO) was formally organized by two traditional leaders living as expatriates in Jidda, Saudi Arabia: Rashid Lucman, a former congressman and sultan among his people in Lanao Province, and Salipada Pendatun, an ex-congressman and member of the Maguindanao nobility of Cotabato Province. They proclaimed the BMLO to be the leader of the Muslim struggle in the Philippines.

Instrumental as he was in having Misuari and other MNLF commanders trained abroad and because of his claimed traditional prerogatives, Lucman felt that he rightly should have full control of the MNLF. But this was not possible as long as Misuari, who belonged to another ethnolinguistic group and a different social class, was chairman. Consequently, the BMLO conspired with Salamat Hashim, the vice chairman of the MNLF Central Committee, to claim or seize leadership of the MNLF on the grounds that Misuari had leftist leanings, was suspicious and secretive, and had abandoned the collegial character of the committee. Salamat Hashim was a nephew of Pendatun and related to the Maguindanao nobility; he had received extensive religious training at al-Azhar. In December 1977, Salamat issued an instrument of takeover and informed the OIC accordingly. But Misuari, with the aid of his loyal followers, held fast to his position and expelled Salamat Hashim. In response, Salamat asserted his independence and transferred his base of operations to Cairo. Because the BMLO had failed to control him or the MNLF, by 1978 there were three groups claiming to head the Muslim movement in the Philippines: the MNLF–Misuari faction, the MNLF–Salamat faction, and the BMLO.

When the Iranian revolution broke out, the leaders of the MNLF–Misuari faction and the BMLO hailed it as a reassertion of Islamic principles. It was reported that in May 1979 Rashid Lucman visited Ayatollah Khomeini, who promised that he would form a committee to offer "tangible" support for Muslim liberation movements, including those in the Philippines.[5] However, subsequent events indicated that no real commitment was ever made to the BMLO by any high-ranking Iranian official.

The case of the MNLF–Misuari faction was different. In June 1979 Misuari, heading a five-man delegation, appeared in Teheran to attend an international conference against imperialism. On June 9 the delegation was able to visit Ayatollah Khomeini in Qum. Imam Khomeini prayed openly for the success of the Muslim revolutionary struggle in the Philippines and assured Misuari that "the victory of the Islamic Revolution of Iran would not be complete until the oppressed Bangsamoro Muslims in the southern Philippines won their victory." The MNLF delegation also had the opportunity to meet Prime Minister Mehdi Bazargan, Ayatollah Montazeri, and Ayatollah Ali Khamenei, then imam of a Teheran mosque. The Iranian foreign ministry assured Misuari that relations between Iran and the MNLF would be based on the principle that all Muslims are brothers and that General Rafael M. Ileto, the Philippine ambassador, had already been informed that future relations between Iran and the Philippines would be contingent on Philippine treatment of the Moro people. Soon after, the Iranian government promised on the state television network that Iran would give every possible assistance to the oppressed Muslims in the Philippines. The MNLF delegation was extensively interviewed by the Iranian press.[6]

The Iran visit was a true morale booster for Misuari and his aides, particularly after what they had to endure from BMLO intrigues, Salamat Hashim's breakaway, and the surrender of several top MNLF commanders to the Philippine government. One can speculate that officials of Iran's new regime might have been wary about dealing with the BMLO, whose leadership represented dynastic and vested interests in traditional Moro society. Misuari and his delegation members, who were relatively young men, must have appeared as sincere and dedicated. At any rate, compared with the other factions, Misuari commanded the largest fighting group.

On October 2, 1979, Abu Sharif, commander of the Islamic Revolutionary Guards (*Pasdaran*), declared in Kermanshah that his organization "will never rest until the complete liberation of Palestine, Lebanon, Eritrea, the Philippines and Iran is achieved."[7] That this statement, later quoted in *Kayhan International*, was unexpectedly reported in a Manila daily most likely reflects the Philippine government's stand that the MNLF was nearly washed up. On October 15, Ali Akbar

Monifar, the Iranian oil minister, suddenly announced that in response to the "massacre" of Muslims by the Philippine regime, Iran had suspended the export of crude oil to the country and would not supply "a single drop of oil so long as oppression and massacre of Muslims continue there."[8]

The Philippine ambassador to Iran said that he was not officially informed of the action and disclosed that his country received 10,000 barrels of oil daily (about 4.16 percent of the annual oil import). Philippine officials were disturbed not only by the charge of massacre but also because they stood to lose about 800,000 barrels of oil already promised by contract. An additional worry was that other oil-exporting Muslim countries might follow suit or use the oil-embargo weapon in retaliation for the Philippine regime's dragging its feet in fully implementing the Tripoli Agreement of 1976. Economic officials were also disappointed, for when Iran's revolutionary government took power, it actually increased oil exports to the Philippines based on an early policy to help poor developing countries—a policy that appeared to some observers as idealistic if not naive. On November 6 Iran's oil embargo against the Philippines became fully effective.

Official reaction to Monifar's announcement was immediate. Manuel Collantes, the acting foreign minister, opined that perchance the oil minister had been misquoted, while denying that the military had perpetuated a massacre. He added that the government had adhered to the cease-fire, was implementing the Tripoli Agreement, and had even held a plebiscite to choose officials to head the "autonomous regions." The defense minister also denied the massacre, although he admitted isolated cases of "some incidents involving civilians." The Muslim head of the office for Muslim affairs in the foreign ministry likewise denied the Iranian charge and countered with a lengthy narration of what the government was doing for Muslims, how the rate of pilgrims to Mecca was increasing every year, and so on. Not to be outdone, a group of Muslims associated with the government accused Misuari of supplying false information to Iranian authorities. A Manila newspaper editorial went so far as to suggest that an Iranian fact-finding mission be invited to the country to discover the falsity of the massacre charge.[9]

Interestingly enough, even before the oil embargo some local political observers had commented on the growing coldness of the new Iranian government toward Filipinos and the Philippine government. Jesus

Bigornia, a columnist who often reflected the government's stand on many issues, attributed this attitude to the suspicion of Iranian authorities that his country was still sympathetic to the Shah.[10] There might be something to this opinion, since Imelda Marcos had attended the Shah's celebration of the 2,500th anniversary of the Achaemenid Empire and had visited the Shah himself on at least one occasion regarding oil imports. But the major reason for cooler relations was probably the growth of Iranian sympathy for the plight of the Moros as expounded by Misuari.

Following the embargo announcement, Philippine officials, especially those in the education ministry, became increasingly watchful of Iranian students, if not hostile to some of them. It was no coincidence that Bigornia, in his column of October 18, 1979, claimed that a disgruntled Iranian student, who had since left Manila for Australia, had revealed that an Iranian revolutionary committee in Teheran was supplying aid to Moro rebels in the southern Philippines through Iranian "students." These Iranians were allegedly under instruction from Teheran and had military training as well as combat experience, having fought rebels in northern Iran. Bigornia then strongly recommended that the government start to investigate such "students" who threatened national security.[11] Henceforth, many Iranians in the Philippines would not find life as easy as when they first arrived during the Shah's regime.

The Iranian oil embargo represented a victory for the MNLF. It was likewise hailed by the BMLO, which had advocated that oil-exporting Muslim countries apply sanctions to the Philippines to force it to grant further concessions to the Moros. However, unlike Misuari, who had reverted to his original demand for secession instead of autonomy, the BMLO continued its agitation for the full implementation of the Tripoli Agreement. For when this was accomplished, BMLO leaders expected to return to the country and take over the leadership of the autonomous region. But Marcos, while clearly hedging on the full implementation of the agreement, was announcing to the world that it was in fact being fulfilled. Failing to convince the OIC, he countered with the argument that since there were three organizations claiming leadership of the Muslims, he did not know with whom to negotiate—in spite of the fact that the OIC had recognized the MNLF with Misuari as its chairman.

The Philippines

In truth, the new Iranian government had never made a secret of its policy to use Iranian oil to support Islamic causes. This explains why the BMLO, in a position paper presented at the tenth OIC conference in Fez, in May 1979, requested that Iran apply oil sanctions to force the Philippines to adhere to the letter of the Tripoli Agreement and lift martial law from Muslim provinces. The paper also pointed out that "The Arab nations should also use its oil for non-Arabs who are victims of genocide because they are Muslims," while suggesting that the Arabs ought to assume some responsibility for the Moros since it was Arabs who had introduced Islam to the Philippines—not to mention that the Muslims there had always supported Arab causes, in exchange for which the Moros had become targets of retaliation by the enemies of Islam.[12] Not long after the start of the Iranian oil embargo, a junior BMLO officer, harking back to the BMLO position paper, bluntly declared in Jidda that the Iranians had made the right move and the proper thing for Saudi Arabians to do was to follow it. Saudi officials were not at all amused by this suggestion, which they deemed unusually impudent, and it was only the intercession of some compassionate souls that prevented the immediate deportation of the BMLO officer.

Misuari himself was more diplomatic and circumspect on the issue of a general oil embargo and saw to it that Arab sensitivities were not hurt. In a talk in London during an international conference on the Prophet Muhammad held in April 1980, he stated:

> The predicament of Marcos and his regime has been exacerbated by the cut-off of petroleum from the Islamic countries, particularly the heroic brotherly Islamic Republic of Iran. This decision was a victory for Islamic solidarity and a clear sign that genuine Islamic unity and solidarity is possible and inevitable. The MNLF and our sympathizers in the world shall continue their campaign until not a drop of petroleum shall come to the Philippines.[13]

In the same talk, Misuari appealed to all oil-producing Muslim countries to stop the sale of oil to "the criminal Marcos regime until the genocidal war ceases and the oppressed Bangsamoro people win their final bid for freedom and independence." To allow Marcos to receive oil and loans only served the further oppression of Muslims and was thus "no different from the supply of armaments Marcos and his repressive regime obtained from the Zionist entity and the imperialistic world led by the United States of America." He then recommended that the conference pass a resolution expressing political and material support for the MNLF cause before the next annual OIC conference slated to be held in Islamabad the following May.[14]

In November 1980, the MNLF office in Teheran was given official recognition by the Iranian government. A reception hosted by the director of the office to mark the occasion was attended by the representatives of at least six embassies of Muslim nations accredited to Iran. It was around this time that Iranian officials tried to bring about a reconciliation between Salamat Hashim and Misuari. The former was invited to Teheran, but considering the strained relations between Iran and Egypt, Salamat's host country, he found it prudent not to accept.

On June 6, 1982, Misuari and a large delegation arrived in Teheran at the invitation of the Iranian government to attend a week-long seminar on world Muslim movements sponsored by the Islamic Revolutionary Guards. They remained in Iran until July 4, and in the course of the stay the delegation members were able to visit Ayatollah Khomeini once again. They also had meetings with Ayatollah Montazeri, President Ali Khamenei, Foreign Minister Ali Akbar Velayati, Deputy Foreign Minister Ahmad Azizi, and Sayyid Mehdi Hashemi, all of whom assured Misuari and his group of Iran's full support for the MNLF's demand for self-determination and independence for the Bangsamoro people. In particular, Khamenei promised "political, economic and other forms of support" for the Bangsamoro revolution.[15] While in Teheran, Misuari was interviewed by the press and took the opportunity to condemn Israel's "atrocious act of aggression against the people of Lebanon and against the Palestinian Revolution," while affirming the unity and solidarity of the Bangsamoro people "with the heroic Palestinian and Lebanese peoples."[16] Members of his delegation were invited to give talks before different audiences on the Bangsamoro struggle. In addition, *Kayhan International* published a series of articles by Abdurashad Asani, the MNLF's information director, on the "genocide" of Muslims in the Philippines.

For all practical purposes, the MNLF office in Teheran (provided by the government) was treated as an embassy. There the MNLF would receive formal greetings and messages from Iran's highest political and religious officials on the occasion of important Islamic festivals and political events. MNLF representatives were also granted easy access to the press. For the next few years, MNLF officers would present a series of well-planned lectures on the problems of the Bangsamoro people before Iranian universities, schools and other groups all over the country.

To highlight Iran's firm anti-imperialistic stand as well as to reassure Misuari and the MNLF of continued support, Foreign Minister Velayati made an announcement broadcast by state radio on November 9, 1982, that his country would not sell oil to the United States, Israel, South Africa, or the Philippines.[17]

Further interest in closer ties with the MNLF was evidenced by the courtesy call paid to Misuari by Mehdi Shamlu, Iran's ambassador to Libya, and Muhammad Reza Shaker, a senior Iranian diplomatic official, in the MNLF Office in Tripoli on April 24, 1983, for discussion of mutual interest. The following month, Hamid Fekri, a member of Iran's political affairs department, visited the same office for an exchange of ideas with MNLF leaders.[18]

Visits and contacts such as these led many political observers to conclude that Iran was taking over the main support of the MNLF from Libya, whose aid was now judged as flagging, and that Misuari's chief base was now in Teheran. On the basis of reports from the intelligence community, Manila journalists wrote about suspected clandestine meetings between Iranian visitors and MNLF sympathizers in the country; they also reported that Iranians with combat experience had gone to the southern Philippines and that MNLF men were being trained in Iran to serve as future commanders.

Benigno Aquino, Jr., who was by now out of the Philippines, had tried in May and July 1981 to unite the various Muslim organizations preparatory to their later joining a political opposition group he would lead. On June 23, 1983, he testified on possible Iran–MNLF relations before the Subcommittee on Asian and Pacific Affairs of the U.S. House Committee on Foreign Relations:

Quality-wise, the MNLF appears to have better trained core commanders [than the Communist-led New People's Army]. Most of these commanders were trained in Middle Eastern training camps: Libya, Syria and Iran. The MNLF is not only better trained but better equipped and better funded. The MNLF leadership reported a major coup last year when Ayatollah Khomeini's regime reportedly established a $30 million escrow fund for the MNLF with which to purchase arms and ammunition. In a deal involving the PLO's Yasir Arafat, Iran supplied the funds and the PLO supplied the weapons from its arsenals in Syria.[19]

One may wonder where Aquino got his facts as well as question the veracity of the huge financial amount reported, especially considering Iran's simultaneous involvement in a very costly war. It may be that Aquino's source of information desired to isolate Misuari from the so-called moderate Muslim countries, principally Saudi Arabia and Egypt. Husain Haqqani, a perceptive observer of Bangsamoro affairs who had been in the Philippines for some time, points out that "Misuari's decision to throw in his lot with regimes like Iran, Libya and Syria has also helped his critics in their attempt to discredit him with the rest of the Islamic world."[20] Indeed, some of the most violent critics of Misuari came from the Jidda-based BMLO, which had often claimed it was backed by Saudi Arabia.

As is well known, one of the first and strongest supporters of Misuari and the MNLF has been Libya. Once Misuari had based himself there, it was natural and logical for him to try to secure a supplementary base in Damascus. An additional base in Teheran was compelling for several reasons. As Haqqani observes:

> Differences within the Islamic world are also reflected in the division in Moro ranks. Given its Islamic nationalist ideology and commitments to revolutionary struggle, the Misuari-led MNLF has grown closer to the present Iranian leadership, besides maintaining its original links with Libya and Syria. The other groups [BMLO, etc.] have concentrated on activities attracting support from Saudi Arabia, which has played an active role in pressuring the Philippine government in favour of the Moros, on behalf of the Organization of the Islamic Conference.[21]

It is crucial to note that in contrast to Libya, Saudi Arabia, and many other Muslim countries that continued to insist on the Tripoli Agreement as the framework of Muslim autonomy and peace, Iran stood for the self-determination and independence of the Bangsamoro people. Unlike Indonesia and Malaysia, which are with the Philippines members of the Association of Southeast Asian Nations (ASEAN),

The Philippines

Iran is under no political constraints in dealing with the MNLF re-garding its Islamic aims. Misuari has always maintained that Marcos never intended to implement the Tripoli Agreement in its entirety; Marcos's own actions as well as statements by high-ranking Philippine officials that the agreement had become a dead letter confirmed Mis-uari's contention. Moreover, even before martial law days, Misuari had consistently held that only through independence and as a separate people could the Moros be free to implement Islamic law and institu-tions. He was persuaded to sign the agreement by strong pressure from Libya and other OIC countries. In addition, he wished to dem-onstrate to all of them that the first to violate the agreement would be Marcos and his regime.

It was almost inevitable that sooner or later top Iranian officials and MNLF leaders would achieve a common understanding. One need not be unduly surprised if the Khomeini government, apart from its moral support, also gave some modest material aid to the MNLF within the constraints of Iran's limited and much-needed resources. Significantly, Iran's hospitality did not isolate the MNLF–Misuari faction from the so-called moderate Muslim countries. Misuari and his closest associates continued to travel freely throughout Saudi Arabia, Pakistan, and the Gulf states, where he was invariably treated with a courtesy not much different from that accorded to a head of state. Recent reports have in-dicated that after a visit to the Grand Sheikh of al-Azhar, where one of his sons is studying, Misuari was promised that the sheikh would recommend to the proper authorities that the MNLF be allowed to open an information office in Cairo.

Regarding the plight of the Muslims in the Philippines, the coun-tries of the Muslim world have shown a united concern and sympathy. Fully aware of this, Misuari tried to keep links with many of them while carefully treading a fine line and not unduly favoring one over the other. In speeches before the OIC and other international Muslim bodies, he would simply express his "prayers for an immediate and honourable end to the Gulf War"[22] or "fervent prayers for the triumph of peace in the Iran-Iraq wars in the true spirit of Islamic unity and brotherhood."[23] In February 1988, during the Islamic Unity Confer-ence held in Islamabad, a neutral body composed of Muslim dignitar-ies, ulama, intellectuals, and *mujahidin* was formed to explore ways and means to end the Iran-Iraq war. Misuari was one of the chosen members, and this was a virtual recognition of his close contacts with Iran as well as his good relations with many Arab countries.[24]

Iranian Students in the Philippines

In the late 1960s, young Iranians began enrolling in Philippine universities and colleges, attracted by the relatively low cost of education and the use of English as the medium of instruction. On the eve of the Iranian revolution, there were at least 2,500 Iranian students in the Philippines. On February 12, 1979, some 700 of them broke into the Iranian embassy in Manila, cheered the victory of the revolution, tore down all the Shah's pictures, and replaced them with pictures of Ayatollah Khomeini as the ambassador and his staff looked on helplessly. Leaders of the students charged that the ambassador had not been sympathetic when, in November 1978, some of them had demonstrated against the Shah. The next day the embassy was closed.

In August 1979, about 2,000 Iranian and local Muslim students demonstrated near a Manila mosque against President Carter and Israeli Prime Minister Begin for the ceaseless Israeli raids on Lebanon. They also condemned the Israeli occupation of Jerusalem and the expulsion of Palestinians from Palestine. In September, Iranian students, with the help of some embassy staff, were able to clear their embassy of other officials believed to be loyal to the Shah. In the second week of November, more than 200 Iranian students held an anti-Shah and anti-American demonstration in front of their embassy. In response, Marcos immediately instructed the defense minister to ban all demonstrations by foreigners. On the same day, November 15, the ministry of education announced that it was reviewing the records of all Iranian students (estimated at 3,500) for reduced academic loads or failures to discover those who were staying in the country illegally. These threats, however, failed to intimidate Iranian students, whose quality of protest was judged as "very violent" by Filipino police standards. Later that month, a rumor that Iranian students were preparing to demonstrate before the U.S. Embassy led an armed police force to cordon and guard the embassy, but no demonstrators appeared. Consequently, the subsequent demonstration by local Muslims near the U.S. Embassy on November 30, 1979, was believed by intelligence authorities to have been inspired or abetted by Iranian students.

Following this demonstration, the ministry of education announced on December 5 its new policy of limiting the number of foreign students: Only 750 new applicants would be allowed to enroll for the academic year 1980–81, with half of this number reserved for ASEAN students; no new Iranian students would be accepted. The ministry explained that this decision had nothing to do with the hostage crisis in Iran but was due to the fact that the Iranians constituted the largest number of foreign students in the Philippines, that is, 2,324 out of a total of 6,831.[25] Within two days, reports circulated that some education ministry officials received death threats from anonymous callers demanding that the ban on new foreign students be lifted. This did not, however, deter the ministry from rejecting 120 new requests by Iranian students for study permits and recommending the deportation of thirty other Iranian students. In addition, twenty-one Iranian students were denied entry to the country by the Commission of Immigration and Deportation (CID) for lack of proper documentation.

The arrival in Manila of Ayatollah Hosein Nuri as an emissary of Ayatollah Khomeini on January 11, 1980, was probably the result of the education ministry's actions and the corresponding complaints by Iranian students. In a press conference at the Iranian Embassy, Nuri descibed how Khomeini had received reports concerning the "insecurity and hardships" faced by Iranian students, especially in their dealings with police. He claimed that there were about 4,000 Iranian students in the Philippines. Nuri took the opportunity to thank the government for the release of demonstrators arrested in the November 30 incident while interceding for the release of those still detained. Curiously Nuri stated that one reason for the Iranian oil embargo was the harsh treatment of and discrimination against Iranian students. He did not fail to mention that there were at least 1,500 Filipino workers still in Iran.

After Nuri's departure Carlos P. Romulo, the Philippine foreign minister, denied that Iranian students were maltreated and proceeded to enumerate the rights of all foreign students. He also expressed regrets that the Ayatollah had chosen to air his grievances before the press rather than before the pertinent government officials.[26]

The year 1980 was marked by a series of well-planned demonstrations by Iranian students. For example, on April 7, some 200 of them assembled at their embassy for an anti-Egyptian and anti-American demonstration, but they failed to march before the Egyptian Embassy due to strong military and police cordons. As far as Manila residents were concerned, political demonstrations reflecting particularly Iranian issues such as the extradition of the Shah were met with either indifference or idle curiosity. But the anti-Egyptian slogans were resented by not a few local Muslims. The Egyptian government had granted hundreds of scholarships to Moro students, and a large segment of the younger local ulama were graduates of al-Azhar. Moreover, in general Arabs have a special place in the hearts of most Moros.

However, some of the so-called Iranian demonstrations were actually religious gatherings, such as the celebration of the end of the fasting month of Ramadan or a funeral procession bearing a dead student to the airport for burial in Iran. Gatherings of this sort were normally tolerated by the police and always joined by Moro classmates or personal friends of the Iranians. But the police were always on the alert to see to it that such events were not transformed into a march to the U.S. Embassy. Cultural differences and lack of proper communication often led to misunderstandings between Iranian students and the police. It should be noted that Iranian political demonstrations usually involved an average of 250 students, while a religious gathering would involve something like 500 or more participants.

On August 7, a visiting Ayatollah, Reza Reghabi, confirmed in an interview at the Iranian Embassy that the MNLF had set up an office in Teheran and had asked for material aid. He also frankly declared that "Iranians supported the Filipino Muslims' secessionist movement war in principle, but that the granting of material aid would be discussed by their parliament."[27] This remark was not played up much in the press since the Marcos government's stand was that the MNLF was virtually isolated. The next day, a group of some 300 Iranian students, carrying placards calling the United States "the Great Satan" and protesting the expulsion of Iranian nationals from the United States, were prevented from marching to the U.S. Embassy by a strong antiriot police force. Thirteen demonstrators were detained by the police. On August 13, some 170 Iranian students staged a hunger strike in their embassy and in a Manila mosque to protest the detentions. They claimed that the August 8 demonstration was actually a religious festival marking the end of Ramadan. The detained students were released. On October 18, the education ministry rejected study permits for an additional 350 foreign students (mostly Iranians) who reportedly failed to submit proper financial statements regarding their studies and stay. By this time, not more than 600 Filipino workers were left in Iran.[28]

In January 1981, martial law was lifted, although Marcos's authoritarian regime continued. Meanwhile, Iranian students experienced division and conflict in their own ranks. In February, a group of them stormed their own embassy to protest a reduction of their allowances. Some 200 of them were detained by police authorities for disturbing the peace, and immigration officials commenced deportation proceedings against some of them. While in detention the students went on a hunger stirke, demanding the ousting of four of their embassy officials. By the end of the year, there were two noticeable factions among the students: one pro-Khomeini, the other anti-Khomeini. Some local Muslims were reportedly aiding the pro-Khomeini faction in harassing the other group, which had claimed that embassy officials were giving financial aid to Muslims in the south. The violence between both groups often reached alarming proportions, with injuries to police and scores of Iranians being hospitalized. In one incident, 200 Iranians were hauled to Fort Bonifacio. While Iranian Embassy officials agreed that the Philippine government must deal strongly with Iranians breaking the law, editorials in some daily papers urged authorities to "kick the Iranian troublemakers out." In 1982, the dailies carried reports of a "death squad" out to eliminate anti-Khomeini students. Some Iranians identified thirty-two "death squad" members and claimed that their embassy had formed a core of "Islamic Guards," one of whom was reported as saying that in accordance with the Iranian constitution, the Islamic revolution had to be exported. It was further alleged that the "Guards" had received arms and ammunition from the MNLF in exchange for financial support.[29]

On April 17, 1983, a fire virtually destroyed the Muslim district in Quiapo in downtown Manila, rendering more than 3,000 families homeless. Lack of water and the alleged indifference of the firemen were blamed for the almost total devastation. Iranian students residing nearby came out in full force to try to save Muslim properties and guard them from outside looters. Political differences were temporarily put aside; it was a simple case of Muslims helping other Muslims in great need. Never were Moro families more grateful to the Iranian students, who had asked nothing in return.

The following August, Manila newspapers in a series of sensational headlines, editorials, and columns, raised a furor about a "killer squad" of militant Iranian students out to liquidate pro-Shah or anti-Khomeini students and reported that these so-called students were actually "intelligence officers." There were reports of the disappearance of at least nine Iranian students, five of whom were well known for their past pro-Shah activities, and that the harassment of anti-Khomeini students had been going on for more than nine months. An Iranian Embassy spokesman countered that such charges were part of a "black propaganda" against his government. The Iranian Muslim Students of the Philippines (IMSP) issued a statement to the effect that most of them had come to the country before the revolution to escape the Shah's harsh repression of Iranian campuses and in recognition of the high standards of Philippine educational institutions. In addition, some 200 Iranian students picketed the education ministry on August 18, denouncing the propaganda on "killer squads." Some non-Muslim Filipino students joined them to denounce the "fascistic repressive tendencies" of the state, while demanding that the Iranians be afforded the basic right to express themselves freely.

Meanwhile, the education ministry announced that no new Iranian students would be issued temporary permits for enrollment the following October and indicated it was recommending the deportation of at least twenty-five "undesirable" Iranians. In a matter of a few days, the commissioner of immigration and deportation ordered the immediate deportation of some 200 Iranian students for lack of study permit extensions. (At this time, the education ministry reported that out of 900 Iranian students enrolled in 32 institutions, just over half (489 students) had permits; the remaining 411 did not.

But the deportation order, which affected nearly 10 percent of the Iranian student population, caused some of those who raised the hysteria against Iranians to have second thoughts. One columnist became concerned that those students with "petro dollars" might use bribery to remain in the country, while financially hard-up, anti-Khomeini students returned to Iran might be "jumping from the frying pan to the fire."[30] Another columnist even commented that many Iranian students wanted to remain not simply because of the relatively low cost of education but because the atmosphere of academic freedom in Philippine institutions was quite different from that in Iran during the Shah's regime.[31]

According to the testimony of Khosrau Minuchehr, a former labor attaché in the Iranian Embassy, there was indeed a "killer squad" out to harass anti-Khomeini students and force them to return to Iran, and some "students" were, in reality, intelligence officers. Significantly Minuchehr added that it was incorrect to label all Iranian students as either pro- or anti-Khomeini since the majority were not ideologically motivated but simply desired "to be left alone with their books and studies."[32]

On August 22, 1983, former Senator Benigno Aquino, Jr., the symbol and hope of the Philippine political opposition, was assassinated at the Manila International Airport. This was the big story for weeks, and news about Iranian students, who had decided to keep a low profile, disappeared from the front pages of the dailies.[33]

But there were those who maintained that the presence of a large number of Iranian students was a threat to national security. On November 16, 1983, a columnist quoted extensively from an editorial of the *Payam-e-Vahdat* (*Message of Unity*), a weekly published by Iranian students, which stated that Iran had produced five million propaganda items in the form of books, articles, and manifestos in the revolution. Some of these materials had been distributed in the Philippines to promote revolution:

> These we have distributed among our Filipino brothers in this country and we say that we have awakened them from their slumber. We have succeeded in enlightening and effectively provoking the Filipino masses—Muslims and Christians alike—to take overt actions against the corrupt regime of prostitutes and dictator. We have witnessed them stage grand demonstrations and rallies all over the country and most recently in Cebu. They have learned what we have taught them in the art and science of revolution and can proudly say now that they have their underground movements patterned after the one we started in Iran.[34]

This self-congratulatory assertion certainly disregarded the existence of an ongoing Muslim armed struggle against the Marcos regime since 1972, the endemic Communist insurgency, the Philippines' long history of large-scale, well-organized labor and peasant demonstrations since the beginning of this century, as well as violent student demonstrations since the late 1960s. Moro students, especially in the urban centers like Manila, could not help but be exposed to the international issues raised by their Iranian classmates and friends. Much of the Iranian literature—both political and religious—had found its way to the Muslim south. Many MNLF field commanders had shown familiarity with the ideas of Ayatollah Khomeini, and some claimed outright to have been influenced by them. In time, many Muslim homes openly displayed pictures of Khomeini, who was regarded as a spiritual leader. During the peaceful demonstrations by Muslims marking the twentieth anniversary of Bangsamoro Freedom Day, held in various cities and towns in the southern Philippines on March 18, 1988, huge pictures of Nur Misuari and Ayatollah Khomeini were paraded together, especially in the city of Zamboanga. Indeed, to many Moros, Khomeini had come to symbolize the Islamic Revolution itself.

Conclusions

The sympathy that the Islamic Republic of Iran had shown for the struggle of the Bangsamoro people for self-determination and independence, the courtesy and hospitality granted to Nur Misuari and the MNLF, and Iran's moral support and tangible forms of aid gave the Muslim movement in the Philippines a much-needed boost. Expressions of support by many Iranian students for the rights of Moros were made despite the restrictions of martial law and the authoritarian Marcos regime. Their actions often placed the Iranian students under military surveillance, earned for them bad publicity in a government-controlled press, subjected them to unnecessary humiliations, and increased their difficulties in a country whose non-Muslim majority generally showed no understanding of the significance of the revolution in Iran. Thus, Moro sympathy for the Iranian students and the revolution itself is readily understandable.

Together with the OIC, Iran recognized the MNLF, with Misuari as its chairman, as the leader of the Philippine Muslim movement. But unlike other Muslim countries, Iran did not push Misuari to negotiate with the Philippine government under the principle of an autonomy "within the realm of the sovereignty and territorial integrity of the Republic of the Philippines," as the OIC resolutions put it. Of the four rival groups that claimed to speak for the Moros, the MNLF reverted to its original stand for secession, while the other three groups consistently opted for autonomy. Of these three, the BMLO withered away with the death of Lucman in 1985 and the earlier return of Pendatun to serve in the government (although not for long since he also soon passed away). The MNLF–Salamat faction, now known as the Moro Islamic Liberation Front (MILF), is relatively weak but has a few thousand armed followers. The third, known as the MNLF–Reform group, or the Pundato faction, which was originally encouraged and supported by the BMLO to displace the MNLF–Misuari faction, has also fallen into the limbo of forgotten movements since its top leader, Dimas Pundato, accepted a government job in Manila. By its own internal logic and ideology, the Iranian government recognized which of the four groups was the most revolutionary and therefore most worthy of support.

The cease-fire in the Gulf and the consequent new directions of Iranian foreign policy will undoubtedly affect Iran's future relations with the MNLF and the Philippines. But as long as their original Islamic orientation is not abandoned, the Bangsamoro people can expect the same sympathy from Iran and the MNLF will continue to hope for the same support they have always enjoyed.

Notes

1. *Bulletin Today* (Manila), October 24, 1979; and *Foreign Broadcast Information Service Daily Reports—Asia and Pacific*, October 23, 1979.
2. *FBIS Daily Reports—Asia and Pacific*, December 10, 1979.
3. Out of a total population of about 55 million, at least 5 million Filipinos are Muslims. Ten ethnolinguistic groups are identified as Muslim, the largest of these being the Maguindanao, the Marano, the Tausug, the Samal, and the Yakan. By comparison, 85 percent of the total population is Catholic.
4. For background information on the armed rebellion and genesis of the MNLF, see T.J.S. George, *Revolt in Mindanao: The Rise of Islam in Philippine Politics* (Kuala Lumpur: Oxford University Press, 1980); Peter G. Growing, *Muslim Filipinos: Heritage and Horizon* (Quezon City, Philippines: New Day Publishers, 1979); and Cesar A. Majul, *The Contemporary Muslim Movement in the Philippines* (Berkeley: Mizan Press, 1985).
5. *Far Eastern Economic Review*, June 8, 1979.
6. *Mahardika* (Official Organ of the Moro National Liberation Front) 9, no. 1 (1982): 1; *Dansalan Quarterly* (Iligan City, Philippines) 1, no. 2 (January 1980): 133; and *Far Eastern Economic Review*, June 22, 1979.
7. *Bulletin Today*, October 4, 1979.
8. *Bulletin Today*, October 17, 1979.
9. *Evening Express* (Manila), October 18, 1979.
10. *Bulletin Today*, September 7, 1979. This observation was Bigornia's reaction to the alleged ill-treatment of some Filipino musicians and singers stranded in the Teheran airport by immigration officials. If the report is true, one possible reason for the treatment may be the newly acquired "puritanical" stance of some Iranian officials.
11. *Bulletin Today*, October 18, 1979.
12. The Supreme Council of the Bangsa Moro Liberation Organization (BMLO), "The Bangsa Moro Struggle" (Paper submitted to the Tenth Islamic Conference of Foreign Ministers, Fez, Morocco, 8 May 1979, Mimeographed), 15–17.
13. Nur Misuari, "The Bangsamoro Right to Self-Determination" (Address

given at the International Conference on the Prophet Muhammad and His Message sponsored by the Organization of the Islamic Conference and organized by the Islamic Council of Europe, London, 11–15 April 1980, Pamphlet), 16.

14. Ibid., 18–19. At this time, the Philippines received 75 percent of its oil from the Middle East, principally Saudi Arabia. Although the Saudis did not follow the Iranian example, they did cancel some contracts granting additional oil in response to Marcos's hedging on the full implementation of the Tripoli Agreement. Saudi Arabia also exercised subtle forms of pressure to force Marcos to renew negotiations with Misuari.

15. *Mahardika* 9, no. 1 (1982): 8.

16. *Mahardika* 9, no. 2 (1982): 1.

17. *Mahardika* 9, no. 4 (1982).

18. *Moro National Liberation Front: MNLF Newsbriefs* (Diplomatic Circulations, Office of the Director, Tripoli, Libya), no. 2, May 6, 1983; and ibid., no. 6, June 3, 1983.

19. "Prepared Statement of ex-Senator Benigno S. Aquino Jr." (Testimony before the Subcommittee on Asian and Pacific Affairs, Committee on Foreign Affairs, U.S. House of Representatives, 23 June 1983, Mimeographed), 10.

20. Husain Haqqani, "Factionalism Stalks the Moro Camp," *Arabia: The Islamic World Review*, June 1983: 38.

21. Ibid.

22. Committee on Information, "Address of the MNLF Chairman Professor Nur Misuari at the Seventeenth Islamic Foreign Ministers Conference held in Amman, Hashemite Kingdom of Jordan, March 21–25, 1988" (Mahardika Press, July 1988), 13.

23. Committee on Information, "Speech of the MNLF Chairman Professor Nur Misuari at the Ninth World General Assembly of the World Muslim Congress (*Motamar al-Alam al-Islami*) held in Karachi, Pakistan, on March 30 to April 2, 1988" (Mahardika Press, July 1988), 19.

24. *Mahardika* 14, no. 2 (March–April 1988): 6.

25. Figures for Iranian students given by the education ministry were always higher than those reported by the Commission of Immigration and Deportation; in fact, the education ministry was not too sure of its figures.

26. For more details on Ayatullah Nuri's visit, see *Bulletin Today*, January 12, 13, 15, and 19, 1980. In his column of January 20, Jesus Bigornia commented that Romulo's remarks could have embarrassed the Ayatollah and suggested that it might be wise for the Philippines to close its embassy in Teheran, presumably to avoid another hostage-taking incident like that at the American Embassy in November 1979. (Bigornia also revealed that in 1979, General Ileto, the Philippine ambassador to Iran, made a special trip to Manila to persuade the government to relax some of its rules regarding Iranian students, since students in Teheran had threatened to demonstrate in protest of this treatment before the Philippine Embassy. Actually, Nuri's purpose in making the trip was to acquaint himself with the problems of Iranian students in various parts of the world.

27. *FBIS Daily Reports—Asia and Pacific*, August 8, 1980.

28. In 1978, the number of Filipino workers in Iran rose to about 6,000. Within a few months after the Shah's flight, the number dropped to 2,000. In April 1980, the number was down to 1,300.

The Philippines

29. Jesus Bigornia, column in *Bulletin Today*, April 25, 1982.

30. Ibid., August 22, 1983.

31. Apolonio Batalla, column in *Bulletin Today*, August 21, 1983.

32. See Jesus Bigornia, column in *Bulletin Today*, April 25, 1982; and *Bulletin Today*, August 16 and 17, 1983. Minuchehr is also the likely source of the information that among the Iranian students, 15 percent were pro-Khomeini while only 5 percent were anti-Khomeini.

33. The news report that on December 2, 1983, a time bomb wrapped in an Iranian newspaper (another report indicates that the wrapper was Christmas paper) was discovered by an alert guard in an extension office of the U.S. Embassy in Manila and later defused failed to arouse much attention in the city. In April 1984, the suspected leader of the alleged "hit squad" and his two closest associates were asked to leave the country.

34. Jesus Bigornia, column in *Bulletin Today*, November 16, 1983.

PART V

Africa

14

Islamization in the

Sudan and the

Iranian Revolution

JOHN O. VOLL

A FORMAL PROGRAM OF Islamization of state and society began in the Sudan in September 1983 when Jafar Numayri, then president of the country, issued a series of proclamations known as the "September Laws." These laws commanded adherence to Islamic regulations in business, public behavior, and family morality, and instituted traditional Muslim judicial procedures and punishments. This Islamization program was initiated during a time when the world's attention was drawn to what many call the resurgence of Islam. The Iranian revolution, which had overthrown the Shah in early 1979 and led to the establishment of an Islamic republic, provided an important rallying point in the resurgence experience. A key question, then, is whether or not the Iranian revolution itself had any significant impact on developments in the Sudan. Answering this question leads to the more general issue of the relationship between the internal evolution of Sudanese society and events in the broader Islamic world.

The Sudanese Islamization process unfolded in a society that was aware of the Islamic revolution in Iran. Most Sudanese Muslims knew of the events that had led to the overthrow of the Shah and the establishment of an Islamic republic, and most responded favorably. However, beyond this general awareness, the Iranian revolution seems to have had little direct impact on the Sudan. The basic developments of Islamization and Islamic revivalism in the country during the 1970s and 1980s were primarily shaped by the long traditions of Sudanese history. However, in the broader historical sense, the Iranian revolution helped to shape the Sudanese Islamization experience through the impact of the era's more general Islamic resurgence. The relationship between Sudanese Islamization and this broader resurgence is worth examining because it provides some insights into both the modern Islamic experience and recent Sudanese history.

The Sudan and the Iranian Revolution

Many of the specific questions that analysts ask when they try to define the impact of the Iranian revolution do not fit the Sudanese situation very closely. This is true of questions like whether or not local Shiites have been inspired to opposition by the Iranian example. In the Sudan, where there is no significant Shii population, the question is irrelevant. However, other questions are profoundly relevant because they raise such issues as the nature of the Islamic experience and the impact of the Islamic resurgence in the Sudan.

IRAN AND INTERNAL SUDANESE DEVELOPMENTS

One such question is whether or not the Iranian revolution has encouraged the development of Islamically oriented opposition movements. In more general terms, one might ask how the Iranian revolution has affected the ways in which Sudanese Muslims view their own government.

Although Sudanese Muslims were aware of developments in Iran in the late 1970s, these events did not have a major impact on the way the Sudanese viewed their government. Between 1978 and 1983, Numayri, head of the Sudan's military-dominated government, was actively developing a more Islamic state ideology, though it does not seem his efforts were inspired by Iran's experience. As early as 1978, he had brought the leader of the major modern revivalist movement, Hasan al-Turabi of the Sudanese Muslim Brotherhood, into his government as part of a national reconciliation program. In addition, Numayri himself had been consciously working to identify his governmental programs more explicitly with Islam, as was reflected by the publication of his book *The Islamic Path: Why?*[1]

In this context, the Iranian revolution had relatively little impact on the ways that Sudanese Muslims viewed their government. The Numayri regime was becoming explicitly more Islamic in tone as events in Iran gathered momentum, but at most the revolution reinforced existing developments in the Sudan.

This leads to a second question that is often asked by analysts: Why has an Iran-style revolution not taken place anywhere but in Iran? The answer for the Sudan is complex.

Numayri's Islamization program removed what pressure there might have been in the early 1980s for an Islamic revolution in the country. The Sudanese Muslim Brotherhood had some reservations about the Numayri program, but the group cooperated with him almost up until he was overthrown in 1985. This cooperation was based on the tactical decision that a self-defined program of Islamization, however imperfect it might be, was better than nothing.

An Islamic revolution led by other groups in the Sudan was more likely and, in fact, had been attempted in various ways. In 1970, the Sudanese Mahdists, whose movement began with the revolution of the Mahdi in the 1880s and is now the country's single largest Muslim group, attempted to overthrow Numayri. At that time, Numayri, who had come to power through a military coup in 1969, was in the radical socialist phase of his regime. The Mahdists were crushed by the government's military forces. Throughout the 1970s, other attempts to overthrow Numayri led by various Islamic forces, especially the Mahdists and the Muslim Brotherhood, also failed because of the regime's military strength.

Thus, even before the Iranian revolution, there were in the Sudan a number of Islamically based opposition movements that attempted to take over the government. However, none of these attempts were "Iranian-style" revolutions, for there were no plans to replace the existing regime with an actively Islamic fundamentalist state. Indeed, it was Numayri himself, not his opposition, who initiated a formal Islamization program for the Sudan. In September 1984 Numayri proclaimed himself the Imam of the country at a government-sponsored international conference on Islamization.[2]

In this context, it is clear that the Iranian revolution could not replicate itself in the Sudan because Islamic opposition and advocacy took different forms in the two countries. By the early 1980s, opposition to Numayri grew for many reasons, but his Islamization program had preempted explicitly Islamic opposition. Thus, when the Sudanese revolution came in 1985–86, even though many of the country's major Muslim groups were joined together in opposition, Islam could not be the unifying force in the revolutionary movement.

A third question regarding the impact of the Iranian revolution is its possible influence on relations between Muslims and non-Muslims. This is a very important issue in the Sudan, since as many as one-third of the Sudanese are non-Muslim; they are concentrated primarily in the southern regions of the country. Relations between Muslims and non-Muslims are thus tied to regional rivalries between northern and southern Sudanese, and religious pluralism is an important dimension in the continuing civil war in the Sudan.

Numayri's Islamization program worsened relations between Muslims and non-Muslims in the country. The imposition of Islamic law and criminal punishments for Muslims and non-Muslims alike raised grave fears among non-Muslim Sudanese. In general, the authoritarian implementation of Numayri's program (which recalled forced Islamization programs under a previous military ruler) helped arouse militant opposition among the non-Muslim Sudanese.

The Iranian revolution did not create tensions between northerners and southerners or between Muslims and non-Muslims in the Sudan; those tensions are the legacy of decades of conflict. When southerners expressed their opposition to domination by the Muslim north, they did not make reference to the Iranian experience, although individual rights in a state engaged in an Islamization program were discussed.[3] Opposition to "Numayrism" was frequently expressed, but few if any spoke of the problems of "Khomeinism." However, the suppression of some non-Muslims in Iran after the revolution may have added to the fears of Sudanese non-Muslims that such repression was an inherent characteristic of any contemporary program of active Islamization.

SUDANESE RELATIONS WITH IRAN

Historically, relations between Iran and the Sudan have been limited, the people in both countries have their primary ties to other areas. However, since the Iranian revolution, both the Sudanese government and at least one opposition group have established relations with Iran's revolutionary government.

The Sudanese group most sympathetic to the general goals of Iran's Islamic revolution is the Sudanese Muslim Brotherhood. Hasan al-Turabi, the movement's leader, was one of the first Sudanese to pay an official visit to Iran after the revolution. Turabi's visit reflected the sympathy of the Brotherhood for the aims of the Islamic movement, but it did not indicate any formal ties between the group and the new government of Iran. Turabi avowed his support for the goal of active Islamization of society while openly expressing his reservations about some of the ways that the Iranian government was implementing its programs.

The views of the Sudanese Muslim Brotherhood are closer to those found in the writings of Ali Shariati than they are to those of Ayatollah Khomeini. The brotherhood itself is not primarily an ulama organization and has not advocated a special role for the ulama in Sudanese affairs. Instead Turabi often speaks of a "new ulama," promoting the involvement of Islamically informed citizens representing both secular and clerical professions. Therefore, while the Sudanese Muslim Brotherhood represents a relatively large and influential group that is sympathetic to the ideals of the Iranian revolution, it is not tied to the specific policies and programs of the Islamic Republic of Iran.

There is no other major group in the Sudan that has more direct or closer ties to Iran than those claimed by the Muslim Brotherhood. Any other explicitly pro-Iranian groups in the country are very small and reflect the views of individual intellectuals or opportunists rather than a significant social or political force. Although observers of other sub-Saharan areas like Nigeria have informally reported that there are small groups who, with Iranian support, have started to call themselves Shii, this phenomenon does not seem to have occurred on any important scale in the Sudan.

As a result of these limited ties, the Sudanese government, both under Numayri and after his overthrow in 1985, has not undertaken highly visible measures to counter Iranian influence. In fact, the appeal of the Iranian revolution, rather than being countered by government actions, was used, especially under Numayri, to provide support for Sudanese Islamization efforts.

Government leaders have, however, separated issues of Islamic identity from those of Arab and Sudanese diplomacy. For example, the Iranian revolution posed some diplomatic problems for Numayri, who had to balance public approval of the Islamic successes in Iran with the more private but strong ties of his government to the United States and Egypt. Closely associated with the United States and strongly dependent on that country's aid, Numayri also maintained close relations with Egypt under Anwar Sadat and his successor, Husni Mubarak. The resolution of the American hostage crisis in Iran helped ease this diplomatic problem.

A similar balancing act was required in Sudanese policy regarding the Iran-Iraq war: While there has been no opposition to Iran as an Islamic state, the Sudan did oppose Iran's fighting an Arab state. However, Sudanese leaders have generally sought to minimize their involvement in global and regional conflicts, and the Sudan attempts to act as a mediator more often than it actively joins one particular side in an international dispute.[4] In like manner, the Sudanese involvement in any of the disputes involving Iran has been to work for conflict resolution rather than either strongly advocating or actively opposing the Iranian position.

We have seen that the emergence of a government-supported program of Islamization in the Sudan does not seem to have been directly inspired by the Iranian revolution. Indeed, the relationship between the Sudan's Islamization program and the Iranian revolution tends to disprove those hypotheses that view the Islamic resurgence as a tightly bound network of events or even some form of international conspiracy. The most visible evidence of Islamic resurgence in the Sudan in the late 1970s and early 1980s appears instead to have deep roots in the history of the Sudan itself.

The Sudanese Context of Islamization

No country or region in the modern era exists in total isolation from the rest of the world. In the diverse contemporary experiences that are described as the Islamic resurgence, there are some universal themes but there are also important local dimensions. In the specific case of the Sudan, the local dimensions are those indigenous factors that have played an important role in the visible Islamic resurgence. These internal factors need to be examined in order to assess the impact of "external" forces and Iranian influences in the country.

Islamization in the Sudan is not simply the political program of a single individual. The process is also a historical phenomenon that is still unfolding. In one sense, Sudanese Islamization is a process of social change in which members of a growing portion of the population identify themselves as Muslims and in which institutions are gradually adapted to conform to expectations of Muslims. Such a social evolution is not, however, usually thought of as a "resurgence" of Islam but is more accurately viewed as an unconscious development of social institutions.

A second dimension of this long-term process is the self-conscious actions of individuals and groups to reform or intensify the Islamic character of Sudanese society. This enhancement of Islamic character is what is usually described as Islamic revivalism or resurgence. In this sense Islamization is not new to the Sudan and was not initiated by Numayri. There have been many "Islamization programs" in Sudanese history, and these have provided the foundations of the thought and actions of contemporary Muslim leaders and groups in the Sudan.

Each of the major contemporary Islamic institutions in the Sudan has its roots in a self-conscious Islamization effort. The nature of these efforts and the institutions they produced reflect the evolution of Islamic society in the Sudan.

EARLY SUDANESE ISLAMIZATION:
ISLAMIC CENTERS AND HOLY FAMILIES

Muslims came to the regions of the Nile Valley south of Egypt in the very first centuries of Islamic history. However, the development of Islamic communities in the region took a long time. The process of Islamization was originally an unconscious and gradual one resulting from migrations and intermarriage.

Self-conscious and intentional Islamization of the region began in the sixteenth century, when the Funj sultanate emerged as a "newly Islamized kingdom."[5] One important traditional Sudanese account describes this process in terms of personalities. The *Kitab Tabaqat* says that at the time the Funj state was established "there were, in that land, no famous schools of knowledge nor reading of the Koran. It is said that a man might divorce his wife and another might marry her on the same day, without regard for the required period of waiting. [This was the case] until al-Shaykh Mahmud al-Araki came from Egypt and instructed the people about the required period of waiting."[6] Mahmud al-Araki was one of many Muslim teachers who came to the Sudan and consciously worked to Islamize the people and society.

By the end of the eighteenth century, many centers of Islamic instruction and piety had been established in what is now the northern Sudan. Such a center usually included a tomb of a pious ancestor, a school, and a residence for the "holy family" who managed the center.[7]

In some areas, as control by the sultans or tribal notables weakened, the family and its organization would provide basic political services as well.

Later reformers and modernizers have tended to criticize these Islamic centers as the manifestations of a style of "popular" Islam that incorporated local customs of which legalistic fundamentalists (and modernizers) would not approve. However, these establishments never lost sight of their original purpose, which was the conscious instruction of the people in the correct ways of Islam, and they remained dedicated to the education and Islamization of their society. In this sense, the families in charge of these centers, who form a respected elite, are the heir to Mahmud al-Araki and his efforts to bring about a more rigorous adherence to Islam in the Sudan.

In the twentieth century, representatives of this established elite have had little national political visibility, but they have enjoyed significant local influence. Politically, their primary mode of operation has been to cooperate quietly with whatever government is in power in order to protect their local interests. Members of the holy families were often elected to parliament in the days of civilian government or, under military rule, were appointed to various local posts.

In the last years of Numayri's rule, some members of this elite were actively mobilized in support of the government.[8] Most visible among them was Nayal Abu Garoon, from a minor, older holy family, who served as a high-level adviser to Numayri and a compiler of the actual legislation of Islamization in 1983–84. Although he and others lost their positions of power with the overthrow of Numayri, the families themselves did not lose their considerable influence in local areas. Their followers continue their political activism, and members of the old establishment became members of the new parliament.

This increased involvement in national affairs and the support for the formal Islamization program are certainly a significant part of the Sudanese Islamic resurgence of the 1970s and 1980s. The transition to a more active role by the traditional elite came during the 1970s, but it seems to have been the result of local conditions and motivations. As the political system developed under Numayri, there were more opportunities for the older Islamic groups to come forward, since the other "national" Muslim organizations were in opposition and much of the leadership was in exile. There is little indication that the changing role of the heirs of Mahmud al-Araki was tied specifically to the Iranian revolution, nor does it represent a sudden conversion to the cause of Islamization. Instead, the political involvement of the holy families reflects a continuing commitment to that cause, now emerging in a new format.

Another aspect of this changing role is reflected in the career of Hasan al-Turabi, the leader of the Muslim Brotherhood in the Sudan. Turabi is probably the most prominent contemporary descendant of a major holy family from the Funj era. The tomb center of the Awlad Turabi remains a respected part of the old establishment, while Hasan Turabi has become the leader of the most recent Islamic institution in the Sudan. Both the old and new establishments are dedicated to the effective Islamization of Sudanese society, although they work in different ways. The transition from the traditional Islamic center to the modern fundamentalist style of the Muslim Brotherhood was easier and more satisfying for Sudanese Muslims than accepting a more secularized mode of modernization. The institutions and traditions associated with the first conscious Islamization program have not disappeared from the Sudanese scene and may, in fact, continue to play an important role, shaped particularly by the local Sudanese context.

NATIONAL MUSLIM ESTABLISHMENTS AND ISLAMIZATION

In the Sudan today there are two large Muslim organizations that are active in national politics and the Islamization effort, the *Khatmiyyah Tariqah*, a Sufi brotherhood, and the Mahdist movement. In contrast to the old, decentralized elite of traditional saintly families and separate centers of piety, these groups represent centrally organized structures. Both the Khatmiyyah and the Mahdist movement are part of the tradition of Islamic resurgence in the Sudan.

The Khatmiyyah Tariqah. The Khatmiyyah is a Sufi brotherhood (*tariqah*) that came to the Sudan during the Islamic revival of the early nineteenth century. Muhammad Uthman al-Mirghani (1793–1853), the founder of the tariqah, was a student of Ahmad ibn Idris, one of the major revivalist teachers of the era, and he brought a new spirit of Islamization to the Sudan.[9]

The Khatmiyyah won followers in a number of different parts of the northern Sudan. The brotherhood went beyond the locally centered structures of the older holy families and the parochialism of local tribal organizations to build a regionwide, relatively centralized organization with the Mirghani family at its core. Moreover, the Khatmiyyah's teachings were more cosmopolitan, reflecting the views of the reform-ist ulama of the Middle East. By creating an organization that inte-grated smaller local groupings into a broader, Islamically committed structure, the Khatmiyyah was an important development in the con-tinuing Islamization of the Sudan.

The Khatmiyyah and the Mirghani family have had political signifi-cance from the very beginning. When the brotherhood's founder ar-rived in the early nineteenth century, his reformist views caused ten-sions within the Funj court, which was facing an invasion from Egypt. By the 1820s, most of the country had come under the control of the Ottoman governor of Egypt, and the Mirghanis cooperated closely with the Turko-Egyptian government of the Sudan. As an ally of the Egyptians, the Mirghani family opposed the Sudanese Islamic revolu-tionary regime of the Mahdi, which arose in the 1880s.

During the twentieth century, the Khatmiyyah maintained its politi-cal significance, usually in association with some other group. For the first decades, Sayyid Ali al-Mirghani, the leader of the order at that time, cooperated closely with the British, who had conquered the Su-dan by 1898. Then, in the era of nationalism, Khatmiyyah leaders sup-ported the idea of union with Egypt rather than the creation of a sep-arate, independent Sudan. Sayyid Ali became the patron of the National Unionist party of Ismail al-Azhari, an activist and leading spokesman for the emerging generation of educated, nationalist-oriented Sudanese in the 1940s.

The Khatmiyyah provides a clearly Islamic organizational allegiance for a significant portion of the Sudanese population, but its specific political role is difficult to define. The brotherhood has cooperated with the various governments rather than working to create alternative systems of political authority. In this position the Khatmiyyah has sel-dom provided an Islamic voice of opposition, and the Mirghani leaders have been reluctant to advocate actively any specific Islamization pro-grams. Instead their role has been to minimize the impact of secularist ideas and maintain a sense of Islamic identity. Sayyid Ali al-Mirghani, for example, broke with Ismail al-Azhari in the mid-1950s at least partly on the issue of secularization and the role of the major Islamic groups in politics.

Traditionally, the leaders of the Mirghani family, especially Sayyid Ali (who died in 1969), have maintained that they are not political leaders and have no aspirations for political office. However, they do wield significant political influence through patronage and mediation. The sons of Sayyid Ali—Sayyid Muhammad Uthman, who is Ali's successor as the leader of the tariqah, and Sayyid Ahmad—are more directly involved in the political arena. They have been party leaders rather than informal counselors and, in post-Numayri civilian politics, hold formal political offices. They are currently leaders in the Democratic Unionist party, an alliance with politicians in the tradition of Ismail al-Azhari.

The Mirghanis have been associated with "respectable" Islam of a nonradical but reformist style, continuing the renewalist mode of those who created the tariqah and brought it to the Sudan. They fought against the more militant and socially upsetting Mahdist movement in the nineteenth century and continue to oppose similar groups in the twentieth. Occasional political alliances with twentieth-century Mahdist leaders have been formed to reduce the influence of yet more socially upsetting groups, like the secularists in al-Azhari's group in the 1950s and the fundamentalists of the Muslim Brotherhood in more recent times.

During the late 1970s, in the era of the Iranian revolution, Muhammad Uthman al-Mirghani took the lead in organizing the Islamic Revival Committee (IRC) in an effort to unify the various Sufi brotherhoods in the Sudan. The goal was to defend the brotherhoods against criticism by fundamentalists and also to provide an organizational structure for presenting the Islamic message as understood by the Khatmiyyah and like-minded Muslims. In 1980, the IRC was active in student politics, especially at the Omdurman Islamic University.[10]

The increased social activism and political involvement of the Khatmiyyah represents a form of Islamic revivalism. It arose primarily out of the social and political conditions in the Sudan in the late 1970s and continued throughout the 1980s. This revivalism was not specifically a response to the Iranian revolution.

The Mirghani family has always based its prestige on its identification with Islamic leadership. This has not produced fundamentalist-style political platforms, but it has meant that over the years the Mirghanis have supported moderate proposals for an Islamic constitution for the Sudan. In this role, they follow a relatively narrow path between more secularist reformist ideas and the proposals and programs of the politically activist Mahdists or, more recently, the fundamentalists. Khatmiyyah participation in the Islamic resurgence of the past decade fits well into the patterns already set by earlier Muslim leaders in the nineteenth and twentieth centuries.

The Mahdist Movement. The second major national Muslim establishment is based on the movement begun by Muhammad Ahmad, who declared himself the Mahdi in 1881. The Mahdi proclaimed a mission of revitalizing Muslim society and established a major state in the Sudan, defeating the Turko-Egyptian rulers in the 1880s. Although his successor, the Khalifah Abdullahi, was not part of the Mahdi's family, it is that family that has provided leadership for the movement since the conquest of the Mahdist state in 1898 by British and Egyptian forces.

During the twentieth century, Mahdist leadership has been relatively realistic and pragmatic, a change from the movement's more messianic mood in the nineteenth century. Sayyid Abd al-Rahman, a son of the Mahdi, helped to transform his father's followers, called the Ansar, from a group of fighters engaged in holy war into an organization that could operate effectively as a nationalist movement and then as a political party. But regardless of the format of the movement, its leadership has continued to hold firmly to an active involvement in the political arena in order to further the conscious Islamization of Sudanese society and to create a "righteous political order."[11]

In practice, this struggle for political righteousness often meant nothing more than active support for leaders of Mahdist background or politicians willing to work with the Mahdist leaders. However, it would be a mistake to assume that even modern-educated Mahdist leaders would be willing or politically able to advocate a secularist program. When Sadiq al-Mahdi, a great-grandson of the Mahdi and leader of Ummah party (the Mahdist political party) in the 1960s, made tentative efforts toward "modernizing" the party, it caused considerable controversy among the Ansar.

Sadiq al-Mahdi's recent career reflects the special character of Mahdist ideas of Islamization in the Sudan. The Mahdists have consistently supported some form of Islamic identification for the Sudanese state. They have also maintained the nineteenth-century tradition of working to "purify" Muslim practices in the Sudan. In this sense, the Mahdist movement has been clearly and directly identified with the ideal of Islamization. However, the Mahdists refused to recognize Numayri's

Islamization program begun in 1983, and Sadiq al-Mahdi was imprisoned because of his public opposition to Numayri's program. Advocates of Islamization may be rivals as well as allies.

Ironically, Sadiq al-Mahdi came to appear as the defender of Numayri's Islamization program in the years following Numayri's ousting. In 1986 Sadiq became prime minister in the first post-Numayri civilian government, and he faced the task of dismantling the old regime's political system, including the September Laws issued by Numayri. Sadiq had vigorously opposed the September Laws as an improper Islamization program, but their repeal became tied to the issue of secularization of the state, to which Sadiq was also opposed. Faced with this dilemma, Sadiq chose to maintain the Islamic identification rather than be seen as the leader responsible for de-Islamizing the state.

The Mahdist commitment to an Islamic state is long-standing. Sadiq's opposition to Numayri and his later resistance to secularizing the state are both demonstrations of the continuity of the Mahdist tradition. As in the case of the Khatmiyyah, an outside inspiration like the Iranian revolution was unnecessary for the development of the Mahdist positions.

NEW ISLAMIC FORCES AND VISIONS

In addition to the older institutions and movements, the Sudan has been involved in new types of Islamic experiences that have had significance in recent years and which reflect the diversity among the country's potential programs of Islamization. Three Islamic visions exemplify this diversity. They are the program of the Sudanese Muslim Brotherhood, the teachings of Mahmoud Mohamed Taha, and the Islamization program of Jafar Numayri.

The Sudanese Muslim Brotherhood. The Muslim Brotherhood began in the Sudan in the years immediately following World War II. In its early days the group emphasized intellectual issues and gained support among students and the educated but had limited impact in the broader political arena. Indeed, it seemed unlikely that the brotherhood would ever be a viable source of political leadership, given the power and mass support of the old national establishments. But over the years this situation has gradually changed, as was graphically shown in the results of the 1986 elections, when the Muslim Brotherhood won a significant number of votes even in relatively rural bastions of the Khatmiyyah and Ansar.

The movement's program is the active Islamization of society. Brotherhood leaders like Hasan Turabi support the Islamization of law and the concrete implementation of its provisions understood in a strict and legalistic manner. Part of this perspective is an opposition to the divisions in the Muslim community implied by the existence of "sects" like the Khatmiyyah and the Ansar. Since its beginnings, the brotherhood has been antisectarian as well as antisecular. In addition, the organization has consistently advocated peaceful persuasion over militant revolution and has participated in and supported democratic parliamentary politics. The basic method of Islamization advocated by Turabi has been social transformation "from the bottom up" rather than a forced or unilaterally imposed program of Islamization.

The Muslim Brotherhood's approach is reflected in the changing relations between Turabi and Numayri. For almost a decade, the brotherhood was part of the civilian political opposition to Numayri's military regime. Then in 1978, Turabi participated in the "national reconciliation" and became attorney general of the Sudan, charged with leading the effort to bring existing Sudanese law into conformity with Islamic law. His committee worked carefully but slowly to transform the country's legal structure. When Numayri decided to hasten this process and began a more rapid—and arbitrary—process of Islamization, Turabi was removed from his post. The Islamization program imposed by Numayri was not the creation of Turabi and the brotherhood group, nor did it reflect the methods consistently advocated by the group.

Thus, by 1978 the Muslim Brotherhood had been able to shift Sudanese policy in the direction of Islamization of the legal system, and by the early 1980s the organization had become an important political force. The movement was strong among students and modern-educated Sudanese and had begun to attract followers from outside this elite. The Muslim Brotherhood is clearly an important part of the Sudan's Islamic resurgence, but its main lines of activity and success were not directly shaped by the Iranian revolution.

The Republican Brotherhood. During the twentieth century the Sudan has witnessed a remarkable variety of intellectually and socially significant developments in Islamic thought and organization. The transformation of Mahdism and the emergence of the Muslim Brotherhood are only the two most visible such developments. However, the formation of another group, the Republican Brotherhood, shows the range of this dynamism.

The Republican Brothers and Sisters are the followers of Mahmoud Mohamed Taha. The movement has its origins in the years following World War II when Taha developed distinctive ideas about the need for a revitalization of Islam. By the late 1960s he had formed the Republican Brotherhood, whose members became increasingly vocal, preaching publicly in the major cities of the Sudan. The organization remained small and urban based but had some influence among educated Sudanese, especially students. The movement received international visibility when Taha Mahmoud was executed by Numayri's government in early 1985.

Taha argued that "present-day industrialized Western civilization has reached the end of its development. It has obviously failed to answer the needs of human society."[12] He also argued that Islam could provide the solution to the current crisis state of humanity, but his interpretation of Islam was significantly different from that of any other major Islamic group. His views challenged those of both the old establishment and the new fundamentalists. For Taha, Islamization of society was the ultimate goal, but the first step was a radical reinterpretation of the meaning of Islam for humanity. In his words, it is now time for "the second message of Islam."

The small but visible Republican Brotherhood provides a clearly developed intellectual alternative to the more standard approaches to the issues of Islamization. In this way, the movement fulfills an important, though limited, function. Moreover, the Republican Brotherhood was the only Islamic group of any significance in the Sudan to condemn the Iranian revolution from the very beginning. Its position was that the "so-called Islamic revolution in Iran contravenes fundamental rules of *Sharia Islamiah*."[13]

The roots of the Republican Brotherhood reach back before the era of the Islamic resurgence of the 1970s, and its message was clearly defined before the Iranian revolution. However, the context of the revolution heightened the distinctiveness of the Republican message. In this sense, the Iranian experience may have had some impact, although it was not a major force in the development of the movement created by Mahmoud Mohamed Taha.

Numayri and Islamization. Jafar Numayri's policies in the early

1980s represent yet another mode of Islamization in the Sudan, different in many ways from the other Islamization efforts. Rather than being part of a broader evolution, Numayri's Islamization was an abrupt policy initiative on the part of an individual who controlled the state.

Numayri has been discredited by his inept handling of many issues in Sudanese politics in the early 1980s. He wasted a large reservoir of political good will that he had built up through the 1972 agreement providing for special autonomy for the southern Sudan and his national reconciliation policies of the late 1970s. In the early 1980s Numayri began to emphasize the idea of Islamization, which, if it had been managed properly, might have recouped some support for his regime in the northern Sudan. However, Numayri insisted upon a style of Islamization that suited his own militantly authoritarian mode of rule but pleased virtually no one else and was not accepted as fully legitimate by any major Muslim group in the northern Sudan. Numayri was forced to go to the less well-known holy families for support.

While Numayri's program was dramatic in terms of the abruptness of its implementation, it did not represent significant new interpretations but was drawn somewhat eclectically from existing compilations of Islamic law. The actual decrees were put together rapidly, usually under the direction of Numayri's close advisers, notably Nayal Abu Garoon and Awad al-Jid Muhammad Ahmad. In 1984, when discussing the materials that they used in compiling these decrees, neither of these advisers mentioned the Iranian revolution or the writings of Iranians as a source of content or inspiration.[14]

Numayri's program has been characterized as "intellectually conservative but, in its starkness, it is revolutionary in social and political terms."[15] The roots of this Islamization effort may lie partly in the broader context of the Islamic resurgence, but they are also embedded within the Sudanese situation itself. Numayri's interest in Islamizing state and society in the Sudan did not suddenly appear in the fall of 1983. Although his regime had originally been self-consciously Arab socialist, by the mid-1970s Numayri had stepped away from leftist-oriented ideological positions. In 1978 he established the committee for the Islamization of laws with Turabi as chair. In 1983 the book *Al-Nahj al-Islami: Limadha?* (*The Islamic Path: Why?*) was published with Numayri credited as author. In this book the major focus was still Arab identity but with a greater emphasis on Islam than had been the case in his earlier pronouncements on Arab socialism. Thus, what was new about the Islamization program of 1983 was not that Numayri had suddenly "discovered" Islam but that he had moved from Arab nationalist and Muslim Brotherhood versions to his own special program of imposed Islamization. In this context, his growing emphasis on Islam as a factor in his policies came before the Iranian revolution, and in the 1980s the Iranian experience had little direct impact on the form that Sudanese Islamization took.

Conclusions

The conscious and unconscious processes of Islamization have deep historical roots in the Sudan. Each of the major Muslim groups and institutions reflects a style of Islamization that continues to have significance in the country today. These Islamization efforts both received inspiration from and gave support to the broader Islamic resurgence of the 1970s. However, the basic character of Islamization in the contemporary Sudan reflects the internal dynamics of Sudanese society more than internal inspiration.

The September Laws were an abrupt departure from the more evolutionary approach that all Islamic establishments had adopted during the twentieth century. Numayri's Islamization program was also different in that it was the imposed policy of a single individual, while other approaches involved the efforts of an established Muslim class, organization, or institution. Numayri created a legal structure that continues to play a significant role, but he left no committed social grouping or organization to carry on his mode of Islamization.

The social and political leaders of the Sudan have never been as secularized as similar figures in the Middle East and Africa. Major political parties and power groups in the Muslim parts of the country maintain a significant Islamic identity. However, the 1970s was a time of increased visibility for a more explicit and fundamentalist affirmation of Islam, as evidenced by the growth of the Muslim Brotherhood and the implementation of Numayri's program. This increasing affirmation took place within the broader Islamic world of which the Iranian revolution was a prominent feature. In this way, Numayri and others involved in the Islamization of the Sudan, however defined, are true contemporaries of the Iranian revolutionaries. In broad historical terms, they are all mutual participants in creating the spirit of Islamic resurgence that characterizes the era. One must, however, avoid seeing in this phenomenon a direct causal relationship between developments in Iran and the Sudan.

Notes

1. Jafar Numayri, *Al-Nahj al-Islami: Limadha?* (Cairo: al-Maktab al-Masri al-Hadith, 1398).

2. John L. Esposito, "Sudan," in *The Politics of Islamic Revivalism*, ed. Shireen T. Hunter (Bloomington: Indiana University Press, 1988), 197.

3. See, for example, the position statements by leaders of the major opposition group, the Sudan People's Liberation Movement, in John Garang, *John Garang Speaks*, ed. Mansour Khalid (London: KPI, 1987).

4. John O. Voll and Sarah Potts Voll, *The Sudan: Unity and Diversity in a Multicultural State* (Boulder, Colo.: Westview Press, 1985), 125.

5. Yusuf Fadl Hasan, *The Arabs and the Sudan* (Edinburgh: Edinburgh University Press, 1967), 180.

6. Muhammad al-Nur bin Dayf Allah, *Kitab al-Tabaqat fi Khusus al-Awliya wa al-Salihin wa al-Ulama wa al-Shuara fi al-Sudan*, ed Yusuf Fadl Hasan (Khartoum: Khartoum University Press, 1971), 39–40.

7. The development of these types of centers is discussed in P.M. Holt, *Studies in the History of the Near East* (London: Frank Cass, 1973), Part II.

8. See, for example, the discussion of the Badrab of Um Dubban in Idris Salim El Hassan, "On Ideology: The Case of Religion in Northern Sudan" (Ph.D. diss., University of Connecticut, 1980).

9. For a discussion of the significance of Ahmad ibn Idris, see Rex S. O'Fahey and Ali Salih Karrar, "The Enigmatic Imam: The Influence of Ahmad ibn Idris," *International Journal of Middle East Studies* 19, no. 2 (May 1987): 205–20. For discussions of the Khatmiyyah Tariqah, see John O. Voll, *A History of the Khatmiyyah Tariqah in the Sudan* (Ph.D. diss., Harvard University, 1969); Ali Salih Karrar, *The Sufi Brotherhoods in the Sudan Until 1900* (Ph.D. diss., University of Bergen, 1985); for twentieth-century developments in the movement, see Ahmad al-Shahi, "A Noah's Ark: The Continuity of the Khatmiyya Order in Northern Sudan," *British Society for Middle Eastern Studies Bulletin* 8, no. 1 (1981): 13–29.

10. Descriptions of the Islamic Revival Committee and its activities on university campuses can be found in Azhari Abdel Rahman, "Pacific Student Politics" and "Spreading the Word," both in *Sudanow* (November 1980).

11. Informative discussions of the transition from the older style of activism to a more modern mode can be found in Lidwien Kapteijns, *Mahdist Faith and Sudanic Tradition: The History of the Masalit Sultanate, 1870–1930* (London: KPI, 1985), and Hassan Ahmed Ibrahim, "Imperialism and Neo-Mahdism in the Sudan: A Study of British Policy Towards Neo-Mahdism," *International Journal of African Historical Studies* 13 (1980): 214–39. A discussion of the evolution of modern Mahdist political organization is found in Gabriel Warburg, *Islam, Nationalism, and Communism in a Traditional Society: The Case of Sudan* (London: Frank Cass, 1978), especially Chapter 1. See also Vincent Andrew, *Religion and Nationalism in a Traditional Society: Ideological Leadership and the Role of the Umma Party as a Force*

for Social Change in the Northern Sudan (Ph.D. diss., University of Pennsylvania, 1988).

12. Mahmoud Mohamed Taha, *The Second Message of Islam*, trans. Abdullahi Ahmed An-Naim (Syracuse: Syracuse University Press, 1987), 53. An-Naim's Introduction gives biographical information about Taha; the book as a whole is the major presentation of his views.

13. Quoted from a 1980 Republican Brotherhood pamphlet by Paul J. Magnarella, "The Republican Brothers: A Reformist Movement in the Sudan," *The Muslim World* 72, no. 1 (January 1982): 17.

14. Interviews by John L. Esposito and John O. Voll with Nayal Abu Garoon and Awad al-Jid Muhammad Ahmad, August 1984.

15. John O. Voll, *The Political Impact of Islam in the Sudan: Numayri's Islamization Program* (Washington, D.C.: U.S. Department of State, 1984), 104–5.

15

Islamic Revivalism in Nigeria:

Homegrown or Externally

Induced?

IBRAHIM A. GAMBARI

NIGERIA'S POPULATION has been estimated to number about 116.2 million people, 40 percent of whom are believed to belong to the Islamic faith. This makes Nigeria the country with the largest concentration of Muslims west of the Gulf region. The vast majority of these believers are Sunni Muslims. Christianity, the competing religion in Nigeria, is the faith claimed by 35 percent of the population. Other Nigerians belong to what are loosely termed traditional African religions.[1]

Nigeria's religious pluralism has a regional dimension, although not a neat one. The overwhelming majority of the population in the northern states (formerly one single region) are Muslims, while Christianity has strong roots in the southern, and eastern parts of Nigeria. Nonetheless, there are relatively small but significant Christian minority groups in northern Nigeria, especially around southern Zaria Province (Kaduna State) and in Plateau and Gongola states. There are also important Muslim communities in the former Western Region, constituting by some estimates almost half of the entire population of that part of Nigeria.

The religious diversity of Nigerian peoples is compounded by years of interethnic rivalries and the north-south dichotomy, all of which have contributed to the political tensions, crises, and conflicts that have undermined the nation's peace and stability and, on one occasion, even threatened the corporate existence of the country as a single entity. We shall return to this point later in the discussion.

Despite the domestic ingredients for potential and actual conflicts in Nigeria, there are strong feelings among many politically aware Nigerians that the country possesses the human and material resources to lead black Africa. Furthermore, the country's geopolitical situation and its religious diversity create a strong potential for Nigeria's playing a pivotal role in Afro-Arab relations within the African continent and between black Africa and the Islamic world as a whole. Although such hopes and aspirations for Nigeria have not been fully realized, they have not been abandoned either—in spite of the recent economic downturn in the country, which is now highly dependent on the export of crude oil.

Because of Nigeria's Muslim majority and its modern status as a nation, the impact of Iran's Islamic revolution on that country is worthy of consideration. In the Nigerian context, the issue is whether the rise of Islamic fundamentalism and the increasingly controversial demand for the application of *Sharia* (Islamic laws) are homegrown phenomena or directly attributable to Iranian influence.

It is, of course, debatable whether the Shia Islamic revolution in Iran—or indeed any revolution in one country—can be successfully exported to other countries. No doubt there are those groups within Iran, in some Western political circles, and among segments of Muslim populations in countries outside the Gulf region that have active interests in promoting the idea of the exportability of the Iranian revolution. The notion may turn out to be a myth rather than an operational reality. Still, the idea of an Islamic revolution has had great appeal beyond Iran where it was successfully carried out.

Islamic revivalism in Nigeria and the growing demand for Sharia are in fact homegrown. Given Nigeria's insignificant Shii population, the diversity of religious beliefs, and the country's ethnic and regional identifications, the import value of the Iranian revolution as a Shii movement is extremely limited.

Nonetheless, Ayatollah Khomeini's leadership and the idea of Islamic revolution touched responsive chords in Nigeria's Islamic community, especially among the downtrodden Muslims in the north. The version of Islamic fundamentalism conceived and operationalized in Iran was skillfully used by local leaders of Islamic revivalism to galvanize the struggle against the growing corruption and excessive materialism of Nigeria's political establishment. In a fragile state with an overstretched security apparatus, the continued assault on the secular nature of the regime and the increasing pressures for the extension of the Sharia throughout the country constitute serious problems for policy makers in Nigeria.

Nigeria's recent history and its entrenched cultural, political, and religious configurations suggest that the country cannot live without periodic expressions of Islamic revivalism, but neither can Nigeria survive an attempt to establish an Islamic republic there. The Khomeini-style model of an Islamic republic, if engineered for Nigeria, would cause fatal problems for the corporate existence of the country as a multireligious and ethnically plural state. Perhaps a more appropriate model for present-day Nigeria is the experience of Egypt as that country seeks to manage Islamic fundamentalist impulses and pressures while trying to maintain a secular state. In this light it is significant that Nigerian President Ibrahim Babangida successfully concluded a state visit to Egypt in February 1989; a similar visit to Iran would have caused serious political problems in Nigeria despite the two countries' membership in OPEC.

Current Manifestations of Islamic Revivalism in Nigeria

Within the last decade or so three major manifestations of Islamic revivalism have rocked the balance between the state and religious faiths in Nigeria. The earliest such manifestation was the Maitatsine movement, whose violent activism inflicted severe property damage and casualties in a number of northern towns and cities. The leader of the movement was nicknamed "Maitatsine" perhaps as an uncomplimentary reference to his notorious proclamation "*Wanda ba ta yarda ba Allah tatsine*" (May God curse whoever disagrees with me).[2] The second manifestation was the heated Sharia debates in the Constituent Assemblies of 1978 and 1988–89 whose task was to prepare the constitution for the return to civilian rule under the Second and Third Republic respectively. Finally, there was the controversy surrounding Nigeria's membership in the Organization of the Islamic Conference (OIC) that poisoned interreligious relationships and led to serious clashes between Muslims and Christians in Kaduna State in 1987. These expressions of Islamic revivalism, which also created crises for state and society in Nigeria, are worth a closer look.

Maitatsine, whose real name was Muhammadu Murawa, migrated to Nigeria from the neighboring country of Cameroon and organized a movement whose supreme guide was the Koran. Regarded as a heretic because he proclaimed himself a Muslim prophet, Maitatsine and his followers incited eleven days of bloody rioting in the northern city of Kano in December 1980. It took the combined efforts of the police, army, and air force to subdue the disturbances, which some described as "Maitatsine's Holy War" and which cost the lives of five thousand people and millions of *niara* in damages to private and public property.

Although Maitatsine was believed to have friends in high places (including prominent politicians, businessmen, and civil servants) who patronized him for charms and other manifestations of special spiritual powers, his followers were mostly young men recruited from the pool of dispossessed youths who had moved to Nigeria's towns and cities from outlying rural areas. The degree of fanaticism with which Maitatsine's followers resisted the state security and military forces was truly extraordinary.[3] Although Maitatsine himself was killed in the bloody confrontation in Kano and although that uprising was suppressed, the movement went on to perpetuate large-scale violence in some other northern cities, notably Maiduguri and its outskirts (October 1982) and Gombe and Bauchi (1984–85).

There have been a number of official and scholarly explanations for the Maitatsine phenomenon. For example, there is the argument that the modern Nigerian state, in its neocolonial form, has promoted and in turn become a hostage to corrupt elements in the society. Maitatsine's total opposition to such corruption found a ground swell of support among the abject poor in the urban communities of northern Nigeria. There was also the background of the deteriorating economic and political conditions in Nigeria as a whole and in the northern states in particular—a situation that contributed to the downfall of constitutional government and the return to military rule in Nigeria by January 1984. According to Sulyman Nyang, Muhammadu Murawa fits into a pattern often identified by social scientists in their examination of sociological problems: "He can be identified with the Mahdist motif . . . ; he can be perceived as a system challenger who saw modernization and corruption in Nigerian society as obscenities that deserved to be wiped out for good; he can be viewed as a Muslim heretical leader who abused his followers' fidelity and loyalty."[4] In any event, Maitatsine and the movement that survived him were directly involved in popular uprisings against the authorities and individuals inside and outside the Islamic faith who were considered to be less than pure according to the dictates of the Koran.

The Maitatsine movement was clearly the most violent of the Nigerian Islamic groups whose members Peter Clarke refers to as the radical reformists or fundamentalists.[5] Other radicals include the supporters of the Islamic scholar and popular writer Ibrahim Suleiman, and the followers of the influential Sheik Abubakar Gumi, the former Grand Khadi (Chief Judge) of the Sharia Court of Appeal in the old Northern Region and founder of the Izala movement. In addition, there are fundamentalists in such Muslim organizations as the Jamaatu Nasir Islam (Society for the Victory of Islam), the Muslim Students Society, and the Young Muslim Association of Nigeria.

On the other end of the spectrum are those Islamists sometimes referred to as moderates. These include members of the Muslim Association of Nigeria; Muslim segments of the political elite, such as senior officials or members of the National party of Nigeria, the major political party during the country's Second Republic (1979–83); retired or serving senior military officers; a few academics in the universities; and religious leaders.[6]

While the methods and approaches of the so-called moderate and radical Islamic revivalists may differ, both groups are united in their support of certain principles, such as the availability of Sharia to Muslims, its incorporation into the federal legal structure, and opposition to a Western-type secular republic.[7] This unity on the part of Muslim activists often alarmed non-Muslims in both the north and south and occasionally provoked reactions from Christian radical and activist groups. The resulting conflicts of perceptions and mistrust have helped create a climate of religious intolerance in Nigeria since the end of the 1970s.

Another major crisis of state and religion was precipitated by the debates in the Constituent Assembly of 1978, formed to help manage the transition from military to civilian rule which culminated in the presidential election and the establishment of the Second Republic in 1979. Most Muslim members of the Constituent Assembly supported the proposal to establish a Federal Sharia Court of Appeal to serve as an intermediary between the Sharia courts in the northern states and the Supreme Court of Nigeria. These supporters argued that Sharia courts were the proper, most accessible, and relatively inexpensive avenues for obtaining justice in Islamic communities throughout the world, and those courts became the symbol of political freedom and equality for Muslims in Nigeria.[8]

On the opposing side were Christian members of the assembly who saw in the Sharia issue, especially the proposed Federal Sharia Court of Appeal, the threat of Muslim domination in Nigeria. The rhetoric on both sides was strident, and the entire assembly appeared to be headed toward disintegration. Finally, however, the assembly reached a compromise whereby there was to be no federal Sharia court, but in cases where appeals from the states' Sharia courts were necessary, a special committee of the Supreme Court, composed of justices versed in Islamic law, would be constituted to hear them.[9] This uneasy compromise was designed to save the assembly from collapse and to prevent the derailment of the transition to civilian rule.

Therefore, it was no surprise that the compromise on the Sharia embodied in the 1979 constitution came under new challenge by some members of the next Constituent Assembly, established in 1988 to prepare an amended constitution for a third experiment in civilian government. Once again, the controversy surrounding the Sharia issue was contentious. So extreme were the positions taken by several Christian and Muslim members of the assembly that the federal military government had to step in to stop the acrimony by declaring the compromise embodied in the 1979 constitution as the final resolution of the issue.

The decade between the two assemblies was marked by the Maitatsine uprisings and the violent form of Islamic revivalism that instilled fear and suspicion in the minds of some Christian Nigerians. Moreover, Chief M.K.O. Abiola, a leading Muslim leader and former vice president of ITT, had been using his considerable wealth and the pages of the newspapers he owned to advocate the establishment of Sharia courts in the southwestern part of Nigeria, where the ratio of Muslims to Christians is about even. Many Christians could concede the operation of Sharia courts in the overwhelmingly Muslim-dominated north and even acquiesce to the constitutional compromise on the Sharia at the federal level, but the spread of Islamic laws and institutions to the predominantly Christian south was totally unacceptable. The battle lines on this issue were clearly demarcated.

The atmosphere of growing religious intolerance was further aggravated by the controversy surrounding the issue of Nigeria's membership in the Organization of the Islamic Conference (OIC). Previously, under the military regime of General Yakubu Gowan (a Christian), Nigeria enjoyed an observer status in the organization. Gowan probably felt that involvement with the OIC would facilitate Nigeria's relationship with other members of OPEC with largely Muslim populations and also keep his government aware of those matters affecting Muslims being discussed at the OIC. But the decision to apply for full membership was made almost in secret by the federal government in 1986 without much consultation or staff involvement. Therefore, when news of the country's changed status in the OIC was leaked to the public, there were great outbursts against the decision on the part of some Christian groups and leaders. While the Christians favored Nigeria's withdrawal from the OIC, the Muslims supported full membership with equal vehemence, and the old fears and suspicions once again came to the fore. Extremists on both sides even threatened to tear the country apart and to start a second civil war over the issue.

At the core of this controversy are differing perceptions of Nigeria as a political and religious entity. On the one hand is the feeling among the politically aware and religiously activist Muslims that in the Western-style secular state of Nigeria their Islamic culture and way of life are being constantly undermined. On the other hand many Christian leaders insist on the retention of precisely that secularism as the minimum condition for ensuring the survival and continued existence of Nigeria as a democratic and pluralistic state.[10]

Despite a tentative compromise whereby the government created a Religious Affairs Council to look into the consequences of Nigeria's membership in the OIC, the relationship between the leaders of major Muslim and Christian organizations took a sharp turn for the worse. The Religious Affairs Council had difficulties holding productive meetings and did not succeed in reducing the tension between the extremists of both sides.

It was in this environment that extensive rioting broke out in Kaduna State on March 7, 1987. Over one hundred churches and several mosques were burnt down, other property was damaged, and several lives were lost before the security forces were able to restore order.[11] The carnage was ignited by what appeared to be a minor incident in the relatively small town of Kafanchan in Kaduna State. Although that state has a large Muslim majority, Kafanchan is predominantly Christian; the town is located in the southern Zaria Province, which historically contained large Christian populations. As descendants of converts to Christianity, the majority of the people of Kafanchan hold tightly to their faith, and the relationship between them and the larger Muslim population of Kaduna State has not always been smooth. It was the preaching at a state teacher's college in Kafanchan by a Christian recently converted from Islam that ignited the rioting. Muslim students in the audience, offended by what they perceived to be derogatory references to Islam and the Koran in the sermon, physically attacked the preacher, starting a melee that soon spread to the town. As minorities in Kafanchan, the Muslims there were reported to have suffered several casualties as well as destruction of some private properties and public mosques. When news of the incident spread to other parts of the largely Muslim state of Kaduna, retaliatory attacks were made against churches and Christian communities. The initial caution and lack of decisive action by the security forces probably prolonged the disturbances. In the end, the combined military and police forces succeeded in bringing the situation under control, thus limiting the crisis to one state.

The reactions to the riot were varied. The military governor of Kaduna State, Lieutenent Colonal Umar, himself a Muslim, came out strongly against the retaliatory actions taken by the Muslims. He reminded his fellow believers that their religion was one of peace and cited references to both the Koran and the Bible to buttress his appeal for calm, tolerance, and the restoration of peace. The influential Academic Staff Union of Universities (ASUU) at the Zaria branch of Ahmadu Bello University condemned the religious disturbances, attributing the outburst to machinations by powerful bourgeoisie and reactionary elements in Nigeria using religion as a cover for their nefarious activities. The union called on the federal government to guarantee life and property to all citizens of Nigeria, pay compensation to the families and communities that suffered casualties, and reaffirm the secular nature of the Nigerian state.[12] In a nationwide broadcast, President Babangida characterized the disturbances as a "civilian equivalent of an attempted military coup d'état" and warned all those groups and individuals attempting the overthrow of his government under the cover of religion to desist from their treasonable actions or face severe penalties. As is usual in Nigeria, a judicial commission of inquiry was established to look into the root causes of the disturbances, and a tribunal was set up for the trial and sentencing of the indicted individuals.

Nigeria

In general, the disturbances were aided by and seriously accelerated the deterioration of interreligious relationships in Nigeria. Indeed, it was a miracle that the riots, once they started, were confined to only one Nigerian state.

Islamic Revivalism in Nigeria: The Link to Iran

On a cursory examination, it would indeed appear that the Islamic revolution in Iran with all its factionalism and religious fervor had direct influence on the Maitatsine uprisings and on what that movement symbolized. Several factors seem to support this linkage. First, the Maitatsine uprisings and the Islamic revivalist impulse as represented by the growing demand for Sharia in Nigeria took place just as the process of establishing an Islamic republic was reaching its climax in Iran.

Second, both the Iranian Islamic revolutionary impulse and the forces represented by Maitatsine were grassroots, popular uprisings against corrupt political and social establishments. In both instances, new confidence in the Islamic faith was visibly demonstrated by the Muslim fundamentalists. Their enthusiasm surged as the spirit of their adversaries faded.

Third, there was the "martyr" factor common to Maitatsine's followers and those of Ayatollah Khomeini. In both movements, masses of young men went into desperate battle at the behest of their respective leaders in order to defend Islam, and many were killed in the struggle. Consider, for example, the Maitatsine riots in the Yan Awaki district of Kano in December 1980. In the direct confrontation between Maitatsine's followers and the military armored cars that moved in to overpower them, the former "just came out of their houses [and] stood there to be mowed down by guns on account of their faith."[13] Some of those who witnessed this supreme sacrifice said that the Maitatsine followers were "completely off their heads."[14] The real explanation may well have been the strongly held belief shared by this group and by Khomeini's fundamentalist followers that those who lost their lives in the cause of purifying Islam as directed by their leader would go straight to paradise.

Fourth, like the Iranian revolution, the Islamic revivalist movement in Nigeria was urban centered. The pace of urbanization has accelerated dramatically in Nigeria, especially since the "oil boom" of the 1970s. Approximately 30 percent of Nigeria's population live in urban areas, the rate of urbanization is steadily increasing at the rate of 5–6 percent annually.

Fifth, the Nigerian authorities have claimed that some of the hard-core members of the increasingly radical Muslim Students Society—especially those operating at Ahmadu Bello University in Zaria and Bayero University in Kano—were trained overseas.[15] At closed sessions of the judical commissions of inquiry into the religious riots in the northern cities in the early 1980s, security agencies are believed to have mentioned Iran as well as Libya as two of the foreign countries offering financial and material support to some of the Islamic fundamentalist groups in Nigeria. Such charges have been vehemently denied by some of those alleged recipients.[16]

Sixth, the anti-imperialist and anti-Zionist postures of the Iranian revolutionaries strongly appealed to the Islamic revivalists in Nigeria where there were, in fact, some historical antecedents for such sentiments. According to Peter Clarke, "the arrival of colonial forces in West Africa represented for the Mahdists signs of the last days, while Western colonial institutions were seen as the work of *daggal*, the anti-Christ. They rejected the 'pact' that they saw Muslim rulers entering into with colonial authorities."[17] Even after their defeat at the hands of British colonial authorities, Mahdist leaders such as Mai Ahmadu (the emir of Missau) and Mai Wurno (son of Sultan Attahiru) fled, *hijra* style, from Nigeria to the Sudan so as to avoid Christian rule, which they perceived as synonymous with paganism and as a fate worse than death.[18]

More recently, a leader of one Nigeria's Islamic revivalist groups who was questioned about his movement's relationship with Iran replied that Khomeini "is the only one in the world today acting on the principal of Quran and Sunna of the Prophet." He also added the more revealing comment that the Ayatollah "is also working hard to see the liberation of Masjid-al-awsa from the Jews in Jerusalem."[19]

Finally, the success of the Islamic revolution in Iran probably ignited the transformation of the Maitatsine movement from a passive to an aggressive force. Events in Iran were not as remote as the geographic distance of the country implies, for many Muslims in Nigeria, especially in the north, have an active interest in developments in the Arab world. The pilgrimages to the holy cities of Mecca and Medina involving thousands of Nigerian Muslims annually are important sources of information. Nigerians also have easy access to overseas broadcasts in local languages by Voice of America, British Broadcasting Corporation, Voice of Moscow, Middle Eastern News Agencies, and so on. Also available is the cultural and religious literature disseminated by the Arab and Muslim embassies operating in Nigeria.

Notwithstanding the strong pointers to a direct connection between Iran's Islamic revolution and local Muslim revivalist groups, there are more compelling factors indicating that the revivalist trends and activities in Nigeria are essentially homegrown. First, the most violent of Nigeria's Islamic revivalist groups, the Maitatsine sect, drew heavily on the Mahdi tradition of the North. While the triumph of Khomeini's movement may well have served as additional inspiration, the Maitatsine movement "demonstrated many of the features of an Islamic millenarian tradition, and of the Mahdist movement which was an important factor in the nineteenth-century history of Islam in that region."[20] Indeed, Shehu Usman Dan Fodio, prior to his establishment of the Sokoto caliphate, and Muhammadu Bello, his son and successor as head of the caliphate (which later spread to what became known as the Northern Region of Nigeria), appeared to have supported the Mahdist tradition.[21]

In addition, the Sokoto caliphate headed by the sultan or *Sarkin Musulumi* (Commander of the faithful) and subordinate emirs had given northern Nigeria the experience of theocratic governance beginning in the early nineteenth century. Although colonial rule and post-independence democratization of the powers of the emirs had transformed the theocracies into local agents of Nigeria's state and federal governments, the emirs and the sultan (Sarkin Musulumi) continue to exercise considerable influence, if not ultimate power, in the public affairs of their respective domains in the northern states and even beyond.

Therefore, the Maitatsine sect and neofundamentalist groups in Nigeria were not motivated by the desire to establish an Islamic republic as such but by the need to purify Islam locally from the corrupt state to which they felt it had descended. They were able to recruit fervent followers from the growing pool of unemployed youths in the urban centers created by the country's worsening economic crisis. The general discontent in the country in the late 1970s and early 1980s was especially acute in the urban areas. Moreover, over half of Nigeria's population is sixteen years of age or younger; in Iran, youth constitute a similar proportion of the country's total population.

Gambari

Kano is the most urbanized area in northern Nigeria. That city has long enjoyed a tradition, accelerated in the post–World War II years, of Islamic reform and fundamentalist movements such as Wahhabi radicalism and Reformed Tijaniyya. Clarke suggests that several Nigerians may have joined the latter movement with the clear expectation that the Mahdi would emerge from the Tijaniyya sect.[22] In any event, the Reformed Tijaniyya were particularly active in Kano, and historically, that city's political culture has rested on the notion that the primary boundaries of communal loyalties are indeed religious.[23]

In many northern cities, there was the additional factor of the development of *talakawa* (poor masses) nationalism. Even the bourgeoisie and petit bourgeoisie (such as traders, craftsmen, and salaried employees) and some ulama had *talakawa* origins in these major cities.[24] When political avenues were closed to the growing urban population (especially during periods of military rule), the urban dwellers directed their energies toward Islamic nationalism. As the author of a recent study of the relationship between Islam and urban labor in northern Nigeria aptly observed, "radical Islamic populist ideologies exist and appear attractive to the impoverished urban masses of Muslims in Northern Nigeria."[25]

Finally, the challenges posed by the intra- and interreligious conflicts in Nigeria must be placed in the proper context with other powerful factors propelling the country's political life, including ethnicity, regionalism, and growing class antagonisms. From the country's independence to the civil war (1960–1970) in particular, competition for political power in Nigeria has taken place largely within the framework of ethnic and regional divisions.[26] Since then, religious differences and tensions have been added to the country's political contours. Nonetheless, religion has not replaced ethnicity as the driving force of Nigeria's political interactions but has served to reinforce the elements of ethnic, regional, and increasing class antagonisms in the country.

Nigeria's northern Muslims are fearful of the prospects of economic and political domination by the largely Christian south, especially given that region's earlier and more pervasive contacts with Westernization and the consequent higher standards of education, literacy, and access to civil service jobs. This fear probably informed the "Northernization" policy adopted by the regional government in the north to promote the employment of local residents in senior and midlevel positions in the areas' civil service. The northern leadership also demanded that the distribution of central government public service jobs, political appointments and even the location of national public-owned industries should reflect the "federal character" of Nigeria. These policies and demands were often resented by southern Nigerians, who began to have fears of their own that the Muslims might use their demographic weight to attempt to impose Islamic laws, culture, and even rule on the country.

Which Way Forward in Nigeria?

Islamic revivalism was an essentially homegrown phenomenon, especially in northern Nigeria with its tradition of indigenous theocracies, Mahdism, the Sharia courts system, and various Islamic reform movements and brotherhoods. This homegrown Islamic revivalism has been intensified by the higher degree of materialism and official corruption, the apparent departure from the principles and precepts of the Koran and Sunna on the part of the ruling class, and by the country's worsening economic situation, especially in the urban centers.

Nonetheless, the victory of Ayatollah Khomeini and his followers and the establishment of the Islamic Republic of Iran probably galvanized the latent impulse toward Islamic reform and revivalism in Nigeria. Still, Islamic revivalists and fundamentalists in Nigeria are not a single, united group. At one extreme is the Maitatsine sect, which has used violence to achieve some of its goals. There are also radical students on college campuses for whom Islam has been an effective tool for challenging the establishment inside and outside the universities. In addition, there are the more traditional leaders of Sunni Muslims who nonetheless actively support the extension of Sharia throughout Nigeria. The extreme factionalization among the Islamic revivalists has made it impossible for them to even attempt to capture state power. Instead, each time they have been involved in uprisings or interreligious disturbances, the state has succeeded in suppressing them—although with increasing difficulties and costs.

The final question to be raised here concerns the future of secularism in the Nigerian state. There is likely to be further accommodation and compromises over the Sharia issue, but as of now, the consensus in Nigeria appears to be that maintaining the secular nature of the state is the most effective way to govern and preserve the country's religious and ethnic pluralism. Nonetheless, opponents of secularism still exists and their number and boldness are growing. The Nigerian state may

Gambari

succeed in suppressing the more violent manifestations of Islamic revivalism, but it has not succeeded in destroying the underlying impulses and constituencies of that movement. Should the downturn in the economy persist and the environment of official laxity and corruption continue unabated in Nigeria, the urban and even the rural poor will likely be empowered to aid the proponents of Islamic fundamentalism in effectively challenging the secular state. This probability could cause serious problems for the successful implementation of the present military government's transition program for a return to civilian, democratic rule.

Notes

1. Demographic data are from Federal Survey Department, National Population Bureau, cited in *Country Profile: Nigeria* (London: The Economist Intelligence Unit, 1988–89), 10–11.

2. Sulyman S. Nyang, "West Africa," in *Politics of Islamic Revivalism*, ed. Shireen Hunter (Bloomington: Indiana University Press, 1988), 219.

3. Peter Clarke, "The Maitatsine Movement in Northern Nigeria in Historical and Current Perspective," in R. Hackett, *New Religious Movements in Nigeria* (Lewisport, NY: Mellen, 1987), 115.

4. Nyang.

5. Peter Clarke, "Islamic Reform in Contemporary Nigeria: Methods and Aims," *Third World Quarterly* 10, no. 2 (April 1988): 521.

6. Ibid.

7. Ibid., 522.

8. For details, see David D. Laitin, *Hegemony and Culture: Politics and Religious Change among the Yoruba* (Chicago: University of Chicago Press, 1986), 6–9.

9. Ibid.

10. Nyang, 220.

11. Clarke, "Islamic Reform," 527–28.

12. Ahmadu Bello University (Zaria, Nigeria), press release (Mimeographed, March 13, 1987).

13. Clarke, "The Maitatsine Movement," 115.

14. Ibid.

15. The training consisted of Islamic education and jurisprudence at Qum (Iran).

16. "No Shiites Here," *Abuja Newsday*, July 1, 1988, p. 1.

17. Clarke, "The Maitatsine Movement," 99.

18. Ibid.

19. "Interview with 'Shiite' leader, Uztaz Aliyu" in *Abuja Newsday*, July 1, 1988, p. 7.

20. Clarke, "The Maitatsine Movement," 95.

21. Ibid., 97–98.

22. Ibid., 103.

23. See John Paden, *Religion and Political Culture in Kano* (Berkeley and Los Angeles: University of California Press, 1973).

24. Paul M. Lubeck, *Islam and Urban Labor in Northern Nigeria: The Making of a Muslim Working Class* (Cambridge: Cambridge University Press, 1986).

25. Ibid., 309.

26. For studies of postindependence political developments in Nigeria, see F.A.O. Schwarz, Jr., *Nigeria: The Tribes, the Nation or the Race: The Politics of Independence* (Cambridge: MIT Press, 1965); and S.K. Panter-Brick, *Nigerian Politics and Military Rule: Prelude to the Civil War* (London: Athlone Press, 1970).

16

The Global Impact of

the Iranian Revolution:

A Policy Perspective

JOHN L. ESPOSITO AND JAMES P. PISCATORI

ITS FRIENDS AND FOES alike agree that the Iranian revolution has had a major impact upon the Muslim world and the West. For some, it has been a source of inspiration and motivation; for others, revolutionary Iran has symbolized an ominous threat to the stability of the Middle East and the security of the West because it has been associated with terrorism, hostage-taking, attacks on embassies, and the promotion of revolutionary activities. Indeed, for the Reagan administration, Iran often seemed synonymous with worldwide terrorism and revolution.

Contemporary Iran began the first decade of its existence with the twin goals of institutionalizing the revolution and exporting it. The first goal was largely achieved, and in fairly short order. A constitution was adopted for the new Islamic Republic of Iran, providing for an elected parliamentary form of government under the guidance of Islamic law. The Ayatollah Khomeini became the *velayat-e faqih*, the ultimate legal authority and the supreme religiopolitical guide for state and society. Lay leaders Mehdi Bazargan and Abul Hasan Bani-Sadr provided only a brief transitional leadership; in 1981 the clergy moved quickly and effectively to consolidate control of the government and its major institutions and to suppress domestic opposition.

The result has been a significant transformation in Iranian society. A new ruling elite, consisting of clergy and clerically approved sons of the revolution, controls the government and bureaucracy. Its members are no longer primarily from the urban, Westernized middle class but are drawn from a spectrum that is broader geographically, economically, educationally, and socially. Moreover, the state now exercises greater control over the economy, ostensibly to fulfill its revolutionary goal of creating a more socially just society for the disinherited or oppressed masses. The government, having taken over banking, insurance, foreign trade, and major industries, has paid off its foreign debt and created an independent economy, less beholden to foreign investment and capital. In fact as well as in theory, the revolution has profoundly altered the political and social landscape of Iran.

From its earliest days, the Islamic Republic of Iran has proclaimed the second goal—the export of the revolution—as a cornerstone of its foreign policy. No other aspect of the Iranian revolution has captured as much media attention and struck as much fear in the hearts of Western and Muslim governments. Militants and their critics alike have tended toward hyperbole when discussing Iranian revolutionary activities; both the acrimonious diatribes of Iran and the overreaction of its opponents have made it difficult to distinguish rhetoric from reality.

Mythologizing the Revolution

The reality of Iranian revolutionary politics and the politics of Islamic revivalism is complex and belies the simple assumptions that were common in the early days of the revolution and have continued in certain circles since then. It is not an exaggeration to say that the Western, especially the U.S., understanding of Iranian politics in general and of the global impact of the Iranian revolution in particular has often been hampered by misperceptions. These have sometimes gained such currency among policy makers, academic analysts, and journalists that they have virtually reached the level of myth. Four such misperceptions have been especially widespread.

First, one common misperception is that the Iranian revolution is a narrowly sectarian, Shii revolution. However, from its earliest days the revolution has deliberately projected a universalist image and harbored universalist aspirations. Ayatollah Khomeini, for example, emphasized that the revolution is rooted in the common tenets of Islam and proclaimed its relevance for all the world's oppressed. This vision is embodied in Iran's constitution: "The Islamic Republic of Iran is to base its overall policy on the coalition and unity of the Islamic nation. Furthermore, it should exert continuous effort until political, economic, and cultural unity is realized in the Islamic world" (Principle 11).

In the aftermath of the revolution, many Islamic student activists, regardless of their sectarian affiliation, looked to Iran as an example. Thus, the Sunni students of the Islamic Association (al-Jamaah al-Islamiyyah) at Cairo University declared that "the revolution of the Iranian people . . . is worthy of our deep study so that we may extract the lesson, learn from it, derive incentives and benefit from the study."[1] Indeed, at the elite and popular levels the revolution was scarcely perceived as solely a Shii victory. Many Muslims regarded it as the triumph of Islam over satanic forces as well as a triumph of the Third World over American neoimperialism.

This is not to suggest, however, that the Sunni-Shii tension is entirely absent. In societies in which significant Shii minorities feel deprived, it is only natural for them to feel a kinship with a country in which Shiism is predominant, just as it is only natural for the Sunni majority to find the Iranian example less attractive. Thus, the Sunni Mujahidin in Afghanistan have looked to Pakistan, while Shii groups have had closer ties to Iran.

The second myth proposes confusion and disorganization as the defining characteristics of Iran's revolution. While all revolutions tend to strike observers as chaotic, regular patterns of social and political behavior soon establish themselves. Even in the midst of the disorder that followed the fall of the strongly centralized and pervasive Pahlavi regime, basic institutions of state and society were created or reconstituted. As early as January 1979, revolutionary committees (*komitehs*) appeared to regulate basic social services as the old state disintegrated. In March 1979, only one month after Khomeini's return to Iran, a referendum was approved that replaced the monarchy with an Islamic republic. In August, a Council of Experts was elected to prepare a new constitution, which was subsequently ratified in November. In January 1980, presidential elections were held, and in the following March and May, the Islamic republican party won a majority of seats in the new parliament. The revolution continued to institutionalize itself with the creation of a revolutionary court system, later incorporated within the Ministry of Justice, and a clerical supervisory body, the Council of Guardians.[2]

The Global Impact of the Revolution

In contrast to the myth of a chaotic revolution, the third myth holds that the Iranian revolution is all too predictable. It is assumed that because the ideology that guides the regime is based on Islamic doctrine, policy prescriptions are predetermined and clear. In fact, Islamic beliefs are subject to a variety of interpretations, as the differences between Ayatollah Khomeini and the French-educated intellectual Ali Shariati demonstrate. Even among clergy with similar backgrounds and training, significant differences of opinion exist, as evidenced by the disagreement between Khomeini and the more senior Ayatollah Shariatmadari over the nature of clerical rule. In addition, parliamentary debates often reflect significant differences of interpretation. For example, in recent years the parliament and Council of Guardians have been at loggerheads over the issue of land reform—the sanctity of private property versus state expropriation and redistribution in the name of Islamic social justice.

This myth is also deceptive because it ignores the inherent fluidity and inevitable pragmatism of all revolutions. Iran's relationship with the Soviet Union exemplifies these characteristics. One might have expected that Islam's antipathy to Marxist atheism and Khomeini's hostility toward the superpowers ("Neither East nor West") would have precluded relations with the Soviet Union. The reality, however, was more complex. From 1979 to mid-1983, at a time when relations with the United States had collapsed, the Iranians maintained correct, if cool, diplomatic relations with the Soviet Union, purchased Soviet weapons (via North Korea), and tolerated the Marxist Tudeh party at home. The seemingly unyielding holy war with Iraq also illustrates this point. Although Ayatollah Khomeini repeatedly insisted that there would be no cessation of fighting until the fall of Saddam Hussein's regime in Baghdad, several leading clerics often demurred as reverses on the battlefield took place. Ali Akbar Hashemi Rafsanjani, speaker of parliament, could be just as adamant as Khomeini, and he eventually succeeded in inducing the Ayatollah to accept the cease-fire with Iraq—a decision Khomeini considered "more deadly than taking poison"[3]— when it became clear that neither the economy nor public morale would support further sacrifices.

The internal debate over the resolution of the Iran-Iraq war belies a fourth and final myth: that there are no Iranian moderates. This characterization became conventional as a result of the hostage crisis of 1979–81 in which the image of unreasonable, armed mullahs was reinforced by the U.S. government's inability to negotiate with a regime unwilling or unable to prevail on student militants. This perception was reconfirmed by the attempt to trade arms for hostages during the Iran-Contra affair. To most critics, the failure of this policy was best explained by the absence of any real moderates in Iran's government rather than by the misguided nature of the policy itself. Yet, this self-serving mythologizing about the composition of the Iranian elite obscures the complex reality of shifting factions within a constantly changing environment. The division between radicals and moderates is a gross simplification; even Khomeini himself sometimes appeared "leftist" and sometimes "rightist." With regard to land reform, for example, he pointedly cited a Prophetic tradition to the effect that wealth must be shared with the poor. But at the same time, he did not rescind existing laws protecting private property, and, cognizant of his *bazaari* supporters, he did not mandate greater government control of the economy. While factionalism is endemic to most political systems, it is particularly pronounced in revolutionary situations.

The foregoing myths have tended to distort current Western thinking about the impact the revolution has had outside Iran's own borders. The belief that the revolution is quintessentially Shii, for example, encouraged the assumption that the Shii generally would be more receptive to Iranian revolutionary ideas than would the Sunnis. The attempted coup d'état in December 1980 in Bahrain—with its majority Shii population—seemed to support this assumption; yet even there no general uprising took place. In Iraq, the Shii, who constitute at least 60 percent of the population and the majority of the military rank and file, resisted the repeated calls of the Ayatollah to regard the war as a Shii holy war rather than a nationalist struggle. Most of the Shii in Kuwait and in the Eastern Province of Sauda Arabia also proved unresponsive to sectarian appeals.

The presumption of Iranian ideological clarity has similarly bedeviled Western understanding of the export of Iran's revolution. This presumption has prevailed despite evidence that Iranian leaders themselves are uncertain, or at least divided, over how to proceed—even on as basic an issue as whether the revolution is to be exported primarily by example or by the sword. Khomeini himself advocated a variety of means: cultural transformation, religious propagation, mass communications, and armed struggle. He once proclaimed: "We want Islam to spread everywhere . . . but this does not mean that we intend to export it by the bayonet." Yet he also said: "If governments submit and behave in accordance with Islamic tenets, support them; if not, fight them without fear of anyone."[4] Another area of basic uncertainty can be seen in the debate over whether primacy should be given to building the revolution at home or to exporting it abroad.

In addition to ambiguities such as these, Iranian decision makers have not been unaware of the political constraints on their freedom of action. As in other policy areas, Iranians have demonstrated flexibility in pursuing their goals. Despite years of calling for the overthrow of Gulf regimes, they saw benefits in maintaining regular contacts—even in the midst of the Iran-Iraq war—with these regimes. Since the cease-fire of August 1988, Iran has moved to improve relations with several member countries of the Gulf Cooperation Council (GCC), notably the United Arab Emirates and Oman.

Global Impact of the Iranian Revolution

The revolution's impact on other Muslim states has depended at least as much on conditions in the particular state and region concerned as on Iran's own efforts. Any analysis, therefore, must depend primarily on a country-by-country or regional examination and take into account such factors as the composition of local elites, the nature of indigenous Islamic groups and opposition movements, and other significant local factors.

The chapters of this book undertake such an analysis, and the survey of the Muslim world that they present reveals four different ways in which Iran's global impact has been experienced. First, in two countries (Lebanon and Bahrain) Iranian intervention has been tangible and significant; second, in a larger group of countries Iran's example and encouragement have confirmed and accelerated preexisting Islamic political trends (Egypt, Tunisia, Nigeria, the USSR, Pakistan, and the Philippines); third, Iran has played a more general role in stimulating Islamic political thinking and ideology (Egypt, the Sudan, Malaysia, and Indonesia); and fourth, Iran's example and activities provided both the reason and the pretext for certain governments (Iraq, Egypt, Tunisia, and Indonesia) to justify control and suppression of Islamically oriented opposition movements.

Iran has intervened directly in some Muslim countries, and in a few of them its intervention has significantly affected the course of events. Lebanon is the prime example: Iran's intervention has dramatically altered the political environment in which the local Shii population has challenged the Lebanese state.

In most Islamic countries, revolutionary Iran's influence has been indirect, with Iran serving primarily as exemplar rather than direct participant. This was particularly true during the early period after the revolution, when both Sunnis and Shia across the Islamic world were applauding the courage and faith of the revolutionaries, and Iran was equated with Islamic revivalism and fundamentalism. Iran's example served as a catalyst to local Muslim activists whose own grievances now seemed neither unique nor insurmountable. Spontaneous political outbursts occurred in such diverse places as Saudi Arabia, Pakistan, Kuwait, and Bahrain. Representatives of Muslim organizations from the Middle East as well as South and Southeast Asia traveled to Teheran immediately after the revolution. Anwar Sadat's support of the Shah and denunciation of Ayatollah Khomeini as a lunatic was the exception that proved the rule. Even the nervous emirs of the Gulf remained cautiously silent in the face of such a popular cause.

The most pervasive way in which revolutionary Iran has influenced the Muslim world is on the level of ideas and ideology. Characteristic of the Islamic revival has been the worldwide dissemination of the ideas of such Sunni ideologues as the Egyptians Hasan al-Banna and Sayyid Qutb, the Pakistani Abul Ala Mawdudi, and the Indian Abul Hasan Ali Nadvi. As a result of the revolution, the writings of two Iranian ideologues, Khomeini and Ali Shariati, have been widely translated and distributed throughout the Muslim—and indeed the non-Muslim—world. Shariati in particular has gained wide currency from Egypt to Malaysia. Egyptian militants have claimed Shariati as one of their inspirers, as have Tunisian activists.[5] In Malaysia and Indonesia, the writings of Shariati are widely available, and influential journals such as *Prisma* and *Dakwah* have given considerable attention to his thought.[6] As a consequence, Shariati's ideas, and to a lesser extent Khomeini's, have influenced students and intellectuals as well as political activists. Whether or not there is a direct connection between ideas and oppositional activity, it is certainly true that the postrevolutionary generation of Muslims across the world accepts that Islam provides a blueprint for political and social reform.

Even as it encourages Islamic opposition movements, the Iranian revolution has been used by governments to legitimate their control or co-optation of these movements. Highlighting the political excesses of

The Global Impact of the Revolution

the revolution, the executions and violations of human rights, the failures of economic and social reform, and the sectarian nature of the regime in postrevolutionary Iran, many governments have attacked their own Islamic critics and dissident groups by explicitly linking them to Iran. In Tunisia, for example, the Bourguiba government hoped to discredit Muslim activists by labeling them "Khomeinists" and, in particular, attempted to discredit the Islamic Tendency Movement (MTI) by declaring that all Tunisians belonged to "the Islamic tendency." Similarly, the Egyptian government has attempted to tarnish the reputation of the Islamic opposition by calling at least one such group the Ansar Khomeini (Companions of Khomeini). The implication was not only that the Islamic opposition was extremist and fanatic but also that it was un-Egyptian, appealing to foreign models.

In Southeast Asia, the Indonesian government has constantly warned of the dangers of "deviant Islam," often attributed to Libya and Iran. In a number of instances, the Suharto regime has accused opposition groups of Iranian backing and antigovernment activities. Iran was thought to be behind one group, the Islamic Revolution Board; and the mere fact that one editor wrote a column under the title of "The Advice of Ayatollah Khomeini" was sufficient to merit the charge that he was engaged in the "stirring-up of Islamic revolution" and earn for him a thirteen-year sentence. The minister of religious affairs underscored the image of a pernicious Iran by explicitly juxtaposing the false practice of Islam that Iran preaches with "true Islam": "Although the extremist movement [in Indonesia] became stronger since the Islamic Revolution in 1979, the Muslims generally do not favor the militant approach."[7] Thus, governments invoke the specter of an extremist Iran, intolerant and in turmoil, to combat the opposition's image of a successful Islamic revolution, thereby enhancing their ability to delegitimize the opposition.

Policy Perspectives

The picture we have painted is of a complex, multidimensional revolution that is neither as ideologically fixed and persistently menacing as its critics hold nor as flexible and benign as its defenders believe. It is difficult to maintain such a complex, nuanced view because of the baggage of the recent past, including the seizure of the American Embassy in Teheran in November 1979 and the release of the hostages in January 1981; Iranian support for the bombings, hijackings, and other acts of violence in the Middle East; the virulent anti-Western propaganda; and, more recently, the political impact of the Salman Rushdie affair.

Yet it is evident that the United States and Iran share congruent long-term interests. Iran has obvious geopolitical importance because of its relatively large population (by the turn of the century, Iran's population will be twice that of the other Gulf states combined), oil and gas wealth, proximity to the Soviet Union and domination of the vital Strait of Hormuz. In terms of U.S. interests, Iran is also significant because of its relation to neighboring countries that are of great importance to the United States, including Turkey and Pakistan as well as the oil-rich states of the Gulf.

With regard to the Gulf states, Iran's strategic importance has increased appreciably since the Iran-Iraq cease-fire, because Iran can now serve as a counterweight to Iraq. Member nations of the GCC face an Iraq that regards itself as the principal regional, if not Arab, state and possesses a large and experienced military. Although Iraq suffered tremendous losses in the war with Iran and must undergo a difficult period of reconstruction, the country has already shown its willingness to pursue an activist foreign policy in the Middle East. In response to this, the GCC members, which had once bankrolled the Iraqi war effort but were careful not to burn all their bridges to Iran, are automatically wary of Iraqi intentions and, as a consequence, may be open to an improved relationship with Iran.

It is true, of course, that by joining Egypt, Jordan, and North Yemen in the Arab Cooperation Council and by signing a nonaggression treaty with Saudi Arabia in 1989, Iraq has signaled its acceptance of the basic status quo in the Middle East. Yet, however reassuring this may be, the Gulf states are unlikely to forget persistent Iraqi claims to Kuwait, or at least to its islands, and Iraq's use of chemical weapons in the war with Iran as well as against parts of its own population. The larger historical record shows that the Gulf emirs are capable of living with a dominant Iran, but they did fear an Iran intent upon exporting its revolution. The changed political environment makes Iran relatively less threatening to the local states, even while Iraq may seem more threatening to them. The U.S. policy toward the Gulf, which seeks to maintain the stability of the region and close ties with the GCC, cannot afford to be indifferent to this new environment.

As for Iran, its long-term interests also lie in improved relations with the United States. Like it or not, the United States plays a domi-

The Global Impact of the Revolution

nant role in the international system within which Iran must function. Although Iran has a European option in reconstructing its economy and military, the United States possesses advantages in both areas that cannot be ignored. And as the Iranians survey their regional environment, concern with Iraq on the one hand and with the Soviet Union on the other is inevitable. It would be prudent for an Iranian state concerned about Iraqi designs to be attentive to the dangers of U.S. preferential support for Iraq. Similarly, the United States could provide a political counterbalance to the Russian bear to the north, which twice in this century has occupied Iranian territory.

Despite these long-term interests, it must be said that the short-term policy options are limited. The time is not auspicious. Iran's negative image of the United States has been reaffirmed by a series of events: the attack on the USS *Stark* in May 1987, which, though launched by the Iraqis, was blamed on the adverse environment created by the Iranians; American naval engagements with Iranian forces in October 1987; the shooting down of an Iranian civilian airliner in July 1988 by the USS *Vincennes*; and President Reagan's renewal of the economic embargo against Iran in November 1988. For the United States, which has regarded Iran as its nemesis since 1979, the Iran-Contra affair in particular has left a legacy of mistrust toward an excessively factionalized Iranian government and an abiding suspicion that normal relations are impossible; as Secretary of State George Shultz put it, "Our guys . . . got taken to the cleaners."[8] Khomeini's pronouncement of a death sentence on Salman Rushdie, author of *The Satanic Verses*, prompted widespread unrest in the Islamic world and reinforced the public image of an intolerant Islam and a vindictive Iran. The Bush administration supported the decision of the European Community to withdraw diplomatic representation from Teheran as a result of the Rushdie affair.

Yet, with the passing of Khomeini, new options may arise, and we should not lose sight of the pragmatic streak that emerged in Iran from the mid-1980s to 1989. Time after time, the Iranian government had to adjust its plans for the reform of the economy, the export of the revolution abroad, and the conduct of the war with Iraq. Ideology, though still vehemently defended by significant leaders and groups, receded. Even Hussein Musavi-Khamenei, the prime minister, who favored a centrally planned economy and had criticized foreign domination of the Iranian economy, suggested in 1988 that Iran might turn to outside sources for loans and expertise.[9] At the same time, leaders such as Hashemi Rafsanjani and Ali Akbar Velayati, the foreign minister, were instrumental in bringing the war to an end and, until the Rushdie affair, in repairing relations with European countries. Perhaps the strongest indicator of the triumph of state interests over Islamic ideology was Khomeini's categorical statement to the president of the republic in January 1988 that "the government is empowered to unilaterally revoke any Shariah [Islamic law] agreements which it has concluded with the people when those agreements are contrary to the interests of the country or of Islam."[10] The ascent to power of Rafsanjani and Khamenei in the wake of Khomeini's death may provide new opportunities for pragmatism and for repairing international relations.

Finally, responses in the Muslim world to the Iranian experience, to Iran's attempt to export the revolution, and to the Rushdie affair have demonstrated the multiple voices of Islam. Muslims, like the followers of other major religions, represent a spectrum of religious and political positions or orientations. Given the force of Islamic revivalism from Rabat to Kuala Lumpur, U.S. responses to Iran affect not only U.S.-Iranian relations but also, and more importantly, Muslim perceptions of the United States. This in turn affects long-term relations of the United States with the moderate majority of Islamic activists or "fundamentalists" who today are often part of the mainstream in Egypt, Tunisia, the Sudan, Kuwait, Pakistan, and Malaysia.

The vast majority of Islamic organizations and movements do not espouse violent revolution but, wherever possible, seek to bring about sociopolitical change within their established governmental systems. This approach is exemplified by the Islamic Tendency Movement (MTI) in Tunisia, the Muslim Brotherhood in the Sudan, and the Malaysian Muslim youth movement (ABIM). These groups run clinics and schools, day-care and social centers, banks and legal aid societies. Their members participate in parliamentary elections, work in the bureaucracy, and have held cabinet posts in the Sudan, Pakistan, and Malaysia. Like many others in the developing world, Muslims are wary and sometimes critical of the United States (as well as of Europe and the Soviet Union), but they are not necessarily anti-American. It is the perception of U.S. policy as anti-Islamic that has the potential to radicalize these moderates. Therefore, U.S. policy makers need to keep in

The Global Impact of the Revolution

mind this moderate majority while formulating present responses to Iran, interpreting Islamic politics in general, and undertaking long-range policy planning.

As policy makers look to the future of the U.S.-Iranian relationship, very little is certain. No one can deny that bad blood has characterized the relationship and that a new era has been consistently elusive. But what is also indisputable is that contacts and exchanges between two antagonists, however indirect, are more likely to lead to an improvement of relations than would no contacts at all. Intensifying these contacts and keeping the lines of communication open—if only through U.S. allies—seem warranted by the pragmatic trend that has emerged within the Iranian government and by the new regional environment that has resulted from the cease-fire in the Gulf war.

Notes

1. Islamic Student Association of Cairo University, "Lessons from Iran," in *Islam in Transition: Muslim Perspectives,* ed. John J. Donohue and John L. Esposito (New York: Oxford University Press, 1982), 246.

2. Shahrough Akhavi, "Iran: Implementation of an Islamic State," in *Islam in Asia: Religion, Politics, and Society*, ed. John L. Esposito (New York: Oxford University Press, 1987), 32.

3. *Independent* (London), July 21, 1988.

4. Ruholla Khomeini, *Sahifeye Nur* (Teheran: Vezarate Ershad, 1364/1985), 18: 129 and 17: 141, as cited in Farhang Rajaee, "Iranian Ideology and Worldview: The Cultural Export of Revolution" (this volume).

5. Saad Eddin Ibrahim, "The Anatomy of Egypt's Militant Islamic Groups," *International Journal of Middle East Studies* 12 (December 1980): 435.

6. Fred R. von der Mehden, "Malaysian and Indonesian Islamic Movements and the Iranian Connection" (this volume).

7. *Berita Harian* (Kuala Lumpur), October 1, 1987, as cited in von der Mehden, pp. 244, 253 (this volume).

8. Secretary of State George P. Shultz, testimony before the Joint House-Senate Iran-Contra Investigation Hearings, July 23, 1987, as cited in *Report of the Congressional Committees Investigating the Iran-Contra Affair,* 100th Congress, 1st Sess., November 13, 1987 (Washington, D.C.: U.S. Government Printing Office, 1987) 245.

9. Fouad Ajami, "Iran: The Impossible Revolution," *Foreign Affairs* 67 (Winter 1988–89): 147.

10. Ayatollah Khomeini's letter to President Seyyed Ali Khamenei, broadcast on Teheran Home Service, January 7, 1988, as reported in *BBC Summary of World Broadcasts—Middle East,* January 8, 1988.

Contributors

Shahrough Akhavi is professor of government and international studies, University of South Carolina. He is the editor of the Middle East Series (State University of New York Press), book review editor of *Iranian Studies*, and author of articles about Egyptian and Iranian politics and *Religion and Politics in Contemporary Iran*.

Lisa Anderson is associate professor of political science and acting director of the Middle East Institute at Columbia University. She is author of *The State and Social Transformation in Tunisia and Libya 1830–1980*, as well as articles on North African politics, history, and political theory.

John L. Esposito is director of the Center for International Studies and professor of religious studies at the College of the Holy Cross. He was president of the Middle East Studies Association and of the American Council for the Study of Islamic Societies. Among his publications are *Islam and Politics, Islam: The Straight Path, Women in Muslim Family Law, Voices of Resurgent Islam,* and *Islam in Asia*.

Ibrahim Gambari is ambassador and permanent representative of Nigeria to the United Nations, professor of political science at Ahmadu Bello University in Zaria, Nigeria, and former foreign minister of Nigeria (1984–85). He has held several teaching positions in the United States, including visiting professor at the School of Advanced International Studies of The Johns Hopkins University. He has contributed articles to periodicals and is author of *Nigerian Foreign Policy at Cross-Roads: Defending the Nation's Interest in the 1980s*.

David E. Long is professor of Middle East politics at the Coast Guard Academy. He has served with the Department of State and was chief of the department's Near East Research Division, a member of the Policy Planning Staff, and deputy director of the Office of Counter-Terrorism. He has written extensively on Saudi Arabia and the Gulf. Among his publications are *The Hajj Today: A Survey of the Contemporary Pilgrimage to Makkah* and *The United States and Saudi Arabia: Ambivalent Allies*.

Cesar Adib Majul is professor emeritus, University of the Philippines. After receiving his Ph.D. from Cornell University, he was for many years professor of Islamic studies, political science, and philosophy at the University of the Philippines. He is a prolific writer on Islam in Asia, whose publications include *The Contemporary Muslim Movement in the Philippines, The Muslims of the Philippines,* and *Islam and Development: A Collection of Essays*.

Augustus Richard Norton is associate professor of comparative politics in the Department of Social Sciences, United States Military Academy. He is author, coauthor, or editor of several books, including *Amal and the Shi'a: Struggle for the Soul of Lebanon*, and senior editor of *The International Relations of the PLO*.

Martha Brill Olcott is professor and chairman of the Department of Political Science at Colgate University. She is author of *The Kazakhs* and editor and principal contributor of the *Soviet Multinational State*. She has written articles on Soviet nationality problems in general and conditions in Central Asia in particular. A frequent traveler to the USSR, she is working on *Soviet Central Asia in Modern Times*.

James P. Piscatori is senior lecturer at the University of Wales and former associate professor of Middle Eastern studies at the School of Advanced International Studies of The Johns Hopkins University. In 1985 he was International Affairs Fellow of the Council on Foreign Relations. He is author or editor of several books, including *Islam in a World of Nation-States* and *Islam in the Political Process*.

Farhang Rajaee, educated at the Universities of Virginia, Oklahoma, and Tehran, is assistant professor at the Iranian Academy of Philosophy in Tehran. Among his publications is *Islamic Values and World Views: Khomeyni on Man, the State, and International Politics*. He is also translator of several English works into Persian.

R.K. Ramazani holds the Harry F. Byrd Chair Professorship of Government and Foreign Affairs at the University of Virginia, where he has taught since 1954. His latest books are *Revolutionary Iran: Challenge and Response in the Middle East* and *The Gulf Cooperation Council: Record and Analysis*. He is also coauthor and editor of *Iran's Revolution: The Search for Consensus*.

Philip Robins is head of the Middle East Programme at the Royal Institute of International Affairs, Chatham House. He is author of *The Future of the Gulf, Politics and Oil in the 1990s* and has written extensively on the politics of Iraq.

Olivier Roy is currently a researcher at the Centre National de Recherche Scientifique in Paris. He has made seven journeys with the resistance forces in Afghanistan and is author of *Islam and Resistance in Afghanistan* and of articles on Iran and Afghanistan.

John Voll is professor of history and chair of the Department of History at the University of New Hampshire. Among his publications are *The Sudan: Unity and Diversity in a Multicultural State, Islam: Continuity and Change in the Modern World*, and *Historical Dictionary of the Sudan*.

Fred R. von der Mehden is Albert Thomas Professor of Political Science at Rice University. He is author or editor of scholarly articles and books, including *Religion and Nationalism in Southeast Asia, Southeast Asia 1930–1970, Politics of the Developing Nations, Issues of Political Development,* and *Religion and Modernization in Southeast Asia*.

Index

Index